Maker Innovations Series

Jump start your path to discovery with the Apress Maker Innovations series! From the basics of electricity and components through to the most advanced options in robotics and Machine Learning, you'll forge a path to building ingenious hardware and controlling it with cutting-edge software. All while gaining new skills and experience with common toolsets you can take to new projects or even into a whole new career.

The Apress Maker Innovations series offers projects-based learning, while keeping theory and best processes front and center. So you get hands-on experience while also learning the terms of the trade and how entrepreneurs, inventors, and engineers think through creating and executing hardware projects. You can learn to design circuits, program AI, create IoT systems for your home or even city, and so much more!

Whether you're a beginning hobbyist or a seasoned entrepreneur working out of your basement or garage, you'll scale up your skillset to become a hardware design and engineering pro. And often using low-cost and open-source software such as the Raspberry Pi, Arduino, PIC microcontroller, and Robot Operating System (ROS). Programmers and software engineers have great opportunities to learn, too, as many projects and control environments are based in popular languages and operating systems, such as Python and Linux.

If you want to build a robot, set up a smart home, tackle assembling a weather-ready meteorology system, or create a brand-new circuit using breadboards and circuit design software, this series has all that and more! Written by creative and seasoned Makers, every book in the series tackles both tested and leading-edge approaches and technologies for bringing your visions and projects to life.

More information about this series at https://link.springer.com/bookseries/17311

Beginning MicroPython with the Raspberry Pi Pico

Build Electronics and IoT Projects

Charles Bell

Apress®

Beginning MicroPython with the Raspberry Pi Pico: Build Electronics and IoT Projects

Charles Bell
Warsaw, VA, USA

ISBN-13 (pbk): 978-1-4842-8134-5   ISBN-13 (electronic): 978-1-4842-8135-2
https://doi.org/10.1007/978-1-4842-8135-2

Managing Director, Apress Media LLC: Welmoed Spahr
Acquisitions Editor: Aaron Black
Development Editor: James Markham
Coordinating Editor: Jessica Vakili

Distributed to the book trade worldwide by Springer Science+Business Media New York, 233 Spring Street, 6th Floor, New York, NY 10013. Phone 1-800-SPRINGER, fax (201) 348-4505, e-mail orders-ny@springer-sbm.com, or visit www.springeronline.com. Apress Media, LLC is a California LLC and the sole member (owner) is Springer Science + Business Media Finance Inc (SSBM Finance Inc). SSBM Finance Inc is a **Delaware** corporation.

For information on translations, please e-mail booktranslations@springernature.com; for reprint, paperback, or audio rights, please e-mail bookpermissions@springernature.com.

Apress titles may be purchased in bulk for academic, corporate, or promotional use. eBook versions and licenses are also available for most titles. For more information, reference our Print and eBook Bulk Sales web page at http://www.apress.com/bulk-sales.

Any source code or other supplementary material referenced by the author in this book is available to readers on the Github repository: https://github.com/Apress/Beginning-MicroPython-with-the-Raspberry-Pi-Pico. For more detailed information, please visit http://www.apress.com/source-code.

Printed on acid-free paper

*I dedicate this book to my brother, Ronald,
who is in our hearts and in our prayers daily.
May God bless you and heal you.*

Table of Contents

About the Author

 **Dr. Charles A. Bell** conducts research in emerging technologies. He is a principal software developer of the Oracle MySQL Development team. He lives in a small town in rural Virginia with his loving wife. He received his Doctor of Philosophy in Engineering from Virginia Commonwealth University in 2005.

Dr. Bell is an expert in the database field and has extensive knowledge and experience in software development and systems engineering. His research interests include microcontrollers, three-dimensional printing, database systems, software engineering, and sensor networks. He spends his limited free time as a practicing maker, focusing on microcontroller projects and refinement of three-dimensional printers.

About the Technical Reviewer

Sai Yamanoor is an embedded systems engineer working for an industrial gases company in Buffalo, NY. His interests, deeply rooted in DIY and open source hardware, include developing gadgets that aid behavior modification. He has published two books with his brother, and in his spare time, he likes to build things that improve quality of life. You can find his project portfolio at `http://saiyamanoor.com`.

Acknowledgments

I would like to thank all of the many talented and energetic professionals at Apress. I appreciate the understanding and patience of my managing editor, Aaron Black; coordinating editor, Jessica Vakili; and development editor, Mark Powers. Each was instrumental in the success of this project. I appreciate their encouragement and guidance as well as patience in dealing with my many questions. I would also like to thank the small army of publishing professionals at Apress for making me look so good in print. Thank you all very much!

I'd like to especially thank the technical reviewer for his patience and attention to detail. Most importantly, I want to thank my wife, Annette, for her unending patience and understanding during the many hours I spent staring into the abyss of a blank page on my laptop or conducting IoT experiments on the dining room table, in the plants on the porch, or plugged into strange places in the house.

Introduction

The Raspberry Pi is the most popular single-board computer platform available. The boards are inexpensive, run the latest fully featured operating systems, and are backed by a growing ecosystem of developers, engineers, enthusiasts, and hobbyists. But raspberrypi.org wasn't done there. Now, we have a Raspberry Pi microcontroller called the Raspberry Pi Pico.

The Raspberry Pi Pico, with a very low cost, small form factor, and system-on-the-chip technology, is enabling many more people to learn, experience, and complete projects that would previously have required special (and expensive) hardware or having to learn a complex programming language – MicroPython. Built on the parent language, Python, MicroPython provides all of the ease of programming and hardware access in Python with a special interpreter built-in that allows the Pico to boot and execute MicroPython code. Nice.

This book presents a beginner's guide to MicroPython and the Raspberry Pi Pico. I cover topics including a tour of the Pico and related hardware, a tutorial on MicroPython programming, what types of sensors exist, how they communicate their values (observations or events), how they can be used in your MicroPython projects, and how to build your own Internet of Things (IoT) projects.

The original version of this book was revised. A correction to this book is available at https://doi.org/10.1007/978-1-4842-8135-2_15

Who This Book Is For

I have written this book with a wide variety of readers in mind. It is intended for anyone who wants to get started building their IoT projects without learning a complicated programming language or those who want to learn how to use components, devices, and sensors with a Raspberry Pi Pico.

Whether you have already been working with IoT projects, or maybe have taken an introductory electronics course, or even have read a good Apress book on the Raspberry Pi, you will get a lot out of this book. Best of all, if you ever wanted to build your own IoT solutions, this book is just what you need!

Most importantly, I wrote this book to meet my own needs. Although there are some excellent books on the Raspberry Pi, sensors, IoT, and MicroPython, I could not find a single reference that showed how to put all of these together.

About the Chapters

There are fourteen chapters, six of which include projects that demonstrate and teach key concepts of building IoT projects. There are also chapters that introduce MicroPython, present an overview of the hardware, and teach you how to program in MicroPython, and there's also an introduction to electronics for beginners.

The project chapters are split into two groups, those projects that require discrete components to form simple IoT solutions and those that use the Grove component system to utilize Grove modules to build more sophisticated IoT projects without soldering.

Depending on your skill level with the chapter topic, you may find some of the projects easier to complete than others. It is my hope that you find the projects challenging and enlightening (but, more importantly, informative) so that you can complete your own projects. The following presents an overview of each chapter.

Chapter 1 – Introducing the Raspberry Pi Pico

In this chapter, you will learn what makes the Pico different from the Raspberry Pi boards, what a microcontroller is, and a demonstration of how easy it is to work with the Raspberry Pi Pico.

Chapter 2 – Introducing MicroPython

You will learn more about MicroPython including an overview of how to get started. The examples in this chapter are intended to give you a taste of what you can do rather than a detailed tutorial. That said, I encourage you to attempt the examples for practice. We will see a detailed tutorial for programming MicroPython in Chapter 3 and take a deeper dive into the software libraries for lower-level hardware support in Chapter 4.

Chapter 3 – How to Program in MicroPython

In this chapter, you will learn some of the basic concepts of Python programming. We begin with the building blocks of the language such as variables, modules, and basic statements and then move into the more complex concepts of flow control and data structures. While the material may seem to come at you in a rush, this tutorial on Python covers only the most fundamental knowledge of the language and how to use it on your PC and Pico. It is intended to get you started writing Python applications quickly.

If you know the basics of Python programming, feel free to skim through this chapter. However, I recommend working through the example projects at the end of the chapter, especially if you've not written many Python applications.

Chapter 4 – Low-Level Hardware Support

The chapter begins with a more detailed look at the GPIO header and pins. In this chapter, you will learn the MicroPython libraries available for you to use in your projects and take a brief look at the low-level hardware support in MicroPython for the Pico. Finally, you will also revisit working with breakout boards to demonstrate some of the libraries and hardware protocols and techniques discussed in previous chapters.

Chapter 5 – Electronics for Beginners

In this chapter, you will see an overview of electronics commonly found in electronics projects. I include an overview of some of the basics, descriptions of common components, and an introduction to sensors. If you are new to electronics, this chapter will give you the extra boost you need to understand the components used in the projects in this book.

If you have experience with electronics either at the hobbyist or enthusiast level or have experience or formal training in electronics, you may want to skim this chapter or read the sections with topics that you may want a refresher.

Chapter 6 – Project: Hello, World! MicroPython Style

This chapter begins the first set of three project chapters that use discrete components to build small IoT projects starting with a very simple example using LEDs and a real-time clock (RTC) module.

The chapter starts with an overview of the project, followed by a list of the required components and how to assemble the hardware. Once the hardware is explained, you will then see how to connect everything and begin writing the code. Each chapter will close with how to execute the project along with a sample of it running and suggestions for embellishing the project.

The chapter also discusses a few best practices and other practical advice for developing projects. These apply to all projects in this chapter and likely any future project you may have in mind.

Chapter 7 – Project: Pedestrian Crossing

The project in this chapter is a simulation. More specifically, you will implement a traffic light and a pedestrian walk button. The walk button is a button pedestrians can use to trigger the traffic signal to change and stop traffic so they can cross the street. This project represents a more complex example of using multiple LEDs as well as writing more sophisticated MicroPython code.

Chapter 8 – Project: Soil Moisture Monitor

The project in this chapter presents more of a challenge because it uses more complex hardware and code to explore combining data logging with data visualization. You will use an OLED made specifically for the Pico using a third-party host board. You will also see how to use an analog sensor that produces analog data that we will then have to interpret. In fact, we will rely on the analog-to-digital conversion (ADC) capabilities of our Pico to change the voltage reading to a value we can use. Finally, we will be reusing the RTC module from Chapter 6.

Chapter 9 – Introducing Grove

This chapter introduces a better alternative to using breadboards and jumper wires. There are component systems designed to unify wiring by providing a modular cabling system to connect modules. One such component system that has been around for a while and is available for use with the Pico is called Grove.

The Grove component system has a rich host of modules we can use to build our projects simply by connecting the hardware together using polarized connectors (you can't plug them in incorrectly). Grove expands your opportunities for building more complex projects, freeing you to concentrate on the code for your project.

This chapter prepares you to use the Grove component system in the next set of projects.

Chapter 10 – Project: Sound Activated Lights

This chapter presents the second set of three projects using the Grove component system. You will learn how to build a simple project that demonstrates how to use a sound sensor and a red-green-blue (RGB) LED to display assorted colors based on the sound detected. The idea is the LED will light up whenever sound is detected, and the color will differ based on the loudness of the sound. So, you will be creating a sound detector.

Chapter 11 – Project: Simon Game

The project for this chapter is designed to demonstrate how to use analog, digital, and I2C devices on the same Grove host adapter to build a Simon game. It works very much like the original game but with an LCD for displaying messages. We will use a Grove Buzzer for sound and two Grove Dual Button modules. For the lights, we will use one Grove RGB LED module.

Chapter 12 – Example: Monitoring Your Environment

The project for this chapter is designed to demonstrate how to use analog, digital, and multiple I2C devices on the same Grove host adapter to build an indoor environment monitor. It uses several sensors to sample the air for gases and dust as well as sample the temperature and barometric pressure. As you will see, this is the most challenging of the projects in this book not only for the number of modules used but also for the complexity of the code.

Chapter 13 – Introducing IoT for the Cloud

In previous chapters, you've seen a number of projects, ranging from very basic to advanced in difficulty. However, the projects did not require to be connected to the Internet nor has there been any mention of using cloud services. While a complete tutorial of IoT cloud services would take several chapters, you will see an overview of what the cloud is and how it is used for IoT solutions. The chapter also presents a concise overview of the popular cloud systems for IoT as well as a short example using two of our earlier projects to give you a sense of what is possible and how projects can be modified to use the Internet.

Chapter 14 – Using ThingSpeak

This chapter presents a popular, easy-to-use, cloud-based IoT data hosting service from MathWorks called ThingSpeak (`www.thingspeak.com`). You will learn how ThingSpeak can allow you to gain more insights about the data. The chapter begins with a brief tour of ThingSpeak and how to get started using it in IoT projects and concludes with examples of how to expand some of the projects in the book to use ThingSpeak.

Tips for Buying Hardware

The hardware list for this book contains a number of common components such as temperature sensors, breadboards, jumper wires, and resistors. Most of these items can be found in electronics stores that stock supplies for electronics enthusiasts.

The appendix has a list of the components used from the project chapters. The appendix includes the name of each component and at least one link to an online vendor that stocks the component. In addition, I include the quantity needed for the chapter and an estimated cost. If you add up all the components needed and sum the estimated cost, the total may be a significant investment for some readers.

Downloading the Code

The code for the examples shown in this book is available on the Apress website, `www.apress.com`. A link can be found on the book's information page under the Source Code/Downloads tab. This tab is located underneath the Related Titles section of the page.

Reporting Errata

Should you find a mistake in this book, please report it through the Errata tab on the book's page at `www.apress.com`. You will find any previously confirmed errata in the same place.

## CHAPTER 1

Introducing the Raspberry Pi Pico

The Raspberry Pi foundation (raspberrypi.org) has changed the world by providing powerful, low-cost computer boards. The Raspberry Pi is by far the biggest selling and most popular of the many small computer boards available. Perhaps even more important is the Raspberry Pi is designed for education. Educators can use the Raspberry Pi to teach computer science, electronics, hardware automation, and Internet of Things (IoT) projects using Python, Java, or C++ programming languages.

Better still, the ability to run a powerful desktop operating system means you can use a Raspberry Pi just like your laptop or desktop to build your project and connect it to other hardware via the general-purpose input/output (GPIO) pins. With those accolades, it was only a matter of time before the Raspberry Pi foundation extended their global dominance.

The Raspberry Pi Pico is a departure from the dominance of the Raspberry Pi small computer boards because it isn't another small computer board. So, it doesn't have the ability to run an operating system, and there are no video ports, no USB host ports, or even a power connector. Rather, the Raspberry Pi Pico is the first microcontroller to use a small Raspberry Pi–based chip (RP2040). Better still, the cost of the Pico is a mere $4.00, and the RP2040 itself is only $1.00.

© Charles Bell 2022
C. Bell, *Beginning MicroPython with the Raspberry Pi Pico*, Maker Innovations Series,
https://doi.org/10.1007/978-1-4842-8135-2_1

Why is this important? It means the Raspberry Pi is one of the newest contenders in the microcontroller field, and, as we will see, the Raspberry Pi foundation has risen to the challenge with a very powerful, very affordable microcontroller that runs one of the world's most popular programming environments – MicroPython (Python for microcontrollers) – making the Raspberry Pi Pico easy to program and easier to use.

In this chapter, we will learn what makes the Pico different from the Raspberry Pi boards, what a microcontroller is, and a demonstration of how easy it is to work with the Raspberry Pi Pico. Let's begin by defining what a microcontroller is and how they are used.

What Is a Microcontroller?

One of the greatest advances in physical computing has been the proliferation of microcontrollers. A microcontroller consists of a processor with a small instruction set, memory, and programmable input/output circuitry contained on a single chip. Microcontrollers are usually packaged with supporting circuitry and connections on a small, printed circuit board.

Microcontrollers are used in embedded systems where small software programs can be tailored to control and monitor hardware devices, making them ideal for use in small projects such as appliances or smart controller boards. Microcontrollers are sometimes called an "embedded controller," "embedded processor," or "microcontroller unit (MCU)."

A typical microcontroller has one or more integrated circuits or a single chip that contains all of the components for the microcontroller. Typically, the processing unit, memory, and I/O circuitry are considered part of the microcontroller. However, microcontrollers often employ other circuits and components such as analog-to-digital converters (ADC), digital-to-analog converters (DAC), and at least one form of serial communication port for programming such as a USB port.

These hardware features make microcontrollers ideal solutions for interfacing with other hardware to perform minimal computational operations while controlling the hardware. In other words, they make excellent programmable controllers.

MICROCONTROLLER VS. MICROPROCESSOR: WHAT IS THE DIFFERENCE?

You may be thinking a microcontroller is just a smaller version of a microprocessor. While some microcontrollers are quite powerful, they are not microprocessors. A microprocessor is designed to maximize computing power on the chip while connecting to a bus (think parallel highway for digital communication) for making use of RAM and input/output (I/O) ports like USB and video graphics, whereas a microcontroller is designed with a much smaller set of dedicated functionality to perform operations with a set of general-purpose input/output (GPIO) pins typically to control hardware components. Thus, a microcontroller has limited computing power, making them useful for hardware automation like a robot, household appliance, etc., whereas a microprocessor is useful for computationally intensive solutions like computers, aircraft, etc.

Now that we have a general idea of what a microcontroller is, let's take a short tour of the Raspberry Pi Pico.

A Tour of the Raspberry Pi Pico

The Raspberry Pi Pico, hence Pico, is a small, green printed circuit board the size of a stick of gum. Along either long side are the GPIO pins with a micro-USB connector on one of the shorter ends. On the other end is a set of debugging pins that you can use for advanced diagnostics. Figure 1-1 shows the Pico from above oriented with the USB port to the right.

Figure 1-1. *The Raspberry Pi Pico – top view (courtesy of raspberrypi.org)*

Notice the GPIO headers on the top and bottom edges. The three pins on the left are the debugging pins. The only other component on the board we need to know about is the *BOOTSEL* (boot selection) switch located in the upper right of the figure. This switch is used to place the Pico in boot mode where it runs the MicroPython platform, or, if held down while the USB cable is connected to your computer, it will connect as a removable drive allowing you to load new files or change the base platform files. We will see how to do this later in this section.

Figure 1-2 shows the underside of the Pico. Notice here we see the GPIO pins are labeled, making it easy to locate a specific pin. The places labeled with "TP" are test points that you can use to test voltage should you need to perform any advanced diagnostics of the board. Once again, the pins on the left are for the Serial Wire Debug (SWD) interface. We will not be using that interface in this book, but you can read more about it in Chapter 6 of the Pico data sheet (book): `https://datasheets.raspberrypi.org/pico/getting-started-with-pico.pdf`.

Figure 1-2. *The Raspberry Pi Pico – bottom view (courtesy of raspberrypi.org)*

The heart of the Pico is the large (relative to the board) black chip located in the center of the board on the top side. This is the RP2040 microprocessor, and it provides all of the features that make up the Pico.

Introducing the RP2040

Let's begin with the name. The name may seem strange at first. Normally, we think the number is some sort of revision or version,[1] but this is not the case for the RP2040. Figure 1-3 depicts the nomenclature of the name. As you can see, it is an encoded phrase to represent four characteristics of the microprocessor. It is likely we will see variants of this microprocessor in the future, and we should expect its name (number) to vary according to this nomenclature.

---

[1] No, this isn't an Edison-like discovery where there were 2039 unsuccessful versions prior to the moment of enlightenment.

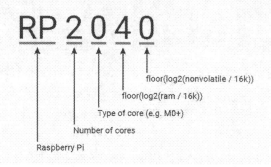

Figure 1-3. *RP2040 nomenclature (courtesy of raspberrypi.org)*

The RP2040 is a single chip combining memory, a dual-core processor, interfaces, and supporting electronics. In many ways, it is a self-contained powerhouse of a microcontroller. The chip is built to deliver high performance with low power consumption. In fact, it can also support extended execution using battery power. And, best of all, it boasts the ability to run MicroPython, making programming very easy to learn breaking the steep programming learning curve common to microcontrollers. In other words, you don't have to have a degree in programming or electronics to be able to use it.

The many features of the RP2040 are listed as follows:

- Dual ARM Cortex-M0+ @ 133MHz

- 264kB on-chip SRAM in six independent banks

- Support for up to 16MB of off-chip flash memory via dedicated QSPI bus

- DMA controller

- Fully connected AHB crossbar

- Interpolator and integer divider peripherals

- On-chip programmable LDO to generate core voltage

- 2 on-chip PLLs to generate USB and core clocks

- 30 GPIO pins, 4 of which can be used as analogue inputs

- Peripherals include

  - 2 UARTs

  - 2 SPI controllers

  - 2 I2C controllers

  - 16 PWM channels

  - USB 1.1 controller and PHY, with host and device support

  - 8 PIO state machines

So, what is all of that mumbo jumbo? For most, these features may not mean a whole lot, but in essence, we're talking about a seriously capable chip. Those features you may be most interested in include the SPI and I2C controllers (2 of each), the 16 pulse-width modulation channels, and the 30 GPIO pins. Suffice to say, it can handle just about anything you would need for your electronics project. Cool!

Tip   For a complete description of the features of the RP2040, see the data sheet at `https://datasheets.raspberrypi.org/rp2040/rp2040-datasheet.pdf`.

The RP2040 microcontroller can be purchased separately, and there are a growing number of vendors building boards around the RP2040. We will see a few of them in a later section. But first, let's look at the hardware of the Pico in more detail.

Pico Hardware Overview

So, what is the Pico? Simply, the Pico is a printed circuit board built around the RP2040 along with supporting circuitry to create a small microcontroller board about the size of a stick of gum. It breaks out (think wiring) all of the interfaces supported by the RP2040 along with power and ground pins to help round out the GPIO pins.

The Pico is a low-cost board that offers more features than any other board in the price range. In fact, you can find the Pico for as little as $4.00! That's amazing considering what you get. For that price, you will get a Pico without headers attached, and you can buy the headers (male or female pins) cut to length. If you do not know how to solder, you can get the Pico with headers soldered on for a couple of dollars more. Even so, it's still well below what you'd expect to pay for a full-featured microcontroller board.

Let's talk about those header pins for a moment. If you look closely, you will see the pins have what appear to be two rows: one hole closer to the center of the board and another half hole on the edge giving the long edges of the board a serrated look. This design, called castellations, allows you to solder the board in a surface mount configuration or use male header pins for use with a breadboard or female header pins to allow the use of jumper wires to connect components to the Pico. Figure 1-4 shows the header in more detail.

Figure 1-4. *Close-up of the Pico header (courtesy of raspberrypi.org)*

Tip   For a complete guide on how to solder headers onto the Raspberry Pi Pico, visit `https://magpi.raspberrypi.org/articles/how-to-solder-gpio-pin-headers-to-raspberry-pi-pico`.

Along with the features of the RP2040, the Pico has been designed with the following features:

- RP2040 microcontroller with 2MB Flash

- Micro-USB-B port for power and data (and for reprogramming the Flash)

- 21x51 1mm thick PCB with 0.1" through-hole pins also with edge castellations

- 40-pin GPIO header

  - Exposes 26 multifunction 3.3V general-purpose I/O (GPIO)

  - 23 GPIO are digital-only and 3 are ADC capable

  - Can be surface mounted as a module

- 3-pin ARM Serial Wire Debug (SWD) port

- Can be powered via the micro-USB, external supplies, or batteries

- High quality, low cost, high availability

- Comprehensive SDK, software examples, and documentation

Tip   For a complete description of the features of the Pico, see the data sheet at `https://datasheets.raspberrypi.org/pico/pico-datasheet.pdf`.

Now that we know more about the features of the Pico, let's look at a few alternatives that use the same RP2040 chip.

WAIT, WHAT ABOUT WIFI? WHERE'S THE WIFI?

Savvy readers may have noticed the Pico does not have a WiFi chip. This is intentional and designed to keep costs low. Does that mean you cannot use WiFi with the Pico? No, it does not. MicroPython fully supports networking protocols, and you can indeed use the Pico with WiFi, but it requires external components to do so. We will see more about how to use the Pico with WiFi in Chapters 13 and 14.

RP2040-Based Alternatives

There are a number of RP2040-based microcontroller boards that have been built around the RP2040. Some offer unique features not found on the Pico, and others are familiar adaptation to existing product lines. All of them get their powerful base from the RP2040 and works the same as the Pico. Some variants are priced several times that of the Pico, but you get a lot more for your money such as Grove connectors, additional components like programmable LEDs, buttons, etc.[2]

---

[2] At the time of this writing, there are several shortages and disruptions of some supply chains. Thus, you may find some boards and components on back order or low stock from vendors.

If you want to try out any of these alternatives, you're welcome to do so. The book will be based on the cheaper Pico, but any of these boards can be used for the projects in this book with some minor adaptations to the wiring. You will find most cost a bit more than the base Pico but, depending on your needs (or familiarity/affinity for a vendor's products), may be worth the extra cost.

Let's look at a few offerings from the most popular vendors including Adafruit (adafruit.com) and SparkFun (sparkfun.com). There are others and more are arriving, but these are the current crop of boards.

Adafruit Feather 2040

Adafruit has a very successful line of small boards under the Feather banner. It's all about powerful features in a lightweight package. It was no surprise that Adafruit adapted the Feather platform for the Raspberry Pi RP2040. This board has the same features as the Pico, but in a slightly different physical layout without castellated headers. It has an 8MB SPI flash chip for storing files, 21 GPIO pins (one more additional ADC), built-in 200mA+ lipoly charger, an RGB NeoPixel for general use, a STEMMA/QT connector for use with their pantheon of STEMMA/QT components (modules), and a USB-C port instead of the micro-USB on the Pico. Figure 1-5 shows the Adafruit Feather RP2040 board. The board costs about $12.00.

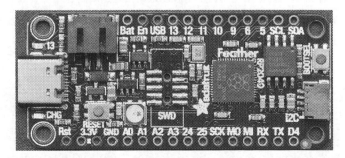

Figure 1-5. *Adafruit Feather RP2040 (courtesy of adafruit.com)*

For a complete description of this board, see `www.adafruit.com/product/4884`.

Adafruit ItsyBitsy RP2040

If you're looking for similar features, but in a slightly smaller package, the Adafruit ItsyBitsy RP2040 may do the trick. Built on their ItsyBitsy platform, this board offers a range of features familiar to that line of boards and all of the features as the Pico, with many of the same features as the Feather RP2040 including two extra GPIO ports, but uses the same micro-USB connector as the Pico. Figure 1-6 shows the Adafruit ItsyBitsy RP2040 board. The board costs about $10.00.

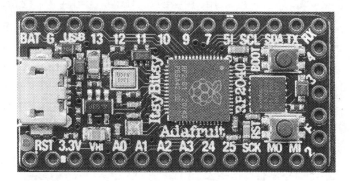

Figure 1-6. *Adafruit ItsyBitsy RP2040 (courtesy of adafruit.com)*

For a complete description of this board, see `www.adafruit.com/product/4888`.

Adafruit QT Py

Yeah, the name is intentional. It is a cutie-pie! This is an extreme version of the RP2040 built to support the Adafruit STEMMA QT line of components. It features a lot of the same features as the other two Adafruit boards but with a tiny footprint and is one of the smallest RP2040 boards on the market. This board has the same features as the Pico as well as the Feather

RP2040 but in an ultra-compact size. It has the same USB-C connector as the Feather RP2040, but only 13 GPIO pins. Despite its small size, it does have a STEMMA/QT connector. It has been fitted with a castellated header, and, since it takes up less space, it offers more versatility with installation. Figure 1-7 shows the Adafruit QT Py board. The board costs about $10.00.

Figure 1-7. *Adafruit QT Py (courtesy of adafruit.com)*

For a complete description of this board, see `www.adafruit.com/product/4900`.

SparkFun Pro Micro – RP2040

The SparkFun Pro Micro RP2040 is one of several RP2040-based boards from SparkFun. Like the Adafruit offerings, it boasts all of the features of the RP2040 along with a WS2812B addressable LED, a boot and reset button, a castellated header, and a Qwiic connector for use with their Qwiic pantheon of I2C devices. It has a USB-C connector instead of the micro-USB on the Pico. Interestingly, it also has a resettable PTC fuse that you can reset should your circuit trip the fuse. In addition, it has 18 GPIO pins, a four-channel ADC with an internal temperature sensor and 12-bit conversion. The board also includes an additional 16MB external QSPI flash chip to store program code, double that of the Feather RP2040. Figure 1-8 shows the SparkFun Pro Micro RP2040. The board costs about $10.00.

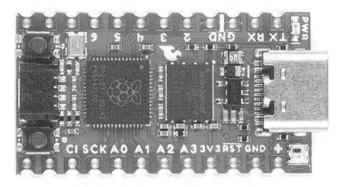

Figure 1-8. *SparkFun Pro Micro RP2040 (courtesy of sparkfun.com)*

For a complete description of this board, see `www.sparkfun.com/products/17717`.

SparkFun Thing Plus – RP2040

The SparkFun Thing Plus is a more compact option that is similar to the Adafruit Feather–sized boards with many of the same features as the SparkFun Pro Micro RP2040 but in a larger format without the castellated header. It has 18 GPIO pins, 16MB flash memory, a JST single-cell battery connector, an addressable WS2812 RGB LED, as well as a Qwiic connector. The board is unique in that it has an SD card slot and mounting holes making it easy to add to projects with enclosures. Figure 1-9 shows the SparkFun Pro Micro RP2040. The board costs about $18.00.

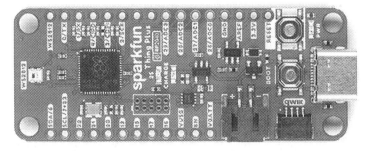

Figure 1-9. *SparkFun Thing Plus – RP2040 (courtesy of sparkfun.com)*

For a complete description of this board, see www.sparkfun.com/products/17745.

SparkFun MicroMod Pi RP2040 Processor

The SparkFun MicroMod Pi RP2040 Processor Board is an interesting deviation from the standard microcontroller board. Instead of building a new board with all of the features, connections, electronics, and headers, SparkFun has come up with a novel idea. They use a modular board for the processor and a separate host board (also called a carrier board) for the rest of the components. That is, you can purchase one of several processors and use with one of several carrier boards.

The SparkFun MicroMod Pi RP2040 Processor Board therefore is a RP2040 mounted on a small card that you can plug into one of the carrier boards. You simply connect it to the carrier board that gives you the inputs and outputs you need for your project. Do you want to use the RP2040 with a different carrier board? No problem! Just switch it to the other one. Cool.

Tip   For more information about the complete line of SparkFun MicroMod products, see www.sparkfun.com/categories/622.

There are several boards you can use, each with a unique set of features. The following lists a few that may be applicable to most projects built with the RP2040 and MicroPython (there are many others):

- *Asset Tracker*: Provides you with tools to monitor and track the location of your assets (www.sparkfun.com/products/17272).

- *Input and Display*: Provides a 2.4" TFT display for data visualization or a visual interface (www.sparkfun.com/products/16985).

- *Weather*: Create your own weather station. It features several sensors: the BME280 temperature, pressure, and humidity sensor, the VEML6075 UV sensor, and the AS3935 Lightning detector (`www.sparkfun.com/products/16794`).

- *Data Logging*: Provides an SD drive and Qwiic connectors for all of your data logging needs (`www.sparkfun.com/products/16829`).

- *Qwiic Versions*: There are two carrier boards designed to support mounting one or two Qwiic modules as well as the RP2040 MicroMod processor. These are great for small projects that use Qwiic components (`www.sparkfun.com/products/17723`, `www.sparkfun.com/products/17724`).

Let's take a look at the double MicroMod Qwiic Carrier Board. Figure 1-10 shows the SparkFun MicroMod Qwiic Carrier Board – double with two Qwiic modules mounted. Notice above the USB-C connector is the MicroMod RP2040 mounted in its slot. The board costs about $12.00.

Figure 1-10. *SparkFun MicroMod Qwiic Carrier Board – double (courtesy of sparkfun.com)*

For a complete description of this board, see `www.sparkfun.com/products/17724`.

The SparkFun MicroMod Pi RP2040 Processor Board is the RP2040 packaged on a small board with an M.2 connector. Connecting your MicroMod Pi RP2040 Processor Board is very easy and the same as mounting a component with an M.2 connector. Just match up the key on the edge connector to the key to the M.2 connector, insert it, and use a screw to fix the module to the carrier. As you surmised, it has all of the same features as the RP2040. The functionality supported depends on the carrier board on which it is employed. Figure 1-11 shows the SparkFun MicroMod RP2040 Processor. The processor costs about $12.00.

Figure 1-11. *SparkFun MicroMod RP2040 Processor (courtesy of sparkfun.com)*

For a complete description of this board, see `www.sparkfun.com/products/17720`.

Arduino Nano RP2040 Connect

The Arduino Nano RP2040 Connect board is one of the most anticipated new RP2040 boards available. It is expected to be widely available by the time this book is in print, and many cannot wait to get hold of one.[3] Why? Because the Arduino has been the king under the mountain of

---

[3] I got mine while writing this chapter!

microcontrollers. If you have used any other microcontroller board, chances are it was an Arduino or Arduino variant.

It comes as no surprise that Arduino.cc would employ the RP2040 on their own format of microcontrollers. Arduino has placed the RP2040 on their Nano format board complete with all of the features of an Arduino Nano plus a NINA WiFi and Bluetooth module! Yes, this board is the first to have onboard WiFi and Bluetooth. There are so many features that it is no wonder the expectations are high for this board. Figure 1-12 shows the Arduino Nano RP2040 Connect. It is slightly smaller than the Pico with fewer GPIO pins but has the castellated header of the Pico and the same micro-USB connector. The board costs about $25.00.

Figure 1-12. *Arduino Nano RP2040 Connect (courtesy of arduino.cc)*

For a complete description of this board, see `https://store.arduino.cc/nano-rp2040-connect-with-headers`. If you plan to use this board, see the online documentation at `https://docs.arduino.cc/hardware/nano-rp2040-connect`.

Note   You must use a special MicroPython image for the Arduino Nano RP2040 despite product descriptions stating support for MicroPython. There is also a port of CircuitPython that works that is very similar to MicroPython (more on that in Chapter 2). See `https://learn.adafruit.com/circuitpython-on-the-arduino-nano-rp2040-connect` for more details.

Pimoroni Pico LiPo

Pimoroni has long been a vendor of excellent and sometimes quirky (in a very cool way) components for microcontrollers and the Raspberry Pi. You may have seen and used one of their many distinctive cases for the Raspberry Pi.

Pimoroni has a product line named Pirate that they use to market products related to the Raspberry Pi including a really cool radio kit[4] that uses a Raspberry Pi Zero WiFi board. They have made a RP2040 Pirate version with extra memory, a USB-C connector, STEMMA/QT and Qwiic connectors, as well as onboard LiPo charging. On top of that, they retained the Pico format along with the castellated header. Figure 1-13 shows the Pimoroni Pico LiPo. The board costs $12.00 and up depending on memory size.

Figure 1-13. *Pimoroni Pico LiPo (courtesy of pimoroni.com)*

For a complete description of this board, see `https://shop.pimoroni.com/products/pimoroni-pico-lipo`.

Now that we have learned about the technical details concerning the Raspberry Pi Pico, the RP2040, and some of the alternative boards available, let's take a look at how to get started using the Pico.

---

[4] `https://shop.pimoroni.com/products/pirate-radio-pi-zero-w-project-kit`

Getting Started with the Pico

While the Pico can be programmed with C++, we will use MicroPython in this book to learn how to build electronics and IoT projects. We choose MicroPython because it is easy to install and the language is easy to learn. But where can you buy one of these little boards?

Where to Buy

The Raspberry Pi has become world known and is available from many online vendors, and some local electronics stores carry them as well. Given our new connected, post-pandemic world where you can order any you want and have it delivered, we can find our Raspberry Pi Pico and all of our accessories online. The following lists a few of the more popular online vendors:

- *The Pi Hut*: Mann Enterprises LTD located in the UK is the premier Raspberry Pi shop. They have just about anything you could need for the Raspberry Pi including the Pico, micro:bit, Arduino, robotics, and more. Check them out at `https://thepihut.com/`.

- *PiShop.US*: The American Raspberry Pi shop located in the United States. They have all things Raspberry Pi, Arduino, and more. Find them at `www.pishop.us/`.

- *Adafruit*: Limor Fried, Adafruit founder and lead engineer, together with a team of talented engineers develop community-driven products and code. They carry many Adafruit designed products for many of the most popular electronics platforms including the Arduino as well as their own brand of Arduino boards, Raspberry Pi, and more. They also host one of the most comprehensive learning systems available. If you need to learn how to do something, check out `https://learn.adafruit.com/`. Chances are you'll find all of your answers there. Also, check out their wares at `www.adafruit.com/`.

- *SparkFun*: Another most excellent online electronics vendor and a favorite of mine, SparkFun is located in the United States and carry a vast line of microcontrollers, discrete components, Arduino, Raspberry Pi, and so much more. You simply will get lost in the depth of their catalog. They are the makers of the Qwiic component system and have many modules to choose from including their own brand of most products. They also host a vast learning website and document every component they sell. If you need help with their products or want to learn how to build something, check out `https://learn.sparkfun.com/`. With excellent customer service and fast shipping, SparkFun should be on your go-to list of vendors. Check out their products at `www.sparkfun.com`.

- *Seeed Studio*: Seeed Studio is located in China. They carry all manner of electronics for all of the major brands as well as they are the makers of the Grove component system, which we will be using later in this book. They also have a vast Wiki devoted to all of their products with ample instructions and documentation. See their Wiki at `https://wiki.seeedstudio.com/`. While transit time for some may be a concern, chances are the nice people at Seeed Studio will have what you need. Look for them at `www.seeedstudio.com/`.

- *Mouser*: One of the largest online electronics stores (their catalog is thousands of pages long) and based in the United States is Mouser. They have almost everything on the planet for the electronics enthusiast. Their website is more industry driven, but if you search for products by name or description, you will find what you need. See `www.mouser.com` for more details.

- *Pimoroni*: A growing online vendor that sells all of their own products directly as well as many accessories for the Arduino and Raspberry Pi. If you want a Pimoroni product but can't find it at a local vendor, get it from the source at `https://shop.pimoroni.com/`.

The Pico is typically sold packaged in a static-free packet without headers. Some vendors offer the Pico with headers attached (Seeed Studio) as well as bundles with the USB cable and more.

Tip   If you want to order new Raspberry Pi products when they are released, The Pi Hut (`https://thepihut.com/`) typically has them in stock the day they are released.

Now that we know where to buy our Pico kit, let's look at what accessories you need to get started.

Required Accessories

The list of required accessories is quite short. In fact, the only thing you need to get started with the Pico is a USB-B female to micro-USB-B male cable. That's it!

Tip   For the most excellent description of USB cables and connectors on the Internet, see `https://learn.sparkfun.com/tutorials/connector-basics/usb-connectors`.

However, that won't get you all you need to do the projects in this book. You will need more components and some electronics to build the projects. Rather than list all those here, you will find a list of required components in each project chapter. For example, you may need a breadboard, jumper wires, and one or more electronic components.

There are some optional and recommended accessories you should consider.

Optional and Recommended Accessories

There are a growing number of accessories available for the Pico. So many, in fact, it is difficult to keep up with the list! Rather than attempt that, this section presents some of the products that have been shown to enhance your experience with the Pico. While some of these may be required or at least optional for the projects in the book, you can get by without them if you're on a tight budget. However, if you have some funds to building a kit for the Pico, these are some of the best options you can find.

There are host boards (not unlike the MicroMod carrier boards from SparkFun), add-on boards, and basic components that you may want to consider. Let's start with the host boards. There are several excellent boards, but we will look at three of the first boards available for the Pico.

One of the host boards that has proven to be a good place to start with basic projects is the Maker Pi Pico Base (without Pico) from Cytron (`https://thepihut.com/products/maker-pi-pico-base-without-pico`). You can get this board with the Pico already soldered in place or with a header ready for you to plug in your Pico with male headers soldered on. The board costs about $9.50 and is available from The Pi Hut.

The Maker Pi Pico Base includes a reset button and access to all GPIO pins on two 20-way pin headers with clear labels. Better still, each pin has an LED indicator to let you know if the pin is in use. Now, that's a nice touch! But it doesn't end there. There are three programmable pushbuttons, an RGB LED, buzzer, audio jack, a micro-SD card slot, and six Grove ports. Most intriguing is the addition of a socket for an ESP-01 WiFi module. Yes, you can provide WiFi for your Pico! Figure 1-14 shows the Maker Pi Pico Base (without Pico).

Figure 1-14. *Maker Pi Pico Base (without Pico) (courtesy of thepihut.com)*

You can find the data sheet with complete details of all of its features at `https://cdn.shopify.com/s/files/1/0176/3274/files/Maker_ Pi_Pico_Datasheet.pdf?v=1617963762`. See `https://github.com/ CytronTechnologies/MAKER-PI-PICO` for example code for the Pico.

Another similar board is from Pimoroni. The Pico Omnibus (Dual Expander) (`https://shop.pimoroni.com/products/pico-omnibus`) is a simple board that contains two mirrored docking ports that mirror the GPIO header of the Pico but with male pins. This allows you to use up to two Pico add-on boards at the same time without having to fuss with soldering stacking headers. The pins are all clearly labeled in white on a black PCB and come with rubber feet you can apply yourself. The board costs about $9.00, and you can find it at thepihut.com or pimoroni.com. Figure 1-15 shows the Pico Omnibus (Dual Expander).

Figure 1-15. *Pico Omnibus (Dual Expander) (courtesy of pimoroni.com)*

You may be wondering what modules you can use with this board. Well, it turns out Pimoroni offers several. Two of those we can use for the projects in this book are the Pico Display Pack (https://shop.pimoroni. com/products/pico-display-pack) and the Pico Wireless Pack (https:// shop.pimoroni.com/products/pico-wireless-pack).

The Pico Display Pack has a 1.14" LCD screen with four buttons and an RGB LED mounted with female headers so you can attach it directly to the bottom of your Pico. Figure 1-16 shows the Pico Display Pack.

Figure 1-16. *Pico Display Pack (courtesy of pimoroni.com)*

The Pico Wireless Pack uses an ESP32 chip to provide 2.4GHz wireless connections for your Pico. It also includes a micro-SD drive for file storage as well as an RGB LED and a programmable button. It is also mounted with female headers so you can attach it directly to the bottom of your Pico. Figure 1-17 shows the Pico Wireless Pack.

Figure 1-17. *Pico Wireless Pack (courtesy of pimoroni.com)*

Tip   If you plan to complete the projects in Chapters 13 and 14 or want to explore the challenge exercises, you should plan on purchasing the Pimoroni Omnibus (Dual Extender), Display Pack, and Wireless Pack.

The last board is the Grove Shield for Pi Pico (`www.seeedstudio.com/Grove-Shield-for-Pi-Pico-v1-0-p-4846.html`). This board is the premier board for using the Grove component system from Seeed Studio. The board features ten Grove connectors, a dual row of GPIO headers to allow access to all pins while the Pico is installed, and a 3.3V/5V power switch, which is needed to support some Grove modules. The board costs about $4.50 and is available from Seeed Studio and other online vendors. It does not come with any bumpers, so you may want to invest in some to attach to the bottom to keep from scratching your workspace/desktop area. Figure 1-18 shows the Grove Shield for the Raspberry Pico.

Figure 1-18. *Grove Shield for the Raspberry Pi Pico (courtesy of seeedstudio.com)*

Seeed Studio also sells a Grove starting kit for the Pico for about $48 (`www.seeedstudio.com/Grove-Starter-Kit-for-Raspberry-Pi-Pico-p-4851.html`), which includes the shield and 12 Grove modules and assorted electronics. If you want to use the Grove system exclusively, this starter kit is a must.

Tip   If you plan to complete the projects in Chapters 9 through 12 or want to explore the challenge exercises, you should plan on purchasing the Grove Shield for the Raspberry Pi Pico.

Now that we've discovered some nice accessories to use with the Pico, let's jump into our first tour of how to use it starting with preparing our PC.

Preparing Your Computer

Fortunately, there isn't much you need to do to configure your computer to work with the Pico. At the barest, you will need to download the MicroPython boot image, which we will see how to do in the next section.

It is highly recommended that you install Python on your computer to help learn how to work with the language. Why? Because MicroPython is a subset of Python and many of the early examples you will see will run on both your PC and the Pico. Thus, it is wise to install Python to help you learn how to write MicroPython. If you don't know how to get started installing Python on your PC, don't worry. We will visit this topic in Chapter 2.

Installing MicroPython on the Pico

Now we're at the meat of our example. Here, we will install MicroPython on our Pico and get it ready for programming. There are two ways to accomplish this: a manual method and an automated process using Thonny. Let's look at both methods. You can choose the one that works best for you.

Manual Install

The process is very simple. First, you download the bootloader file, then place your Pico into USB drive mode, insert it into your PC, then copy the file onto the drive, remove the Pico, and reinsert it. Simple! Let's see it in more detail.

Caution   Do not connect your Pico to your computer yet. You will need to plug it in and unplug it at specific steps in the process. If you've already plugged in the cable, it won't hurt anything, but you will need to disconnect it before your begin.

Begin by visiting https://micropython.org/download/rp2-pico/ rp2-pico-latest.uf2 and download the latest UF2 bootloader file. Make sure you let the download complete before you continue.

Next, locate the *BOOTSEL* switch on your Pico. You will need to press this button and hold it while you connect it to your PC. Figure 1-19 shows the location of the *BOOTSEL* switch.

Figure 1-19. *Locating the BOOTSEL switch*

Next, connect your USB cable to your Pico and press the *BOOTSEL* and hold it when you insert the other end of the USB cable to your PC. Wait about three to five seconds and then release the button. It will mount as a drive with the name *RPI-RP2*. On Windows, you will hear the tone to indicate a new USB device was detected. On Linux and macOS, you will see a new icon appear for the drive.

Be very careful when connecting and disconnecting the USB cable on your Pico boards, especially those with the micro-USB connector. These are very fragile and can be broken easily if the cable is pulled at an angle or twisted. The same is true when using the Pico on a breadboard or host adapter like those shown earlier. Be sure to remove the Pico by grasping it on the sides away from the USB connector.

Caution   The USB connector on the Pico is fragile. Be sure to insert and remove the USB cable directly and never pull the cable at an angle to remove it.

Next, locate the UF2 file you downloaded and simply drag and drop it onto your Pico (shown as a drive on your PC). When the file copy is finished, the Pico will reboot. You can tell by watching the LED on the Pico, and the drive on your PC should disappear. If this does not happen, you can unplug the Pico and plug it back in to get it to boot into MicroPython.

Using Thonny

There is also an automated method to install MicroPython on your PC. If you have worked with the Raspberry Pi and Python, chances are you've run across a nice, small Python integrated development environment (IDE) named Thonny. Thonny is available for most platforms including Linux, Windows, and macOS at `https://thonny.org/`. Simply download the installer for your platform and install it.

After you have installed Thonny and start it for the first time, on some platforms, you will be asked to choose a *language* and *initial settings*. The choices for settings include *Standard* and *Raspberry Pi*. The *Raspberry Pi* settings are simplistic, and you won't see the menu (but you can turn it on by switching the mode). So, you should select the *Standard* option as shown in Figure 1-20.

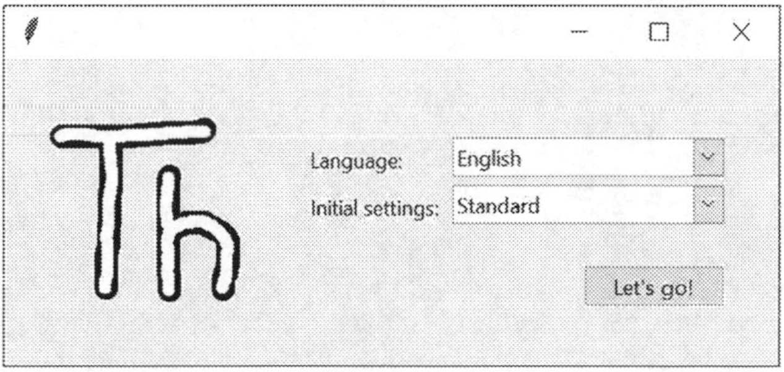

Figure 1-20. *Choose initial settings (Thonny)*

Caution   To perform this process, your Pico should not be connected to your PC. If it is, disconnect it before you continue.

Using Thonny, you can develop Python and MicroPython code and even run the code to test it. The editor is tailored for writing Python code and has many useful tools to help you with your coding. Better still, it does all of this using a simple, uncluttered user interface that is elegant in its simplicity.

But it's not just a fancy editor! You can also connect to your Raspberry Pi Pico to write code and run it. In fact, you can use Thonny to load MicroPython on your Pico. Let's see how to do that. First, launch Thonny without the Pico connected to your computer. Figure 1-21 shows the Thonny IDE on Windows.

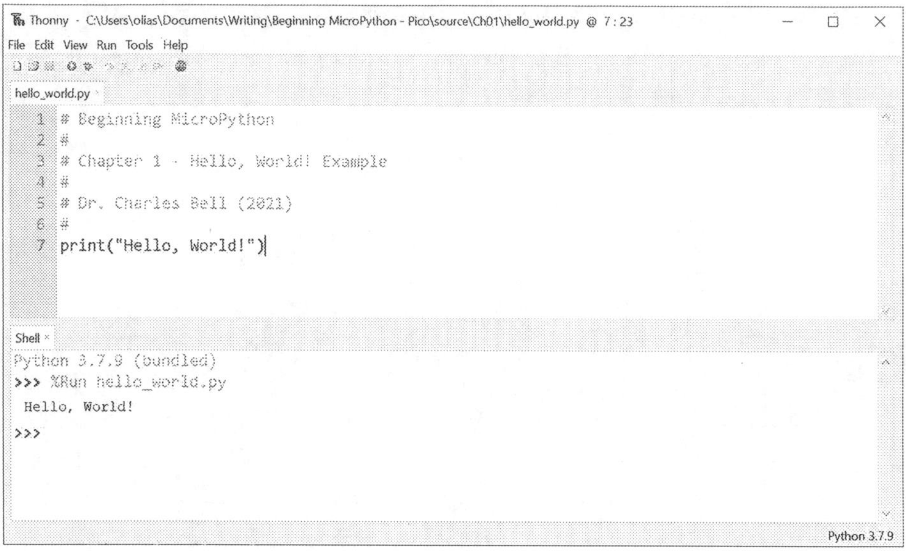

Figure 1-21. *Thonny IDE (Windows 10)*

Notice at the top of the window is a tabbed editor area where you can work on one or more Python files. Below that is the Shell area that you can use to execute your Python code. Here, we see a very simple print statement and its execution. On the right is an area for the documentation and help links. You can close both if you want some more room for the editor.

Notice also in the lower right-hand corner the text *Python 3.7.9*. This is actually an actionable area (think button) that lets you change the base Python interpreter. We will use that in a moment.

Next, locate the *BOOTSEL* switch on your Pico. You will need to press this button and hold it while you connect it to your PC. Figure 1-19 shows the location of the *BOOTSEL* switch. Next, connect your USB cable to your Pico and press the *BOOTSEL* and hold it when you insert the other end of the USB cable to your PC.

Go back to Thonny and click the Python version. Figure 1-22 shows what the menu should look like.

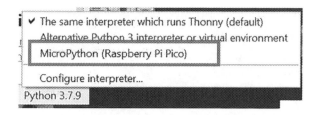

Figure 1-22. *Choose a Python interpreter (Thonny)*

Next, click *MicroPython (Raspberry Pi Pico)*. A dialog box will prompt you to install the latest version of the MicroPython firmware on your Pico. When ready, click *Install* in the dialog that appears as shown in Figure 1-23.

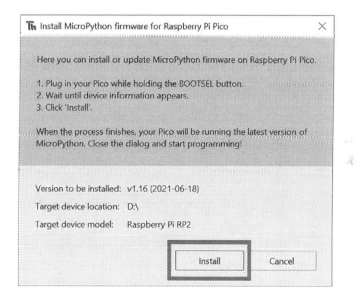

Figure 1-23. *Install MicroPython (Thonny)*

Note If the dialog doesn't appear, ensure you have plugged in your Pico with the *BOOTSEL* pressed. It is OK to try it again.

When the installation is complete, you can click *Close* as shown in Figure 1-24. Now we're ready to begin programming our Pico.

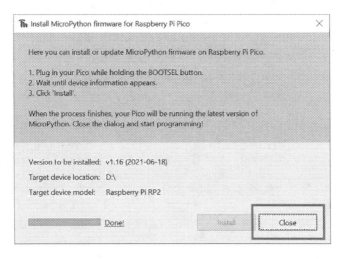

Figure 1-24. *MicroPython install complete (Thonny)*

Your Pico will reboot, and when it is booted, you will see the MicroPython header in the Shell window as shown in Figure 1-25. Just for fun, type help() in the >>> prompt and press enter. This is the basic help for the MicroPython interpreter. We'll see more about how to use this in the next section.

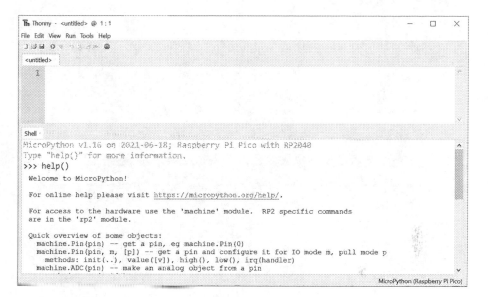

Figure 1-25. *Connected to the Pico (Thonny)*

It is possible on some platforms for the Pico to change COM ports when it is rebooted. If you cannot connect to the Pico with Thonny at this step, try disconnecting and reconnecting the Pico. You can also click the red *Stop* button on the toolbar to stop and restart the Pico connection. Then, in the *Tools* ➤ *Options...* menu on the *Interpreter* tab, select the COM port for the Pico as shown in Figure 1-26 and then click *OK*.

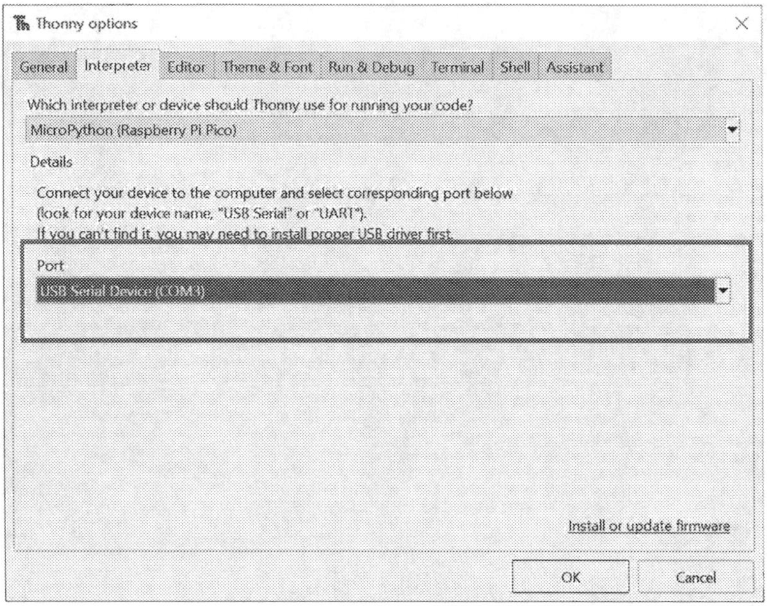

Figure 1-26. *Selecting the COM port for the Pico (Thonny – Windows 10)*

It is also possible the interpreter for the MicroPython Pico will not show up if there is an error communicating with the Pico. In that case, open the options dialog again and choose the `MicroPython (Raspberry Pi Pico)` in the Interpreter drop-down box as shown in Figure 1-27.

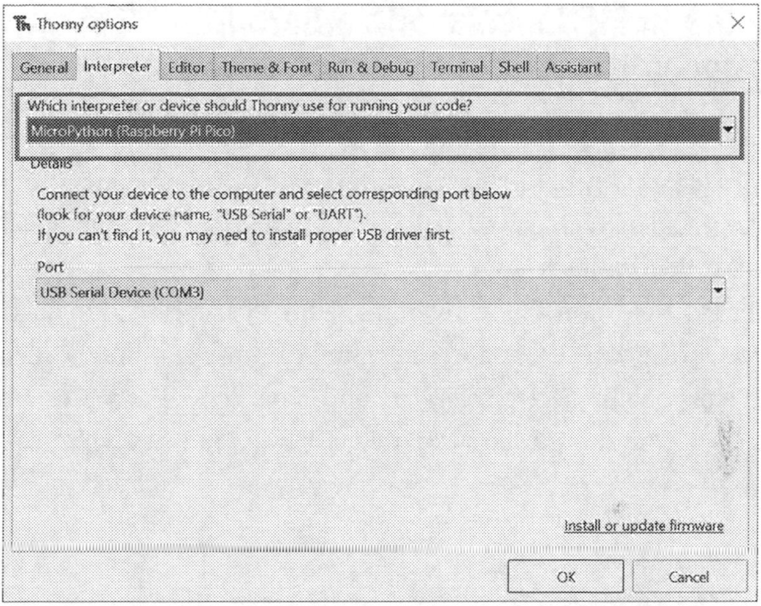

Figure 1-27. Selecting the Python interpreter (Thonny)

Now that our Pico is loaded with the MicroPython boot image, let's see how to connect to it and run some code!

Connecting to the Pico

Now that you have your Pico running MicroPython, now what do you do? Now you need to open a communication link to the MicroPython interpreter. The MicroPython interpreter is called a read-evaluate-print loop (REPL) and is often referred to with that acronym. You can connect to your Pico to execute the REPL feature using either a serial communication utility or a development environment with the same feature. Let's see how to use the communication utility first.

Using the REPL Console with a Serial Communication Utility

If you are using Windows 10, you can use any serial communication utility you'd like. One of the most common is PuTTY (`www.putty.org/`). It is rather aged but works well. If you want to use PuTTY, go ahead and download and install it now.

Once installed, you will be referencing the Pico connection via the COM port. To find the COM port that your Windows computer is using for the Pico, open the *Device Manager* and expand the *Ports (COM & LPT)* section. You should see a USB device similar to what is shown in Figure 1-28.

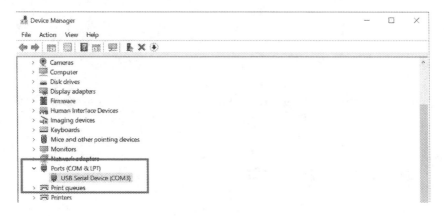

Figure 1-28. *Locating the COM port (Windows 10)*

If you have multiple devices connected, you may need to disconnect the Pico, refresh the device manager, then reconnect the Pico. The COM port that disappears when you disconnect and reappears when you reconnect the Pico is the one you need to use.

Notice the COM port (COM3). We will need that to tell PuTTY which port to use. Now, open PuTTY and select the *Serial* for the *Connection type* and change the *Serial line* to *COM3* (the port shown in your device manager) as shown in Figure 1-29. Click Open to start the terminal.

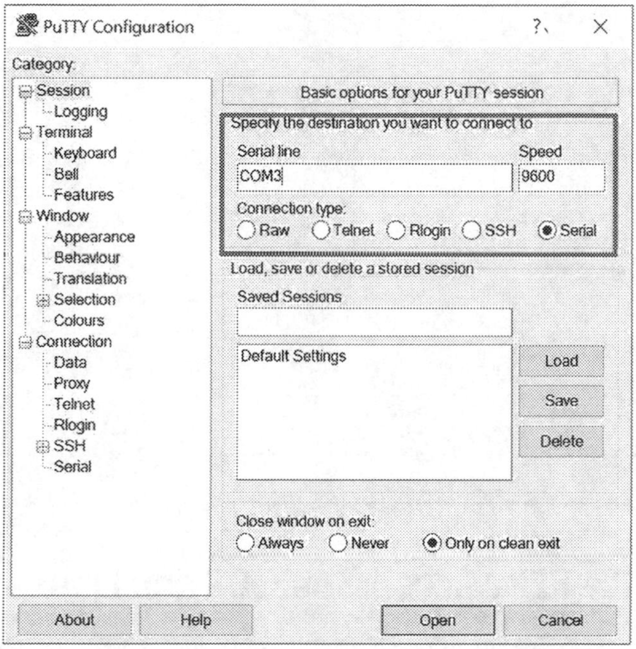

Figure 1-29. *Connecting to the Pico with PuTTY (Windows 10)*

When the terminal opens, you may not see anything at first. If so, you can press *ENTER* a few times and you should see the >>> prompt. You can then enter MicroPython statements and have them execute as demonstrated in Figure 1-30.

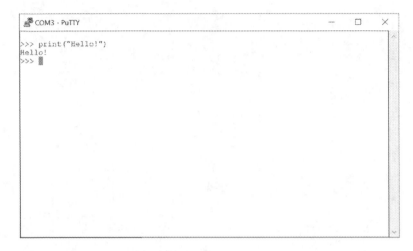

Figure 1-30. *PuTTY terminal (Windows 10)*

Starting the REPL Console (macOS and Linux)

To connect using macOS or Linux, you need to locate the correct device. I demonstrate this with the following command that lists the devices on my macOS system. Do this after you've connected the USB cable to the Pico.

```
% ls /dev/tty.*
/dev/tty.Bluetooth-Incoming-Port      /dev/tty.usbmodem14401
```

Once you see the correct USB device, you can enter the following command to open a screen (terminal) to execute the REPL:

```
% screen /dev/tty.usbmodem14401
```

Once again, you may need to press *ENTER* a few times to get the >>> prompt. Once you do, enter the following statement, and see the results:

```
>>> print("Hello from macOS!")
Hello from macOS!
>>>
```

Tip   There is one oddity with the REPL console. The quit() doesn't work. To exit the console for some Pico boards, you will need to reset the board or kill the connection.

Connecting to the Pico with Thonny

If you followed the instructions in the Thonny section earlier, you have what you need to connect to your Pico via Thonny. Recall, we need only connect our Pico to our PC and then open Thonny and change the Python interpreter. If you have not done that, you should go back and follow the preceding steps to choose the *MicroPython (Raspberry Pi Pico)*.

Once connected, the REPL will appear in the Shell tab as shown in Figure 1-31. You can enter the statement print("Hello from Thonny!") at the >>> prompt and press *ENTER*. You should see the results shown in the figure.

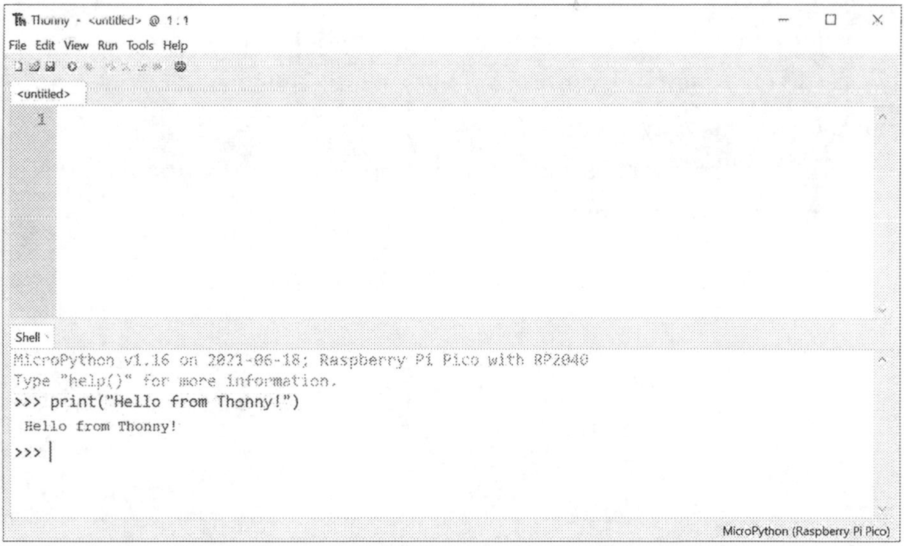

Figure 1-31. Connecting to the Pico with Thonny

If everything worked and you saw the message printed, congratulations! You've just written your first MicroPython code, and you're ready to dive into more MicroPython coding. Yippee!

Summary

There is little doubt that the Raspberry Pi Pico will open a new avenue for Raspberry Pi enthusiasts. The fact that we now have a Raspberry Pi–based microcontroller available at a very low cost and programmable with MicroPython means anyone can start to build electronics projects without the need for lengthy study or a steep learning curve. The subsequent chapters in this book will guide you to becoming proficient in building electronics projects with the Pico.

In this opening chapter, we have discovered what the Pico is, the hardware features available on the board, and we took a look at some of the other RP2040-based microcontroller boards available from other vendors. We also saw some recommended accessories to help make your experience with the Pico better by adding convenience features such as Grove and Qwiic connectors and a fully labeled GPIO header. However, your journey has only begun.

In the next chapter, we will learn more about MicroPython including how to get started programming your Pico.

CHAPTER 2

Introducing MicroPython

Now that we have learned more about the Raspberry Pi Pico and saw a demonstration of how to connect to it from our PC, it is time to learn more about MicroPython – how we can get started, how it works, and examples of what you can do with your own Pico.

Learning MicroPython is very easy even for those who have not had any programming experience. Indeed, all you need to learn MicroPython is a bit of patience and a little time to get used to the syntax and the mechanisms unique to working with MicroPython, the Pico, and the electronics. As we will see, there is a lot you can do with just a little knowledge.

In this chapter, we will learn more about MicroPython including an overview of how to get started. The examples in this chapter are intended to give you a taste of what you can do rather than a detailed tutorial. That said, I encourage you to attempt the examples for practice. We will see a detailed tutorial for programming MicroPython in Chapter 3 and a deeper dive into the software libraries for lower-level hardware support in Chapter 4.

Let's start with a look at what MicroPython is including why it was created and how to get started.

© Charles Bell 2022
C. Bell, *Beginning MicroPython with the Raspberry Pi Pico*, Maker Innovations Series,
https://doi.org/10.1007/978-1-4842-8135-2_2

Note   Since MicroPython runs on many boards, I use the term "boards" to mean any board that runs MicroPython, which includes the Pico.

Getting Started

The use of the Python language for controlling hardware has been around for some time. Users of the Raspberry Pi, pcDuino, and other low-cost computers and similar boards have had the advantage of using Python for controlling hardware. In this case, they used full versions of the Python programming language on the native Linux-based operating system.

While these boards made it possible for those who wanted to develop electronics projects, it required users to buy the board as well as peripherals like a keyboard, mouse, and monitor. Not only that, but users also had to learn the operating system. For those not used to Linux, this can be a challenge in and of itself.

The vision for MicroPython was to combine the simplicity of learning Python with the low cost and ease of use of microcontroller boards, which would permit a lot more people to work with electronics for art and science projects. Beginners would not have to learn a new operating system or learn one of the more complex programming languages. MicroPython was the answer. Figure 2-1 shows the MicroPython logo in the form of a sticker from Adafruit.

Figure 2-1. *MicroPython logo skill badge (courtesy of adafruit.com)*

That's pretty cool, isn't it? It's a snake (a python) on an integrated circuit (chip). You can order this nifty MicroPython sticker (`www.adafruit.com/products/3270`). I recommend getting one of these and displaying it proudly when you finish the book.

Origins

MicroPython[1] was created and is maintained by Damien P. George, Paul Sokolovsky, and other contributors. It was designed to be a lean, efficient version of the Python 3 language and installed on a small microcontroller. Since Python is an interpreted language and thus slower (in general) than compiled languages, MicroPython was designed to be as efficient as possible so that it can run on microcontrollers that normally are slower and have much less memory than a typical personal computer.

---

[1] Copyright 2014–2017, Damien P. George, Paul Sokolovsky, and contributors. Last updated on March 5, 2017.

COMPILED VS. INTERPRETED

Compiled languages use a program, called a compiler, to convert the source code from a human-readable form to a binary executable form. There are a few steps involved in this conversion, but, in general, we take source code and compile it into a binary form. Since it is in binary form, the processor can execute the statements generated directly without any additional steps (again, in general).

Interpreted languages, on the other hand, are not compiled but instead are converted to a binary form (or an intermediate binary form) on the fly with a program called an interpreter. Python 3 provides a Python executable that is both an interpreter and a console that allows you to run your code as you type it in. Python programs run one line of code at a time starting at the top of the file.

Thus, compiled languages are faster than interpreted languages because the code is prepared for execution and does not require an intermediate, real-time step to process the code before execution.

Another aspect is microcontroller boards like the Arduino and similar boards require a compilation step that you must perform on your computer and load the binary executable onto the board first. In contrast, since MicroPython has its interpreter running directly on the hardware, we do not need the intermediate step to prepare the code; we can run the interpreted language directly on the hardware!

This permits hardware manufacturers to build small, inexpensive boards that include MicroPython on the same chip as the microprocessor (typically). This gives you the ability to connect to the board, write the code, and execute it without any extra work.

You may be thinking that to reduce Python 3 to a size that fits on a small chip with limited memory, the language is stripped down and lacking features. That can't be further than the truth. In fact, MicroPython is a complete implementation of the core features of Python 3 including a compact runtime and interactive interpreter. There is support for reading and writing files, loading modules, interacting with hardware such as GPIO pins, error handling, and much more. Best of all, the optimization of Python 3 code allows it to be compiled into a binary requiring about 256K of memory to store the binary and run with as little as 16K of RAM.

However, there are a few things that MicroPython doesn't implement from the Python 3 language. The following sections give you an idea of what you can do with MicroPython and what you cannot do with MicroPython.

MicroPython Features

The biggest feature of MicroPython is, of course, it runs Python. This permits you to create simple, efficiently specified, and easy-to-understand programs. That alone, I think, is its best advantage over other boards like the Arduino. The following lists a few of the features that MicroPython supports. We will see these features in greater detail throughout this book:

- *Interactive interpreter*: MicroPython boards have built in a special interactive console that you can access by connecting to the board with a USB cable. Recall from Chapter 1, the console is called a read-evaluate-print loop (REPL) that allows you to type in your code and execute it one line at a time. It is a great way to prototype your code or just run a project as you develop it.

- *Python standard libraries*: MicroPython also supports many of the standard Python libraries. In general, you can expect to find MicroPython supports more than 80% of the most commonly used libraries. These include parsing JavaScript Object Notation (JSON),[2] socket programming, string manipulation, file input/output, and even regular expression support.

- *Hardware-level libraries*: MicroPython has libraries built-in that allow you to access hardware directly either to turn on or off analog pins, read analog data, read digital data, and even control hardware with pulse-width modulation (PWM) – a way to limit power to a device by rapidly modulating the power to the device, for example, making a fan spin slower than if it had full power.

- *Extensible*: MicroPython is also extensible. This is a great feature for advanced users who need to implement some complex library at a low level (in C or C++) and include the new library in MicroPython. Yes, this means you can build in your own unique code and make it part of the MicroPython feature set.

To answer your question, "What can I do with MicroPython?", the answer is quite a lot! You can control hardware connected to the MicroPython board, write code modules to expand the features of your program storing them for later retrieval (just like you can in Python on a PC), and much more. The hardware you can connect to include turning LEDs on and off, drive servos, read sensors, and even display text on LCDs. Some boards also

---

[2] www.json.org/json-en.html

have networking support in the form of WiFi radios. Just about anything you can do with the other microcontroller boards, you can do with a MicroPython board.

However, there are a few limitations to running MicroPython on the chip.

MicroPython Limitations

The biggest limitation of MicroPython is its ease of use. The ease of using Python means the code is interpreted on the fly. And while MicroPython is highly optimized, there is still a penalty for the interpreter. This means that projects that require a high degree of precision such as sampling data at a high rate or communicating over a connection (USB, hardware interface, etc.) may not run fast enough. For these areas, we can overcome the problem by extending the MicroPython language with optimized libraries for handling the low-level communication.

MicroPython also uses a bit more memory than other microcontroller platforms such as the Arduino. Normally, this isn't a problem but something you should consider if your program starts to get large. Larger programs that use a lot of libraries could consume more memory than you may expect. Once again, this is related to the ease of use of Python – another price to pay.

Finally, as mentioned previously, MicroPython doesn't implement all the features of all the Python 3 libraries. However, you should find it has everything you need to build IoT projects (and more).

ARE MY PYTHON SKILLS APPLICABLE TO MICROPYTHON?

If you've already learned how to program with Python, you may be expecting
to see something that stands out as different or even odd about MicroPython.
The good news is your Python skills are all you need to work with MicroPython.
Indeed, MicroPython and Python use the same syntax; there isn't anything new
to learn. As you will see in the next few chapters, MicroPython implements a
subset of Python libraries but still is very much Python.

What Does MicroPython Run On?

Due to the increasing popularity of MicroPython, there are more options
for boards to run MicroPython being added regularly. Part of this is from
developers building processor- and platform-specific compiled versions of
MicroPython that you can download and install on the board. This is how
the Raspberry Pi Pico works.

ONE MICROPYTHON, MANY BOARDS

There are other microcontroller and microprocessor boards that run
MicroPython natively (installed at the factory) or can be loaded with
MicroPython binaries, for example, the pyboard (`https://micropython.`
`org/`), which was the first MicroPython board created by the implementors
of MicroPython. There is also the WiPy (`https://pycom.io/`), which is an
excellent IoT board. There are also versions of the Espressif (ESP) boards and
Arduino that run MicroPython.

However, some of the other boards use a slightly different mix of MicroPython
libraries because some MicroPython boards have different hardware. Take
care when studying online examples to ensure you are referencing a generic
MicroPython example or one tailored to the Pico. We will focus exclusively on
the Pico in this book.

Next, let's talk about using Python on our PC for experimenting with learning the language.

Experimenting with Python on Your PC

Since MicroPython is Python (just a bit scaled down for optimization purposes), you can run Python on your PC and experiment with the language. I recommend loading Python on your PC even if you already have a MicroPython board. You may find it more convenient to try out things with your PC since you can control the environment better. However, your PC won't be able to communicate with electronic components or hardware like the MicroPython boards, so while you can do a lot more on the PC, you can't test your code that communicates with hardware. But you can test the basic constructs such as function calls, printing messages, and more.

So, why bother? Simply, using your PC to debug your Python code will allow you to get much of your project complete and working before trying it on the MicroPython board. More specifically, by developing the mundane things on your PC, you eliminate a lot of potential problems debugging your code on the MicroPython board. This is the number one mistake novice programmers make – writing an entire solution without testing smaller parts. It is always better to start small and test a small part of the code at a time adding only those parts that have been tested and shown to work correctly.

All you need to get started is to download and install Python 3 (e.g., Python 3.9.6 is the latest, but new versions become available periodically). The following sections briefly describe how to install Python on various platforms. For specific information about platforms not listed here, see the Python wiki at `https://wiki.python.org/moin/BeginnersGuide/Download`.

Caution   There are two versions of Python available – Python 2 and Python 3. Since MicroPython is based on Python 3, you will need to install Python version 3, not Python version 2.

Fortunately, most computers today come with Python installed. If you are not sure, open a terminal window (command window) and type the following command:

```
$ python –version
Python 3.9.6
```

If you get a result similar to what is shown earlier, you've got what you need. If not, you should install Python on your PC. Some computers may have both Python 2 and 3 installed. In this case, you may see a different version than what is shown earlier.

If you saw a version like Python 2.7.X, there is still a chance you have Python 3 on your machine. Some systems have both Python 2 and Python 3 installed. To run Python 3, use the following command:

```
$ python3
```

If Python 3 is not installed or it is an older version, use the following sections to install Python on your system. You should always install the latest version. You can download Python 3 from `www.python.org/downloads/`.

Installing Python 3 on Windows 10

Most Windows machines do not include Python, and you must install it. You can download Python 3 for Windows from `www.python.org/downloads/windows/`. You will find the usual Windows installer options for 32-bit and 64-bit versions as well as a web-based installer and a .zip format. Most people will use the Windows installer option, but if you have advanced needs to install Python manually, you can use the other options.

Once you download Python, you can launch the installer. For example, on my Windows 10 machine, I downloaded the file under the link named Latest Python 3 Release – Python 3.9.6. If you scroll down, you can find the installer you want. For example, I clicked the installer for Windows 64-bit machines. This downloaded a file named `python-3.9.6-amd64.exe`, which I located in my Downloads folder and executed by double-clicking the file.

Like most Windows installer installs, you can step through the various screens agreeing to the license, specifying where you want to install it, and finally initiating the install. Figure 2-2 shows an example of the installer running.

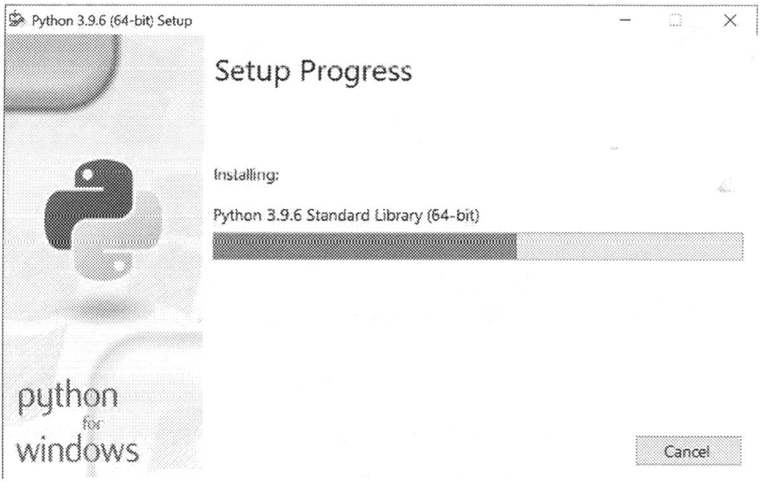

Figure 2-2. *Installing Python 3.9.6 on Windows 10*

Tip   If you get stuck or need more detailed instructions, see the excellent article at How-To Geek: `www.howtogeek.com/197947/how-to-install-python-on-windows/`.

Once the installation is complete, you can try the test in the previous section to verify the installation. If you do not modify your PATH variable, you may need to use the Python console shortcut on the start menu to launch the console.

In fact, if you run the installation and you cannot get Python to launch, you can fix this problem by running the installer again. When you launch the installer a subsequent time, you will be prompted on how to proceed. Click the *Modify* option as shown in Figure 2-3.

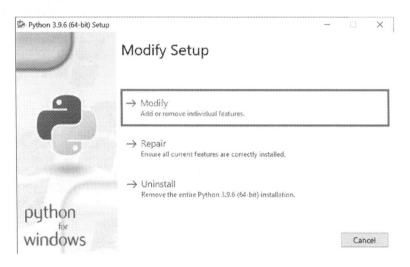

Figure 2-3. *Modify Python 3.9.6 installation on Windows 10*

On the next screen, ensure the *pip* option is chosen and click *Next* as shown in Figure 2-4. Pip is a special Python package installer that you will need to use to install additional Python libraries.

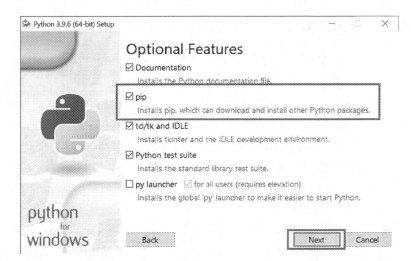

Figure 2-4. *Select Optional Features for Python 3.9.6 install on Windows 10*

On the next screen, ensure there are checkmarks for creating shortcuts and adding the Python command to the environment variables as shown in Figure 2-5.

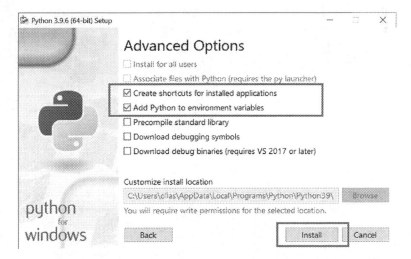

Figure 2-5. *Select Advanced Options for Python 3.9.6 install on Windows 10*

Installing Python 3 on macOS

If you are using macOS, you probably have Python installed since most releases of macOS install Python by default. However, if you were not able to run the Python version command earlier or it wasn't the correct version, you can still download the latest Python 3 from the Python website (`www.python.org/downloads/mac-osx/`). You will find several versions, but you should download the latest version available that matches your hardware. You will find an Intel-based installer and a universal installer. If in doubt, try the universal installer.

Once you download Python, you can launch the installer. For example, on my iMac, I downloaded the latest Python 3 file under the link named Latest Python 3 Release – Python 3.9.6. If you scroll down, you can find the installer you want. For example, I clicked the installer for Intel machines. This downloaded a file named `python-3.9.6-macosx10.9.pkg`, which I located in my `Downloads` folder and executed.

Like most installers, you can step through the various screens agreeing to the license, specifying where you want to install it, and finally initiating the install. Figure 2-6 shows an example of the installer running.

Figure 2-6. *Installing Python 3.9.6 on macOS*

Note   Depending on which version of macOS you are running, and how your security settings are set, you may need to change them to run the installer since it is not signed by an identified developer. See the *Security & Privacy* panel in your *System Preferences*.

Once the installation is complete, you can try the test in the previous section to verify the installation.

Installing Python 3 on Linux

If you are using Linux, the way you install Python will vary based on the platform. For instance, Ubuntu uses apt-get commands, while other distributions have different package managers. Use the default package manager for your platform to install Python 3.6 (or later).

For example, on Debian or Ubuntu, we install the Python 3.9 package using the following commands. The first command updates the packages to ensure we have the latest package references. The second command initiates a download of the necessary files and installs Python:

```
$ sudo apt-get update
$ sudo apt-get install python3.9
```

Once the installation is complete, you can try the test in the previous section to verify the installation.

Running the Python Console

Now let's run some tests on our PC. Recall we can open a Python console by opening a terminal window (command prompt) and entering the command python (or python3 depending on your installation).

Once you see the prompt, enter the following code at the prompt (>>>). This code will print a message to the screen. The \n at the end is a special, nonprinting character that issues a carriage return (like pressing *ENTER*) to move to a new line.

```
print ("Hello, World!")
```

When you enter this code, you will see the result right away. Recall the interpreter works by executing one line of code at a time – each time you press Enter. However, unlike running a program stored in a file, the code you enter in the console is not saved. The following shows an example of running the Python console on Windows 10. Notice I typed in a simple program – the quintessential "Hello, World!" example:

```
C:\> python -version
Python 3.9.6

C:\> python
```

```
Python 3.9.6 (tags/v3.9.6:db3ff76, Jun 28 2021, 15:26:21) [MSC
v.1929 64 bit (AMD64)] on win32
Type "help", "copyright", "credits" or "license" for more
information.
>>> print("Hello, World!")
Hello, World!
>>> quit()

C:\>
```

To quit the console, enter the code quit() as shown earlier. You can also enter the command help() to start the Python help utility. Here, you can enter different commands to get help on Python. For example, at the help prompt, you can type the topics command to get a quick overview of the commands available to use in the interpreter as shown in Listing 2-1. You can press CTRL+C to exit the help utility.

Listing 2-1. Getting Help in the Python Interpreter

```
>>> help()
```

Welcome to Python 3.9's help utility!

If this is your first time using Python, you should definitely check out the tutorial on the Internet at https://docs.python.org/3.9/tutorial/.

Enter the name of any module, keyword, or topic to get help on writing Python programs and using Python modules. To quit this help utility and return to the interpreter, just type "quit".

To get a list of available modules, keywords, symbols, or topics, type "modules", "keywords", "symbols", or "topics". Each module also comes with a one-line summary of what it does; to list the modules whose name or summary contain a given string such as "spam", type "modules spam".

```
help> topics
```

Here is a list of available topics. Enter any topic name to get more help.

ASSERTION	DELETION	LOOPING	SHIFTING
ASSIGNMENT	DICTIONARIES	MAPPINGMETHODS	SLICINGS
ATTRIBUTEMETHODS	DICTIONARYLITERALS	MAPPINGS	SPECIALATTRIBUTES
ATTRIBUTES	DYNAMICFEATURES	METHODS	SPECIALIDENTIFIERS
AUGMENTEDASSIGNMENT	ELLIPSIS	MODULES	SPECIALMETHODS
BASICMETHODS	EXCEPTIONS	NAMESPACES	STRINGMETHODS
BINARY	EXECUTION	NONE	STRINGS
BITWISE	EXPRESSIONS	NUMBERMETHODS	SUBSCRIPTS
BOOLEAN	FLOAT	NUMBERS	TRACEBACKS
CALLABLEMETHODS	FORMATTING	OBJECTS	TRUTHVALUE
CALLS	FRAMEOBJECTS	OPERATORS	TUPLELITERALS
CLASSES	FRAMES	PACKAGES	TUPLES
CODEOBJECTS	FUNCTIONS	POWER	TYPEOBJECTS
COMPARISON	IDENTIFIERS	PRECEDENCE	TYPES
COMPLEX	IMPORTING	PRIVATENAMES	UNARY
CONDITIONAL	INTEGER	RETURNING	UNICODE
CONTEXTMANAGERS	LISTLITERALS	SCOPING	
CONVERSIONS	LISTS	SEQUENCEMETHODS	
DEBUGGING	LITERALS	SEQUENCES	

```
help>
```
You are now leaving help and returning to the Python interpreter. If you want to ask for help on a particular object directly from the interpreter, you can type "help(object)". Executing "help('string')" has the same effect as typing a particular string at the help> prompt.
```
>>>
```

While that demonstrates running Python from your PC, it is not that interesting. Let's see something a bit more complicated.

Running Python Programs with the Interpreter

Suppose your project required you to save data to a file or possibly read data from a file. Rather than try and figure out how to do this on your MicroPython board, we can experiment with files on our PC!

In the next example, I write data to a file and then read the data and print it out. Don't worry too much about understanding the code – just read through it – it's very intuitive. The with statement allows us to open a file and operate on it inside the code block and then automatically close it for us when it exits the code block. Listing 2-2 shows the code for this example. I used a text editor and saved the file as file_io.py.

Listing 2-2. File I/O Example

```
# Step 1: Create a file and write some data
with open("log.txt", "w") as new_file:     # use "write" mode
    new_file.write("1,apples,2.5\n")    # write some data
    new_file.write("2,oranges,1\n")     # write some data
    new_file.write("3,peaches,3\n")     # write some data
    new_file.write("4,grapes,21\n")     # write some data
# Step 2: Open a file and read data
with open("log.txt", "r") as old_file:  # use "read" mode
    # Use a loop to read all rows in the file
    for row in old_file.readlines():
        columns = row.strip("\n").split(",") # split row by commas
        print(" : ".join(columns))  # print the row with colon
        separator
```

I saved the code to a file to show you how you can execute your Python scripts using the Python interpreter using the following command:

```
python ./file_io.py
```

Listing 2-3 shows the results of running the script.

Listing 2-3. Output for the File I/O Example

```
$ python ./file_io.py
1 : apples : 2.5
2 : oranges : 1
3 : peaches : 3
4 : grapes : 21
```

Notice the code changes the separator in the data by exchanging the comma as originally written to a space, colon, and another space. The code does this by splitting the line (string) read into parts by comma. The columns data contains three parts. We use the `join()` method to rejoin the string and print it. Take a moment to read through the code, and you will see these aspects. As you can see, Python is easy to read.

Now that we've experimented briefly with Python on our PC (we will see more of this in the next chapter), let's see how to use MicroPython on our Raspberry Pi Pico. We saw some of this as a demo, but this time you get to try it yourself.

How It Works

Recall that MicroPython is designed to work on small microcontroller platforms. Some of these microcontroller platforms use a special chip that contains the MicroPython binaries (libraries, basic disk I/O, bootstrapping, etc.) as well as the microcontroller, memory, and supporting components.

When you use a MicroPython board – like most microcontrollers – you must first write your code before executing it. If you use the REPL, you're actually executing the code as you write it, and the code is not saved on the board. If you want to store your code and execute it on boot (for example), you must load it onto the board. You can do this in one of two ways. You can use a command-line utility designed to use raw REPL, which allows Python code to be entered and executed on the board from a script to effect file operations, or you can use Thonny to write and copy your program (script file) to the board. Let's see how to use each of these.

Note   Some other MicroPython boards have a USB flash drive that mounts when you connect it to your computer using a USB cable. The Pico does not have this feature, so you must use a utility or Thonny to edit or copy files on the Pico.

File Operations with a Utility

There are several utilities available for working with files on the Pico. All use some form of the raw REPL to execute filesystem operations via Python code to list and copy files. We will see how to use one of the following utilities, but the other options work in a similar fashion:

- *Remote MicroPython shell*: https://github.com/dhylands/rshell

- *mpfshell*: https://github.com/wendlers/mpfshell

- *Adafruit MicroPython tool (ampy)*: https://github.com/scientifichackers/ampy

Let's see how to use the Adafruit MicroPython tool (ampy). You can install ampy using the following command:

```
$ pip3 install adafruit-ampy
```

Once installed, you can use ampy as a command-line tool to execute file operations. Listing 2-4 shows the help feature for ampy.

Listing 2-4. Adafruit MicroPython Tool (ampy) Help

```
ampy --help
Usage: ampy [OPTIONS] COMMAND [ARGS]...

  ampy - Adafruit MicroPython Tool

  Ampy is a tool to control MicroPython boards over a serial
  connection. Using ampy you can manipulate files on the
  board's internal filesystem and even run scripts.

Options:
  -p, --port PORT     Name of serial port for connected
                      board.  Can optionally
                      specify with AMPY_PORT environment
                      variable.  [required]
  -b, --baud BAUD     Baud rate for the serial connection
                      (default 115200).
                      Can optionally specify with AMPY_BAUD
                      environment variable.
  -d, --delay DELAY   Delay in seconds before entering RAW MODE
                      (default 0).
                      Can optionally specify with AMPY_DELAY
                      environment variable.
  --version           Show the version and exit.
  --help              Show this message and exit.
```

Commands:

get   Retrieve a file from the board.

ls   List contents of a directory on the board.

mkdir   Create a directory on the board.

put   Put a file or folder and its contents on the board.

reset   Perform soft reset/reboot of the board.

rm   Remove a file from the board.

rmdir   Forcefully remove a folder and all its children from
        the board.

run   Run a script and print its output.

Here, we see how to use options to connect to our Pico as well as the commands available. We only need to specify the port and optionally the baud rate and then one of the eight commands. For example, if you want to connect to the board on Windows 10 (COM3) with a baud rate of 115200 and list the contents of the filesystem, we use the following command:

```
$ ampy -p COM3 -b 115200 ls
```

If you are using Linux or macOS, you would use the device file such as /dev/tty… in place of COM3.

Note   Adafruit has discontinued the development of ampy to concentrate on their CircuitPython variant, but the utility is the best of the available utilities and easiest to use.

Let's see ampy in action. Begin by creating a file on your PC with the following contents. Save it as hello_pico.py.

```
print("Hello from Pico!")
```

Now, open a terminal on your PC and navigate to the folder where you saved the file. Then, enter the following command to connect to the Pico:

```
$ ampy -p COM3 -b 115200 put hello_pico.py
```

You won't see any output to know if the file copy worked, but you can list the files in the filesystem with the following command:

```
$ ampy -p COM3 -b 115200 ls
/hello_pico.py
```

Here, we see the file was copied. We can run (execute) the file with the following command:

```
$ ampy -p COM3 -b 115200 run hello_pico.py
Hello from Pico!
```

Finally, you can remove the file to save some space on the filesystem for other files. Note that the Pico has only 1.4MB of space to save files.

```
$ ampy -p COM3 -b 115200 rm hello_pico.py
```

As you can see, it is easy to use ampy, but it is not as nice as a GUI. That's where Thonny makes these operations nicer.

File Operations with Thonny

You can perform filesystem operations on your Pico from inside Thonny. You should first connect your Pico board to your PC. Then, simply click the *View* ➤ *Files* menu. You will then see a tool window open that allows you to see the files on both your PC from the current working directory and those on your Pico.

You can right-click any files listed to download them from your Pico to your PC, or you can use the submenu to see all of the available commands as shown in Figure 2-7.

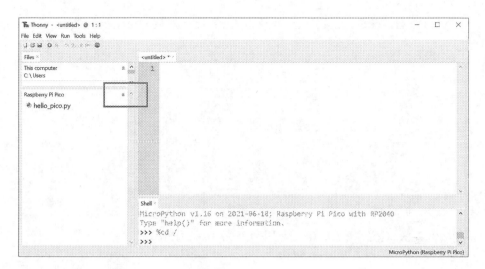

Figure 2-7. *File viewer (Thonny)*

To copy files to the Pico using Thonny, first navigate to the file from your PC in the top part of the file tool window and then select the file as shown in Figure 2-8. Recall, we created the hello_pico.py file in the last section.

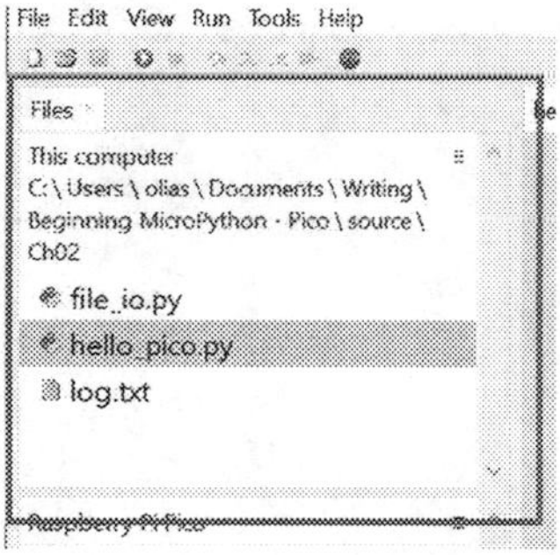

Figure 2-8. *Copy a file to the Pico – select a file (Thonny)*

Next, right-click the file and select *Upload to /* as shown in Figure 2-9.

Figure 2-9. *Copy a file to the Pico – copy (Thonny)*

Now you will see the file on the Pico. You can then open the file by double-clicking it in the Pico section. A new tab will open with square brackets around the name to indicate the file is a remote file. Now you can run it with the run command as shown in Figure 2-10.

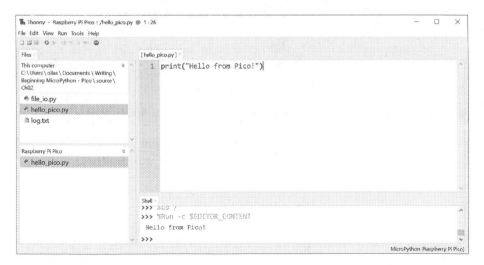

Figure 2-10. *Open and execute a file on the Pico (Thonny)*

As you can see, it is very easy to use Thonny to work with the files on the Pico.

Now it's time to take a tour of what we can do with MicroPython. The following section uses several example projects to show you what you can do with a MicroPython board. Once more, I introduce the examples with a minimal amount of explanation and details about the hardware. We will learn much more about the hardware in Chapter 4.

Off and Running with MicroPython

If you're like me when encountering new technologies, you most likely want to get started as soon as you can. If you already have a Pico, you can follow along with the examples in this section and see a few more examples of what you can do with MicroPython. The examples will use the onboard LED, which can be found to the left of the micro-USB port as shown in Figure 2-11.

Figure 2-11. *Locating the onboard LED (Pico)*

The LED is a single-color (green) LED that you can turn on and off. That might not seem very interesting, but using this simple component will help you get used to creating new code files in Thonny, uploading them to your Pico, and executing them.

Tip   If you're wondering what protocols are supported on the pins, you can visit `https://datasheets.raspberrypi.com/pico/Pico-R3-A4-Pinout.pdf` to see a complete list of the pins and their uses.

You will also learn more about how to interface with the hardware, but don't worry too much about what each line of code does. We'll learn more as we progress to more complex examples.

Example 1 – Blink the LED

In this example, we will write code to turn on the LED on the board. Rather than simply turning it on, let's use a construct called a loop to turn it on and off every 250 milliseconds. Thus, it will flash rather quickly. Before I explain the code, let's look at the completed code. Listing 2-5 shows how the code would look. Don't worry, I'll explain each of the lines of code after the listing.

Listing 2-5. Blink the LED

```
#
# Beginning MicroPython - Chapter 2
#
# Example 1 - Blink the LED
#
# Dr. Charles Bell
#
import time from machine import Pin # Import the Pin class from
the machine library

led = Pin(25, Pin.OUT)  # Get the LED instance (from GPIO pin 25)
```

```
led.off()                # Make sure it's off first
for i in range(0, 20):   # Run the indented code 20 times
    led.on()             # Turn LED on
    time.sleep(0.250)    # Wait for 250 milliseconds
    led.off()            # Turn LED off
    time.sleep(0.250)    # Wait for 250 milliseconds

led.off()                # Turn the LED off at the end
print("Done!")           # Goodbye!
```

The first lines of code are comment lines. These are ignored by MicroPython and are a way to communicate to others what your program is doing. If you are using the REPL console instead of following along with this tutorial, feel free to skip the comment lines when entering the code.

Next is a line of code that is used to import the base hardware library (machine). This library is specific to the Pico and makes available all the components on the board. We also import the time library as we will need to use the sleep() method later to pause execution. This will allow the LED to remain on (or off) for a specific amount of time.

The next two lines of code initialize a variable (led) by using the Pin class from the machine library (Pin) to instantiate a variable of the Pin class representing the onboard LED found on GPIO number 25 (the physical number of the pin). This creates an instance of that object that we can use. In this case, we immediately turn the LED off by calling led.off().

Next is the main portion of the code – a loop! In this case, it is a for loop designed to run the block of code below it as indicated by the indentation 20 times. The for loop uses a counter, i, and the values 1 through 20 as returned by the range(1, 20) function. Within the body of the loop (the indented portion), we first turn the LED on with led.on(), wait 250 milliseconds using the time.sleep () method, then turn the LED off again and wait another 250 milliseconds. We use 0.250 because the sleep() method uses seconds rather than milliseconds. Finally, we turn the LED off and print a message that we're done.

You can enter this code line by line into the REPL console if you'd like, but since we have such a nice IDE with Thonny, let's use that. Start by opening a new file using the *File* ➤ *New* menu and type the lines of code as shown in the listing. Next, let's save the file with the *File* ➤ *Save* menu. This will open a new dialog as shown in Figure 2-12 where you can choose where to save the file. You should choose the *Raspberry Pi Pico* option.

Figure 2-12. *Where to save to? dialog (Thonny)*

Next, you will be shown the save dialog where you can name the file as shown in Figure 2-13. If you have created directories on your Pico, you can navigate to where you'd like to save the file. Name the file example1.py and click OK.

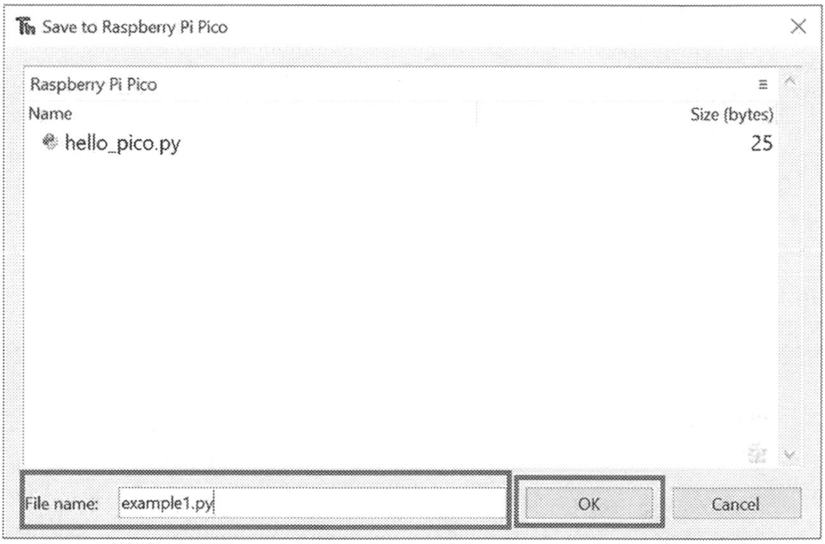

Figure 2-13. *Save dialog (Thonny)*

Next, we can run the example. To do so, you can either click the *Run* button (small green button with an arrowhead on the toolbar) or click the *Run ➤ Run current script* menu. You will see the MicroPython console show in the shell tab as the program executes. You should also see the green LED on the Pico blink rapidly. Figure 2-14 shows an example of the code running in Thonny. If you want it to blink slower, just adjust the time.sleep() calls and increase the value to 0.500 or even 1.0.

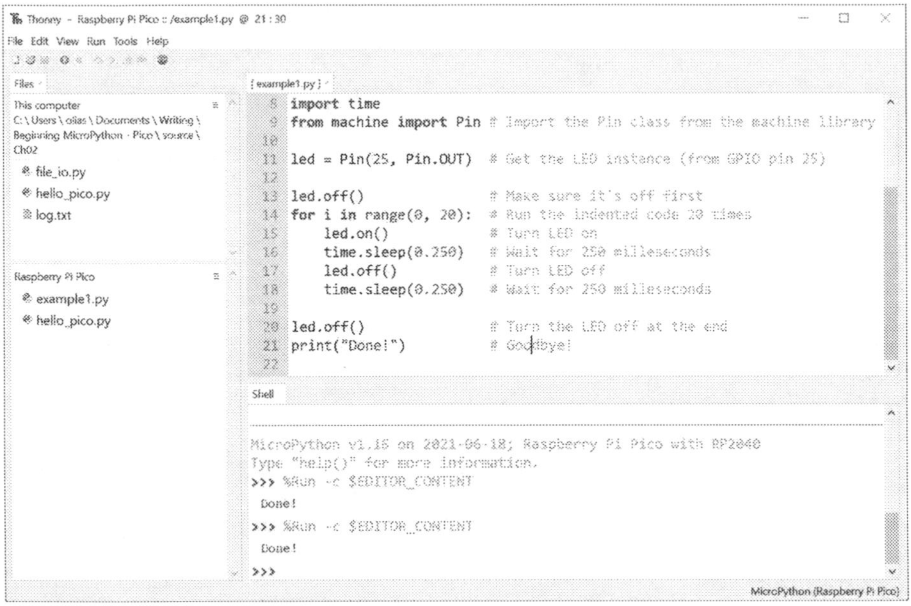

Figure 2-14. *Running example 1 (Thonny)*

If you have been following along with this chapter, you should now see two files on your Pico as shown earlier.

Example 2 – Toggle the LED

Now, let's modify our last example to use a helper function. In this case, we will use the `toggle()` method to turn the LEDs on and off. Basically, whatever state it is in, the `toggle()` sets it to the opposite. Let's shake things up a bit and use a different loop (a `while` loop) with a counter inside the loop, and we'll place out delay and toggle into a method we will create. So, it is like the previous example but, as you will see, demonstrates a bit more complexity. Since it is more complex, I will walk through the code in sections before presenting the completed code.

Recall from the last example, we must import two things: the `Pin` class from the `machine` library and the time library as shown in the following:

```
import time
from machine import Pin
```

Next, we are going to use a new concept called constants. There are simply placeholders for values we will use that never change. They are especially helpful when used in more than one place in the code. We will create one for the time to sleep and another for the maximum number of blinks, which we will use to end the `while` loop. The following shows the correct syntax for the constants:

```
SLEEP_TIME = 0.250          # Time to sleep in milliseconds
MAX_BLINKS = 20             # Max number of blinks
```

Next, we create the new method named `blink_led()` as shown in the following. Here, we define the method with the def clause and indent all of the code we want to include. Here, we call the `toggle()` method and `time.sleep()`. This is a common way to organize your code and make it possible to reuse some lines of code from different places in your code to eliminate duplication:

```
def blink_led():
    led.toggle()                # Toggle the LED
    time.sleep(SLEEP_TIME)
```

Following that, we instantiate a class variable for the pin like we did before, and then we initialize a counting variable for use in the loop. The while loop is written differently than the for loop. In this case, we place a condition at the top of the loop, and the loop is executed so long as the condition is true. To make it false and stop the loop, we simply increment the counter as part of the body of the loop as follows:

```
count = 0                      # Initialize the counter
while count < MAX_BLINKS:      # Run while counter < max
num blinks
```

```
    blink_led()                # Toggle the LED
    count = count + 1          # Increment the counter
```

The rest of the code is the same as the last example. Listing 2-6 shows the completed code. Read through it a few times until you're convinced it will work.

Listing 2-6. Example 2. Toggle the LED

```
#
# Beginning MicroPython - Chapter 2
#
# Example 2 - Toggle the LED
#
# Dr. Charles Bell
#
import time
from machine import Pin

# Constants
SLEEP_TIME = 0.250             # Time to sleep in milliseconds
MAX_BLINKS = 20               # Max number of blinks

# Create a method to toggle the LED and wait 250 milliseconds
def blink_led():
    led.toggle()               # Toggle the LED
    time.sleep(SLEEP_TIME)

led = Pin(25, Pin.OUT)         # Get the LED instance (from
                              GPIO pin 25)
```

```
led.off()                  # Make sure it's off first
count = 0                  # Initialize the counter
while count < MAX_BLINKS:  # Run while counter < max
                           num blinks
    blink_led()            # Toggle the LED
    count = count + 1      # Increment the counter
led.off()                  # Turn the LED off at the end
print("Done!")             # Goodbye!
```

If you're following along, go ahead and save this file on your Pico as example2.py. See the previous example for instructions on how to save the file.

When you run the code by clicking the *Run* button (small green button with an arrowhead on the toolbar) or clicking the *Run ➤ Run current script* menu, you will see the LED turn on and off.

However, there is a bug (defect or logic error) in this code. Can you spot it? I'll give you a hint. Run the code and count how many times the LED turns on.

How many did it turn on? Now, go back and run the first example again. How many times did the LED turn on there? If you discovered the LED turns on 10 times for this example, but 20 for the last example, you've found the artifact (data) that shows the logic error. Now, where is the logic error?

If you're thinking it has something to do with either the blink_led() method or the constant, you're on the right track.

Now, look at our first example. What did we do inside the for loop? We turned it on, waited, then turned it off, and waited some more. That effected a "blink" of the LED, and we did it 20 times.

But in this example, we use toggle(), which only turns the LED on if off and off if on. We did this 20 times too. Do you see where we went wrong?

You may be tempted to fix the issue by changing the constant MAX_ BLINKS to 40 and that would work, but the logic error is actually in the blink_led() method. We should have called the toggle() method twice as shown in the following:

```
def blink_led():
    led.toggle()                # Toggle the LED
    time.sleep(SLEEP_TIME)
    led.toggle()                # Toggle the LED
    time.sleep(SLEEP_TIME)
```

Go ahead and make that change. You should now see the LED illuminate 20 times.

It is this sort of error that we can introduce unknowingly especially if we build our own logic to control hardware.[3] That's why it is always best to let the hardware do the work for us, which we are going to do in the next example.

Example 3 – Timer

This example demonstrates how to use a timer with a callback function, which is simply a method we create to execute when the timer "triggers." That is, we create a function in our code and then tell MicroPython to execute that function when the timer alarm or frequency cycles (also called trigger). This example is based on the previous example, but with a timer instead of a loop.

---

[3] It also illustrates why I prefer specific functions like on() and off() over a helper like toggle(). The code reads more clearly, and it is less likely to introduce logic errors.

We will use the same imports as the last example except with one additional library – the Timer library as shown in the following:

```
import time
from machine import Pin, Timer
```

We still need the SLEEP_TIME constant, but not the MAX_BLINKS constant. The blink_led() is altered slightly, however. We add the timer variable in the parameter list as shown in the following. This is so that we can use the method as a callback for the Timer class:

```
def blink_led(timer):
    led.toggle()            # Toggle the LED
    time.sleep(SLEEP_TIME)
    lcd.toggle()            # Toggle the LED
    time.sleep(SLEEP_TIME)
```

Next, we set up the pin as before and initiate a Timer class instance variable as follows:

```
led = Pin(25, Pin.OUT)      # Get the LED instance (from
                            # GPIO pin 25)
timer = Timer()             # Get the timer instance
led.off()                   # Make sure it's off first
```

Now we can set up the timer using a frequency of 2.0, which means fire (call) the blink_led() method twice per second (or every 500 milliseconds) with a mode of periodic, and we pass in the address of the blink_led() method by not specifying the () as follows:

```
timer.init(freq=2.0, mode=Timer.PERIODIC, callback=blink_led)
time.sleep(10)              # Wait for 10 seconds
timer.deinit()             # Turn off the timer
```

Notice we add a sleep() method to sleep for 10 seconds and then call deinit() for the timer. This will effectively let the code run for 10 seconds blinking the LED twice per second for 20 iterations. We call the deinit() to turn off the timer. Otherwise, the timer will continue to run even when our code has completed. So, yes, you can spawn code to execute by itself. Cool, eh?

Listing 2-7 shows the completed code. Read through it a few times until you're convinced it will work.

Listing 2-7. Example 3. Blink the LED with a Timer

```
#
# Beginning MicroPython - Chapter 2
#
# Example 3 - Blink the LED with a Timer
#
# Dr. Charles Bell
#
import time
from machine import Pin, Timer

# Constants
SLEEP_TIME = 0.250              # Time to sleep in milliseconds

# Create a timer callback method to toggle the LED
def blink_led(timer):
    led.toggle()               # Toggle the LED
    time.sleep(SLEEP_TIME)
    led.toggle()               # Toggle the LED
    time.sleep(SLEEP_TIME)

led = Pin(25, Pin.OUT)         # Get the LED instance (from
                               GPIO pin 25)
timer = Timer()                # Get the timer instance
led.off()                      # Make sure it's off first
```

```
# Use a timer to control the blink twice per second or
# every 500 milliseconds
timer.init(freq=2.0, mode=Timer.PERIODIC, callback=blink_led)
time.sleep(10)              # Wait for 10 seconds
timer.deinit()             # Turn off the timer

led.off()
print("Done!")             # Goodbye!
```

If you're following along, go ahead and save this file on your Pico as `example3.py`. See the previous example for instructions on how to save the file.

When you run the code by clicking the *Run* button (small green button with an arrowhead on the toolbar) or clicking the *Run* ➤ *Run current script* menu, you will see the LED turn on and off. Try to count the number of times the LED is turned on to convince yourself this code works as described.

Here, we see a more complex example of blinking the LED without using a counting loop. While the timer may seem strange, it is much easier and less error-prone than the loop option of the previous examples.

Saving Your Work

If you have followed along thus far, you should have five MicroPython files on your Pico (`hello_pico.py`, `file_io.py`, `example1.py`, `example2.py`, and `example3.py`). Unless you created these on your PC first, you only have copies on your Pico. You can download these to your PC from your Pico using Thonny by right-clicking the file in the Pico section and then choosing *Download to <current_directory>* as shown in Figure 2-15. Repeat until all files have been downloaded to your PC.

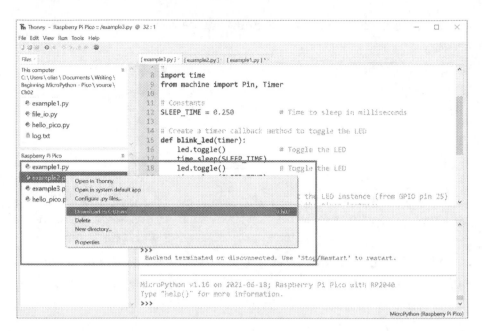

Figure 2-15. *Downloading files from the Pico to your PC (Thonny)*

Summary

MicroPython is a very exciting addition to the microcontroller world. For the first time, beginners do not need to learn a new operating system or a complex programming language like C or C++ to program the microcontroller. MicroPython permits people with some or even no programming experience to experiment with electronics and build interesting projects. Thus, MicroPython provides opportunities for more hobbyists and enthusiasts who just want to get their projects working without a steep learning curve.

In this chapter, we discovered the major features of MicroPython. We also discovered that MicroPython is based on the Python that we find on our PCs. Best of all, we saw firsthand how MicroPython works on the Pico.

In the next chapter, we will dive into a programming tutorial on using Python and MicroPython. The chapter is very much a lightning tour and intended to help guide you to the point where you can write (and understand) the examples in this book.

CHAPTER 3

How to Program in MicroPython

Now that we have a basic understanding of the Pico and have had a short introduction to MicroPython, we are ready to learn more about programming in MicroPython. Mastering MicroPython is very easy, and some may suggest it doesn't require any formal training to use. This is largely true and thus you should be able to write MicroPython scripts with only a little bit of knowledge about the language.

Given that MicroPython is a subset of Python, we can learn the basics of the Python language first through examples on our PC. Thus, this chapter presents a crash course on the basics of Python programming including an explanation about some of the most commonly used language features. As such, this chapter will provide you with the skills you need to understand the Python examples in this book and available on the Internet. The chapter also demonstrates how to program in Python through examples that you can run on your PC or your Pico. So, let's get started!

Note   I use the term Python to describe programming concepts in this chapter that apply to both MicroPython and Python. Concepts unique to MicroPython use the term MicroPython.

C. Bell, *Beginning MicroPython with the Raspberry Pi Pico*, Maker Innovations Series, https://doi.org/10.1007/978-1-4842-8135-2_3

Now let's learn some of the basic concepts of Python programming. We will begin with the building blocks of the language such as variables, modules, and basic statements and then move into the more complex concepts of flow control and data structures. While the material may seem to come at you in a rush, this tutorial on Python covers only the most fundamental knowledge of the language and how to use it on your PC and Pico. It is intended to get you started writing Python applications quickly.

If you know the basics of Python programming, feel free to skim through this chapter. However, I recommend working through the example projects at the end of the chapter, especially if you've not written many Python applications.

The following sections present many of the basic features of Python programming that you will need to know to understand the example projects in this book.

Basic Concepts

Python is a high-level, interpreted, object-oriented scripting language. One of the biggest goals of Python is to have a clear, easy-to-understand syntax that reads as close to English as possible. That is, you should be able to read a Python script and understand it even if you haven't learned the language. Python also has less punctuation (special symbols) and fewer syntactical machinations than other languages. The following lists a few of the key features of Python:

- An interpreter processes python at runtime. No external (separate) compiler is used.

- Python supports object-oriented programming constructs by way of a class.

- Python is a great language for the beginner-level programmers and supports the development of a wide range of applications.

- Python is a scripting language but can be used for a wide range of applications.

- Python is very popular and used throughout the world giving it a huge support base.

- Python has few keywords, simple structure, and a clearly defined syntax. This allows the student to pick up the language quickly.

- Python code is more clearly defined and visible to the eyes.

Recall that Python is available for download (`python.org/downloads`) for just about every platform that you may encounter or use – even Windows! Python is a very easy language to learn with very few constructs that are even mildly difficult to learn. Rather than toss out a sample application, let's approach learning the basics of Python in a Python-like way: one step at a time.

Code Blocks

The first thing you should learn is that Python does not use a code block demarcated with symbols like other languages. More specifically, code that is local to a construct such as a function or conditional or loop is designated using indentation. Thus, the lines below that are indented (by spaces or, gasp, tabs) so that the starting characters align for the code body of the construct.

Tip   Examples like the following are designed to show concepts in action. As such, some of the syntax is a mock-up (also called pseudo) Python code and may not execute if used verbatim.

```
if (expr1):
    print("inside expr1")
    print("still inside expr1")
else:
    print("inside else")
    print("still inside else")
print("in outer level")
```

Here, we see a conditional or if statement. Notice the function call print() is indented. This signals the interpreter that the lines belong to the construct above it. For example, the two print statements that mention expr1 form the code block for the if condition (and executes when the expression evaluates to true). Similarly, the next two print statements form the code block for the else condition. Finally, the non-indented lines are not part of the conditional and thus are executed after either the if or else depending on the expression evaluation.

As you can see, indentation is a key concept to learn when writing Python. Even though it is very simple, making mistakes in indentation can result in code executing that you did not expect or worse errors from the interpreter.

There is one special symbol that you will encounter frequently. Notice the use of the colon (:) in the preceding code. This symbol is used to terminate a construct and signals the interpreter that the declaration is complete, and the body of the code block follows. We use this for conditionals, loops, classes, and functions.

Note   I use "program" and "application" interchangeably with "script" when discussing Python. While, technically, Python code is a script, we often use it in contexts where "program" and "application" are more appropriate.

Comments

One of the most fundamental concepts in any programming language is the ability to annotate your source code with nonexecutable text that not only allows you to make notes among the lines of code but also forms a way to document your source code.

To add comments to your source code, use the pound sign (#). Place at least one at the start of the line to create a comment for that line, repeating the # symbols for each subsequent line. This creates what is known as a block comment as shown. Notice I used a comment without any text to create whitespace. This helps with readability and is a common practice for block comments:

```
#
# Beginning MicroPython - Chapter 3
#
# Example Python application.
#
# Created by Dr. Charles Bell
#
```

You can also place comments on the same line as the source code. The compiler will ignore anything from the pound sign to the end of the line. For example, the following shows a common style of documenting variables:

```
zip = 35012              # Zip or postal code
address1= "123 Main St." # Store the street address
```

Arithmetic

You can perform many mathematical operations in Python including the usual primitives, but also logical operations and operations used to compare values. Rather than discuss these in detail, I provide a quick reference in Table 3-1 that shows the operation and example of how to use the operation.

Table 3-1. *Arithmetic, Logical, and Comparison Operators in Python*

Type	Operator	Description	Example
Arithmetic	+	Addition	`int_var + 1`
	-	Subtraction	`int_var - 1`
	*	Multiplication	`int_var * 2`
	/	Division	`int_var / 3`
	%	Modulus	`int_var % 4`
	-	Unary subtraction	`-int_var`
	+	Unary addition	`+int_var`
Logical	&	Bitwise and	`var1&var2`
	|	Bitwise or	`var1|var2`
	^	Bitwise exclusive or	`var1^var2`
	~	Bitwise complement	`~var1`
	and	Logical and	`var1and var2`
	or	Logical or	`var1or var2`

(*continued*)

Table 3-1. (*continued*)

Type	Operator	Description	Example
Comparison	==	Equal	expr1==expr2
	!=	Not equal	expr1!=expr2
	<	Less than	expr1<expr2
	>	Greater than	expr1>expr2
	<=	Less than or equal	expr1<=expr2
	>=	Greater than or equal	expr1>=expr2

Bitwise operations produce a result on the values performed on each bit. Logical operators (and, or) produce a value that is either true or false and are often used with expressions or conditions.

Output to Screen

We've already seen a few examples of how to print messages to the screen but without any explanation about the statements shown. While it is unlikely that you would print output from your MicroPython board for projects that you deploy, learning Python is much easier when you display messages to the screen.

Some of the things you may want to print are variable values, which is to communicate what is going on inside your program. This can include simple messages (strings), but can also include the values of variables, expressions, and more.

As we have seen, the built-in print() function is the most common way to display output text contained within single or double quotes. We have also seen some interesting examples using another function named format(). The format() function generates a string for each argument passed. These arguments can be other strings, expressions, variables, etc. The function is used with a special string that contains replacement keys delimited by curly braces { } (called string interpolation[1]). Each replacement key contains either an index (starting at 0) or a named keyword. The special string is called a format string. Let's see a few examples to illustrate the concept. You can run these yourself either on your PC or your MicroPython board. I include the output so you can see what each statement does:

```
>>> a = 42
>>> b = 1.5
>>> c = "seventy"
>>> print("{0} {1} {2} {3}".format(a,b,c,(2+3)))
42 1.5 six 5
>>> print("{a_var} {b_var} {c_var}{0}".format((3*3),c_var=c,b_
var=b,a_var=a))
42 1.5 six 9
```

Notice I created three variables (we will talk about variables in the next section) assigning them different values with the equal symbol (=). I then printed a message using a format string with four replacement keys labeled using an index. Notice the output of that print statement. Notice I included an expression at the end to show how the format() function evaluates expressions.

The last line is more interesting. Here, I use three named parameters (a_var, b_var, c_var) and used a special argument option in the format() function where I assign the parameter a value. Notice I listed them in a different order. This is the greatest advantage of using named parameters; they can appear in any order but are placed in the format string in the position indicated.

---

[1] https://en.wikipedia.org/wiki/String_interpolation

As you can see, it's just a case of replacing the { } keys with those from the format() function, which converts the arguments to strings. We use this technique anywhere we need a string that contains data gathered from more than one area. We can see this in the preceding examples.

Tip   See https://docs.python.org/3/library/string. html#formatstrings for more information about format strings.

Now let's look at how we can use variables in our programs (scripts).

Tip   For those who have learned to program in another language like C or C++, Python allows you to terminate a statement with the semicolon (;); however, it is not needed and considered bad form to include it.

Variables and Statements

Python is a dynamically typed language, which means the type of the variable (the type of data it can store) is determined by context as it is encountered or used. This contrasts with other languages such as C and C++ where you must declare the type before you use the variable.

Variables in Python are simply named memory locations that you can use to store values during execution. We store values by using the equal sign to assign the value. Python variable names can be anything you want, but there are rules and conventions most Python developers follow. The rules are listed in the Python coding standard.[2]

---

[2] www.python.org/dev/peps/pep-0008/

Tip   See `www.python.org/dev/peps/pep-0008` for the PEP8 coding guidelines and complete list of the rules and standards.

However, the general, overriding rule requires variable names that are descriptive, have meaning in context, and can be easily read. That is, you should avoid names with random characters, forced abbreviations, acronyms, and similar obscure names. By convention, your variable names should be longer than a single character (with some acceptable exceptions for loop counting variables) and short enough to avoid overly long code lines.

WHAT IS A LONG CODE LINE?

Most will say a code line should not exceed 80 or even 100 characters, but this harkens from the darker days of programming when we used punched cards that permitted a maximum of 80 characters per card and later display devices with the same limitation. With modern, widescreen displays, this is not as big a deal, but I still recommend keeping lines short to ensure better readability. No one likes to scroll down to read!

Thus, there is a lot of flexibility in what you can name your variables. There are additional rules and guidelines in the PEP8 standard, and should you wish to bring your project source code up to date with the standards, you should review the PEP8 naming standards for functions, classes, and more.

The following shows some examples of simple variables and their dynamically determined types:

```
# floating point number
length = 10.0
# integer
```

```
width = 4
# string
box_label = "Tools"
# list
car_makers = ['Ford', 'Chevrolet', 'Dodge']
# tuple
porsche_cars = ('911', 'Cayman', 'Boxster')
# dictionary
address = {"name": "Joe Smith", "Street": "123 Main", "City":
"Anytown", "State": "New Happyville"}
```

So, how did we know the variable width is an integer? Simply because
the number 4 is an integer. Likewise, Python will interpret "Tools" as a
string. We'll see more about the last three types and other types supported
by Python in the next section.

Types

As mentioned, Python does not have a formal type of specification
mechanism like other languages. However, you can still define variables
to store anything you want. In fact, Python permits you to create and use
variables based on context, and you can use initialization to "set" the data
type for the variable. The following shows several examples:

```
# Numbers
float_value = 9.75
integer_value = 5

# Strings
my_string = "He says, he's already got one."

print("Floating number: {0}".format(float_value))
print("Integer number: {0}".format(integer_value))
print(my_string)
```

For situations where you need to convert types or want to be sure values are typed a certain way, there are many functions for converting data. Table 3-2 shows a few of the more commonly used type conversion functions. I discuss some of the data structures in a later section.

Table 3-2. *Type Conversion in Python*

Function	Description
int(x [,base])	Converts x to an integer. Base is optional (e.g., 16 for hex)
long(x [,base])	Converts x to a long integer
float(x)	Converts x to a floating-point
str(x)	Converts object x to a string
tuple(t)	Converts t to a tuple
list(l)	Converts l to a list
set(s)	Converts s to a set
dict(d)	Creates a dictionary
chr(x)	Converts an integer to a character
hex(x)	Converts an integer to a hexadecimal string
oct(x)	Converts an integer to an octal string

However, you should use these conversion functions with care to avoid data loss or rounding. For example, converting a float to an integer can result in truncation. Likewise, printing floating-point numbers can result in rounding.

Now let's look at some commonly used data structures including this strange thing called a dictionary.

Basic Data Structures

What you have learned so far about Python is enough to write the most basic programs and indeed more than enough to tackle the example project later in this chapter. However, when you start needing to operate on data – either from the user or from sensors and similar sources – you will need a way to organize and store data as well as perform operations on the data in memory. The following introduces three data structures in order of complexity: lists, tuples, and dictionaries.

Lists

Lists are a way to organize data in Python. It is a free-form way to build a collection. That is, the items (or elements) need not be the same data type. Lists also allow you to do some interesting operations such as adding things at the end, beginning, or at a special index. The following demonstrates how to create a list:

```
# List
my_list = ["abacab", 575, "rex, the wonder dog", 24, 5, 6]
my_list.append("end")
my_list.insert(0,"begin")
for item in my_list:
  print("{0}".format(item))
```

Here, we see I created the list using square brackets ([ ]). The items in the list definition are separated by commas. Note that you can create an empty list simply by setting a variable equal to [ ]. Since lists, like other data structures, are objects, there are several operations available for lists such as the following:

- append(x): Add x to the end of the list

- extend(l): Add all items to the end of the list

- `insert(pos,item)`: Insert an item at a position pos

- `remove(value)`: Remove the first item that matches (`==`) the value

- `pop([i])`: Remove and return the item at position `i` or end of list

- `index(value)`: Return the index of the first item that matches

- `count(value)`: Count occurrences of the value

- `sort()`: Sort the list (ascending)

- `reverse()`: Reverse sort the list

Lists are like arrays in other languages and very useful for building dynamic collections of data.

Tuples

Tuples, on the other hand, are a more restrictive type of collection. That is, they are built from a specific set of data and do not allow manipulation like a list. In fact, you cannot change the elements in the tuple. Thus, we can use tuples for data that should not change. The following shows an example of a tuple and how to use it:

```
# Tuple
my_tuple = (0,1,2,3,4,5,6,7,8,"nine")
for item in my_tuple:
  print("{0}".format(item))
if 7 in my_tuple:
  print("7 is in the list")
```

Here, we see I created the tuple using parentheses (). The items in the tuple definition are separated by commas. Note that you can create an empty tuple simply by setting a variable equal to (). Since tuples, like other data structures, are objects, there are several operations available such as the following, including operations for sequences such as inclusion, location, etc.:

- `x in t`: Determine if t contains x
- `x not in t`: Determine if t does not contain x
- `s + t`: Concatenate tuples
- `s[i]`: Get element i
- `len(t)`: Length of t (number of elements)
- `min(t)`: Minimal (smallest value)
- `max(t)`: Maximal (largest value)

If you want even more structure with storing data in memory, you can use a special construct (object) called a dictionary.

Dictionaries

A dictionary is a data structure that allows you to store key, value pairs where the data is assessed via the keys. Dictionaries are a very structured way of working with data and the most logical form we will want to use when collecting complex data. The following shows an example of a dictionary:

```
# Dictionary
my_dictionary = {
  'first_name': "Chuck",
  'last_name': "Bell",
  'age': 36,
  'my_ip': (192,168,1,225),
```

```
  42: "What is the meaning of life?",
}
# Access the keys:
print(my_dictionary.keys())
# Access the items (key, value) pairs
print(my_dictionary.items())
# Access the values
print(my_dictionary.values())
# Create a list of dictionaries
my_addresses = [my_dictionary]
```

There is a lot going on here! We see a basic dictionary declaration that uses curly braces to create a dictionary. Inside that, we can create as many key, value pairs we want separated by commas. Keys are defined using strings (I use single quotes by convention, but double quotes will work) or integers, and values can be any data type we want. For the my_ip attribute, we are also storing a tuple.

Following the dictionary, we see several operations performed on the dictionary from printing the keys, printing all the values, and printing only the values. The following shows the output of executing this code snippet from the Python interpreter:

```
[42, 'first_name', 'last_name', 'age', 'my_ip']
[(42, 'what is the meaning of life?'), ('first_name', 'Chuck'),
('last_name', 'Bell'), ('age', 36), ('my_ip', (192, 168,
1, 225))]
['what is the meaning of life?', 'Chuck', 'Bell', 36, (192,
168, 1, 225)]
'42': what is the meaning of life?
'first_name': Chuck
'last_name': Bell
'age': 36
'my_ip': (192, 168, 1, 225)
```

As we have seen in this example, there are several operations (functions or methods) available for dictionaries including the following. Together, this list of operations makes dictionaries a very powerful programming tool:

- `len(d)`: Number of items in d

- `d[k]`: Item of d with key k

- `d[k] = x`: Assign key k with value x

- `del d[k]`: Delete an item with key k

- `k in d`: Determine if d has an item with key k

- `d.items()`: Return a list (view) of the (key, value) pairs in d

- `d.keys()`: Return a list (view) of the keys in d

- `d.values()`: Return a list (view) of the values in d

Best of all, objects can be placed inside other objects. For example, you can create a list of dictionaries like I did earlier, a dictionary that contains lists and tuples, and any combination you need. Thus, lists, tuples, and dictionaries are a powerful way to manage data for your program.

In the next section, we will learn how we can control the flow of our programs.

Statements

Now that we know more about the basics of Python, we can discover some of the more complex code concepts you will need to complete your project such as conditional statements and loops.

Conditional Statements

We have also seen some simple conditional statements – statements designed to alter the flow of execution depending on the evaluation of one or more expressions. Conditional statements allow us to direct execution of our programs to sections (blocks) of code based on the evaluation of one or more expressions. The conditional statement in Python is the if statement.

We have seen the if statement in action in our example code. Notice in the example, we can have one or more (optional) else phrases that we execute once the expression for the if conditions evaluate to false. We can chain if/else statements to encompass multiple conditions where the code executed depends on the evaluation of several conditions. The following shows the general structure of the if statement. Notice in the comments how I explain how execution reaches the body of each condition:

```
if (expr1):
    # execute only if expr1 is true
elif ((expr2) or (expr3)):
    # execute only if expr1 is false *and* either expr2 or
      expr3 is true
else:
    # execute if both sets of if conditions evaluate to false
```

While you can chain the statement as much as you want, use some care here because the more elif sections you have, the harder it will become to understand, maintain, and avoid logic errors in your expressions.

There is another form of conditional statement called a ternary operator. Ternary operators are more commonly known as conditional expressions in Python. These operators evaluate something based on a condition being true or not. They became a part of Python in version 2.4. Conditional expressions are a shorthand notation for an if-then-else construct used (typically) in an assignment statement as shown in the following:

```
variable = value_if_true if condition else value_if_false
```

Here, we see if the condition is evaluated to true, the value preceding the if is used, but if the condition evaluates to false, the value following the else is used. The following shows a short example:

```
>>> numbers = [1,2,3,4]
>>> for n in numbers:
...     x = 'odd' if n % 2 else 'even'
...     print("{0} is {1}.".format(n, x))
...
1 is odd.
2 is even.
3 is odd.
4 is even.
>>>
```

Conditional expressions allow you to quickly test a condition instead of using a multiline conditional statement, which can help make your code a bit easier to read (and shorter).

Loops

Loops are used to control the repetitive execution of a block of code. There are three forms of loops that have slightly different behaviors. All loops use conditional statements to determine whether to repeat execution or not. That is, they repeat as long as the condition is true. The two types of loops are while and for. I explain each with an example.

The while loop has its condition at the "top" or start of the block of code. Thus, while loops only execute the body if and only if the condition evaluates to true on the first pass. The following illustrates the syntax for a while loop. This form of loop is best used when you need to execute code only if some expression(s) evaluate to true. For example, iterating through a collection of things whose number of elements is unknown (loop until we run out of things in the collection):

```
while (expression):
    # do something here
```

For loops are sometimes called counting loops because of their unique form. For loops allow you to define a counting variable and a range or list to iterate over. The following illustrates the structure of the for loop. This form of loop is best used for performing an operation in a collection. In this case, Python will automatically place each item in the collection in the variable for each pass of the loop until no more items are available:

```
for variable_name in list:
  # do something here
```

You can also do range loops or counting loops. This uses a special function called range() that takes up to three parameters, range([start], stop[, step]), where start is the starting number (an integer), stop is the last number in the series, and step is the increment. So, you can count by 1, 2, 3, etc. through a range of numbers. The following shows a simple example:

```
for i in range(2,9):
    # do something here
```

There are other uses for range() that you may encounter. See the documentation on this function and other built-in functions at https://docs.python.org/3/library/functions.html for more information.

Python also provides a mechanism for controlling the flow of the loop (e.g., duration or termination) using a few special keywords as follows:

- `break`: Exit the loop body immediately

- `continue`: Skip to the next iteration of the loop

- `else`: Execute code when the loop ends (not executed if the loop was stopped with a break statement)

There are some uses for these keywords, particularly break, but it is not the preferred method of terminating and controlling loops. That is, professionals believe the conditional expression or error handling code should behave well enough to not need these options.

Modularization

The last group of topics are the most advanced and include modularization (code organization). As we will see, we can use functions to group code, to eliminate duplication, and to encapsulate functionality into objects.

Including Modules

Python applications can be built from reusable libraries that are provided by the Python environment. They can also be built from custom modules or libraries that you create yourself or download from a third party. These are often distributed as a set of Python code files (e.g., files that have a file extension of `.py`). When we want to use a library (function, class, etc.) that is included in a module, we use the import keyword and list the name of the module. The following shows some examples:

```
import os
import sys
```

The first two lines demonstrate how to import a base or common module provided by Python. In this case, we are using or importing modules for the os and sys modules (operating system and Python system functions).

Tip   It is customary to list your imports in alphabetical order with built-in modules first, then third-party modules listed next, and finally your own modules.

Functions

Python allows you to use modularization in your code. While it supports object-oriented programming by way of classes (a more advanced feature that you are unlikely to encounter for most Python GPIO examples), on a more fundamental level you can break your code into smaller chunks using functions.

Functions use a special keyword construct (rare in Python) to define a function. We simply use def followed by a name for the function and a comma-separated list of parameters in parentheses. The colon is used to terminate the declaration. The following shows an example:

```python
def print_dictionary(the_dictionary):
    for key, value in the_dictionary.items():
        print("'{0}': {1}".format(key, value))

# define some data
my_dictionary = {
  'name': "Chuck",
  'age': 37,
}
```

You may be wondering what this strange code does. Notice the loop is assigning two values from the result of the items() function. This is a special function available from the dictionary object. The items() function returns the key, value pairs, hence the names of the variables.

The next line prints out the values. The use of formatting strings where the curly braces define the parameter number starting at 0 is common for Python 3 applications. See the Python documentation for more information about formatting strings (https://docs.python.org/3/library/string.html#format-string-syntax).

The body of the function is indented. All statements indented under this function declaration belong to the function and are executed when the function is called. We can call functions by name providing any parameters as follows. Notice how I referenced the values in the dictionary by using the key names:

```
print_dictionary(my_dictionary)
print(my_dictionary['age'])
print(my_dictionary['name'])
```

This example together with the preceding code, when executed, generates the following:

```
$ python
Python 3.9.6 (tags/v3.9.6:db3ff76, Jun 28 2021, 15:26:21) [MSC
v.1929 64 bit (AMD64)] on win32
Type "help", "copyright", "credits" or "license" for more
information.
>>> def print_dictionary(the_dictionary):
...     for key, value in the_dictionary.items():
...         print("'{0}': {1}".format(key, value))
...
>>> # define some data
>>> my_dictionary = {
```

```
...    'name': "Chuck",
...    'age': 37,
... }
>>> print_dictionary(my_dictionary)
'name': Chuck
'age': 37
>>> print(my_dictionary['age'])
37
>>> print(my_dictionary['name'])
Chuck
>>>
```

Now let's look at the most complex concept in Python – object-oriented programming.

Classes and Objects

You may have heard that Python is an object-oriented programming language. But what does that mean? Simply, Python is a programming language that provides facilities for describing objects (things) and what you can do with the object (operations).

Objects are an advanced form of data abstraction where the data is hidden from the caller and only manipulated by the operations (methods) the object provides. But before we start learning object-oriented programming in Python, let's look at some of the terminology common to the technique.

Object-Oriented Programming (OOP) Terminology

Like any technology or concept, there comes a certain number of terms that you must learn to be able to understand and communicate with others about the technology. We've seen some of these thus far in the book. The following briefly describes some of the terms you will need to know to learn more about object-oriented programming:

- *Attribute*: A data element in a class.

- *Class*: A code construct used to define an object in the form of attributes (data) and methods (functions) that operate on the data. Methods and attributes in Python can be accessed using dot notation.

- *Class instance variable*: A variable that is used to store an instance of an object. They are used like any other variable and, combined with dot notation, allow us to manipulate objects.

- *Constructor*: A special method that is executed once each time the class is instantiated. Thus, you would place any startup or initialization code you need to run once in the constructor.

- *Instance*: An executable form of a class created by assigning a class to a variable initializing the code as an object.

- *Inheritance*: The inclusion of attributes and methods from one class in another.

- *Instantiation*: The creation of an instance of a class.

- *Method overloading*: The creation of two or more methods with the same name but with a different set of parameters. This allows us to create methods that have the same name but may operate differently depending on the parameters passed.

- *Polymorphism*: Inheriting attributes and methods from a base class adding additional methods or overriding (changing) methods.

109

There are many more OOP terms, but these are the ones you will encounter most often.

Python Object Syntax

The syntax we use in Python is the class statement, which you can use to help make your projects modular. By modular, we mean the source code is arranged to make it easier to develop and maintain. Typically, we place classes in separate modules (code files), which helps organize the code better. While it is not required, I recommend using this technique of placing a class in its own source file. This makes modifying the class or fixing problems (bugs) easier.

So, what are Python classes? Let's begin by considering the construct as an organization technique. We can use the class to group data and methods together. The name of the class immediately follows the keyword class followed by a colon. You declare other class methods like any other method except the first argument must be self, which ties the method to the class instance when executed.

FUNCTION VS. METHOD – WHAT IS THE DIFFERENCE?

I prefer to use terms that have been adopted by the language designers or community of developers. For example, some use "function," but others may use "method." Still others may use subroutine, routine, procedure, etc. It doesn't matter which term you use, but you should strive to use terms consistently. One example, which can be confusing to some, is I use the term method when discussing object-oriented examples. That is, a class has methods, not functions. However, you can use function in place of method, and you'd still be correct (mostly).

Accessing the data is done using one or more methods by using the class (creating an instance) and using dot notation to reference the data member or function. Let's look at an example. Listing 3-1 shows a complete class that describes (models) the most basic characteristics of a vehicle used for transportation. I created a file named vehicle.py to contain this code.

Listing 3-1. Vehicle Class

```
#
# Beginning MicroPython - Chapter 3
#
# Class Example: A generic vehicle
#
# Dr. Charles Bell
#
class Vehicle:
    """Base class for defining vehicles"""
    axles = 0
    doors = 0
    occupants = 0

    def __init__(self, num_axles, num_doors):
        self.axles = num_axles
        self.doors = num_doors

    def get_axles(self):
        return self.axles

    def get_doors(self):
        return self.doors
```

```
def add_occupant(self):
    self.occupants += 1

def num_occupants(self):
    return self.occupants
```

Notice a couple of things here. First, there is a method with the name __init__(). This is the constructor and is called when the class instance is created. You place all your initialization code like setting variables in this method. We also have methods for returning the number of axles, doors, and occupants. We have one method in this class to add occupants.

Also notice we address each of the class attributes (data) using self.<name>. This is how we can ensure we always access the data that is associated with the instance created.

Let's see how this class can be used to define a family sedan. Listing 3-2 shows code that uses this class. We can place this code in a file named sedan.py.

Listing 3-2. Using the Vehicle Class

```
#
# Beginning MicroPython - Chapter 3
#
# Class Example: Using the generic Vehicle class
#
# Dr. Charles Bell
#
from vehicle import Vehicle

sedan = Vehicle(2, 4)
sedan.add_occupant()
sedan.add_occupant()
```

```
sedan.add_occupant()
print("The car has {0} occupants.".format(sedan.num_
occupants()))
```

Notice the first line imports the `Vehicle` class from the vehicle module. Notice I capitalized the class name but not the file name. This is a very common naming scheme. Next in the code, we create an instance of the class. Notice I passed in 2, 4 to the class name. This will cause the __init__ () method to be called when the class is instantiated.

The variable, `sedan`, becomes the class instance variable (object) that we can manipulate, and I do so by adding three occupants and then printing out the number of occupants using the method in the `Vehicle` class.

We can run the code on our PC using the following command. As we can see, it tells us there are three occupants in the vehicle when the code is run. Nice.

```
$ python ./sedan.py
The car has 3 occupants.
```

Now, let's see how we can use the vehicle class to demonstrate inheritance. In this case, we will create a new class named `PickupTruck` that uses the vehicle class but adds specialization to the resulting class. Listing 3-3 shows the new class. I placed this code in a file named `pickup_truck.py`. As you will see, a pickup truck is a type of vehicle.

Listing 3-3. Pickup Truck Class

```
#
# Beginning MicroPython - Chapter 3
#
# Class Example: Inheriting the Vehicle class to form a
# model of a pickup truck with maximum occupants and maximum
```

```
# payload.
#
# Dr. Charles Bell
#
from vehicle import Vehicle

class PickupTruck(Vehicle):
    """This is a pickup truck that has:
    axles = 2,
    doors = 2,
    __max occupants = 3
    The maximum payload is set on instantiation.
    """

    occupants = 0
    payload = 0
    max_payload = 0

    def __init__(self, max_weight):
        super().__init__(2,2)
        self.max_payload = max_weight
        self.__max_occupants = 3

    def add_occupant(self):
        if self.occupants < self.__max_occupants:
            super().add_occupant()
        else:
            print("Sorry, only 3 occupants are permitted in the
            truck.")

    def add_payload(self, num_pounds):
        if (self.payload + num_pounds) < self.max_payload:
            self.payload += num_pounds
        else:
            print("Overloaded!")
```

```
def remove_payload(self, num_pounds):
    if (self.payload - num_pounds) >= 0:
        self.payload -= num_pounds
    else:
        print("Nothing in the truck.")

def get_payload(self):
    return self.payload
```

Notice a few things here. First, notice the class statement: `class PickupTruck(Vehicle):`. When we want to inherit from another class, we add the parentheses with the name of the base class. This ensures Python will use the base class, allowing the derived class to use all its accessible data and memory. If you want to inherit from more than one class, you can (called multiple inheritance), just list the base (parent) classes with a comma-separated list.

Next, notice the `__max_occupants` variable. Using two underscores in a class for an attribute or a method name, makes it private to the class. That is, it should only be accessed from within the class. No caller of the class (via a class variable/instance) can access the private items nor can any class that was derived from the class. It is always a good practice to hide the attributes (data).

You may be wondering what happened to the occupant methods. Why aren't they in the new class? They aren't there because our new class inherited all that behavior from the base class. Not only that, but the code has been modified to limit occupants to exactly three occupants.

I also want to point out the documentation I added to the class. We use documentation strings (strings that use a set of three double quotes before and after) to document the class. You can put documentation here to explain the class and its methods. We'll see a good use of this a bit later.

Finally, notice the code in the constructor. This demonstrates how to call the base class method, which I do to set the number of axles and doors. We could do the same in other methods if we wanted to call the base class method's version.

Now, let's write some code to use this class. Listing 3-4 shows the code we used to test this class. Here, we create a file named `pickup.py` that creates an instance of the pickup truck, adds occupants, and payload, then prints out the contents of the truck.

Listing 3-4. Using the PickupTruck Class

```
#
# Beginning MicroPython - Chapter 3
#
# Class Example: Exercising the PickupTruck class.
#
# Dr. Charles Bell
#
from pickup_truck import PickupTruck

pickup = PickupTruck(500)
pickup.add_occupant()
pickup.add_occupant()
pickup.add_occupant()
pickup.add_occupant()
pickup.add_payload(100)
pickup.add_payload(300)
print("Number of occupants in truck = {0}.".format(pickup.num_
occupants()))
print("Weight in truck = {0}.".format(pickup.get_payload()))
pickup.add_payload(200)
pickup.remove_payload(400)
pickup.remove_payload(10)
```

Notice I add a couple of calls to the add_occupant() method, which the new class inherits and overrides. I also add calls so that we can test the code in the methods that check for excessive occupants and maximum payload capacity. When we run this code, we will see the results as shown in the following:

```
$ python ./pickup.py
Sorry, only 3 occupants are permitted in the truck.
Number of occupants in truck = 3.
Weight in truck = 400.
Overloaded!
Nothing in the truck.
```

Once again, I ran this code on my PC, but I can run all this code on the MicroPython board and will see the same results.

There is one more thing we should learn about classes: built-in attributes. Recall the __init__() method. Python automatically provides several built-in attributes each starting with __ that you can use to learn more about objects. The following lists a few of the operators available for classes:

- __dict__: Dictionary containing the class namespace
- __doc__: Class documentation string
- __name__: Class name
- __module__: Module name where the class is defined
- __bases__: The base class(es) in order of inheritance

The following shows what each of these attributes returns for the preceding PickupTruck class. I added this code to the pickup.py file:

```
print("PickupTruck.__doc__:", PickupTruck.__doc__)
print("PickupTruck.__name__:", PickupTruck.__name__)
print("PickupTruck.__module__:", PickupTruck.__module__)
```

```
print("PickupTruck.__bases__:", PickupTruck.__bases__)
print("PickupTruck.__dict__:", PickupTruck.__dict__)
```

When this code is run, we see the following output:

```
Sorry, only 3 occupants are permitted in the truck.
Number of occupants in truck = 3.
Weight in truck = 400.
Overloaded!
Nothing in the truck.
PickupTruck.__doc__: This is a pickup truck that has:
    axles = 2,
    doors = 2,
    __max occupants = 3
    The maximum payload is set on instantiation.
```

```
PickupTruck.__name__: PickupTruck
PickupTruck.__module__: pickup_truck
PickupTruck.__bases__: (<class 'vehicle.Vehicle'>,)
PickupTruck.__dict__: {'__module__': 'pickup_truck', '__doc__':
'This is a pickup truck that has:\n    axles = 2,\n    doors
= 2,\n    __max occupants = 3\n    The maximum payload is
set on instantiation.\n    ', 'occupants': 0, 'payload':
0, 'max_payload': 0, '__init__': <function PickupTruck.__
init__ at 0x0000023ADF7B7C10>, 'add_occupant': <function
PickupTruck.add_occupant at 0x0000023AE1150820>, 'add_payload':
<function PickupTruck.add_payload at 0x0000023AE11508B0>,
'remove_payload': <function PickupTruck.remove_payload at
0x0000023AE1150940>, 'get_payload': <function PickupTruck.get_
payload at 0x0000023AE11509D0>}
```

You can use the built-in attributes whenever you need more information about a class. Notice the `_PickupTruck__max_occupants` entry in the dictionary. Recall that we made a pseudo-private variable, `__max_occupants`. Here, we see how Python refers to the variable by prepending the class name to the variable. Remember, variables that start with two underscores (not one) should be considered private to the class and only usable from within the class.

Tip   See `https://docs.python.org/3/tutorial/classes.html` for more information about classes in Python.

Now, let's see a few examples of Python programs that we can use to practice. Like the previous examples, you can write and execute these either on your PC or on your MicroPython board.

Learning Python by Example

The best way to learn how to program in any language is practicing with examples. In this section, I present several examples that you can use to practice coding in Python. You can use either your Pico or your PC to run these examples. I present the first two examples using my PC and the second two using the Pico.

Tip   For the adventurous, I also include some challenges (modifications to the code) for you to work out on your own. I encourage you to try these so that you can get more hands-on experience coding in Python.

How Do I Create and Execute Python Files?

I also use Thonny to create the file, save it, and execute it. However, if you'd rather use a different editor, you may do so and execute the scripts using the python command as shown in the examples.

To open a new file in Thonny, click the *File* ➤ *New* menu, press *CTRL+N*, or click the *New* button on the far left of the toolbar. Recall, we can save the file using the *File* ➤ *Save* menu, press *CTRL+S*, or click the *Save* button on the toolbar (third from the left and looks like a diskette[3]). Finally, to run the script in the current open tab in the editor window, click the *Run* ➤ *Run current script* menu, press *F5*, or click the *Run* button on the toolbar (fourth from the left and looks like a green dot with an arrow in the center).

I explain the code in detail for each example and show example output when you execute the code as well as a challenge for you to try a modification or two of each example on your own. I encourage you to implement these examples and figure out the challenge yourself as practice for the projects later in this book.

Example 1: Using Loops

This example demonstrates how to write loops in Python using the for loop. The problem we are trying to solve is converting integers from decimal to binary, hexadecimal, and octal. Often with hardware projects, we need to see values in one or more of these formats, and in some cases, the sensors we use (and the associated documentation) use hexadecimal rather than decimal. Thus, this example can be helpful in the future not only for how to use the for loop but also how to convert integers into different formats.

---

[3] Ah, a diskette. Also called a floppy drive. The old standby of computers from a bygone era. See https://en.wikipedia.org/wiki/Floppy_disk

Write the Code

The example begins with a tuple of integers to convert. Tuples and lists can be iterated through (values read in order) using a for loop. Recall a tuple is read only, so in this case since it is input, it is fine, but in other cases where you may need to change values, you will want to use a list. Recall, the syntactical difference between a tuple and a list is the tuple uses parentheses and a list uses square brackets.

The for loop demonstrated here is called a "for each" loop. Notice I used the syntax "for value in values," which tells Python to iterate over the tuple named values fetching (storing) each item into the value variable each iteration through the tuple.

Finally, I use the print() and format() functions to replace two placeholders {0} and {1} to print out a different format of the integer using the methods bin() for binary, oct() for octal, and hex() for hexadecimal that do the conversion for us.

Listing 3-5. Converting Integers

```
#
# Beginning MicroPython - Chapter 3
#
# Example: Convert integer to binary, hex, and octal
#
# Dr. Charles Bell
#

# Create a tuple of integer values
values = (12, 450, 1, 89, 2017, 90125)

# Loop through the values and convert each to binary, hex,
and octal
for value in values:
```

```
print("{0} in binary is {1}".format(value, bin(value)))
print("{0} in octal is {1}".format(value, oct(value)))
print("{0} in hexadecimal is {1}".format(value, hex(value)))
```

Execute the Code

You can save this code in a file named conversions.py on your PC and then open a terminal (console window) and run the code with the command python ./conversions.py (or python3 if you have multiple versions of Python installed). Figure 3-1 shows the code executing in Thonny.

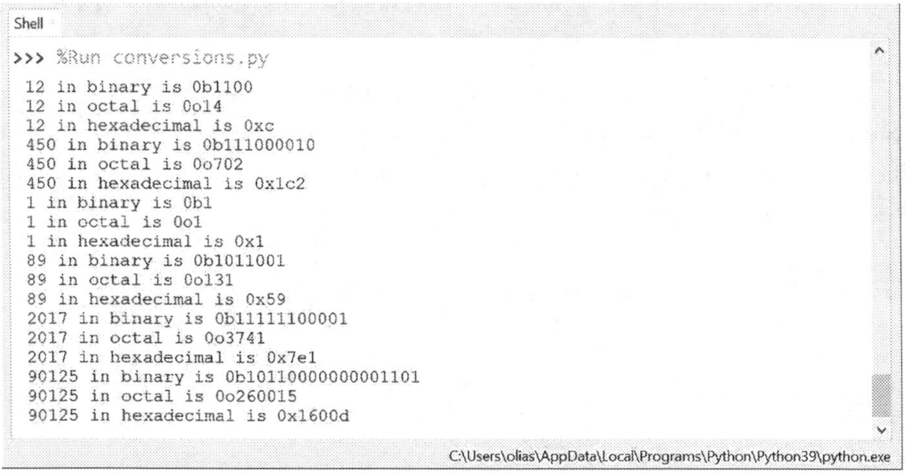

```
Shell
>>> %Run conversions.py
 12 in binary is 0b1100
 12 in octal is 0o14
 12 in hexadecimal is 0xc
 450 in binary is 0b111000010
 450 in octal is 0o702
 450 in hexadecimal is 0x1c2
 1 in binary is 0b1
 1 in octal is 0o1
 1 in hexadecimal is 0x1
 89 in binary is 0b1011001
 89 in octal is 0o131
 89 in hexadecimal is 0x59
 2017 in binary is 0b11111100001
 2017 in octal is 0o3741
 2017 in hexadecimal is 0x7e1
 90125 in binary is 0b10110000000001101
 90125 in octal is 0o260015
 90125 in hexadecimal is 0x1600d
                           C:\Users\olias\AppData\Local\Programs\Python\Python39\python.exe
```

Figure 3-1. Executing Python in Thonny

Listing 3-6 shows the command and output if you choose to run the code from the command line.

Listing 3-6. Conversions Example Output

```
$ python ./conversions.py
12 in binary is 0b1100
12 in octal is 0o14
```

```
12 in hexadecimal is 0xc
450 in binary is 0b111000010
450 in octal is 0o702
450 in hexadecimal is 0x1c2
1 in binary is 0b1
1 in octal is 0o1
1 in hexadecimal is 0x1
89 in binary is 0b1011001
89 in octal is 0o131
89 in hexadecimal is 0x59
2017 in binary is 0b11111100001
2017 in octal is 0o3741
2017 in hexadecimal is 0x7e1
90125 in binary is 0b10110000000001101
90125 in octal is 0o260015
90125 in hexadecimal is 0x1600d
```

Notice all the values in the tuple were converted.

Note   The rest of the examples in this chapter will use a listing of the output for brevity and readability.

Your Challenge

To make this example better, instead of using a static tuple to contain hard-coded integers, rewrite the example to read the integer from arguments on the command line along with the format. For example, the code would be executed like the following:

```
$ python ./conversions.py 123 hex
123 in hexadecimal is 0x7b
```

To read arguments from the command line, use argparse (https://docs.python.org/3/howto/argparse.html). If you want to read the integer from the command line, you can use the argparse module to add an argument by name as follows:

```
import argparse

# Setup the argument parser
parser = argparse.ArgumentParser()

# We need two arguments: integer, and conversion
parser.add_argument("original_val")
parser.add_argument("conversion")

# Get the arguments
args = parser.parse_args()
```

When you use the argument parser (argparse) module, the values of the arguments are all strings, so you will need to convert the value to an integer before you use the bin(), hex(), or oct() method.

You will also need to determine which conversion is requested. I suggest use only hex, bin, and oct for the conversion and use a set of conditions to check the conversion requested. Something like the following would work:

```
if args.conversion == 'bin':
    # do conversion to binary
elif args.conversion == 'oct':
    # do conversion to octal
elif args.conversion == 'hex':
    # do conversion to hexadecimal
else:
    print("Sorry, I don't understand, {0}.".format(args.
    conversion))
```

Notice the last else communicates that the argument was not recognized. This helps to manage user error.

There is one more thing about the argument parser you should know. You can pass in a help string when adding arguments. The argument parser also gets you the help argument (-h) for free. Observe the following. Notice I added a couple of strings using the help= parameter:

```
# We need two arguments: integer, and conversion
parser.add_argument("original_val", help="Value to convert.")
parser.add_argument("conversion", help="Conversion options:
hex, bin, or oct.")
```

Now when we complete the code and run it with the -h option, we get the following output. Cool, eh?

```
$ python3 ./conversions.py -h
usage: conversions.py [-h] original_val conversion

positional arguments:
  original_val  Value to convert.
  conversion    options: hex, bin, or oct.

optional arguments:
  -h, --help    show this help message and exit
```

Example 2: Using Complex Data and Files

This example demonstrates how to work with the JavaScript Object Notation[4] (JSON) in Python. In short, JSON is a markup language used to exchange data. Not only is it human readable, but it can also be used directly in your applications to store and retrieve data to and from other applications, servers, and even MySQL. In fact, JSON looks familiar to

---

[4]www.json.org/json-en.html

programmers because it resembles other markup schemes. JSON is also very simple in that it supports only two types of structures: (1) a collection containing (name, value) pairs and (2) an ordered list (or array). Of course, you can also mix and match the structures in an object. When we create a JSON object, we call it a JSON document.

The problem we are trying to solve is writing and reading data to/from files. In this case, we will use a special JSON encoder and decoder module named json that allows us to easily convert data in files (or other streams) to and from JSON. As you will see, accessing JSON data is easy by simply using the key (sometimes called fields) names to access the data. Thus, this example can be helpful in the future not only for how to use read and write files but also how to work with JSON documents.

Write the Code

This example stores and retrieves data in files. The data is basic information about pets including the name, age, breed, and type. The type is used to determine broad categories like fish, dog, or cat.

We begin by importing the JSON module (named json), which is built-in to the MicroPython platform. Next, we prepare some initial data by building JSON documents and storing them in a Python list. We use the json.loads() method to pass in a JSON formatted string. The result is a JSON document that we can add to our list. The examples use a very simple form of JSON documents – a collection of (name, value) pairs. The following shows an example of one of the JSON formatted strings used:

```
{"name":"Violet", "age": 11, "breed":"dachshund", "type":"dog"}
```

Notice we enclose the string inside curly braces and use a series of key names, a colon, and a value separated by commas. If this looks familiar, it's because it is the same format as a Python dictionary. This demonstrates my comment that JSON syntax looks familiar to programmers.

The JSON method, json.loads(), takes the JSON formatted string and then parses the string checking for validity and returns a JSON document. We then store that document in a variable and add it to the list as shown in the following:

```
parsed_json = json.loads('{"name":"Violet", "age": 11,
"breed":"dachshund", "type":"dog"}')
pets.append(parsed_json)
```

Once the data is added to the list, we then write the data to a file named my_data.json. To work with files, we first open the file with the open() function, which takes a file name (including a path if you want to put the file in a directory) and an access mode. We use "r" for read and "w" for write. You can also use "a" for append if you want to open a file and add to the end. Note that the "w" access will overwrite the file when you write to it. If the open() function succeeds, you get a file object that permits you to call additional functions to read or write data. The open() will fail if the file is not present (and you have requested read access) or you do not have permissions to write to the file.

In case you're curious what the other access modes are, Table 3-3 shows the list of modes available for the open() function.

Table 3-3. *Python File Access Modes*

Mode	Description
R	Opens a file for reading only. The file pointer is placed at the beginning of the file. This is the default mode
Rb	Opens a file for reading only in binary format. The file pointer is placed at the beginning of the file. This is the default mode
r+	Opens a file for both reading and writing. The file pointer is placed at the beginning of the file

(continued)

Table 3-3. (*continued*)

Mode	Description
rb+	Opens a file for both reading and writing in binary format. The file pointer is placed at the beginning of the file
W	Opens a file for writing only. Overwrites the file if the file exists. If the file does not exist, creates a new file for writing
wb	Opens a file for writing only in binary format. Overwrites the file if the file exists. If the file does not exist, creates a new file for writing
w+	Opens a file for both writing and reading. Overwrites the existing file if the file exists. If the file does not exist, creates a new file for reading and writing
wb+	Opens a file for both writing and reading in binary format. Overwrites the existing file if the file exists. If the file does not exist, creates a new file for reading and writing
A	Opens a file for appending. The file pointer is at the end of the file if the file exists. That is, the file is in the append mode. If the file does not exist, it creates a new file for writing
ab	Opens a file for appending in binary format. The file pointer is at the end of the file if the file exists. That is, the file is in the append mode. If the file does not exist, it creates a new file for writing
a+	Opens a file for both appending and reading. The file pointer is at the end of the file if the file exists. The file opens in the append mode. If the file does not exist, it creates a new file for reading and writing
ab+	Opens a file for both appending and reading in binary format. The file pointer is at the end of the file if the file exists. The file opens in the append mode. If the file does not exist, it creates a new file for reading and writing

Once the file is open, we can write the JSON documents to the file by iterating over the list. Iteration means to start at the first element and access the elements in the list one at a time in order (the order they appear in the list). Recall, iteration in Python is very easy. We simply say, "for each item in the list" with the for loop as follows:

```
for pet in pets:
  // do something with the pet data
```

To write the JSON document to the file, we use the json.dumps() method, which will produce a JSON formatted string writing that to the file using the file variable and the write() method. Thus, we now see how to build JSON documents from strings and then decode (dump) them to a string.

Once we've written data to the file, we then close the file. However, we can use the with clause that will manage the close file operation for us. Without the with clause, you would need to manually close the file with the close() function. You can then reopen it and read data from the file. In this case, we use another special implementation of the for loop. We use the file variable to read all of the lines in the file with the readlines() method and then iterate over them with the following code:

```
with open("my_data.json", "r") as json_file:
    for pet in json_file.readlines():
      // do something with the pet string
```

We use the json.loads() method again to read the JSON formatted string as read from the file to convert it to a JSON document, which we add to another list. Now the data has been read back into our program, and we can use it. Finally, we iterate over the new list and print out data from the JSON documents using the key names to retrieve the data we want. Listing 3-7 shows the completed code for this example.

Listing 3-7. Writing and Reading JSON Objects to/from Files

```
#
# Beginning MicroPython - Chapter 3
#
# Example: Storing and retrieving JSON objects in files
#
# Dr. Charles Bell
#
import json

# Prepare a list of JSON documents for pets by converting JSON
# to a dictionary
pets = []
parsed_json = json.loads('{"name":"Violet", "age": 11,
"breed":"dachshund", "type":"dog"}')
pets.append(parsed_json)
parsed_json = json.loads('{"name": "Mister", "age": 16,
"breed":"siberian khatru", "type":"cat"}')
pets.append(parsed_json)
parsed_json = json.loads('{"name": "Spot", "age": 13,
"breed":"koi", "type":"fish"}')
pets.append(parsed_json)
parsed_json = json.loads('{"name": "Charlie", "age": 11,
"breed":"dachshund", "type":"dog"}')
pets.append(parsed_json)

# Now, write these entries to a file. Note: overwrites the file
with open("my_data.json", "w") as json_file:
    for pet in pets:
        json_file.write(json.dumps(pet))
        json_file.write("\n")
```

```
# Now, let's read the JSON documents then print the name and
age for all of the dogs in the list
my_pets = []
with open("my_data.json", "r") as json_file:
    for pet in json_file.readlines():
        parsed_json = json.loads(pet)
        my_pets.append(parsed_json)

print("Name, Age")
for pet in my_pets:
    if pet['type'] == 'dog':
        print("{0}, {1}".format(pet['name'], pet['age']))
```

Notice the loop for writing data. We added a second write() method passing in a strange string (it is actually an escape character). The \n is a special character called the newline character. This forces the JSON formatted strings to be on separate lines in the file and helps with readability.

Tip   For a more in-depth look at how to work with files in Python, see https://docs.python.org/3/tutorial/inputoutput. html#reading-and-writing-files.

So, what does the file look like? The following is a dump of the file using the more utility, which shows the contents of the file. Notice the file contains the JSON formatted strings just like we had in our code:

```
$ more my_data.json
{"age": 11, "breed": "dachshund", "type": "dog", "name": "Violet"}
{"age": 16, "breed": "siberian khatru", "type": "cat", "name":
"Mister"}
{"age": 12, "breed": "koi", "type": "fish", "name": "Spot"}
```

```
{"age": 11, "breed": "dachshund", "type": "dog", "name":
"Charlie"}
```

Now, let's see what happens when we run this script.

Execute the Code

You can save this code in a file named rw_json.py on your PC and then open a terminal (console window) and run the code with the command python ./rw_json.py (or python3 if you have multiple versions of Python installed). The following shows the output:

```
$ python ./rw_json.py
Name, Age
Violet, 11
Charlie, 11
```

While the output may not be very impressive, by completing the example, you've learned a great deal about working with files and structured data using JSON documents.

Your Challenge

To make this example more of a challenge, you could modify it to include more information about your pets. I suggest you start with a simple text file and type in the JSON formatted strings for your pets. To increase the complexity, try adding information that is pertinent to the type of pet. For example, you could add some keys for one or more pets, other keys for other pets, and so on. Doing so will show one of the powers of JSON documents; collections of JSON documents do not have to have the same format.

Once you have this file, modify the code to read from the file and print out all the information for each pet by printing the key name and value. Hint: You will need to use special code to print out the key name and the value called "pretty printing." For example, the following code will print out the JSON document in an easily readable format. Notice we use the sort_keys option to print the keys (fields), and we can control the number of spaces to indent:

```
for pet in my_pets:
    print(json.dumps(pet, sort_keys=True, indent=4))
```

When run, the output will look like the following:

```
{
    "age": 11,
    "breed": "dachshund",
    "name": "Violet",
    "type": "dog"
}
...
```

Example 3: Using Functions

This example demonstrates how to create and use functions. Recall functions are used to help make our code more modular. Functions can also be a key tool in avoiding duplication of code. That is, we can reuse portions of code repeatedly by placing them in a function. Functions are also used to help isolate code for special operations such as mathematical formulae.

The problem we're exploring in this example is how to create functions to perform calculations. We will also explore a common computer science technique called recursion where a function calls itself repeatedly. I will also show you the same function implemented in an iterative manner (typically using a loop). While some would advise avoiding recursion, recursive functions are a bit shorter to write but can be more difficult to debug if something goes wrong. The best advice I can offer is that almost every recursive function can be written as iterative functions, and novice programmers should stick to iterative solutions until they gain confidence using functions.

Write the Code

This example is designed to calculate a Fibonacci series.[5] A Fibonacci series is calculated as the sum of the two preceding values in the series. The series begins with 1 followed by 1 (nothing plus 1), then $1 + 1 = 2$, and so on. For this example, we will ask the user for an integer and then calculate the number of values in the Fibonacci series. If the input is 5, the series is 1, 1, 2, 3, 5.

We will create two functions: one to calculate the Fibonacci series using code that iteratively calculates the series and one to calculate the nth Fibonacci number using a recursive function. Let's look at the iterative function first.

To define a function, we use the syntax `def func_name(<parameters>):` where we supply a function name and a list of zero or more parameters followed by a colon. These parameters are then usable inside the function. We pass in data to the function using the parameters. The following shows the iterative version of the Fibonacci series code. We name this function `fibonacci_iterative`:

```
def fibonacci_iterative(count):
    i = 1
    if count == 0:
        fib = []
    elif count == 1:
```

---

[5] https://en.wikipedia.org/wiki/Fibonacci_number

```
        fib = [1]
    elif count == 2:
        fib = [1,1]
    elif count > 2:
        fib = [1,1]
        while i < (count - 1):
            fib.append(fib[i] + fib[i-1])
            i += 1
    return fib
```

This code simply calculates the first N values in the series and returns them in a list. The parameter count is the number of values in the series. The function begins by checking to see if the trivial values are requested: 0, 1, or 2 whose values are known. If the count value is greater than 2, we begin with the known series [1, 1] and then use a loop to calculate the next value by adding the two previous values together. Take a moment to notice how I use the list index to get the two previous values in the list (i and i-1). We will use this function and the list returned directly in our code to find a specific value in the series and print it.

Now let's look at the recursive version of the function. The following shows the code. We name this function fibonacci_recursive:

```
def fibonacci_recursive(number):
    """Calculate the Nth Fibonacci as a recursive function."""
    if number == 0:
        return 0
    if number == 1:
        return 1
    # Call our self counting down.
    value = fibonacci_recursive(number-1) + fibonacci_
    recursive(number-2)
    return value
```

In this case, we don't return the entire series; rather, we return the specific value in the series – the nth value. Like the iterative example, we do the same thing regarding the trivial values returning the number requested. Otherwise, we call the same function again for each number. It may take some time to get your mind around how this works, but it does calculate the nth value.

Now, you may be wondering where you place functions in the code. We need to place them at the top of the code. Python will parse the functions and continue to execute statements following the definitions. Thus, we place our "main" code after our functions.

The main code for this example begins with requesting the nth value for the Fibonacci series and then uses the recursive function first to calculate the value. We then ask the user if they want to see the entire series, and if so, we use the iterative version of the function to get the list and print it out. We print out the nth value and give the option again to see the entire series to show the result is the same using both functions.

Finally, we will place all of the main executable code into a function named main(), which we will call with a special technique that tests to see if the file has been executed. More specifically, if the __name__ parameter is equal to "main", we call the main() function. This technique allows you to attempt an import statement without executing the main body of code. This enables us to reuse any functions defined in the file. The code for this technique is shown as follows:

```
def main():
    # Main code goes here

if __name__ == '__main__':
    main()
```

Listing 3-8 shows the completed code for the example. We will name this code fibonacci.py.

Listing 3-8. Calculating Fibonacci Series

```
#
# Beginning MicroPython - Chapter 3
#
# Example: Fibonacci series using recursion
#
# Calculate the Fibonacci series based on user input
#
# Dr. Charles Bell
#

# Create a function to calculate Fibonacci series (iterative)
# Returns a list.
def fibonacci_iterative(count):
    """Calculate Fibonacci as an iterative function."""
    i = 1
    if count == 0:
        fib = []
    elif count == 1:
        fib = [1]
    elif count == 2:
        fib = [1,1]
    elif count > 2:
        fib = [1,1]
        while i < (count - 1):
            fib.append(fib[i] + fib[i-1])
            i += 1
    return fib

# Create a function to calculate the nth Fibonacci number
(recursive)
```

```python
# Returns an integer.
def fibonacci_recursive(number):
    """Calculate the Nth Fibonacci as a recursive function."""
    if number == 0:
        return 0
    elif number == 1:
        return 1
    else:
        # Call our self counting down.
        value = fibonacci_recursive(number-1) + fibonacci_
        recursive(number-2)
        return value

# Main code
def main():
    print("Welcome to my Fibonacci calculator!")
    index = int(input("Please enter the number of integers in
    the series: "))

    # Recursive example
    print("We calculate the value using a recursive
    algorithm.")
    nth_fibonacci = fibonacci_recursive(index)
    print("The {0}{1} Fibonacci number is {2}."
        "".format(index, "th" if index > 1 else "st", nth_
        fibonacci))
    see_series = str(input("Do you want to see all of the
    values in" " the series? "))
    if see_series in ["Y","y"]:
        series = []
        for j in range(1,index+1):
```

```
        series.append(fibonacci_recursive(j))
    print("Series: {0}: ".format(series))

# Iterative example
print("We calculate the value using an iterative
algorithm.")
series = fibonacci_iterative(index)
print("The {0}{1} Fibonacci number is {2}."
        "".format(index, "th" if index > 1 else "st",
        series[index-1]))
see_series = str(input("Do you want to see all of the values "
                        "in the series? "))
if see_series in ["Y","y"]:
    print("Series: {0}: ".format(series))

print("bye!")


if __name__ == '__main__':
    main()
```

Take a few moments to read through the code. While the problem being solved is a bit simpler than the previous example, there is a lot more code to read through. When you're ready, connect your MicroPython board and create the file. You create the file on your PC for this example and name it fibonacci.py. We'll copy it to our MicroPython board in the next section.

Tip   For a more in-depth look at how to create and use your own functions, see `https://docs.python.org/3/tutorial/controlflow.html#defining-functions`.

Now, let's see what happens when we run this script. Recall, we will be running this code on our MicroPython board, so if you're following along, be sure to set up your board and connect it to your PC.

Execute the Code

Recall from Chapter 3, when we want to move code to our Pico, we need to create the file and then upload it to the Pico and then execute it.

We can do this in Thonny by creating a new file and then saving it. Thonny will ask us where to save the file. Choose the *Raspberry Pi Pico* option when prompted. If you have already created the file on your PC, you can upload the file to your Pico by right-clicking the file and choosing Upload to /. Once the file is on your Pico, you can execute it.

You will be prompted for the data as shown in the following. Notice we enter an integer for calculating the Nth Fibonacci number, and then we are asked if we want to see all of the values. The first attempt uses the recursive version and the second the iterative:

```
Welcome to my Fibonacci calculator!
Please enter the number of integers in the series: 13
We calculate the value using a recursive algorithm.
The 13th Fibonacci number is 233.
Do you want to see all of the values in the series? Y
Series: [1, 1, 2, 3, 5, 8, 13, 21, 34, 55, 89, 144, 233]:
We calculate the value using an iterative algorithm.
The 13th Fibonacci number is 233.
Do you want to see all of the values in the series? Y
Series: [1, 1, 2, 3, 5, 8, 13, 21, 34, 55, 89, 144, 233]:
bye!
```

There is another way we can execute the file. Recall, we used the main() function technique to execute the main code if the file is executed. We can also import the file and use any functions in the file. To do this, open the REPL console (or connect to your Pico via Thonny) and enter the following code:

```
>>> import fibonacci
>>> fibonacci_recursive(7)
13
>>> fibonacci_iterative(7)
[1, 1, 2, 3, 5, 8, 13]
```

Go ahead and try it yourself.

When you're done experimenting the example, remember to close the terminal and eject the drive for the flash before you unplug it.

Your Challenge

To make this example a bit more challenging, modify the code to search a Fibonacci series for a specific integer. Ask the user to provide an integer and then determine if the value is a valid Fibonacci value. For example, if the user enters 144, the code should tell the user that value is valid and is the twelfth value in the series. While this challenge will require you rewrite most of the code for the "main" functionality, you must figure out how to use the functions in a new way.

Example 4: Using Classes

This example ramps up the complexity considerably by introducing an object-oriented programming concept: classes. Recall from earlier that classes are another way to modularize our code. Classes are used to model data and behavior on that data. Further, classes are typically placed in their own code module (file) that further modularizes the code. If you need to modify a class, you may need only change the code in the class module.

The problem we're exploring in this example is how to develop solutions using classes and code modules. We will be creating two files: one for the class and another for the main code. Since this code is more complex, we will execute it first on our PC by creating the files there and then upload them to the Pico and execute them there.

Write the Code

This example is designed to convert Roman numerals to integers. That is, we will enter a value like VIII, which is eight, and expect to see the integer 8. To make things more interesting, we will also take the integer we derive and convert it back to Roman numerals. Roman numerals are formed as a string using the characters I for 1, V for 5, X for 10, L for 50, C for 100, D for 500, and M for 1000. Combinations of other numbers are done by adding the character numerical value together (e.g., 3 = III) or a single, lower character before a character to indicate the representative minus that character (e.g., 4 = IV). The following shows some examples of how this works:

```
3 = III
15 = XV
12 = XII
24 = XXIV
96 = LXLVI
107 = CVII
```

This may sound like a lot of extra work but consider this: if we can convert from one format to another, we should be able to convert back without errors. More specifically, we can use the code for one conversion to validate the other. If we get a different value when converting it back, we know we have a problem that needs to be fixed.

To solve the problem, we will place the code for converting Roman numerals into a separate file (code module) and build a class called Roman_Numerals to contain the methods. In this case, the data is a mapping of integers to Roman numerals:

```
# Private dictionary of roman numerals
__roman_dict = {
    'I': 1,
    'IV': 4,
    'V': 5,
    'IX': 9,
    'X': 10,
    'XL': 40,
    'L': 50,
    'XC': 90,
    'C': 100,
    'CD': 400,
    'D': 500,
    'CM': 900,
    'M': 1000,
}
```

Notice the two underscores before the name of the dictionary. This is a special notation that marks the dictionary as a private variable in the class. This is a Python aspect for information hiding, which is a recommended technique to use when designing objects; always strive to hide data that is used inside the class.

Notice also that instead of using the basic characters and their values, I used several other values too. I did this to help make the conversion easier (and cheat a bit). In this case, I added the entries that represent the one value previous conversions such as 4 (IV), 9 (IX), etc. This makes the conversion a bit easier (and more accurate).

We will also add two methods: convert_to_int(), which takes a Roman numeral string and converts it to an integer, and convert_to_roman(), which takes an integer and converts it to a Roman numeral. Rather than explain every line of code in the methods, I leave it to you to read the code to see how it works.

Simply, the convert to integer method takes each character and gets its value from the dictionary summing the values. There is a trick there that requires special handling for the lower value characters appearing before higher values (e.g., IX). The convert to Roman method is a bit easier since we simply divide the value by the highest value in the dictionary until we reach zero. Listing 3-9 shows the code for the class module, which is saved in a file named roman_numerals.py.

Listing 3-9. Roman Numeral Class

```
"""roman_numerals.py"""
#
# Beginning MicroPython - Chapter 3
#
# Example: Roman numerals class
#
# Convert integers to roman numerals
# Convert roman numerals to integers
#
# Dr. Charles Bell
#

class Roman_Numerals:
    """Roman Numerals class"""

    # Private dictionary of roman numerals
    __roman_dict = {
        'I': 1,
```

```
        'IV': 4,
        'V': 5,
        'IX': 9,
        'X': 10,
        'XL': 40,
        'L': 50,
        'XC': 90,
        'C': 100,
        'CD': 400,
        'D': 500,
        'CM': 900,
        'M': 1000,
    }

    def convert_to_int(self, roman_num):
        """Convert Roman numeral to integer"""
        value = 0
        for i in range(len(roman_num)):
            if i > 0 and self.__roman_dict[roman_num[i]] >
                self.__roman_dict[roman_num[i - 1]]:
                value += self.__roman_dict[roman_num[i]] - 2 *
                self.__roman_dict[roman_num[i - 1]]
            else:
                value += self.__roman_dict[roman_num[i]]
        return value

    def __find_numeral(self, find_value):
        """Search the dictionary for the Roman numeral"""
        return [item[0] for item in
self.__roman_dict.items() if item[1] == find_value][0]

    def convert_to_roman(self, int_value):
        """Convert integer to Roman numeral"""
```

```
    # First, sort the dictionary by value

    roman_values = sorted(list(self.__roman_dict.values()))
    # Prepare the string
    roman_str = ""
    remainder = int_value
    # Loop through the values in reverse
    for i in range(len(roman_values)-1, -1, -1):
        count = int(remainder / roman_values[i])
        if count > 0:
            for j in range(0,count):
                roman_str += self.__find_numeral(roman_
                values[i])
            remainder -= count * roman_values[i]
    return roman_str
```

Notice the function named __find_numeral(). This is a special list operation to search the __roman_dict dictionary to find the Roman number by value. Why is this needed? It is needed because the Pico MicroPython core does not return dictionary values in order. Thus, we either must sort the dictionary (an unnecessary step) or search for the value and return the key or, in this case, the Roman numeral. The following shows a simplified version of this code that works the same way without the special list function:

```
def __find_numeral_search(self, find_value):
    """Search the dictionary for the Roman numeral using a
    search"""
    for key in self.__roman_dict.keys():
        if self.__roman_dict[key] == find_value:
            return key
    return None
```

If you're following along with the chapter, go ahead and create a file on your PC for this code and name it `roman_numerals.py`. We'll copy it to our Pico in the next section.

Now let's look at the main code. For this, we simply need to import the new class from the code module as follows. This is a slightly different form of the import directive. In this case, we're telling Python to include the `roman_numerals` class from the file named `Roman_Numerals`:

```
from roman_numerals import Roman_Numerals
```

Note   If the code module were in a subfolder, say `roman`, we would have written the `import` statement as `from roman import Roman_Numerals` where we list the folders using dot notation instead of slashes.

The rest of the code is straightforward. We first ask the user for a valid Roman numeral string and then convert it to an integer and use that value to convert back to Roman numerals printing the result. So, you see having the class in a separate module has simplified our code, making it shorter and easier to maintain. Listing 3-10 shows the complete main code saved in a file named simply `roman.py`.

Listing 3-10. Converting Roman Numerals

```
#
# Beginning MicroPython - Chapter 3
#
# Example: Convert roman numerals using a class
#
# Convert integers to roman numerals
# Convert roman numerals to integers
```

```
#
# Dr. Charles Bell
#

from roman_numerals import Roman_Numerals

roman_str = input("Enter a valid roman numeral: ")
roman_num = Roman_Numerals()

# Convert to roman numerals
value = roman_num.convert_to_int(roman_str)
print("Convert to integer:        {0} = {1}".format(roman_
str, value))

# Convert to integer
new_str = roman_num.convert_to_roman(value)
print("Convert to Roman Numerals: {0} = {1}".format(value,
new_str))

print("bye!")
```

If you're following along with the chapter, go ahead and create a file on your PC for this code and name it roman.py. We'll copy it to our Pico in the next section.

Tip   For a more in-depth look at how to work with classes in Python, see https://docs.python.org/3/tutorial/classes.html.

Now, let's see what happens when we run this script. Recall, we will be running this code on our MicroPython board, so if you're following along, be sure to set up your board and connect it to your PC.

Execute the Code

If you haven't created the files, do that now and save them on your
PC. Then, open a terminal and use the python ./roman.py command to
execute it, or you can execute it with the Run command in Thonny. When
you execute the code, you will be prompted to enter the Roman numeral.
Try executing it several times and entering some valid and invalid Roman
numerals. You should get results similar to the following:

```
$ python ./roman.py
Enter a valid roman numeral: VI
Convert to integer:        VI = 6
Convert to Roman Numerals: 6 = VI
bye!

$ python ./roman.py
Enter a valid roman numeral: IIV
Convert to integer:        IIV = 5
Convert to Roman Numerals: 5 = V
bye!

$ python ./roman.py
Enter a valid roman numeral: MMXXI
Convert to integer:         MMXXI = 2021
Convert to Roman Numerals: 2021 = MMXXI
bye!
```

Notice the second execution. Here, we entered an invalid Roman
numeral but got an answer anyway (rather than an error). Clearly, this is
an area where we can improve the code.

Now let's upload the files to the Pico and execute them. Use Thonny
to do this. When you run the roman.py file, you should see output similar
to the following. Run it a few times until you are convinced it is working
correctly:

```
Enter a valid roman numeral: XIV
Convert to integer:        XIV = 14
Convert to Roman Numerals: 14 = XIV
bye!
```

Your Challenge

There isn't much to add for this example to improve it other than perhaps some user friendliness (nicer to use). If you want to improve the code or the class itself, I suggest adding a new method named validate() used to validate a Roman numeral string. This method can take a string and determine if it contains a valid series of characters. Hint: To start, check the string has only the characters in the dictionary.

However, you can use this template to build other classes for converting formats. For example, as an exercise, you could create a new class to convert integers to hexadecimal or even octal. Yes, there are functions that will do this for us, but it can be enlightening and satisfying to build it yourself. Go ahead, give it a go – create a new class to convert integers to other formats. I would suggest doing a hexadecimal to integer function first, and when that is working correctly, create the reciprocal to convert integers to hexadecimal.

A more advanced challenge would be to rewrite the class to accept a string in the constructor (when the class variable is created) and use that string to do the conversions instead of passing the string or integer using the convert_to* methods. For example, the class could have a constructor and private member as follows:

```
__roman_str = ""
...
def __init__(self, name):
        self.name = name
```

When you create the instance, you will need to pass the string or else you will get an error that a required parameter is missing.

```
roman_str = input("Enter a valid roman numeral: ")
roman_num = Roman_Numerals(roman_str)
```

For More Information

Should you require more in-depth knowledge of Python, there are several excellent books on the topic. I list a few of my favorites in the following. A great resource is the documentation on the Python site: `python.org/doc/`.

- *Pro Python, Second Edition* (Apress 2014) J. Burton Browning , Marty Alchin

- *Learning Python, 5th Edition* (O'Reilly Media 2013) Mark Lutz

- *Automate the Boring Stuff with Python: Practical Programming for Total Beginners* (No Starch Press 2015), Al Sweigart

Summary

Wow! That was a wild ride, wasn't it? I hope that this short crash course in Python has explained enough about the sample programs shown so far that you now know how they work. This crash course also forms the basis for understanding the other Python examples in this book.

If you are learning how to work with IoT projects and don't know how to program with Python, learning Python can be fun given its easy-to-understand syntax. While there are many examples on the Internet you can use, very few are documented in such a way as to provide enough information for someone new to Python to understand or much less get started and deploy the sample! But at least the code is easy to read.

This chapter has provided a crash course in Python that covers the basics of the things you will encounter when examining most of the smaller example projects. We discovered the basic syntax and constructs of a Python application including a walk-through of building a real Python application that blinks an LED. Through that example, we learned how to work with headless applications including how to manage a startup background application.

In the next chapter, we'll dive deeper into the Pico hardware. We will see more about the special libraries available for use in your projects written for running on the Pico.

CHAPTER 4

Low-Level Hardware Support

The previous chapters have given us a foundation of what is possible when programming the Pico in MicroPython. However, there is far more about the Pico than what has been presented in the previous chapters. In fact, there are many layers to the Pico hardware support including libraries that contain helpful constructs and classes you will need in order to work with the hardware connected to your Pico.

While we've had a quick look at how to work with the Pico including a presentation on several forms of Python projects and a tutorial in programming in Python, we are only just beginning to learn what is possible with the Pico. It is now time to learn more about the available hardware-related software libraries.

In this chapter, we will look at the MicroPython libraries available for you to use in your projects and have a brief look at the low-level hardware support in MicroPython for the Pico. Finally, we will also revisit working with breakout boards to demonstrate some of the libraries and hardware protocols and techniques discussed in previous chapters.

Before we jump into looking at the Pico hardware and supporting software, let's take a more detailed look at the GPIO header and pins.

© Charles Bell 2022
C. Bell, *Beginning MicroPython with the Raspberry Pi Pico*, Maker Innovations Series,
https://doi.org/10.1007/978-1-4842-8135-2_4

The Pico GPIO Header

We learned a bit about the general-purpose input/output (GPIO) header and the pins included in the last chapter. The GPIO pins are arranged in a very specific layout that isn't completely linear. More specifically, the GPIO pin number does not map directly to the physical pin number.

Where people can go wrong is not knowing (or not verifying) the GPIO header layout, which can lead to the wrong pins being used for electronics and can result in unexpected behavior, things not working at all, or even damaged components. Thus, like all successful endeavors, you need to consult a map before you begin. Figure 4-1 shows a drawing that illustrates the GPIO pins available on the Pico.

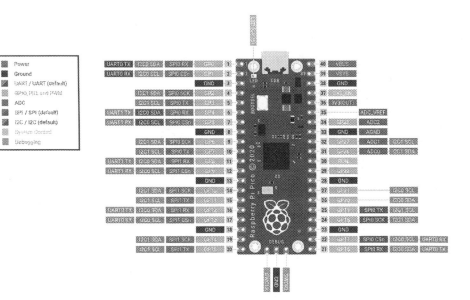

Figure 4-1. *Pico GPIO pins (courtesy of raspberrypi.org)*

Here, we see there are pins labeled (starting from closest to the board) by a physical number, logical GPIO name/number, then any low-level interfaces or mechanisms supported. Some pins can be programmed to operate in different modes or for different hardware features. For example, look at physical pins 31 and 32. Here, we see the pins can act as analog pins (indicated with ADC) as well as an I2C interface (more on that later). Also notice there are a number of pins marked as ground (GND), and those related to power located on physical pins 36, 37, 39, and 40.

Now, let's take a look at the core MicroPython software libraries available that provide advanced capabilities we can exploit in our projects.

Note   This chapter contains only a subset of the much larger documentation found at `https://datasheets.raspberrypi.org/pico/pico-datasheet.pdf`.

MicroPython Libraries

The libraries available in MicroPython mirror those in Python. In fact, the libraries in the firmware (sometimes called the application programming interface or API or firmware API) comprise a great deal of the same libraries in Python.

There are some notable exceptions for standard libraries where there is an equivalent library in MicroPython, but it has been renamed to distinguish it from the Python library. In this case, the library has either been reduced in scope by removing the less frequently used features or modified in some ways to fit the MicroPython platform – all to save space (memory).

There are also libraries that are specific to MicroPython and the hardware that provide functionality that may or may not be in some general Python releases. These libraries are designed to make working with the microcontroller and hardware easier.

Thus, there are three types of libraries in the firmware: those that are standard and mostly the same as those in Python, those that are specific to MicroPython, and those specific to the hardware. There is another type of library sometimes called user-supplied or simply custom libraries. These are libraries (APIs) we create ourselves that we can deploy to our board and thereby make functionality available to all our projects. We will see an overview of all types of libraries in this section.

Rather than simply paraphrase or (gasp) copy the existing documentation, we will see overviews of the libraries in the form of quick reference tables you can use to become familiar with what is available. We will also see some code snippets designed to help you learn how to work with some of the more common libraries.

Let's begin with a look at those libraries in MicroPython that are "standard" Python libraries.

Built-In and Standard Libraries

MicroPython is a specialized and trimmed-down version of Python we can use on our PC. It contains much of the same libraries as Python, but with some differences. We call these libraries "built-in," but it is more correct to name them "standard" libraries since these libraries are the same as those in Python.

They have the same classes with the same functions as those in Python. So, you can write a script on your PC and execute it there and then execute the same script unaltered on your MicroPython board. Nice! As you can surmise, this helps greatly when developing a complex project.

In this section, we will explore the standard Python libraries beginning with a short overview of what is available followed by details on how to use some of the more common libraries.

Tip   See `https://datasheets.raspberrypi.org/` `pico/raspberry-pi-pico-python-sdk.pdf` for complete documentation of the built-in libraries for MicroPython on the Pico. You can also check out the overview at `https://docs.` `micropython.org/en/latest/rp2/quickref.html`.

Overview

The standard libraries in MicroPython contain objects that you can use to perform mathematical functions, operate on programming structures, work with transportable documents (a document store) through JSON, interact with the operating system and other system functions, and even perform calculations on time.

Table 4-1 contains a list of the current standard MicroPython libraries. The first column is the name we use in our import statement, the second is a short description, and the third contains a link to the online documentation with abbreviated links for brevity.

Note   All links start with `https://docs.micropython.org/en/latest/`.

Table 4-1. *Standard Python Libraries in MicroPython*

Library	Description	Documentation
cmath	Mathematical functions for complex numbers	library/cmath.html
gc	Control the garbage collector	library/gc.html
math	Mathematical functions	library/math.html
uarray	Arrays of numeric data	library/uarray.html
uasyncio	Asynchronous I/O scheduler	library/uasyncio.html
ubinascii	Binary/ASCII conversions	library/ubinascii.html
ucollections	Collection and container types	library/ucollections.html
uerrno	System error codes	library/uerrno.html

(continued)

Table 4-1. (*continued*)

Library	Description	Documentation
uhashlib	Hashing algorithms	library/uhashlib.html
uio	Input/output streams	library/uio.html
ujson	JSON encoding and decoding	library/ujson.html
uos	Basic "operating system" services	library/uos.html
ure	Simple regular expressions	library/ure.html
uselect	Wait for events on a set of streams	library/uselect.html
ustruct	Pack and unpack primitive data types	library/ustruct.html
usys	System-specific functions	library/usys.html
utime	Time-related functions	library/utime.html
uzlib	zlib decompression	library/uzlib.html
_thread	Multithreading support	library/_thread.html

Note   The MicroPython standard library includes additional libraries not currently part of the Pico firmware. For example, the uheapq, ussl, and usocket libraries are not currently included, but may be added in later releases.

As you can see, there are many libraries that begin with u to signify they are special versions of the Python equivalent libraries. That is, if you need access to the original Python version – if it exists – you can still access it by using the original name (without the u prefix). In this case, MicroPython will attempt to find the module by the original name and, if not there, default to the MicroPython version. For example, if we wanted to use the original io library, we could use import io. However, if there is no module named io on the platform, MicroPython will use the MicroPython version named uio.

Next, we will look at some of the more commonly used standard libraries and see some code examples for each. But first, there are two categories of standard functions we should discuss.

INTERACTIVE HELP FOR LIBRARIES

A little-known function named help() can be, well, very helpful when learning about the libraries in MicroPython. You can use this function in a REPL session to get information about a library. The following shows an excerpt of the output for the uos library:

```
>>> help(uos)
object <module 'uos'> is of type module
    __name__ -- uos
  uname -- <function>
  urandom -- <function>
  chdir -- <function>
  getcwd -- <function>
  listdir -- <function>
  mkdir -- <function>
  remove -- <function>
  rename -- <function>
  rmdir -- <function>
  stat -- <function>
  statvfs -- <function>
  ilistdir -- <function>
  mount -- <function>
  umount -- <function>
```

```
    VfsFat -- <class 'VfsFat'>
    VfsLfs2 -- <class 'VfsLfs2'>
>>>
```

Notice we see the names of all the functions and, if present, constants. This can be a real help when learning the libraries and what they contain. Try it!

Now let's look at examples of some of the more commonly used standard libraries. What follows is just a sampling of what you can do with each of the libraries. See the online documentation for a full description of all the capabilities.

sys

The sys library provides access to the execution system such as constants, variables, command-line options, streams (stdout, stdin, stderr), and more. Most of the features of the library are constants or lists. The streams can be accessed directly, but typically we use the print() function, which sends data to the stdout stream by default. The following shows the most commonly used functions in this library, and Listing 4-1 contains a demonstration of the sys library:

- sys.argv: List of arguments passed to the script from the command line

- sys.exit(r): Exit the program returning the value r to the caller

- sys.modules: List of modules loaded (imported)

- sys.path: List of paths to search for modules – can be modified

- sys.platform: Display the platform information such as Linux, MicroPython, etc.

- sys.stderr: Standard error stream

- sys.stdin: Standard input stream

- sys.stdout: Standard output stream

- sys.version: The version of Python currently
  executing

Listing 4-1. Demonstration of the sys Library Features

```
# Beginning MicroPython - Chapter 4: Listing 4-1
# Example use of the sys library
import sys
print("Modules loaded: " , sys.modules)
sys.path.append("/my_libs")
print("Path: ", sys.path)
sys.stdout.write("Platform: ")
sys.stdout.write(sys.platform)
sys.stdout.write("\n")
sys.stdout.write("Version: ")
sys.stdout.write(sys.version)
sys.stdout.write("\n")
sys.exit(1)
```

Notice we start with the import statement, and after that, we can print
the constants and variables in the sys library using the print() function.
We also see how to append a path to our search path with the sys.path.
append() function. This is very helpful if we create our own directories
on the flash memory drive to place our code. Without this addition, the
import statement will fail unless the code module is in the lib directory.

At the end of the example, we see how to use the stdout stream to
write things to the screen. Note that you must provide the carriage return
(newline) command to advance the output to a new line (\n). The print()

function takes care of that for us. The following shows the output of running this script on the Pico:

```
Modules loaded:  {'rp2': <module 'rp2' from 'rp2.py'>}
Path:  ['', '/lib', '/my_libs']
Platform: rp2
Version: 3.4.0
```

Notice the addition of the my_libs folder. We add this so that we could import modules from that directory. If you place your modules in a subfolder, and don't include the subfolder in the import statement, you must add the folder to the system path.

uio

The uio library contains additional functions to work with streams and stream-like objects. There is a single function named uio.open() that you can use to open files (but most people use the built-in function named open()) as well as classes for byte and string streams. In fact, the classes have similar file functions such as read(), write(), seek(), flush(), close(), as well as a getvalue() function, which returns the contents of the stream buffer that contains the data. Listing 4-2 shows a demonstration of the uio library.

Listing 4-2. Demonstration of the uio Library Features

```
# Beginning MicroPython - Chapter 4: Listing 4-2
# Example use of the uio library
# Note: change uio to io to run this on your PC!
import uio
try:
    fio_out = uio.open('data.bin', 'wb')
    fio_out.write(b"\x5F\x9E\xAE\x09\x3E\x96\x68\x65\x6C\x6C\x6F")
```

```
    fio_out.write(b"\x00")
    fio_out.close()
except Exception as err:
    print("ERROR (writing):", err)

# Read the binary file and print out the results in hex and char.
try:
    fio_in = uio.open('data.bin', 'rb')
    print("Raw,Dec,Hex from file:")
    byte_val = fio_in.read(1)  # read a byte
    while byte_val:
        print(byte_val, ",", ord(byte_val), hex(ord(byte_val)))
        byte_val = fio_in.read(1)  # read a byte
    fio_in.close()
except Exception as err:
    print("ERROR (reading):", err)
```

In this example, we first open a new file for writing and write an array of bytes to the file. The technique used is passing the hex values for each byte to the write() function. When you read data from sensors, they are typically in binary form (a byte or string of bytes). You signify a byte with the escape \x as shown.

After writing the data to the file, we then read the file one byte at a time by passing 1 to the read() function. We then print the values read in their raw form (the value returned from the read(1) call) as a decimal value and a hex value. The bytes written contain a secret word (one obscured by using hex values) – can you see it?

This is like how you would use the normal built-in functions, which we saw in the last chapter. The following shows the output when run on the Pico:

```
Raw,Dec,Hex from file:
b'_' , 95 0x5f
b'\x9e' , 158 0x9e
b'\xae' , 174 0xae
b'\t' , 9 0x9
b'>' , 62 0x3e
b'\x96' , 150 0x96
b'h' , 104 0x68
b'e' , 101 0x65
b'l' , 108 0x6c
b'l' , 108 0x6c
b'o' , 111 0x6f
b'\x00' , 0 0x0
```

If you're curious what the file looks like, you can use a utility like hexdump to print the contents as shown in the following. Can you see the hidden message?

```
$ hexdump -C data.bin
00000000   5f 9e ae 09 3e 96 68 65   6c 6c 6f 00
|_...>.hello.|
0000000c
```

ujson

The ujson library is one of those libraries you are likely to use frequently when working with data in an IoT project. It provides encoding and decoding of JavaScript Object Notation (JSON) documents. This is because many of the IoT services available either require or can process JSON documents. Thus, you should consider getting into the habit of formatting your data in JSON to make it easier to integrate with other systems. The library implements the following functions that you can use to work with JSON documents:

- `ujson.dumps(obj)`: Return a string decoded from a JSON object

- `ujson.loads(str)`: Parse the JSON string and return a JSON object. Will raise an error if not formatted correctly

- `ujson.load(fp)`: Parse the contents of a file pointer (a file string containing a JSON document). Will raise an error if not formatted correctly

Recall we saw a brief example of JSON documents in the last chapter. That example was written exclusively for the PC, but a small change makes it possible to run it on the Pico. Let's look at a similar example. Listing 4-3 shows an example of using the `ujson` library.

Listing 4-3. Demonstration of the ujson Library Features

```
# Beginning MicroPython - Chapter 4: Listing 4-3
# Example use of the ujson library
# Note: change ujson to json to run it on your PC!
import ujson

# Prepare a list of JSON documents for pets by converting JSON
to a dictionary
vehicles = []
vehicles.append(ujson.loads('{"make":"Chevrolet",
"year":2015, "model":"Silverado", "color":"Pull me over red",
"type":"pickup"}'))
vehicles.append(ujson.loads('{"make":"Yamaha", "year":2009,
"model":"R1", "color":"Blue/Silver", "type":"motorcycle"}'))
```

```
vehicles.append(ujson.loads('{"make":"SeaDoo", "year":1997,
"model":"Speedster", "color":"White", "type":"boat"}'))
vehicles.append(ujson.loads('{"make":"TaoJen", "year":2013,
"model":"Sicily", "color":"Black", "type":"Scooter"}'))

# Now, write these entries to a file. Note: overwrites the file
json_file = open("my_vehicles.json", "w")
for vehicle in vehicles:
    json_file.write(ujson.dumps(vehicle))
    json_file.write("\n")
json_file.close()

# Now, let's read the list of vehicles and print out their data
my_vehicles = []
json_file = open("my_vehicles.json", "r")
for vehicle in json_file.readlines():
    parsed_json = ujson.loads(vehicle)
    my_vehicles.append(parsed_json)
json_file.close()

# Finally, print a summary of the vehicles
print("Year Make Model Color")
for vehicle in my_vehicles:
    print(vehicle['year'],vehicle['make'],vehicle['model'],
    vehicle['color'])
```

The following shows the output of the script running on the Pico:

```
Year Make Model Color
2015 Chevrolet Silverado Pull me over red
2009 Yamaha R1 Blue/Silver
1997 SeaDoo Speedster White
2013 TaoJen Sicily Black
```

uos

The uos library implements a set of functions for working with the base operating system. Some of the functions may be familiar if you have written programs for your PC. Most functions allow you to work with file and directory operations. The following lists several of the more commonly used functions:

- uos.chdir(path): Change the current directory

- uos.getcwd(): Return the current working directory

- uos.listdir([dir]): List the current directory if dir is missing or list the directory specified

- uos.mkdir(path): Create a new directory

- uos.remove(path): Delete a file

- uos.rmdir(path): Delete a directory

- uos.rename(old_path, new_path): Rename a file

- uos.stat(path): Get the status of a file or directory

In this example, we see how to change the working directory so that we can simplify our import statements. We also see how to create a new directory, rename it, create a file in the new directory, list the directory, and finally clean up (delete) the changes. Listing 4-4 shows the example for working with the uos library functions.

Listing 4-4. Demonstration of the uos Library Features

```
# Beginning MicroPython - Chapter 4
# Example use of the uos library
# Note: change uos to os to run it on your PC!
import sys
import uos
```

```
# Create a function to display files in directory
def show_files():
    files = uos.listdir()
    sys.stdout.write("\nShow Files Output:\n")
    sys.stdout.write("\tname\tsize\n")
    for file in files:
        stats = uos.stat(file)
        # Print a directory with a "d" prefix and the size
        is_dir = True
        if stats[0] > 16384:
            is_dir = False
        if is_dir:
            sys.stdout.write("d\t")
        else:
            sys.stdout.write("\t")
        sys.stdout.write(file)
        if not is_dir:
            sys.stdout.write("\t")
            sys.stdout.write(str(stats[6]))
        sys.stdout.write("\n")

# List the current directory
show_files()

# Create a directory
uos.mkdir("test")
show_files()
```

While this example is a little long, it shows some interesting tricks. Notice we created a function to print out the directory list rather than printing out the list of files returned. We also checked the status of the file to determine if the file was a directory or not, and if it is, we printed a d to signal the name refers to a directory. We also used the stdout stream to control formatting with tabs (\t) and newline (\n) characters.

Now let's see the output. The following shows the output when run on the Pico. Note: If you run this a second time, be sure to delete the new directory created.

```
Show Files Output:
    name      size
    data.bin      12
    example1.py       632
    example2.py       946
    example3.py       939
    fibonacci.py      2259
    hello_pico.py       25
    listing_04_01.py        380
    listing_04_02.py        794
    listing_04_03.py        1411
    listing_04_04.py        907
    my_data.json        268
    my_vehicles.json        377
    roman.py        621
    roman_numerals.py       1839

Show Files Output:
    name      size
    data.bin      12
    example1.py       632
    example2.py       946
    example3.py       939
    fibonacci.py      2259
    hello_pico.py       25
    listing_04_01.py        380
    listing_04_02.py        794
    listing_04_03.py        1411
    listing_04_04.py        907
```

```
my_data.json      268
my_vehicles.json      377
roman.py      621
roman_numerals.py      1839
```

There are also built-in functions that are not part of any specific library, and there are exceptions that allow us to capture error conditions. Let's look at those before we dive into some of the more commonly used standard libraries.

Built-In Functions and Classes

Python comes with many built-in functions – functions you can call directly from your script without importing them. There are many classes that you can use to define variables, work with data, and more. They're objects so you can use them to contain data and perform operations (functions) on the data. We've seen a few of these in the examples so far.

Let us see some of the major built-in functions and classes. Table 4-2 includes a short description of each. You should look through this list and explore the links for those you find interesting and refer to the list when developing your projects so that you can use the most appropriate function or class. You may be surprised how much is "built-in."

Table 4-2. *MicroPython Built-In Functions and Classes*

Name	Description
abs(x)	Return the absolute value of a number
all(iterable)	Return True if all elements of the iterable are true (or if the iterable is empty)
any(iterable)	Return True if any element of the iterable is true
bin(x)	Convert an integer number to a binary string
class bool([x])	Return a Boolean value, i.e., one of True or False
class bytearray([source [, encoding[, errors]]])	Return a new array of bytes
class bytes([source[, encoding[, errors]]])	Return a new "bytes" object, which is an immutable sequence of integers in the range $0 <= x < 256$
callable(object)	Return True if the object argument appears callable, False if not
chr(i)	Return the string representing a character whose Unicode code point is the integer i
classmethod(function)	Return a class method for a function
class complex([real[, imag]])	Return a complex number with the value real + imag*1j or convert a string or number to a complex number
delattr(obj, name)	This is a relative of setattr(). The arguments are an object and a string. The string must be the name of one of the object's attributes
class dict()	Create a new dictionary

(*continued*)

Table 4-2. (*continued*)

Name	Description
dir([object])	Without arguments, return the list of names in the current local scope. With an argument, attempt to return a list of valid attributes for that object
divmod(a,b)	Take two (noncomplex) numbers as arguments and return a pair of numbers consisting of their quotient and remainder when using integer division
enumerate(iterable, start=0)	Return an enumerate object. The iterable must be a sequence, an iterator, or some other object which supports iteration
eval(expression, globals=None, locals=None)	Evaluate an expression using globals and locals as dictionaries in a local namespace
exec(object[, globals[, locals]])	Execute a set of Python statements or object using globals and locals as dictionaries in a local namespace
filter(function, iterable)	Construct an iterator from those elements of the iterable for which the function returns true
class float([x])	Return a floating-point number constructed from a number or string
class frozenset ([iterable])	Return a new frozenset object, optionally with elements taken from the iterable
getattr(object, name[, default])	Return the value of the named attribute of the object. The name must be a string

(continued)

Table 4-2. (*continued*)

Name	Description
globals()	Return a dictionary representing the current global symbol table
hasattr(object, name)	The arguments are an object and a string. The result is True if the string is the name of one of the object's attributes, False if not
hash(object)	Return the hash value of the object (if it has one). Hash values are integers
hex(x)	Convert an integer number to a lowercase hexadecimal string prefixed with "0x"
id(object)	Return the "identity" of an object
input([prompt])	If the prompt argument is present, it is written to standard output without a trailing newline. The function then reads a line from input, converts it to a string (stripping a trailing newline), and returns that
class int(x)	Return an integer object constructed from a number or string x, or return 0 if no arguments are given
isinstance(object, classinfo)	Return true if the object argument is an instance of the classinfo argument or of a (direct, indirect, or virtual) subclass thereof
issubclass(class, classinfo)	Return true if the class is a subclass (direct, indirect, or virtual) of classinfo
iter(object[, sentinel])	Return an iterator object

(*continued*)

Table 4-2. (*continued*)

Name	Description
`len(s)`	Return the length (the number of items) of an object
`class list([iterable])`	List sequence
`locals()`	Update and return a dictionary representing the current local symbol table
`map(function, iterable, ...)`	Return an iterator that applies a function to every item of the iterable, yielding the results
`max([iterable|arg*])`	Return the largest item in an iterable or the largest of two or more arguments
`class memoryview(obj)`	Return a "memory view" object created from the given argument
`min([iterable|arg*])`	Return the smallest item in an iterable or the smallest of two or more arguments
`next(iterator[, default])`	Retrieve the next item from the iterator by calling its __next__() method
`class object0`	Return a new featureless object. The object is a base for all classes
`oct(x)`	Convert an integer number to an octal string
`open(file, mode='r', buffering=-1, encoding=None, errors=None, newline=None, closefd=True, opener=None)`	Open a file and return a corresponding file object. Use close() to close the file

(continued)

Table 4-2. (*continued*)

Name	Description
`ord(c)`	Given a string representing one Unicode character, return an integer representing the Unicode code point of that character
`pow(x, y[, z])`	Return x to the power y; if z is present, return x to the power y, modulo z (computed more efficiently than pow(x, y) % z)
`print(*objects, sep=' ', end='\n', file=sys.stdout, flush=False)`	Print objects to the text stream file, separated by sep and followed by end. sep, end, file, and flush, if present, must be given as keyword arguments
`class property(fget=None, fset=None, fdel=None, doc=None)`	Return a property attribute
`range([stop|[start, stop[, step]]])`	Range sequence
`repr(object)`	Return a string containing a printable representation of an object
`reversed(seq)`	Return a reverse iterator
`round(number[, ndigits])`	Return a number rounded to ndigits precision after the decimal point
`class set([iterable])`	Return a new set object, optionally with elements taken from the iterable
`setattr(object, name, value)`	This is the counterpart of getattr(). The arguments are an object, a string, and an arbitrary value

(*continued*)

Table 4-2. (*continued*)

Name	Description
class slice(start, stop[, step])	Return a slice object representing the set of indices specified by range(start, stop, step)
sorted(iterable[, key] [, reverse])	Return a new sorted list from the items in the iterable
staticmethod(function)	Return a static method for a function
class str(object)	Return a str version of an object
sum(iterable[, start])	Sum the start and the items of an iterable from left to right and return the total
super([type[, object-or-type]])	Return a proxy object that delegates function calls to a parent or sibling class of a type
class tuple([iterable])	Tuple sequence
type(object)	Return the type of an object
zip(*iterables)	Make an iterator that aggregates elements from each of the iterables

Now let's talk about a topic we haven't talked a lot about – exceptions. Exceptions are part of the built-in module for Python and can be a very important programming technique you will want to use. Perhaps not right away, but eventually you will appreciate the power and convenience of using exceptions in your code.

Exceptions

There is also a powerful mechanism we can use in Python (and MicroPython) to help manage or capture events when errors occur and execute code for a specific error. This construct is called exceptions, and the exceptions (errors) we can capture are called exception classes.

It uses a special syntax called the try statement (also called a clause since it requires at least one other clause to form a valid statement) to help us capture errors as they are generated.

Exceptions can be generated anywhere in code with the raise() function. That is, if something goes wrong, a programmer can "raise" a specific, named exception, and the try statement can be used to capture it via an except or else clause. Table 4-3 shows the list of exception classes available in MicroPython along with a short description of when (how) the exception could be raised.

Table 4-3. *MicroPython Exception Classes*

Exception Class	Description of Use
AssertionError	An assert() statement fails
AttributeError	An attribute reference fails
Exception	Base exception class
ImportError	One or more modules failed to import
IndexError	Subscript is out of range
KeyboardInterrupt	Keyboard *CTRL+C* was issued or simulated
KeyError	Key mapping in the dictionary is not present in the list of keys
MemoryError	Out of memory condition
NameError	A local or global name (variable, function, etc.) is not found
NotImplementedError	An abstract function has been encountered (it is incomplete)
OSError	Any system-related error from the operating system
RuntimeError	Possibly fatal error encountered on execution

(continued)

Table 4-3. (*continued*)

Exception Class	Description of Use
StopIteration	An iterator's next function signaled no more values in an iterable object
SyntaxError	Code syntax error encountered
SystemExit	The sys.exit() function was called or simulated
TypeError	A function or operation is applied to an inappropriate type (like type mismatch)
ValueError	The right type but wrong value found (like out of bounds)
ZeroDivisionError	Mathematical function results in division by zero

The syntax for the try statement is shown as follows. Each part of the construct is called a clause:

```
try_stmt   ::=  try1_stmt | try2_stmt
try1_stmt ::=  "try" ":" code block
               ("except" [expression ["as" identifier]] ":"
               code block)+
               ["else" ":" code block]
               ["finally" ":" code block]
try2_stmt ::=  "try" ":" code block
               "finally" ":" code block
```

Notice there are four clauses: try, except, else, and finally. The try clause is where we put our code (code block) – one or more lines of code that will be included in the exception capture. There can be only one try, else, and finally, but you can have any number of except clauses naming an exception class.

In fact, the except and else go together such that if an exception is detected running any of the lines of code in the try clause, it will search the except clauses, and if and only if no except clause is met, it will execute the else clause. The finally clause is used to execute after all exceptions are processed and executed.

Notice also that there are two versions of the statement: one that contains one or more except and optionally an else and finally, and another that has only the try and finally clauses.

Let's look at one of the ways we can use the statement to capture errors in our code. Suppose you are reading data from a batch of sensors and the libraries (modules) for those sensors raise ValueError if the value read is out of range or invalid. It may also be the case that you don't want the data from any other sensors if one or more fail. So, we can use code like the following to "try" to read each of the sensors and, if there is a ValueError, issue a warning and keep going or, if some other error is encountered, flag it as an error during the read. Note that typically we would not stop the program at that point; rather, we would normally log it and keep going. Study the following until you're convinced exceptions arc cool:

```
values = []
print("Start sensor read.")
try:
    values.append(read_sensor(pin11))
    values.append(read_sensor(pin12))
    values.append(read_sensor(pin13))
    values.append(read_sensor(pin17))
    values.append(read_sensor(pin18))
except ValueError as err:
    print("WARNING: One or more sensors valued to read a
    correct value.", err)
```

```
except:
    print("ERROR: fatal error reading sensors.")
finally:
    print("Sensor read complete.")
```

Another way we can use exceptions is when we want to import a module (library) but we're not sure if it is present. For example, suppose there was a module named piano.py that has a function named keys() that you want to import, but the module may or may not be on the system. In this case, we may have other code we can use instead creating our own version of keys(). To test if the module can be imported, we can place our import inside a try block as shown in the following. We can then detect if the import fails and take appropriate steps:

```
# Try to import the keys() function from piano. If not present,
# use a simulated version of the keys() function.
try:
    from piano import keys
except ImportError as err:
    print("WARNING:", err)
    def keys():
        return(['A','B','C','D','E','F','G'])
print("Keys:", keys())
```

If we added code like this and the module were not present, not only can we respond with a warning message, but we can also define our own function to use if the module isn't present.

Finally, you can raise any exception you want including creating your own exceptions. Creating custom exceptions is an advanced topic, but let's see how we can raise exceptions since we may want to do that if we write our own custom libraries. Suppose you have a block of code that is reading values, but it is possible that a value may be out of range. That is, too large for an integer, too small for the valid range of values expected, etc. You can simply raise the ValueError passing in your custom error message as follows with the raise statement and a valid exception class declaration:

```
raise ValueError("ERROR: the value read from the sensor ({0})
is not in range.".format(val_read))
```

You can then use the try statement to capture this condition since you know it is possible and work your code around it. For example, if you were reading data, you could elect to skip the read and move on – continue the loop. However, if this exception were to be encountered when running your code and there were no try statements, you could get an error like the following, which, even though is fatal, is still informative:

```
Traceback (most recent call last):
  File "<stdin>", line 1, in <module>
ValueError: ERROR: the value read from the sensor (-12) is not
in range.
```

You can use similar techniques as shown here to make your MicroPython code more robust and tolerant of errors. Better still, you can write your code to anticipate errors and react to them in a graceful, controlled manner.

MicroPython-Specific Libraries

There are also libraries that are built expressly for the MicroPython system. These are libraries designed to help facilitate using MicroPython on the hardware and are specific to the MicroPython implementation of Python. Let's look at a few of the more common MicroPython libraries and see some code examples for each. What follows is just a sampling of what you can do with each of the libraries. See the online documentation for a full description of all the capabilities.

machine

The machine library contains functions related to the hardware providing an abstraction layer that you can write code to interact with the hardware. Thus, this library is the main library you will use to access features like timers, communication protocols, CPUs, and more. Since this functionality is communicating directly with the hardware, you should take care when experimenting to avoid changing or even potentially damaging the performance or configuration of your board. For example, using the library incorrectly could lead to lockups, reboots, or crashes.

Caution   Take care when working with the low-level machine library to avoid changing or even potentially damaging the performance or configuration of your Pico.

Since the machine library is a low-level hardware abstraction, we will not cover it in depth in this chapter. Rather, we will see more of the hardware features in the next chapter. In the meantime, let's explore another interesting gem of MicroPython knowledge by showing you how to discover what a library contains through the help function. For example, Listing 4-5 shows an excerpt of what is reported through the REPL console when we issue the statement help(machine) on the Pico. While it doesn't replace a detailed explanation or even a complete example, it can be useful when encountering a library for the first time.

Listing 4-5. The machine Library Help

```
>>> help(machine)
>>> object <module 'umachine'> is of type module
  __name__ -- umachine
  unique_id -- <function>
  soft_reset -- <function>
```

```
reset -- <function>
reset_cause -- <function>
bootloader -- <function>
freq -- <function>
idle -- <function>
lightsleep -- <function>
deepsleep -- <function>
disable_irq -- <function>
enable_irq -- <function>
time_pulse_us -- <function>
mem8 -- <8-bit memory>
mem16 -- <16-bit memory>
mem32 -- <32-bit memory>
ADC -- <class 'ADC'>
I2C -- <class 'I2C'>
SoftI2C -- <class 'SoftI2C'>
Pin -- <class 'Pin'>
PWM -- <class 'PWM'>
RTC -- <class 'RTC'>
Signal -- <class 'Signal'>
SPI -- <class 'SPI'>
SoftSPI -- <class 'SoftSPI'>
Timer -- <class 'Timer'>
UART -- <class 'UART'>
WDT -- <class 'WDT'>
PWRON_RESET -- 1
WDT_RESET -- 3
```

Notice there is a lot of information there! What this gives us most is the list of classes we can use to interact with the hardware. Here, we see there are classes for UART, SPI, I2C, PWM, and more.

Custom Libraries

Building your own custom libraries may seem like a daunting task, but it isn't. What is possibly a bit of a challenge is figuring out what you want the library to do and making the library abstract (enough) to be used by any script. The rules and best practices for programming come into play here such as data abstraction, API immutability, etc.

In this section, we will look at how to organize our code modules into a library (package) that we can deploy (copy) to our Pico and use in all our programs. This example, while trivial, is a complete example that you can use as a template should you decide to make your own custom libraries.

For this example, we will create a library with two modules: one that contains code to perform value conversions for a sensor and another that contains helper functions for our projects – general functions that we want to reuse. We will name the library my_helper. It will contain two code modules: sensor_convert.py and helper_functions.py. Recall we will also need an __init__.py file to help MicroPython import the functions correctly, but we will get back to that in a moment. Let's look at the first code module.

We will place the files in a directory named my_helper (same as the library name). This is typical convention, but you can put whatever name you want, but you must remember it since we will use that name when importing the library in our code.

There are two ways to go about creating the files. You can create them on your PC and then upload them to the Pico, or you can create them on the Pico directly using Thonny. We will use the Thonny method.

First, connect your Pico to your PC and then open Thonny. Make sure it connects to the Pico. Then, we will create a new folder named my_helper on the Pico. You can do this by right-clicking the Pico section of the file viewer in Thonny and choose *New directory....* Once you have the folder created, double-click it and then create a new file named __init__.py and save it on the Pico. Create the other files the same way: `sensor_convert.py` and `helper_functions.py`. Once created, you should see the directory and three files as shown in Figure 4-2.

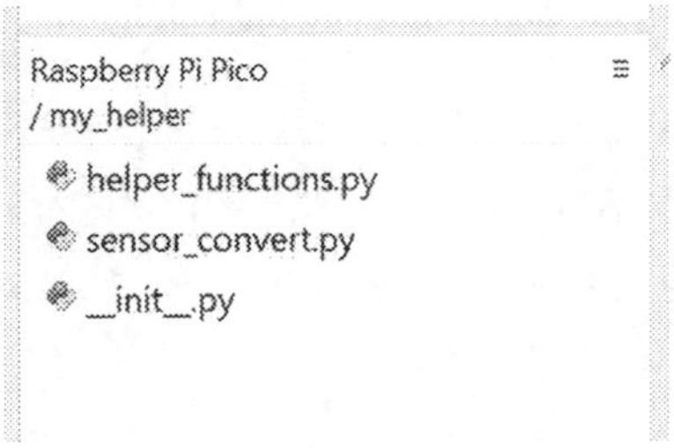

Figure 4-2. *New directory and files (Thonny)*

Now let's look at the code. The first module is named `helper_functions.py` and contains a helper function for formatting a time data structure to print the time in a more pleasing format. Listing 4-6 shows the complete code for the module.

Listing 4-6. The helper_functions.py Module

```
#
# Beginning MicroPython - Chapter 4
#
# Example module for the my_helper library
# This module contains helper functions for general use.
#

# Format the time (epoch) for a better view
def format_time(tm_data):
    # Use a special shortcut to unpack tuple: *tm_data
    return "{0}-{1:0>2}-{2:0>2} {3:0>2}:{4:0>2}:{5:0>2}".
    format(*tm_data)
```

The second code module is named `sensor_convert.py` and contains functions that are helpful in converting sensor raw values into a string for qualitative comparisons. For example, the function `get_moisture_level()` returns a string based on the threshold of the raw value.

The data sheet for the sensor will define such values, and you should use those in your code until and unless you can calibrate the sensor. In this case, if the value is less than the lower bound, the soil is dry, and if greater than the upper bound, the soil is wet. Listing 4-7 shows the complete code for the module.

Listing 4-7. The sensor_convert.py Module

```
#
# Beginning MicroPython - Chapter 4
#
# Example module for the my_helper library

# This function converts values read from the sensor to a
# string for use in qualifying the moisture level read.

# Constants - adjust to "tune" your sensor

_UPPER_BOUND = 400
_LOWER_BOUND = 250

def get_moisture_level(raw_value):
    if raw_value <= _LOWER_BOUND:
        return("dry")
    elif raw_value >= _UPPER_BOUND:
        return("wet")
    return("ok")
```

Now let's go over the __init__.py file. This is a very mysterious file that developers often get very confused about. If you do not include one in your library directory, you should import what you want to use manually.

That is, with something like import my_helper.helper_functions. But
with the file, you can do your imports at one time allowing a simple import
my_helper statement, which will import all the files. Let's look at the __
init__.py file. The following shows the contents of the file:

```
# Metadata
__name__ = "Chuck's Python Helper Library"
__all__ = ['format_time', 'get_moisture_level']
# Library-level imports
from my_helper.helper_functions import format_time
from my_helper.sensor_convert import get_moisture_level
```

Notice on the first line we use a special constant to set the name of
the library. The next constant limits what will be imported by the * (all)
option for the import statement. Since it lists all the methods, it's just an
exercise but a good habit to use especially if your library and modules
contain many internal functions that you do not want to make usable to
others. The last two lines show the import statements used to import the
functions from the modules making them available to anyone who imports
the library. The following shows a short example of how to do that along
with how to use an alias. Here, we use myh as the alias for my_helper:

```
>>> import my_helper as myh
>>> myh.get_moisture_level(375)
'ok'
>>> myh.get_moisture_level(35)
'dry'
>>> myh.get_moisture_level(535)
'wet'
```

In case you're wondering, the help function works on this custom library too!

```
>>> help(myh)
object <module 'Chuck's Python Helper Library' from 'my_
helper/__init__.py'> is of type module
  __path__ -- my_helper
  get_moisture_level -- <function get_moisture_level at
  0x2001e610>
  __name__ -- Chuck's Python Helper Library
  __file__ -- my_helper/__init__.py
  format_time -- <function format_time at 0x2001e580>
  helper_functions -- <module 'my_helper.helper_functions' from
  'my_helper/helper_functions.py'>
  __all__ -- ['format_time', 'get_moisture_level']
  sensor_convert -- <module 'my_helper.sensor_convert' from
  'my_helper/sensor_convert.py'>
```

Once you have started experimenting with MicroPython and have completed several projects, you may start to build up a set of functions that you reuse from time to time. These are perfect candidates to place into a library. It is perfectly fine if the functions are not part of a larger class or object. So long as you organize them into modules of like functionality, you may not need to worry about making them classes. On the other hand, if data is involved or the set of functions works on a set of data, you should consider making that set of functions a class for easier use and better quality code.

Low-Level Libraries

While the MicroPython firmware at the most basic of functionality is the same from board to board for all the general Python languages supported and many of the built-in functions, some of the libraries in the MicroPython firmware have a few minor differences from one board to another.

In some cases, there are more libraries or classes available than others or perhaps the classes are organized differently, but most implement the same core libraries in one form or another. The same cannot be said to be true at the lower-level hardware abstraction layers. This is simply because one board vendor may implement different hardware than others. In some cases, the board has features that are not present on other boards. For example, some boards support networking, but the Pico (currently) does not. To keep things brief, we will explore the board-specific libraries for the Pico.

Tip   You can see the differences in the low-level library support for other boards at `https://docs.micropython.org/en/latest/library/index.html`, clicking the links for the other boards listed such as the pyboard, ESP8266, and WIPy. The Pico libraries are listed under the RP2040 section at `https://docs.micropython.org/en/latest/library/rp2.html`.

The low-level libraries for the Pico (also described as RP2040-specific libraries) are encapsulated in a single library named `rp2`. This library contains a number of classes and functions for performing programmable input/output tasks (PIO), accessing the filesystem (flash drive) directly, or working with a state machine. The classes are defined as follows:

- `Flash`: Built-in flash storage

- `PIO`: Advanced PIO

- `StateMachine`: Support for the RP2040's programmable I/O interface

The `PIO` and `StateMachine` classes provide the ability to add additional interfaces or protocols such as additional serial communication support. This is not likely something most Pico projects will require, but it is there should you find you need one more interface than what is provided by the Pico hardware.

With these classes, you can create your own custom low-level hardware access mechanisms. For example, if you have a sensor that needs a specific timing to read data faster than the existing hardware and software library support or a device requires a specific sequence of commands or responses, you can use these classes to essentially use software to form the hardware interface. These special code segments are loaded and run in a special processing core allowing up to eight processes to run. You can find a complete guide to using PIO in Chapter 3 of the RP2040 data sheet book (`https://datasheets.raspberrypi.org/rp2040/rp2040-datasheet.pdf`).

Similarly, the `Flash` class provides the ability to work directly with the flash filesystem. This may be handy if you want to do some low-level data storage, but in general you are encouraged to use the existing higher-level MicroPython libraries for reading and writing files.

Should you wish to explore these classes in greater detail, or you want to learn more about PIO support, you can find example code at `https://github.com/raspberrypi/pico-micropython-examples/tree/master/pio`.

Working with Low-Level Hardware

Working with the low-level hardware (some would just say, "hardware" or "device") is where all the action and indeed the focus (and relative difficulty) of using MicroPython takes place. MicroPython and the breakout board vendors have done an excellent job of making things easier for us, but there is room for improvement in the explanations.

That is, the documentation online is a bit terse when it comes to offering examples of using the low-level hardware. Part of this is because the examples often require additional, specific hardware and software. For example, to work with the I2C interface, you will need an I2C capable breakout board as well as a software library (or drive) to "talk" to the board. Thus, the online examples provide only the most basic of examples and explanations.

Except for the onboard sensors, most low-level communication will be through I2C, one-wire, analog, or digital pins, or using even SPI interfaces. The I2C and SPI interfaces are those where you will likely encounter the most difficulty working with hardware. This is because each device (breakout board) you use will require a very specific protocol. That is, the device may require a special sequence to trigger the sensor or features of the device that differs from other breakout boards. Thus, working with I2C or SPI (and some other) type devices can be a challenge to figure out exactly how to "talk" to them.

Drivers and Libraries to the Rescue!

Fortunately, there are a small but growing number of people making classes and sets of functions to help us work with those devices. These are called libraries or more commonly drivers and come in the form of one or more code modules that you can download, copy to your board, and import the functionality into your program. The developers of the drivers have done all the heavy lifting for you, making it very easy to use the device.

Thus, for most just starting out with MicroPython wanting to work with certain sensors, devices, breakout boards, etc., you should limit what you plan to use to those that you can find a driver that works with it. So, how do you find a driver for your device? There are several places to look.

First and foremost, you should look to the forums and documentation on MicroPython. In this case, don't limit yourself to only those forums that cater to your board of choice. Rather, look at all of them! Chances are you can find a library that you can adapt with only minor modifications. Most of them can be used with very little or even no effort beyond downloading it and copying it to the board. The following lists the top set of forums and documentation you should frequent when looking for drivers:

- *MicroPython Forums*: `https://forum.micropython.org/`

- *MicroPython Documentation*: `https://docs.micropython.org/en/latest/`

- *Adafruit Learning*: `https://learn.adafruit.com/`

- *Pico Documentation*: `www.raspberrypi.org/documentation/rp2040/getting-started/`

There are also a number of documents you can download and read offline. The following are some of the more important Pico documents:

- *Pico Datasheet*: `https://datasheets.raspberrypi.org/pico/pico-datasheet.pdf`

- *RP2040 Datasheet*: `https://datasheets.raspberrypi.org/rp2040/rp2040-datasheet.pdf`

- *Hardware Design Guide*: `https://datasheets.raspberrypi.org/rp2040/hardware-design-with-rp2040.pdf`

- *Pico MicroPython Manual*: `https://datasheets.raspberrypi.org/pico/raspberry-pi-pico-python-sdk.pdf`

Second, use your favorite Internet search engine and search for examples of the hardware. Use the name of the hardware device and "MicroPython" in your search. If the device is new, you may not find any hits on the search terms. Be sure to explore other search terms too.

Once you find a driver, the fun begins! You should download the driver and copy it to your board for testing. Be sure to follow the example that comes with the driver to avoid using the driver in an unexpected way.

This calls to mind one important thing you should consider when deciding if you want to use the driver. If the driver is documented well and has examples – especially if the example is written for the Pico – you should feel safe using it. However, if the driver isn't documented at all or there is no or little sample code or it is written for a specific board, you may not want to use it. There is a good chance it is half-baked, old, a work in progress, or just poorly coded. Not all those that share can share and communicate well.

We will see several examples of libraries as we work through the example projects in this book. As you will see, not all are as simple as downloading and using.

One skill we will need going forward is understanding breakout boards and how to use them. Let's look at how to communicate with breakout boards using the I2C and SPI protocols.

Using Breakout Boards

Breakout boards are one of the key elements hobbyists and enthusiasts will use in creating a MicroPython (or any microcontroller based) IoT solution. This is because breakout boards are small circuit boards that contain all the components needed to support a function such as a sensor, network interface, or even a display. Breakout boards also support one of several communication protocols that require only a few pins to be wired making them very easy to use. In general, they save the developer a lot of time trying to figure out how to design circuits to support a sensor or chip.

There are two methods for working with breakout boards: finding a driver you can use or building your own driver. Building your own driver is not recommended for those new to MicroPython and I2C or SPI. It is much easier to take the time to search for a driver that you can use (or adapt) than to try to write one yourself. This is because you must be able to obtain, read, and understand how the breakout board communicates (understand its protocol). Each board will communicate differently based on the sensor or devices supported. That is, a driver for a BMP180 sensor will not look or necessarily work the same as one for a BME280 sensor. You must be very specific when locating and using a driver.

Searching for a driver can be a tedious endeavor, which requires some patience and perhaps several searches on the forums using different search terms such as "`micropython BME280`". Once you find a driver, you can tell quickly whether it is a viable option by looking at the example included. As mentioned before, if there is no example or the example doesn't resemble anything you've seen in this book or in the online documentation, don't use it.

Let's look at two examples of breakout boards: one that uses the I2C protocol and another that uses the SPI protocol. We will follow a pattern of explaining the examples that is used throughout the book to introduce the project, present the required components, show you how to set up the hardware (connect everything together), write the code, and finally execute it.

THE VALUE OF ONLINE EXAMPLES

If you want to use a breakout board in your IoT project, be sure to spend some time not only in the forums but also looking at various blogs and tutorials such as those on hackaday.com, learn.sparkfun.com, or learn.adafruit.com. The best blogs and tutorials are those that explain not only how to write the code but also what the breakout board does and how to use it. These online references are few, but the ones from these three sites are among the very best. Also, look at some of the videos on the topic too. Some of those are worth the time to watch – especially if they're from the nice folks at Adafruit or SparkFun.

Inter-integrated Circuit (I2C)

The I2C protocol is perhaps the most common protocol that you will find on breakout boards. We've encountered this term a few times in previous chapters, and thus we only know it is a communication protocol. So, what is it?

What Is I2C?

I2C is a fast digital protocol using two wires (plus power and ground) to read data from circuits (or devices). The protocol is designed to allow the use of multiple devices (slaves) with a single master (the MicroPython board). Thus, each I2C breakout board will have its own address or identity that you will use in the driver to connect to and communicate with the device.

Tip   See `https://learn.sparkfun.com/tutorials/i2c` for an in-depth discussion of I2C.

Overview

Let's look at an example of how to use an I2C breakout board. In this example, we want to use an RGB sensor from Adafruit (`www.adafruit.com/product/1334`) to read the color of objects. Yes, you can make your Pico see in color!

What the code will present is four values read from the sensor. We will see the values for the red, green, and blue spectrum as well as the clear light value. The combination of the red, green, and blue values defines the color. You can use a color picker control from one of several websites like `www.rapidtables.com/web/color/RGB_Color.html` to show you the color. This RGB sensor isn't going to give you a 100% color match, but you may be surprised how well it can distinguish colors. Let's get started.

Required Components

Don't worry if you do not have or do not want to purchase the Adafruit RGB sensor breakout board (although it is not expensive). This example is provided as a tutorial for working with I2C breakout boards. We will use another I2C breakout board in one of the example projects later in the book. Figure 4-3 shows the Adafruit RGB sensor. Note that this sensor comes without the header soldered, so you will need to solder a header on the breakout board before you can use it with your Pico.

Figure 4-3. *Adafruit RGB sensor (courtesy of adafruit.com)*

Set Up the Hardware

Wiring the breakout board is also very easy since we need only power, ground, SCL, and SDA connections. SCL is the clock signal, and SDA is the data signal. These pins are labeled on your Pico (or in the documentation) as well as the breakout board. When you connect your breakout board, make sure the power requirements match. That is, some breakout boards can take 5V, but many are limited to 3 or 3.3V. Check the vendor's website if you have any doubts.

We need only to connect the 3V, ground, SDA, SCL, and LED pins. The LED pin is used to turn on the bright LED on the breakout board to signal it is ready to read. We will leave it on for ten seconds so that there is time to read the color value and then display it. We will then wait another five seconds to take the next reading.

But to get this to work, we will need to connect the breakout board to the Pico. If you ordered a Pico with headers or you soldered your own headers to the Pico, we can use what is called a breadboard to host the Pico and use wires called jumper wires to connect the Pico GPIO pins to the pins on the breakout board.

Note   We will discuss breadboards and their use in more detail in the next chapter.

Once you place your Pico on a breadboard, you can use (5) male-to-female jumper wires to connect to the breakout board. Figure 4-4 shows the connections you need to make.

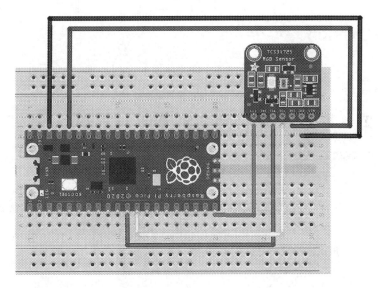

Figure 4-4. *Wiring the RGB sensor*

The connections we will use are shown in Table 4-4, which shows the pin for the Pico in the first three columns depicting the description, physical pin, and GPIO number with the pin on the breakout board in the last column. Recall, physical pins are numbered 1–20 on the left of the USB connector starting at the top and 21–40 on the right starting from the bottom.

Table 4-4. *Connections for the RGB Sensor*

Pico Function	Physical Pin	GPIO Number	RGB Sensor Pin Label
OUT	20	GP15	LED
I2C SDA	11	GP8	SDA
I2C SDC	12	GP9	SCL
3V3	37	N/A	3V3
GND	38	N/A	GND

Write the Code

Once you have the hardware connected, set it aside. We need to download the driver and copy it to the board before we can experiment further. You can find the driver for download on GitHub at https://github.com/adafruit/micropython-adafruit-tcs34725. This is a fully working, tested driver that demonstrates how easy it is to use an I2C breakout board.

Note   This library has been abandoned by Adafruit in an effort to focus on their version of MicroPython named CircuitPython. But don't worry. The library still works very well. We just are not likely to see any updates to the code.

So, how do we find the address of our I2C breakout board? Recall the I2C bus requires each device to have a unique address. The I2C firmware uses this address to know which device it is communicating with, and the device itself will only recognize messages for that specific address.

We check the documentation, or we can check the code for the library. If you open the library you downloaded, you can read through it and look in the initialization code (or constructor) to see what address the library is using. In this case, we find the address in the library is 0x29 as shown in the following, but since the address is a parameter, you can override it if you have another breakout board for the same RGB sensor that is at a different address. This means you can use more than one RGB sensor with the same driver!

```
class TCS34725:
    def __init__(self, i2c, address=0x29):
```

To download the driver, you first navigate to https://github. com/adafruit/micropython-adafruit-tcs34725 and then click the *Download* button and then the *Download Zip* button. Once the file has been downloaded, unzip it. In the resulting folder, you should find the file named tcs34725.py. This is the driver code module. When ready, copy the module to your Pico and place it in the root folder (same folder as the example code).

Now that the driver is copied to our board, we can write the code. In this example, we will set up the I2C connection to the breakout board and run a loop to read values from the sensor. Sounds simple, but there is a bit of a trick to it. We will forego a lengthy discussion of the code and instead offer some key aspects allowing you to read the code yourself to see how it works.

The key components are setting up the I2C, sensor, a pin for controlling the LED, and reading from the sensor. The LED on the board can be turned on and off by setting a pin high (on) or low (off). First, the I2C code is as follows. Here, we initiate an object, then call the init() function setting the bus to master mode. The scan() function returns a list of addresses found on the bus. We can then print out the device addresses. Notice we define the pins for the SDA and SCL I2C operations too.

Tip   If you see an empty set displayed, your I2C wiring is not correct. Check it and try the code again.

```
# Setup the I2C - easy, yes?
sda = Pin(8)
scl = Pin(9)
i2c = SoftI2C(sda=sda,scl=scl,freq=400000)
print("I2C Devices found:", end="")
for addr in i2c.scan():
    print("{0} ".format(hex(addr)))
print("")
```

Notice here we are using something named SoftI2C. This is a special version of the I2C library that supports a different way of communicating with a breakout board. As it turns out, not all I2C devices will work correctly with the firmware implementation of I2C on the Pico. To use the firmware I2C, use the I2C library from the machine module as shown in the following. The only difference beside the name is the first parameter, which tells the I2C we want a master connection:

```
#i2c = I2C(0,sda=sda,scl=scl,freq=400000)
```

It is recommended to try the I2C library first, and if that doesn't work, try the SoftI2C library. This is because the I2C firmware is much faster than the software implementation. We will see specific examples that use I2C and SoftI2C in later chapters.

The next part is the sensor itself. The driver makes this easy. All we need to do is pass in the I2C constructor function as shown:

```
# Setup the sensor
sensor = tcs34725.TCS34725(i2c)
```

Setting up the LED pin is also easy. All we need to do is call the `Pin()` class constructor passing in the pin name (P15) and setting it for output mode as follows:

```
# Setup the LED pin
led_pin = Pin(15, Pin.OUT)
led_pin.value(0)
```

Finally, we read from the sensor with the `sensor.read()` function passing in True, which tells the driver to return the RGBC values. We will then print these out in order. Listing 4-8 shows the completed code. Take a few moments to read through it so that you understand how it works.

Listing 4-8. Using the Adafruit RGB Sensor

```
"""listing_04_06.py"""
#
# Beginning MicroPython - Chapter 4
#
# Example of using the I2C interface via a driver
# for the Adafruit RGB Sensor tcs34725
#
# Requires library:
# https://github.com/adafruit/micropython-adafruit-tcs34725
#
from machine import I2C, SoftI2C, Pin
import sys
import tcs34725
import utime

# Method to read sensor and display results
def read_sensor(rgb_sense, led):
    sys.stdout.write("Place object in front of sensor now...")
    led.value(1)                    # Turn on the LED
```

```
    utime.sleep(5)                    # Wait 5 seconds
    sys.stdout.write("reading.\n")
    data = rgb_sense.read(True)   # Get the RGBC values
    print("Color Detected: {")
    print("    Red: {0:03}".format(data[0]))
    print("  Green: {0:03}".format(data[1]))
    print("   Blue: {0:03}".format(data[2]))
    print("  Clear: {0:03}".format(data[3]))
    print("}\n")
    led.value(0)

# Setup the I2C - easy, yes?
sda = Pin(8)
scl = Pin(9)
i2c = SoftI2C(sda=sda,scl=scl,freq=400000)
print("I2C Devices found:", end="")
for addr in i2c.scan():
    print("{0} ".format(hex(addr)))
print("")

# Setup the sensor
sensor = tcs34725.TCS34725(i2c)

# Setup the LED pin
led_pin = Pin(15, Pin.OUT)
led_pin.value(0)
print("Reading object color every 10 seconds.")
print("When LED is on, place object in front of sensor.")
print("Press CTRL-C to quit.")
while True:
    utime.sleep(10)                    # Sleep for 10 seconds
    read_sensor(sensor, led_pin)   # Read sensor and
                                     display values
```

Once you have the code, you can copy it to your board in the similar manner we did for the driver. All that is left is running the example and testing it.

Execute

After copying the code to the Pico, go ahead and run it from Thonny. Listing 4-9 shows an example of the code running. Note that you will get differing results for each object you test in a mixture of the RGB values as shown.

Listing 4-9. Output from Using the Adafruit RGB Sensor

```
I2C Devices found:0x29
Reading Colors every 10 seconds.
When LED is on, place object in front of sensor.
Press CTRL-C to quit.
Place object in front of sensor now...reading.
Color Detected: {
    Red: 057
  Green: 034
   Blue: 032
  Clear: 123
}
Place object in front of sensor now...reading.
Color Detected: {
    Red: 054
  Green: 069
   Blue: 064
  Clear: 195
}
Place object in front of sensor now...reading.
Color Detected: {
```

```
    Red: 012
  Green: 013
   Blue: 011
  Clear: 036
}
...
```

If you wanted another exercise, you could take these values from the sensor and map them to an RGB LED. Yes, you can do that! Go ahead, try it. See the example GitHub project at https://github.com/JanBednarik/ micropython-ws2812 for inspiration. Tackle it after you've read the next section on SPI.

Serial Peripheral Interface (SPI)

The Serial Peripheral Interface (SPI) is designed to allow sending and receiving data between two devices using a dedicated line for each direction. That is, it uses two data lines along with a clock and a slave select pin. Thus, it requires six connections for bidirectional communication or only five for reading or writing only. Some SPI devices may require a seventh pin called a reset line.

Tip   See https://learn.sparkfun.com/tutorials/serial-peripheral-interface-spi for an in-depth discussion of SPI.

Overview

Let's look at an example of how to use an SPI breakout board. In this example, we want to use the Adafruit Thermocouple Amplifier MAX31855 breakout board (www.adafruit.com/product/269) and a Thermocouple Type-K sensor (www.adafruit.com/product/270) to read high temperatures. It can also read low or room temperature, so don't worry. You won't need to put this in a heater or oven to use it!

In fact, we're going to use this example to show how easy it is to read one of the most common measurements (samples) taken – temperature. Once the code is running, you can simply touch the thermocouple and watch the values respond (change) as it heats up and again when you let go. A touchable project, cool!

Required Components

Don't worry if you do not have or do not want to purchase the Adafruit Thermocouple Amplifier MAX31855 breakout board (although it is not expensive). This example is provided as a tutorial for working with SPI breakout boards. We will use another I2C breakout board in one of the example projects later in the book. Figure 4-5 shows the Adafruit Thermocouple Amplifier and Type-K sensor from Adafruit.

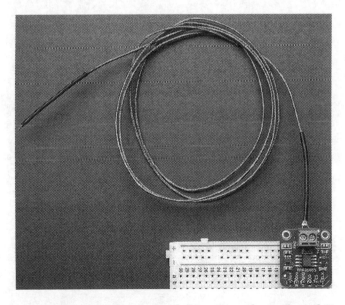

Figure 4-5. *Adafruit Thermocouple breakout board and Type-K sensor (courtesy of adafruit.com)*

The sensor can be used to measure high temperatures either through proximity or touch. The sensor can read temperature in the range –200°C to +1350°C output in 0.25 degree increments. One possible use of this sensor is to read the temperature of nozzles on 3D printers or any similar high heat output. It should be noted that the breakout board comes unassembled, so you will need to solder the header and terminal posts.

Set Up the Hardware

Now, let's see how to wire the breakout board to our Pico. We will use only five wires since we are only reading data from the sensor on the breakout board. This requires a connection to power, ground (GND), the master input (MOSI), clock (CLK), and chip select (CS). We only receive information from the sensor, so the MISO (transmit) pin isn't needed. Figure 4-6 shows the connections.

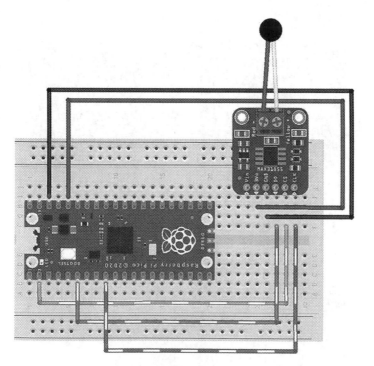

Figure 4-6. *Wiring the Adafruit Thermocouple module*

The connections we will use are shown in Table 4-5, which shows the pin for the Pico in the first three columns depicting the description, physical pin, and GPIO number with the pin on the breakout board in the last column. Recall, physical pins are numbered 1–20 on the left of the USB connector starting at the top and 21–40 on the right starting from the bottom.

Table 4-5. *Connections for the MAX31855*

Pico Function	Physical Pin	GPIO Number	RGB Sensor Pin Label
GND	38	N/A	GND
3V3	37	N/A	3V3
SPI RX/MOSI	6	GP4	SDO
SPI CS	2	GP1	CS
SPI CLK	9	GP6	CLK

Now, let's look at the code!

Write the Code

In this example, we are not going to use a driver; rather, we're going to see how to read directly from the breakout board using SPI. To do so, we first set up an object instance of the SPI interface and then choose a pin to use for chip select (also called code or even slave select). From there, all we need to do is read the data and interpret it. We will read the sensor in a loop and write a function to convert the data.

This is the tricky part. This example shows you what driver authors must do to make using the device easier. In this case, we must read the data from the breakout board and interpret it. We could just read the raw data, but that would not make any sense since it is in binary form. Thus, we can borrow some code from Adafruit that reads the raw data and makes sense of it.

The function is named `normalize_data()` as shown in the following, and it does some bit shifting and arithmetic to transform the raw data to a value in Celsius. This information comes from the data sheet for the breakout board, but the nice folks at Adafruit made it easy for us:

```python
# Create a method to normalize the data into degrees Celsius
def normalize_data(data):
    temp = data[0] << 8 | data[1]
    if temp & 0x0001:
        return float('NaN')
    temp >>= 2
    if temp & 0x2000:
        temp -= 16384
    return (temp * 0.25)
```

Setting up the SPI class is easy. We initiate an SPI object using the class constructor passing in the SPI option. We will use 0 for the first SPI implementation. The other parameters tell the SPI class to set up the SCK, MISO, and MOSI pins (even though we are not using the MOSI pin) and set the baud rate, polarity, and phase (which can be found on the data sheet). We also set the CS pin and turn it on (set to high) after initializing the SPI library. The following shows the code we need to activate the SPI interface:

```python
...
spi_cs = Pin(1)
spi = SPI(0, baudrate=1000000, sck=Pin(6), miso=Pin(4),
mosi=Pin(3))
spi_cs.high()
...
```

Now, let's look at the completed code. Listing 4-10 shows the complete code to use the Thermocouple Amplifier breakout board from Adafruit.

Listing 4-10. The Adafruit Thermocouple Module Example

```python
"""listing_04_07.py"""
#
# Beginning MicroPython - Chapter 4
#
# Example of using the SPI interface via direct access
# for the Adafruit Thermocouple Module MAX31855
#
from machine import Pin, SPI
import utime

# Create a method to normalize the data into degrees Celsius
def normalize_data(data):
    temp = data[0] << 8 | data[1]
    if temp & 0x0001:
        return float('NaN')
    temp >>= 2
    if temp & 0x2000:
        temp -= 16384
    return (temp * 0.25)

spi_cs = Pin(1)
spi = SPI(0, baudrate=1000000, sck=Pin(6), miso=Pin(4),
mosi=Pin(3))
spi_cs.high()

# read from the chip
print("Reading temperature every second.")
print("Press CTRL-C to stop.")
while True:
    spi_cs.low()
    utime.sleep(1)
```

```
print("Temperature is {:05.2F} C".format(normalize_
data(spi.read(4))))
spi_cs.high()
```

Execute

At this point, you can make the hardware connections and plug in your
Pico. Then, you can copy the file to your Pico and run it. Let it run for a few
readings and then try to gently grasp the silver portion (the far end) of the
thermocouple with two fingers. Be sure not to turn the Pico or the breakout
board. You should see a change in temperature. You can let go and also see
the temperature return to near room temperature.

```
Reading temperature every second.
Press CTRL-C to stop.
Temperature is 24.50 C
Temperature is 24.50 C
Temperature is 24.25 C
Temperature is 24.25 C
Temperature is 25.75 C
Temperature is 25.50 C
Temperature is 25.75 C
Temperature is 26.25 C
Temperature is 26.00 C
Temperature is 26.50 C
Temperature is 26.50 C
Temperature is 27.00 C
Temperature is 27.25 C
Temperature is 27.00 C
Temperature is 27.50 C
Temperature is 27.50 C
Temperature is 27.00 C
...
```

Once you run the example, you should see it produce values in degrees Celsius. If you see 00.00, or NaN, you likely do not have the SPI interface connected properly. Check your wiring against the preceding figure. If you see values but they go down when you expose the thermocouple tip to heat, you need to reverse the wires. Be sure to power off the board first to avoid damaging the sensor, breakout board, or your Pico!

Summary

Accessing the low-level hardware through the firmware is where the true elegance and in some cases complexity of using MicroPython begins. We also need to know what breakout boards and devices we want to connect to and if there are drivers or other libraries we can use to access them. In this case, most breakout boards with I2C or SPI interfaces will require some form of a driver.

In this chapter, we explored some of the low-level support in the firmware and specialized support for the Pico in MicroPython and explored some of the more commonly used built-in and MicroPython libraries that we will use in our projects. We also saw a lot of code in this chapter – more than any previous chapter. The examples in this chapter are meant to be examples for you to see how things are done rather than projects to implement on your own (although you're welcome and encouraged to do so). We will see more hands-on projects with a greater level of detail in later chapters.

In the next chapter, we take a short detour in the form of a short tutorial on electronics. If you've never worked with electronics before, the next chapter will give you the information you need to complete the projects in this book and prepare you for an exciting new hobby – building MicroPython IoT projects!

CHAPTER 5

Electronics for Beginners

If you are new to working with hardware and have little or no experience with electronics, you may be curious as to how you can complete the projects in this book. Fortunately, the projects in this book walk you through how to connect the various electronic parts together with your Pico. That is, you can complete the projects without additional skill or experience.

However, if you want to know what the components do, you will need a bit more information than "plug this end in here." This is especially so if something goes wrong. Furthermore, if you want to create projects on your own, you need to know enough about how the components work to successfully complete your project – whether that is completing the examples in this book or examples found elsewhere on the Internet.

Fortunately, you don't need formal training or even a college degree in theory to learn how to work with electronics. You can learn quite a lot about working with electronics at the hobbyist level without devoting months or years of research. To ensure success even at a basic level, you will need to know more than simply how to plug the components together.

Rather than attempt to present a comprehensive tutorial on electronics, which would take several volumes, this chapter presents an overview of electronics for those who want to work with the types of electronic components commonly found in electronics projects. I include

© Charles Bell 2022
C. Bell, *Beginning MicroPython with the Raspberry Pi Pico*, Maker Innovations Series,
https://doi.org/10.1007/978-1-4842-8135-2_5

an overview of some of the basics, descriptions of common components, and a look at sensors. If you are new to electronics, this chapter will give you the extra boost you need to understand the components used in the projects in this book.

If you have experience with electronics either at the hobbyist or enthusiast level or have experience or formal training in electronics, you may want to skim this chapter or read the sections with topics that you may want a refresher.

Let's begin with a look at the basics of electronics. Once again, this is in no way a tutorial that covers all there is to know, but it will get you to the point where the projects make sense in how they connect and use components.

The Basics

This section presents a short overview of some of the most common tools and techniques you will need to use when working with electronics. As you will see, you only need the most basic of tools, and the skills or techniques are not difficult to learn. We will also see an example of a basic electronics kit to help you get started. However, before we get into those, let's look at some of the tools you will need to work on your electronics projects.

Tools

The clear majority of tools you will need to construct your electronics projects are common hand tools (screwdrivers, small wrenches, pliers, etc.). For larger projects or for creating enclosures, you may need additional tools such as power tools, but I will concentrate only on those tools for building the projects. The following is a list of tools I recommend:

- Breadboard

- Breadboard wires (also called jumpers)

- Electrostatic discharge (ESD) safe tweezers

- Helping hands or printed circuit board (PCB) holder

- Multimeter

- Needle-nose pliers

- Screwdrivers – assorted sizes (micro, small)

- Solder

- Soldering iron

- Solder remover

- Tool case, roll, or box for storage

- Wire strippers

However, you cannot go wrong if you prefer to buy a complete electronics toolset such as those from SparkFun (`www.sparkfun.com/categories/47`) or Adafruit (`www.adafruit.com/categories/83`). You can often find electronics kits at major brand electronics stores and home improvement centers. Most electronics kits will have all the hand tools you will need. Some even come with a multimeter, but more often you must buy them separately.

Most of the tools in the list do not need any explanation except to say you should purchase the best tools that your budget permits. The following paragraphs describe some of the tools that are used for special tasks such as stripping wires, soldering, and measuring voltage and current.

Multimeter

A multimeter is one of those tools that you will need when building electronics projects. You will also need it to do almost any electrical repair on your circuits. There are many different multimeters available with prices ranging from inexpensive, basic units to complex, feature-rich, incredibly expensive units. For most electronics projects, a basic unit is all you will need. Most meters come with an instruction booklet that will show you how to use the functions of the meter.

However, if you plan to build more than one project or want to assemble your own electronics, you may want to invest a bit more in a more sophisticated multimeter. Figure 5-1 shows a basic digital multimeter (costing about $10) on the left and a professional multimeter from BK Precision on the right.

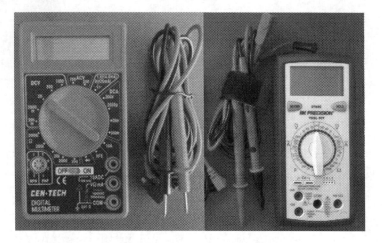

Figure 5-1. Digital multimeters

Notice the better meter has more granular settings and more features. Again, you probably won't need more than the basic unit. You will need to measure voltage, current, and resistance at a minimum. Whichever meter you buy, make sure it has modes for measuring AC and DC voltage, continuity testing (with an audible alert), and checking resistance. I will explain how to use a multimeter in a later section.

Tip   Choose a solder with a low lead content in the 37%–40% range.

Soldering Iron

A soldering iron is not required for using the components in the projects in this book, but some breakout boards may require soldering of the headers. If you plan to build a simple project where you will need to solder wires together, or maybe a few connectors, a basic soldering iron from an electronics store such as Radio Shack is all you will need. Figure 5-2 shows a well-used entry-level Radio Shack soldering iron.

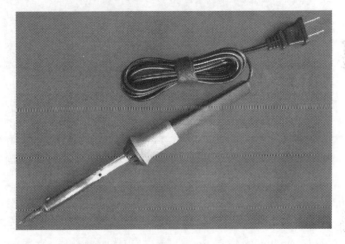

Figure 5-2. Entry-level soldering iron

On the other hand, if you plan to assemble your own electronics, you may want to consider getting a good, professional soldering iron such as a Hakko. The professional models include features that allow you to set the temperature of the wand, have a wider array of tips available, and tend to last a lot longer. Figure 5-3 shows a professional model Hakko soldering iron.

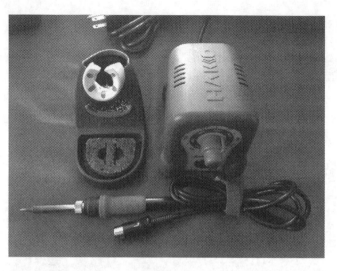

Figure 5-3. *Professional soldering iron*

DO I NEED TO LEARN TO SOLDER?

If you do not know how to solder or it has been a while since you've used a soldering iron, you may want to check out the book *Learn to Solder* by Brian Jepson, Tyler Moskowite, and Gregory Hayes (O'Reilly Media, 2012) or Google how-to videos to find everything you need to learn how to solder.

Wire Strippers

There are several types of wire strippers. In fact, there are probably a dozen or more designs out there. But there are two kinds: ones that only grip and cut the insulation as you pull it off the wire and those that grip, cut, and remove the insulation. The first type is more common and, with some practice, does just fine for most small jobs (like repairing a broken wire); but the second type makes a larger job – such as wiring electronics from bare wire (no prefab connectors) – much faster. As you can imagine, the first type is considerably cheaper. Figure 5-4 shows both types of wire strippers. Either is a good choice.

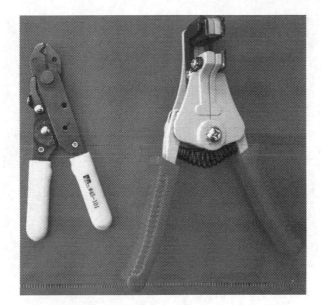

Figure 5-4. *Wire strippers*

ESD IS THE ENEMY

You should take care to make sure your body, your workspace, and your project is grounded to avoid electrostatic discharge (ESD). ESD can damage your electronics – permanently. The best way to avoid this is to use a grounding strap that loops around your wrist and attaches to an antistatic mat like these: `uline.com/BL_7403/Anti-Static-Table-Mats`.

Helping Hands

There is one other tool that you may want to get, especially if you need to do any soldering called helping hands or third hand tool. Most have a pair of alligator clips to hold wires, printed circuit boards, or components while you solder. Figure 5-5 shows an example of a simple helping hands tool.

Figure 5-5. *Helping hands tool*

Now let's look at some of the skills you are likely to need for electronics projects starting with the one tool you will use most – the multimeter.

Using a Multimeter

The electrical skills needed for electronics projects can vary from plugging in wires on a breadboard – as we saw with the projects so far – to needing to solder components together or to printed circuit boards (PCBs). Regardless of whether you need to solder the electronics, you will need to be able to use a basic multimeter to measure resistance and check voltage and current.

A multimeter is a very useful and essential tool for any electronics hobbyist and downright required for any enthusiast of worth. A typical multimeter has a digital display (typically an LCD or similar numeric display), a dial, and two or more posts or ports for plugging in test leads with probe ends. Most multimeters have ports for lower current (that you will use most) and ports for larger current. Test leads use red for positive and black for negative (ground). The ground port is where you plug in the black test lead and is often marked with a dash or COM for common. Which of the other ports you use will depend on what you are testing.

One thing to note on the dial is that there are many settings (with some values repeated) or those that look similar. For example, you will see a set of values (sometimes called a scale) for ohms, one or two sets of values for amperage, and one or two sets of values for volts. The set of values for voltages that has a V with a solid and dashed line is for DC, whereas the range that has a V with a wavy line is for AC. Amperage ranges are marked in the same manner. Figure 5-6 shows a close-up of a multimeter dial labeled with the sets of values I've mentioned.

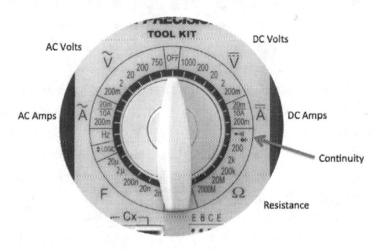

Figure 5-6. *Multimeter dial (typical)*

Tip   When not in use, be sure to turn your multimeter dial to off or one of the voltage ranges if it has a separate off button.

There is a lot you can do with a multimeter. You can check voltage, measure resistance, and even check continuity. Most basic multimeters will do these functions. However, some multimeters have a great many more features such as testing capacitors and the ability to test AC as well as DC.

Let's see how we can use a multimeter to perform the most common tasks we will need for electronics projects: testing continuity, measuring voltage in a DC circuit, measuring resistance, and measuring current.

Testing Continuity

We test for continuity to determine if there is a path for the charged particles to flow. That is, our wires and components are connected properly. For example, you may want to check to ensure a wire has been spliced correctly.

To test for continuity, turn your multimeter dial to the position marked with an audible symbol, bell, or triangle with an arrow through it. Plug the black test lead into the *COM* port and the red test lead in the port marked with *Hz VΩ* or similar. Now you can touch the probe end of the test leads together to hear an audible tone or beep. Some multimeters don't have an audible tone but instead may display "1" or the like to indicate continuity. Check your manual for how your multimeter indicates continuity. Figure 5-7 shows how to set a multimeter to check for continuity including which ports to plug in the test leads. Notice in the photo I simply touched the probes together to demonstrate how to check for continuity. I like to do this just to ensure my multimeter is turned on and in the correct setting.

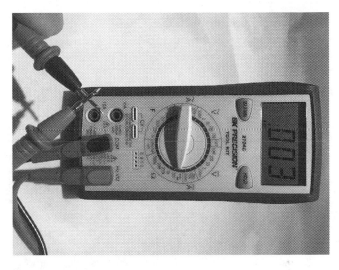

Figure 5-7. *Settings for checking continuity*

Another excellent use for the continuity test is when diagnosing or discovering how cables are wired. For example, you can use the continuity test to discover which connector is connected on each end of the cable (sometimes called wire sorting or ringing out from the old telephone days).

Measuring Voltage

Our electronics projects use DC. To measure voltage in the circuit, we will use the DC range on the multimeter. Notice the DC range has several stops. This is a scale selection. Choose the scale that closely matches the voltage range you want to test. For example, for our electronics projects we will often measure 3.3–12V, so we choose *20* on the dial. Next, plug the black test lead into the *COM* port and the red test lead into the port labeled *Hz VΩ*.

Now we need something to measure! Take any battery you have in the house and touch the black probe to the negative side and the red probe to the positive side. You should see a value appear on the display that is close to the range for the battery. For example, if we used a 1.5V battery, we should see close to 1.5V. It may not be exactly 1.5–1.6V if the battery is depleted. So now you know how to test batteries for freshness! Figure 5-8 shows how to measure voltage of a battery.

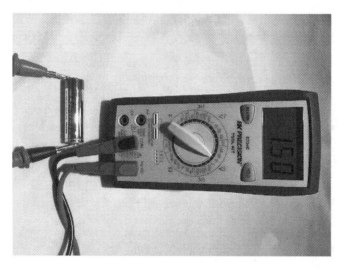

Figure 5-8. *Measuring voltage of a battery*

Notice the readout displays 1.50, which is the correct voltage for this AA battery. If I had reversed the probes – the red one on negative and the black on positive – the display would have read –1.50. This is OK because it shows the current is flowing in the opposite direction of how the probes are oriented.

Note   If you use the wrong probe when measuring voltage in a DC circuit, most multimeters will display the voltage as a negative number. Try that with your battery. It won't hurt the multimeter (or the battery)!

We can use this technique to measure voltage in our projects. Just be careful to place the probes on the appropriate positions and try not to cross or short by touching more than one component at a time with a single probe tip.

Measuring Current

Current is measured as amperage (milliamps – *mA*). Thus, we will use the range marked with an A with a straight and dashed line (not the wavy one – that's AC). We measure current in series. That is, we must place the multimeter in the circuit. This can be a little tricky because we must interrupt the flow of current and put the meter inline.

If you are familiar with how to use a breadboard, you can follow along with this experiment. However, if you haven't used a breadboard, you may want to read through this experiment and then return to it once you finish reading this chapter. For this experiment, we will use a breadboard power supply, an LED, and a resistor. We will wire the circuit such that we will use the multimeter to complete the circuit. Figure 5-9 shows how to set up the circuit with the multimeter inline.

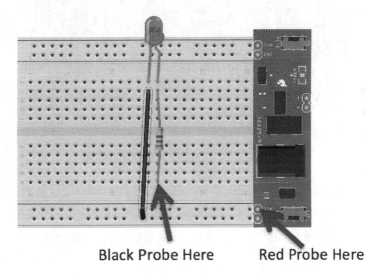

Black Probe Here   Red Probe Here

Figure 5-9. Measuring current

Before powering on your breadboard power supply, plug the black test lead into the COM port and the other test leads into the port labeled mA. Some multimeters use the same port for measuring voltage as well as current. Turn the dial on the multimeter to the 200mA setting. Then power on the breadboard power supply and touch the leads to the places indicated. Be careful to touch only the VCC pin on the breadboard power supply. Once the circuit is powered on, you should see a value on the multimeter. Figure 5-10 shows how to use a multimeter to measure current in a circuit.

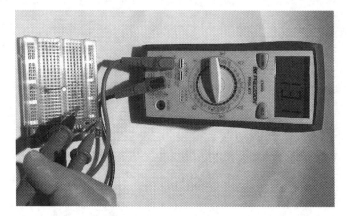

Figure 5-10. *Measuring current*

There is one other tricky thing about measuring current. If you attempt to measure current that is greater than the maximum for the port, you may see an error or cause damage to your meter. This is not desirable, but at least there is a fuse that we can replace should we make a mistake and choose the wrong port.

Measuring Resistance

Resistance is measured in ohms (Ω). The most common component we will use to introduce resistance in a circuit is a resistor. We can test the resistance of the charge through the resistor with our multimeter. To test resistance, choose the ohm scale that is closest to the rating of the resistor. For example, I am going to test a resistor that I believe is about 200 Ohms, but since I am not sure, I will choose the *2k* setting.

Next, plug the black test lead into the *COM* port and the red test lead into the port labeled *HzVΩ*. Now, touch one probe to one side of a resistor and the other probe to the other side. It doesn't matter which side you choose – a resistor works in both directions. Notice the readout. The meter will read one of three things, 0.00, 1, or the actual resistor value.

In this case, the meter reads 0.219, meaning this resistor has a value of 220Ω. Recall, I used the 2k scale, which means a resistor of 1k would read 1.0. Since the value is a decimal, I can move the decimal point to the left to get a whole number.

If the multimeter displays another value such as 0 or 1, it indicates the scale is wrong and you should try a higher scale. This isn't a problem. It just means you need to choose a larger scale. On the other hand, if the display shows 0 or a small number, you need to choose a lower scale. I like to go one tick of the knob either way when I am testing resistance in an unknown component or circuit.

Figure 5-11 shows an example of measuring resistance for a resistor. Notice the display reads 219. I am testing a resistor rated at 220 Ohms. The reason it is 219 instead of 220 is because the resistor I am using is rated at 220 +/– 5%. Thus, the acceptable range for this resistor is 209–231 Ohms.

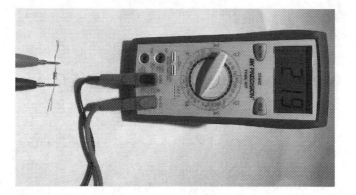

Figure 5-11. *Measuring resistance of a resistor*

Now we know how to test a resistor to discover its rating. As we will see, those rings around the body of the resistor are the primary way we know its rating, but we can always test it if we're unsure, someone has painted over it (hey, it happens), or we're too lazy to look it up.

Now, let's discuss the most fundamental concept you must understand when working with electronics – powering your project!

Powering Your Electronics

Electricity is briefly defined as the flow of electric charge and when used provides power for our electronics – from a common light bulb or ceiling fan to our high-definition television or our new tablet. Whether you are powering your electronics with batteries or a power supply, you are initiating a circuit where electrons flow in specific patterns. There are two forms (or kinds) of power you will be using. Your home is powered by alternating current, and your electronics are powered by direct current.

The term alternating current (AC) is used to describe the flow of charged particles that changes direction periodically at a specific rate (or cycle) reversing the voltage along with the current. Thus, AC systems are designed to work with a specific range of cycles as well as voltage. Typically, AC systems use higher voltages than direct current systems.

The term direct current (DC) is used to describe the flow of charged particles that do not change direction and thus always flow in a specific "direction." Most electronics systems are powered with DC voltages and are typically at lower voltages than AC systems. For example, electronics projects typically run on lower direct current (DC) voltages in the range 3.3–24V.

Tip   For more information about AC and DC current and the differences, see `https://learn.sparkfun.com/tutorials/alternating-current-ac-vs-direct-current-dc`.

Since DC flows in a single direction, components that operate on DC have a positive and a negative "side" where current flows from positive to negative. The orientation of these sides – one to positive and one to negative – is called polarity. Some components such as resistors can operate in "direction," but you should always be sure to connect your components per its polarity. Most components are clearly marked, but those that are not have a well-known arrangement. For example, the positive pole (side) of an LED is the longer of the two legs is called the anode, whereas the negative or shorter leg is called the cathode.

Despite the lower voltages, we mustn't think that they are completely harmless or safe. Incorrectly wiring electronics (reversing polarity) or shorting (connecting positive and negative together) can damage your electronics and in some cases cause overheating, which, in extreme cases, causes electronics to catch fire.

Caution   Don't be tempted to think working with 3.3 or 5.5 volts is "safe." Even a small amount of voltage improperly connected can lead to potentially devastating results. Don't assume low DC voltage is harmless.

Those warnings aside, I have deliberately kept the discussion on power simple. There is far more to electrical current than what I've described here, but enough to get started working with electronic components. Now, let's explore some of the more popular components.

Electronic Components

Aside from learning how to use a multimeter and possibly learning to solder, you also need to know something about the electronic components available to build your projects. In this section, I provide a short list and description of some of the common components in alphabetical order by name that you will encounter when building electronics projects. I also cover breakout boards and logic circuits, which are small circuits built with a set of components that provide a feature or solve a problem. For example, you can get breakout boards for USB host connections, Ethernet modules, logic shifters, real-time clocks, and more.

Button

A button (sometimes called a momentary button) is a mechanism that makes a connection when pressed. More specifically, a button connects two or more poles together while it is pressed. A common (and perhaps overused) example of a button is a home doorbell. When pressed, it completes a circuit that triggers a chime, bell, tone, or music to play. Some older doorbells continue to sound while the button is pressed.

In electronics projects, we will use buttons to trigger events, start and stop actions, and similar operations. A button is a simple form of a switch, but unlike a switch, you must continue to press the button to make the electrical connections. Most buttons have at least two legs (or pins) that are connected when the button is pressed. Some have more than two legs connected in pairs, and some of those can permit multiple connections. Figure 5-12 shows several buttons.

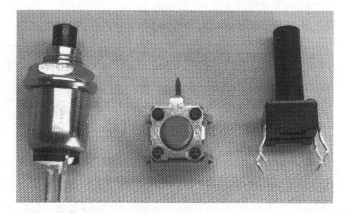

Figure 5-12. Momentary buttons

There is a special variant of a momentary button called a latching momentary button. This version uses a notch or detent to keep the poles connected until it is pushed again. If you've seen a button on a stereo or in your car that remains depressed until pressed again, it is likely a latching momentary button.

There are all kinds of buttons from those that can be used with breadboards (the spacing of the pins allow it to be plugged into a breadboard), can be mounted to a panel, or those made for soldering to printed circuit boards.

Capacitor

A capacitor is designed to store charges. As current flows through the capacitor, it accumulates charge and can discharge after the current is disconnected. In this way, it is like a battery, but unlike a battery, a capacitor charges and discharges very fast. We use capacitors for all manner of current storage from blocking current, reducing noise in power supplies, in audio circuits, and more. Figure 5-13 shows several capacitors.

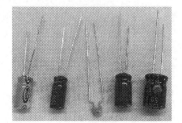

Figure 5-13. *Capacitors*

There are several types of capacitors, but we will most often encounter capacitors when building power supplies for electronics projects. Most capacitors have two legs (pins) that are polarized. That is, one is positive and the other negative. Be sure to connect the capacitor with the correct polarity in your circuit.

Diode

A diode is designed to allow current to flow in only one direction. Most are marked with an arrow pointing to a line, which indicates the direction of flow. A diode is often used as rectifiers in AC-to-DC converters (devices that convert AC to DC voltage), used in conjunction with other components to suppress voltage spikes, or protect components from reversed voltage. Often, it is used to protect against current flowing into a device.

Most diodes are shaped like a small cylinder, are usually black with silver writing, and have two legs. They look a little like resistors. We use a special variant called a Zener diode in power supplies to help regulate voltages. Figure 5-14 shows several Zener diodes.

Figure 5-14. *Diodes*

Fuse

A fuse is designed to protect a device (the entire circuit) from current greater than what the components can safely operate. Fuses are placed inline on the positive pole. When too much current flows through the fuse, the internal parts trigger a break in the flow of current.

Some fuses use a special wire inside that melts or breaks (thereby rendering it useless but protecting your equipment), while other fuses use a mechanism that operates like a switch (many of these are resettable). When this happens, we say the fuse has "blown" or "tripped." Fuses are rated at a certain current in amperage indicating the maximum amps that the fuse will permit to flow without tripping.

Fuses come in many shapes and varieties and can work with AC or DC voltage. Those we will use are of the disposable variety. Figure 5-15 shows an example of two fuses: an automotive-style blade fuse on the left and a glass cartridge fuse on the right.

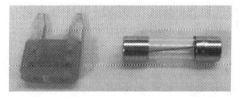

Figure 5-15. *Fuses*

If you are familiar with the electrical panels in your home that house the circuit breakers, they are resettable fuses. So, the next time one of them goes "click" and the lights go out, you can say, "Hey, a fuse has tripped!" Better still, now you know why – you have exceeded the maximum rating of the circuit breaker.

This is probably fine in situations where you accidentally left that infrared heater on when you dropped the toast and started the microwave (it happens), but if you are tripping breakers frequently without any load, you should call an electrician to have the circuit checked.

Light-Emitting Diode (LED)

As we learned in Chapter 3, an LED has two legs where the longer leg
is positive and the shorter negative. LEDs also have a flat edge that
also indicates the negative leg. They come in a variety of sizes ranging
from as small as 3mm to 10mm. Figure 5-16 shows an example of some
smaller LEDs.

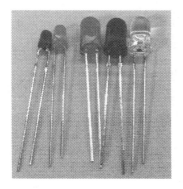

Figure 5-16. *Light-emitting diodes*

Recall we also needed to use a resistor with an LED. We need this to
help reduce the flow of the circuit to lower the current flowing through the
LED. LEDs can be used with lower current (they will burn a bit dimmer
than normal) but should not be used with higher current.

To determine what size resistor we need, we need to know several
things about the LED. This data is available from the manufacturer who
provides the data in the form of a data sheet or, in the case of commercially
packaged products, lists the data on the package. The data we need
includes the maximum voltage, the supply voltage (how many volts are
coming to the LED), and the current rating of the LED.

For example, if I have an LED like the one we used in the last chapter, in this case a 5mm red LED, we find on Adafruit's website (adafruit.com/products/297) that the LED operates at 1.8–2.2V and 20mA of current. Let's say we want to use this with a 5V supply voltage. We can then take these values and plug them into this formula:

```
R = (Vcc-Vf)/I
```

Using more descriptive names for the variable, we get the following:

```
Resistor = (Volts_supply - Volts_forward) / Desired_current
```

Plugging our data in, we get this result. Note that we have mA so we must use the correct decimal value (divide by 1000). In this case, it is 0.020, and we will pick a voltage in the middle:

```
Resistor = (5 - 2.0) / 0.020
         = 3.0 / 0.020
         = 150
```

Thus, we need a resistor of 150 Ohms. Cool. Sometimes, the formula will produce a value that does not match any existing resistors. In that case, choose one closest to the value but a bit larger. Remember, we want to limit and thus err on the side of more restrictive than less restrictive. For example, if you found you need a resistor of 95 Ohms, you can use one rated at 100 Ohms, which is safer than using one rated at 90 Ohms.

Tip   Always err on the side of the more restrictive resistor when the formula produces a value for which there is no resistor available.

Also, if you use LEDs in serial or parallel, the formula is a little different. See https://learn.adafruit.com/all-about-leds for more information about using LEDs in your projects and calculating the size of resistors to use with LEDs.

Relay

A relay is an interesting component that helps us control higher voltages with lower voltage circuits. For example, suppose you wanted to control a device that is powered by 12V from your Pico, which only produces a maximum of 3.3V. A relay can be used with a 3V circuit to turn on (or relay) power from that higher source. In this example, we would use the Pico output to trigger the relay to switch on the 12V power. Thus, relays are a form of switch. Figure 5-17 shows a typical relay and how the pins are arranged.

Figure 5-17. *Relay*

Relays can take a lot of different forms and typically have slightly different wiring options such as where the supply voltage is attached and where the trigger voltage attaches as well as whether the initial state is open (no flow) or close (flow) and thus the behavior of how it controls voltage. Some relays come mounted on a PCB with clearly marked terminals for changing its switching feature and where everything plugs in. If you want to use relays in your projects, always check the data sheet to make sure you are wiring it correctly based on its configuration.

You can also use relays to allow your DC circuit to turn AC appliances on and off like those from Adafruit (www.adafruit.com/product/2935).

Resistor

A resistor is one of the standard building blocks of electronics. Its job is to impede current and impose a reduction in voltage (which is converted to heat). Its effect, known as resistance, is measured in ohms. A resistor can be used to reduce voltage to other components, limiting frequency response, or protect sensitive components from overvoltage. Figure 5-18 shows several resistors.

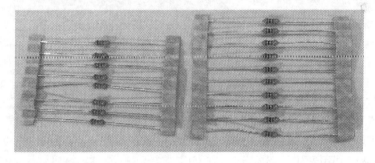

Figure 5-18. *Resistors*

When a resistor is used to pull up voltage (by attaching one end to positive voltage) or pull down voltage (by attaching one end to ground) (resistors are bidirectional), it eliminates the possibility of the voltage floating in an indeterminate state. Thus, a pull-up resistor ensures that the stable state is positive voltage, and a pull-down resistor ensures that the stable state is zero voltage (ground).

Switch

A switch is designed to control the flow of current between two or more pins. Switches come in all manner of shapes, sizes, and packaging. Some are designed as a simple on/off, while others can be used to change current from one set of pins to another. Like buttons, switches come in a variety of mounting options from PCB (also called through hole) to panel mount for mounting in enclosures. Figure 5-19 shows a variety of switches.

Figure 5-19. *Various switches*

Switches that have only one pole (leg or side) are called single-pole switches. Switches that can divert current from one set of poles to another set are called two-pole switches. Switches where there is only one secondary connection per pole are called single-throw switches. Switches that disconnect from one set of poles and connect to another while maintaining a common input are called double-throw switches. These are often combined and form the switch type (or kind) as follows:

- *SPST*: Single pole, single throw

- *DPST*: Double pole, single throw

- *SPDT*: Single pole, double throw

- *DPDT*: Double pole, double throw

- *3PDT*: Three pole, double throw

There may be other variants that you could encounter. I like to keep it straight like this; if I have just an on/off situation, I want a single-throw switch. How many poles depends on how many wires or circuits I want to turn on or off at the same time. For double-throw switches, I use these when I have an "A" condition and "B" condition where I want A on when B is off and vice versa. I sometimes use multiple-throw switches when I want "A," "B," and off situations where I use the center position (throw) as off. You can be very creative with switches!

Transistor

A transistor (a bipolar transistor) is designed to switch current on/off in a cycle or amplify fluctuations in current. Interestingly, transistors used to amplify current replaced vacuum tubes. If you are an audiophile, you likely know a great deal about vacuum tubes. When a resistor operates in switching mode, it behaves like a relay, but its "off" position still allows a small amount of current to flow. Transistors are used in audio equipment, signal processing, and switching power supplies. Figure 5-20 shows two varieties of transistors.

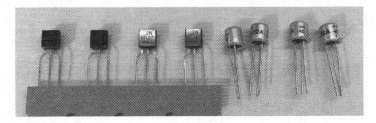

Figure 5-20. *Transistors*

Transistors come in all manner of varieties, packaging, and ratings that make them suitable for one solution or another.

Voltage Regulator

A voltage regulator (linear voltage regulator) is designed to keep the flow of current constant. Voltage regulators often appear in electronics when we need to condition or lower current from a source. For example, we want to supply 5V to a circuit but only have a 9V power supply. Voltage regulators accomplish this (roughly) by taking current in and dissipating the excess current through a heat sink. Thus, voltage regulators have three legs: positive current in, negative, and positive current out. They are typically shaped like those shown in Figure 5-21, but other varieties exist.

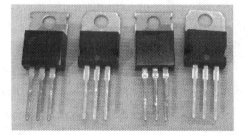

Figure 5-21. *Voltage regulators*

The small hole in the plate that extends out of the voltage regulator is where the heat sink is mounted. Voltage regulators are often numbered to match their rating. For example, an LM7805 produces 5V, whereas an LM7833 produces 3.3V.

An example of using a voltage regulator to supply power to a 3.3V circuit on a breadboard is shown in Figure 5-22. This circuit was designed with capacitors to help smooth or condition the power. Notice the capacitors are rated with uF, which means microfarad.

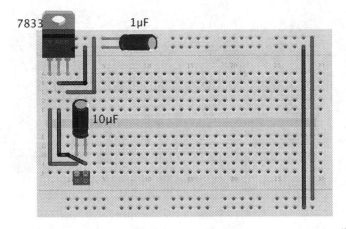

Figure 5-22. *Power supply circuit on a breadboard with voltage regulator*

Breakout Boards

We briefly discussed breakout boards in the last chapter. Recall, breakout boards are our modular building blocks for electronics projects. They typically combine several components together to form a function such as measuring temperature, enabling reading GPS data, communicating via cellular services, and more. Whenever you design a circuit or project, you should consider using breakout boards as much as possible because they simplify the use of the components. Figure 5-23 shows examples of breakout boards.

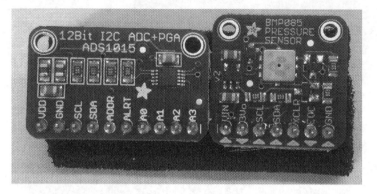

Figure 5-23. *Breakout boards*

For example, notice the breakout board on the left. This is a 128-bit analog-to-digital converter (`www.adafruit.com/product/1083`). Adafruit has designed this board so that all we need to do to use it is to attach power and connect it to our Pico on its I2C bus. An I2C bus is a fast digital protocol that uses two wires (plus power and ground) to read data from circuits (or devices).

Breadboard and Jumper Wires

A breadboard is a special tool designed to allow you to plug in your electrical components and provide interconnectivity in columns so that you can plug the leads of two components into the same column and therefore make a connection. The board is split into two rows, making it easy to use IC in the center of the board. Wires (called jumper wires or simply jumpers) can be used to connect the circuit on the breadboard to the Pico. You will see an example of this later in this chapter.

Figure 5-24 shows a half-sized breadboard from Adafruit. This breadboard is called half since it is one half the normal length of a standard breadboard.

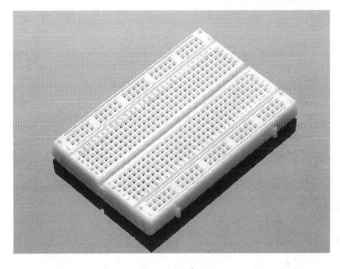

Figure 5-24. *Half-sized breadboard (courtesy of adafruit.com)*

If you already have some components or decide to buy a different basic electronics kit that doesn't come with a breadboard, you can buy a breadboard separately from Adafruit (www.adafruit.com/products/64).

If you use a device with male header pins instead of female header pins, you will need to get a different set of jumper wires. Once again, Adafruit has what you need. If you need male/female jumper wires, order the Premium Female/Male Extension Jumper Wires – 20 x 6 (www.adafruit.com/products/1954). Figure 5-25 shows a set of male/female jumper wires.

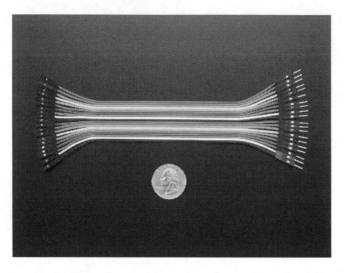

Figure 5-25. *Male/female jumper wires (courtesy of adafruit.com)*

Basic Electronics Kit

The example projects in this book use several common electronic components such as LEDs, switches, buttons, resistors, etc. One of the biggest challenges when learning to work with electronics at the hobbyist level is what to buy. I've talked to some who have made numerous trips to the local electronics store to get what they need seeming to never have the right components no matter what they buy.

Fortunately, electronics retailers have caught on to this problem and now offer a basic electronics kit that contains many of the more common components. Both Adafruit (www.adafruit.com/products/2975) and SparkFun (www.sparkfun.com/products/13973) offer such kits. While you cannot go wrong with either kit, I like the Adafruit kit best since it has more components (e.g., more LEDs).

The Adafruit Parts Pal comes packaged in a small plastic case with a host of electronic components. Figure 5-26 shows the Parts Pal kit.

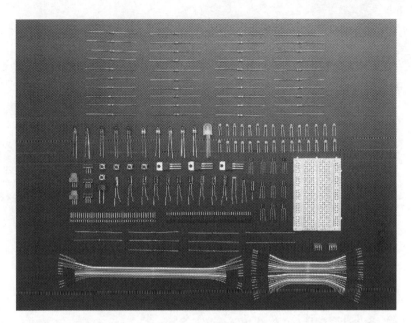

Figure 5-26. *Adafruit Parts Pal (courtesy of adafruit.com)*

The kit includes the following components: prototyping tools, LEDs, capacitors, resistors, some basic sensors, and more. In fact, there are more components in this kit than what you will need for many experiments. Better still, the kit costs only $19.95 making it a good deal (and the case is a great bonus):

- 1x: Storage box with latch

- 1x: Half-sized breadboard

- 20x: Male/male jumper wires – 3" (75mm)

- 10x: Male/male jumper wires – 6" (150mm)

- 5x: 5mm diffused green LEDs

- 5x: 5mm diffused red LEDs

- 1x: 10mm diffused common anode RGB LED

- 10x: 1.0uF ceramic capacitors

- 10x: 0.1uF ceramic capacitors

- 10x: 0.01uF ceramic capacitors

- 5x: 10uF 50V electrolytic capacitors

- 5x: 100uF 16V electrolytic capacitors

- 10x: 560 Ohm 5% axial resistors

- 10x: 1K Ohm 5% axial resistors

- 10x: 10K Ohm 5% axial resistors

- 10x: 47K Ohm 5% axial resistors

- 5x: 1N4001 diodes

- 5x: 1N4148 signal diodes

- 5x: NPN transistor PN2222 TO-92

- 5x: PNP transistor PN2907 TO-92

- 2x: 5V 1.5A linear voltage regulator – 7805 TO-220

- 1x: 3.3V 800mA linear voltage regulator – LD1117-3.3 TO-220

- 1x: TLC555 wide-voltage range, low-power 555 timer

- 1x: Photocell

- 1x: Thermistor (breadboard version)

- 1x: Vibration sensor switch

- 1x: 10K breadboard trim potentiometer

- 1x: 1K breadboard trim potentiometer

- 1x: Piezo buzzer

- 5x: 6mm tactile switches

- 3x: SPDT slide switches

- 1x: 40-pin break-away male header strip

- 1x: 40-pin female header strip

As you can see, there are a lot of components in this kit, making it ideal for beginners. Now, let's learn how to use a breadboard to build circuits.

Using a Breadboard to Build Circuits

If you have been following along with the projects thus far in the book, you have already encountered a breadboard to make a very simple circuit. Recall from Chapter 3 that a breadboard is a tool we use to plug components into to form circuits. Technically, we're using a solderless breadboard. A solder breadboard has the same layout only it has only through-hole solder points on a PCB.

WHY ARE THEY CALLED BREADBOARDS?

In the grand old days of microelectronics and discrete components became widely available for experimentation, when we wanted to prototype a circuit, some would use a piece of wood with nails driven into it (sometimes in a grid pattern) where connections were made (called "runs") by wrapping wire around the nails. Some used a breadboard from the kitchen to build their wire wrap prototypes. The name has stuck ever since.

A breadboard allows us to create prototypes for our circuits or simply temporary circuits without having to spend the time (and cost) to make the printed circuit board. Prototyping is the process of experimenting with a circuit by building and testing your ideas. In fact, once we've got our circuit to work correctly, we can use the breadboard layout to help us design a PCB. Figure 5-27 shows several breadboards.

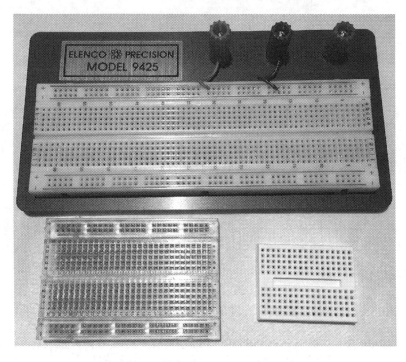

Figure 5-27. *Assorted breadboards*

Recall that most breadboards (there are several varieties) have a center groove (called a ravine) or a printed line down the center of the board. This signifies the terminal strips that run perpendicular to the channel are not connected. That is, the terminal strip on one side is not connected to the other side. This allows us to plug integrated circuits (IC) or chips that are packaged as two rows of pins. Thus, we can plug the IC into the breadboard with one set of pins on each side of the breadboard. We see this in the following example.

Most breadboards also have one or more sets of power rails that are connected together parallel to the ravine. If there are two sets, the sets are not connected together. The power rails may have a colored reference line, but this is only for reference; you can make either one positive with the other negative. Finally, some breadboards number the terminal strip rows. These are for reference only and have no other meaning. However, they can be handy for making notes in your engineering notebook.

Should our circuits require more room than what is available on a single breadboard, you can use multiple breadboards by simply jumping the power rails and continuing the circuit. To facilitate this, some breadboards can be connected using small nubs and slots on the side. Finally, most breadboards also come with an adhesive backing that you can use to mount on a plate or inside an enclosure or similar workspace. If you decide to use the adhesive backing, be forewarned that they cannot be unstuck easily – they stay put quite nicely.

Figure 5-28 shows the nomenclature of a breadboard and how the terminal strips and power rails are connected together.

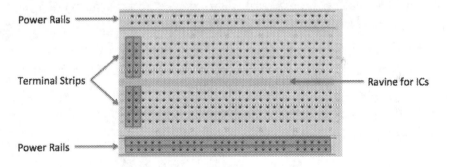

Figure 5-28. *Breadboard layout*

Note   The sets of power rails are not connected together. If you want to have power on both sides of the breadboard, you must use jumpers to connect them.

FRITZING: A BREADBOARDING SOFTWARE APPLICATION

The drawings of breadboards in this book were made with a program named Fritzing (`http://fritzing.org/home/`). This open source application allows you to create a digital representation of a circuit on a breadboard. It is quite handy to use. If you find yourself wanting to design a prototype circuit, using Fritzing can help save you a lot of trial and error. As a bonus, Fritzing allows you to see the same circuit in an electronic schematic or PCB layout view. I recommend downloading and trying this application out.

It is sometimes desirable to test a circuit out separately from code. For example, if we want to make sure all our devices are connected together properly, we can use a breadboard power supply to power the circuit. This way, if something goes horribly wrong, we don't risk damaging our Pico. Most breadboard power supplies are built on a small PCB with a barrel jack for a wall wart power supply, two sets of pins to plug into the power rails on the breadboard, and an off switch (very handy), and some can generate different voltages. Figure 5-29 shows one of my favorite breadboard power supplies from SparkFun (`www.sparkfun.com/products/13157`).

Figure 5-29. *Breadboard power supply*

Now that we know more about how breadboards work, let's discuss the component our electronics projects will employ to collect data: sensors.

What Are Sensors?

A sensor is a device that measures phenomena of the physical world. These phenomena can be things you see, like light, gases, water vapor, and so on. They can also be things you feel, like temperature, electricity, water, wind, and so on. Humans have senses that act like sensors, allowing us to experience the world around us. However, there are some things your sensors can't see or feel, such as radiation, radio waves, voltage, and amperage. Upon measuring these phenomena, it's the sensors' job to convey a measurement in the form of either a voltage representation or a number.

There are many forms of sensors. They're typically low-cost devices designed for a single purpose and with a limited capability for processing. Most simple sensors are discrete components; even those that have more sophisticated parts can be treated as separate components. Sensors are either analog or digital and are typically designed to measure only one thing. But an increasing number of sensor modules are designed to measure a set of related phenomena, such as the USB Weather Board from SparkFun Electronics (`www.sparkfun.com/products/10586`).

The following sections examine how sensors measure data, how to store that data, and examples of some common sensors.

How Sensors Measure

Sensors are electronic devices that generate a voltage based on the unique properties of their chemical and mechanical construction. One of the common misconceptions some have about sensors is they do not manipulate the phenomena (change the event or data) they're designed to measure. Rather, sensors sample some physical variable and turn it into a proportional electric signal (voltage, current, digital, and so on).

For example, a humidity sensor measures the concentration of water (moisture) in the air. Humidity sensors react to these phenomena and generate a voltage that the microcontroller or similar device can then read and use to calculate a value on a scale. A basic, low-cost humidity sensor is the DHT-22 available from most electronics stores (`www.adafruit.com/product/385`). Figure 5-30 shows a typical DHT-22 sensor.

Figure 5-30. *DHT-22 humidity sensor*

The DHT-22 is designed to measure temperature as well as humidity. It generates a digital signal on the output (data pin). Although simple to use, it's a bit slow and should be used to track data at a reasonably slow rate (no more frequently than about once every three or four seconds).

When this sensor generates data, that data is transmitted as a series of high (interpreted as a 1) and low (interpreted as a 0) voltages that the microcontroller can read and use to form a value. In this case, the microcontroller reads a value 40 bits in length (40 pulses of high or low voltage) – that is, 5 bytes – from the sensor and places it in a program variable. The first two bytes are the value for humidity, the second two are for temperature, and the fifth byte is the checksum value to ensure an accurate read. Fortunately, all this hard work is done for you in the form of a special library designed for the DHT-22 and similar sensors.

The DHT-22 produces a digital value. Not all sensors do this; some generate a voltage range instead. These are called analog sensors. Let's take a moment to understand the differences. This will become essential information as you plan and build your sensor nodes.

Analog Sensors

Analog sensors are devices that generate a voltage range, typically between 0 and 5 volts. An analog-to-digital circuit is needed to convert the voltage to a number. But it isn't that simple (is it ever?). Analog sensors work like resistors and, when connected to GPIO pins, often require another resistor to "pull up" or "pull down" the voltage to avoid spurious changes in voltage known as floating. This is because voltage flowing through resistors is continuous in both time and amplitude.

Thus, even when the sensor isn't generating a value or measurement, there is still a flow of voltage through the sensor that can cause spurious readings. Your projects require a clear distinction between OFF (zero voltage) and ON (positive voltage). Pull-up and pull-down resistors ensure that you have one of these two states. It's the responsibility of the A/D converter to take the voltage reading from the sensor and convert it to a value that can be interpreted as data.

When sampled (when a value is read from a sensor), the voltage reading must be interpreted as a value in the range specified for the given sensor. Remember that a value of, say, 2 volts from one analog sensor may not mean the same thing as 2 volts from another analog sensor. Each sensor's data sheet shows you how to interpret these values.

As you can see, working with analog sensors is a lot more complicated than using the DHT-22 digital sensor. With a little practice, you will find that most analog sensors aren't difficult to use once you understand how to attach them to a microcontroller and how to interpret their voltage on the scale in which the sensor is calibrated to work.

Digital Sensors

Digital sensors like the DHT-22 are designed to produce a string of bits using serial transmission (one bit at a time). However, some digital sensors produce data via parallel transmission (one or more bytes at a time). As described previously, the bits are represented as voltage, where high voltage (say, 5 volts) or ON is 1 and low voltage (0 or even –5 volts) or OFF is 0. These sequences of ON and OFF values are called discrete values because the sensor is producing one or the other in pulses – it's either ON or OFF.

Digital sensors can be sampled more frequently than analog signals because they generate the data more quickly and because no additional circuitry is needed to read the values (such as A/D converters and logic or software to convert the values to a scale). Thus, digital sensors are generally more accurate and reliable than analog sensors. But the accuracy of a digital sensor is directly proportional to the number of bits it uses for sampling data.

The most common form of digital sensor is the pushbutton or switch. What, a button is a sensor? Why, yes, it's a sensor. Consider for a moment the sensor attached to a window in a home security system. It's a simple switch that is closed when the window is closed and open when the window is open. When the switch is wired into a circuit, the flow of current is constant and unbroken (measuring positive volts using a pull-up resistor) when the window is closed and the switch is closed, but the current is broken (measuring zero volts) when the window and switch are open. This is the most basic of ON and OFF sensors.

Most digital sensors are small circuits of several components designed to generate digital data. Unlike analog sensors, reading their data is easy because the values can be used directly without conversion (except to other scales or units of measure). Some may suggest this is more difficult than using analog sensors, but that depends on your point of view.

An electronics enthusiast would see working with analog sensors as easier, whereas a programmer would think digital sensors are simpler to use.

Now let's look at some of the sensors available and the types of phenomena they measure.

Examples of Sensors

An electronics project that observes something may use at least one sensor and requires a means to read and interpret the data need from the sensor. You may be thinking of all manner of useful things you can measure in your home or office, or even in your yard or surroundings. You may want to measure the temperature changes in your new sunroom, detect when the mail carrier has tossed the latest circular in your mailbox, or perhaps keep a log of how many times your dog uses his doggy door. I hope that by now you can see these are just the tip of the iceberg when it comes to imagining what you can measure.

What types of sensors are available? The following sections describe some of the more popular sensors and what they measure. I also provide a few hints on how you might want to use the sensor in an electronics project. However, this is just a sampling of the growing array of sensors available. Perusing the catalogs of online electronics vendors like Mouser Electronics (`www.mouser.com`), SparkFun Electronics (`www.sparkfun.com`), and Adafruit Industries (`www.adafruit.com`) will reveal many more examples.

I also include photos of popular examples for some of the sensor types.

Accelerometers

These sensors measure the motion or movement of the sensor or whatever it's attached to. They're designed to sense motion (velocity, inclination, vibration, and so on) on several axes. Some include gyroscopic features. Most are digital sensors. A Wii Nunchuck (or WiiChuck) contains a sophisticated accelerometer for tracking movement. Aha! Now you know the secret of those funny little thingamabobs that came with your Wii! You may want to add accelerometers if your project involves something in motion and the observation of that motion provides useful information.

Audio Sensors

Perhaps this is obvious, but microphones are used to measure sound. Most are analog, but some of the better security and surveillance sensors have digital variants for higher compression of transmitted data. Electronics projects such as home security, child monitoring, ghost hunting, or auditory health can all benefit from integrating audio sensors.

Barcode Readers

These sensors are designed to read barcodes. Most often, barcode readers generate digital data representing the numeric equivalent of a barcode. Such sensors are often used in inventory tracking systems to track equipment through a plant or during transport. They're plentiful, and many are economically priced, enabling you to incorporate them into your own projects. If your project requires capturing data from an object, you may want to consider barcodes.

For example, if you want to sense when parking lot subscribers enter or exit an unattended parking lot, you could position a barcode reader at the gates that read barcodes that you design and distribute to your subscribers. When the car pulls up to the gate, the barcode reader can read the barcode, log the entry, and raise the gate. If you've ever lived in a large city, worked in a controlled office complex, or were a commuter student, you may have encountered parking solutions like this.

Biometric Sensors

A sensor that reads fingerprints, irises, or palm prints contains a special sensor designed to recognize patterns. Given the uniqueness inherent in patterns such as fingerprints and palm prints, they make excellent components for a secure access system. Most biometric sensors produce a block of digital data that represents the fingerprint or palm print. Electronics projects that require a greater level of security may want to include a biometric sensor to help identify the user of the system.

Capacitive Sensors

A special application of capacitive sensors, pulse sensors are designed to measure your pulse rate and typically use a fingertip for the sensing site. Special devices known as pulse oximeters (called pulse-ox by some medical professionals) measure the pulse rate with a capacitive sensor and determine the oxygen content of blood with a light sensor.

If you own modern electronic devices, you may have encountered touch-sensitive buttons that use special capacitive sensors to detect touch and pressure. If your project needs to measure any sort of movement, or respond to touch, capacitive sensors can help provide a futuristic non-tactile interface. The Touch Bar on the latest MacBook Pro is an example of such a solution.

Figure 5-31 shows two examples of touch-sensitive modules that you can buy from Adafruit. In this case, we see breakout boards for a momentary switch (www.adafruit.com/products/1374) and a toggle switch (www.adafruit.com/products/1375).

Figure 5-31. *Touch capacitive sensor breakout boards*

Coin Sensors

This is one of the most unusual types of sensors. These devices are like the coin slots on a typical vending machine. Like their commercial equivalent, they can be calibrated to sense when a certain size of coin is inserted. Although not as sophisticated as commercial units that can distinguish fake coins from real ones, coin sensors can be used to add a new dimension to your projects. A great, practical project for parents would be a coin-operated WiFi station where the children have to buy their own Internet time. Not only will this keep them from using the Internet too much, but it may also help teach them how to budget their allowance. Now, that should keep the kids from spending too much time on the Internet!

Current Sensors

These are designed to measure voltage and amperage. Some are designed to measure change, whereas others measure load. Electronics projects that integrate circuits or need to monitor the flow of electricity will need a current sensor. These may be some of the more esoteric projects, but you can use these sensors to monitor the behavior of existing solutions without modifying them.

For example, if you wanted to adapt sensors to observe a manufacturing machine, you could add sensors that monitor the current to the various components. That is, you may be able to record when voltage is applied to motors, actuators, or even warning lights to determine when (or how much) the devices are activated. However, as a hobbyist, you are more likely interested in building your own multimeter or similar tool.

Flex/Force Sensors

Resistance sensors measure flexes in a piece of material or the force or impact of pressure on the sensor. Flex sensors may be useful for measuring torsional effects or measuring finger movements (like in a Nintendo Power Glove). Flex sensor resistance increases when the sensor is flexed. For example, if you want to create an electronics project that reports your fishing experience in real time, you might want to use a flex sensor on your fishing rod to report every time you cast or got a hit on your lure.

Gas Sensors

There are a great many types of gas sensors. Some measure potentially harmful gases such as LPG and methane and other gases such as hydrogen, oxygen, and so on. Other gas sensors are combined with light sensors to sense smoke or pollutants in the air. The next time you hear that telltale and often annoying low-battery warning beep from your smoke detector, think about what that device contains. Why, It's a sensor node! If your project needs to observe or detect any form of gas, especially if it involves reacting to certain gases or levels thereof, you will need to use the appropriate gas sensors.

Light Sensors

Sensors that measure the intensity or lack of light are special types of resistors: light-dependent resistors (LDRs), sometimes called photoresistors or photocells. Thus, they're analog by nature.

If you own a Mac laptop, chances are you've seen a photoresistor in action when your illuminated keyboard turns itself on in low light. Special forms of light sensors can detect other light spectrums such as infrared (as in older TV remotes). For example, if you want your project to automatically adjust the brightness of its display, a light sensor is the component you need.

The following shows two examples of light sensors. Figure 5-32 shows a typical mini photocell (www.sparkfun.com/products/9088) and Figure 5-33 shows a color sensor (www.adafruit.com/products/1334).

Figure 5-32. *Mini photocell*

Figure 5-33. *Color sensor breakout board*

Liquid Flow Sensors

These sensors resemble valves and are placed inline in plumbing systems. They measure the flow of liquid as it passes through. Basic flow sensors use a spinning wheel and a magnet to generate a Hall effect (rapid ON/ OFF sequences whose frequency equates to how much water has passed). If your electronics project involves any form of liquid such as a garden pond or irrigation system, knowing the flow of the water may be helpful in learning or observing something.

Liquid-Level Sensors

A special resistive solid-state device can be used to measure the relative height of a body of water. One example generates low resistance when the water level is high and higher resistance when the level is low. Like liquid flow sensors, liquid-level sensors are typically used in the same solution. Figure 5-34 shows a typical liquid-level sensor that operates as a switch where the float closes the switch when the water level rises.

Figure 5-34. *Water-level sensor*

Location Sensors

Modern smartphones have GPS sensors for sensing location, and of course GPS devices use the GPS technology to help you navigate. Fortunately, GPS sensors are available in low-cost forms, enabling you to add location sensing to your project. GPS sensors generate digital data in the form of longitude and latitude, and most can also sense altitude. If your project needs to report its location, a GPS sensor can give you very accurate readings. However, like most sensors, GPS sensors can have a degree of inaccuracy. Depending on how close you need to locate something, you may need to spend a bit more on a more accurate GPS sensor.

Magnetic Stripe Readers

These sensors read data from magnetic stripes (like that on a credit card) and return the digital form of the alphanumeric data (the actual strings). Electronics projects that include a security component may want to use a magnetic stripe reader to help identify a user. When combined with a password and a biometric sensor, security can be increased considerably. That is, someone would have to know something (a password or pin), possess something (security card with a magnetic stripe encoded with a key phrase, number, user ID, etc.), and be validated as someone (fingerprint) before gaining access.

Magnetometers

These sensors measure orientation via the strength of magnetic fields. A compass is a sensor for finding magnetic north. Some magnetometers offer multiple axes to allow even finer detection of magnetic fields. This is another sensor that you may not encounter very often, but if your project needs to measure magnetic fields from motors or atmospheric phenomena, you may want to look at magnetometers.

Moisture Sensors

Moisture sensors measure the amount of moisture in a substance (such as soil) or in the air. They typically send data in the form of a voltage reading where low values indicate less moisture. You often find moisture sensors in atmospheric projects or even plant monitoring solutions. Figure 5-35 shows a typical soil moisture sensor. Notice the prongs are the portion of the sensor inserted into the soil.

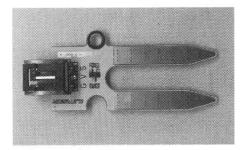

Figure 5-35. *Soil moisture sensor*

Proximity Sensors

Often thought of as distance sensors, proximity sensors use infrared or sound waves to detect distance, movement, or the range to/from an object. Made popular by low-cost robotics kits, the Parallax Ultrasonic Sensor uses sound waves to measure distance by sensing the amount of time between the pulse sent and the pulse received (the echo). For approximate distance measuring, it's a simple math problem to convert the time to distance. If you're building an electronics project that detects movement or proximity such as a motion sensing camera, you may want to use proximity sensors.

The following figures show two types of proximity sensors. Figure 5-36 shows a popular passive infrared sensor (PIR) motion sensor (www.sparkfun.com/products/13285).

Figure 5-36. *PIR motion sensor*

Figure 5-37 shows an ultrasonic sensor (`www.sparkfun.com/products/13959`) used in many projects from robots to drones.

Figure 5-37. *Ultrasonic proximity sensor*

Radiation Sensors

Among the more serious sensors are those that detect radiation. This can also be electromagnetic radiation (there are sensors for that too), but a Geiger counter uses radiation sensors to detect harmful ionizing. In fact, it's possible to build your very own Geiger counter using a sensor and an Arduino (and a few electronic components). This is one sensor that you may not encounter as a hobbyist. However, there are several kits for building your own Geiger counter such as those from Adafruit (`www.adafruit.com/products/483`).

RFID Sensors

Radio frequency identification uses a passive device (sometimes called an RFID tag) to communicate data using radio frequencies through electromagnetic induction. For example, an RFID tag can be a credit card–sized plastic card, a label, or something similar that contains a special antenna, typically in the form of a coil, thin wire, or foil layer that is tuned to a specific frequency.

When the tag is placed near the reader, the reader emits a radio signal; the tag can use the electromagnet energy to transmit a nonvolatile message embedded in the antenna, in the form of radio signals, which is then converted to an alphanumeric string. RFID sensors are another good choice for security systems. If you have pets, you may want to visit your veterinarian to inquire about RFID sensors that act as hidden owner identification tags. If you know the frequency, you can even use it to help detect when your pet goes through a pet door. Figure 5-38 shows an RFID reader (sensor) that you can use to read RFID tags via USB (`www.sparkfun.com/products/9963`).

Figure 5-38. *RFID reader*

Speed Sensors

Like flow sensors, simple speed sensors like those found on many bicycles use a magnet and a reed switch to generate a Hall effect. The frequency combined with the circumference of the wheel can be used to calculate speed and, over time, distance traveled. If your project needs to read movement, you can use a magnetic switch and a magnet to detect rotation. For example, bicycle speedometers often use a magnet and magnetic switch to detect the number of rotations, circumference of the wheel, and frequency of the actions to calculate speed.

Switches and Pushbuttons

These are the most basic of digital sensors used to detect if something is set (ON) or reset (OFF). Even so, you can use switches and buttons to build a user interface, for controlling other devices, or even turning the thing on!

Tilt Switches

These sensors can detect when a device is tilted one way or another. Although very simple, they can be useful for low-cost motion detection sensors. They are digital and are essentially switches. If your project needs to detect when the device is leaning, you can use tilt sensors to trigger at a certain lean angle. For example, some modern motorcycles use tilt sensors to turn on cornering lights – headlamps angled to improve vision around a turn at night.

Touch Sensors

The touch-sensitive membranes formed into keypads, keyboards, pointing devices, and the like are an interesting form of sensor. You can use touch-sensitive devices like these for collecting data from humans. Touch sensors can help you build a user interface for your project that can be presented in a low-profile form or to save space in a console, project box, etc.

Video Sensors

As mentioned previously, it's possible to obtain very small video sensors that use cameras and circuitry to capture images and transmit them as digital data. If you want to incorporate a video element to your project such as a security solution, you can add a camera or video sensor to capture a visual component that can help provide information beyond the incident measurements. That is, you can review a photo and learn more than simply something moved or approached the device. For example, you can build a project that detects movement and takes a photo if something gets close enough or, perhaps, moves faster than a certain threshold.

Weather Sensors

Sensors for temperature, barometric pressure, rain fall, humidity, wind speed, and so on are all classified as weather sensors. Most generate digital data and can be combined to create comprehensive environmental solutions. Figure 5-39 shows a common breakout board for the BMP280 pressure and temperature sensor (`www.adafruit.com/products/2651`).

Figure 5-39. *BMP280 pressure and temperature sensor*

With this and other easy-to-use sensors, it's possible to build your own weather station from about a dozen inexpensive sensors!

Tip   If you want to see more sensors, you can purchase any number of sensors from Adafruit (`www.adafruit.com/category/35`) or SparkFun (`www.sparkfun.com/categories/23`).

Electronics Resources

If you find you need or want to learn more about electronics that I've presented in this chapter or you want to learn more about the electronics you will need for a more advanced project, you may want to consider taking a course at a community college or try a self-paced course on electronics.

One of the best self-paced courses I've found includes the set of electronics books by Charles Platt. I've found these books to be very well written opening the door for many to learn electronics without having to spend years learning the tedious (but no less important) theory and mathematics of electronics. Best of all, they are not written in the dreary textbook fact-fact-fact-question pace. They are written by a world-renowned expert with a gift of presenting the material in an easy to read and comprehend style. I recommend the following books for anyone wanting to learn more about electronics:

- *Make: Electronics, Third Edition* (O'Reilly, 2021), Charles Platt

- *Make: More Electronics* (O'Reilly, 2014), Charles Platt

- *Encyclopedia of Electronic Components Volume 1* (O'Reilly, 2012), Charles Platt

- *Encyclopedia of Electronic Components Volume 2* (O'Reilly, 2014), Charles Platt

- *Encyclopedia of Electronic Components Volume 3* (O'Reilly, 2016), Charles Platt

The third volume in his encyclopedia series includes an in-depth study of sensors, a must for advanced electronics projects.

Summary

Learning how to work with electronics as a hobby or to create an electronics project does not require a lifetime of study or a change of vocation. Indeed, learning how to work with electronics is all part of the fun of experimenting with the Pico! I have met many people who have learned electronics on their own, and while most will admit formal study is essential for mastering the topic, you can learn quite a lot on your own – enough to become proficient working with the basic electronic components typically found in electronics projects.

This chapter presented the basics of electronic components including the use of breadboards, common components, and example circuits. This and a bit of key knowledge of how to use a multimeter will get you a long way toward becoming proficient with electronics. We also learned about one of the key components of an electronics project – sensors. We discovered two ways they communicate (digital and analog) and a bit of what types of sensors are available.

In the next chapter, we will dive into our first electronics project – the equivalent of a "hello, world!" project for your Pico. We'll see how to connect our Pico to a few components and write a MicroPython program to control them. Cool!

## CHAPTER 6

Project: Hello, World! MicroPython Style

Here, we are at the most fun part of this book – working on MicroPython projects! It is at this point that we have learned how to write in MicroPython and now know a lot more about the hardware and even how to use discrete electronics and breakout boards.

This chapter represents an introduction to building MicroPython projects. As such, there are a few more things we need to learn including techniques and procedures for installing and running our projects on our MicroPython boards. This chapter will introduce those things you need to make your MicroPython projects successful. Thus, the chapter is a bit longer and should be considered required reading even if you do not plan to implement the project.

As you will see, the format for all the project chapters is the same; an overview of the project is presented followed by a list of the required components and how to assemble the hardware. Once we have a grasp of how to connect the hardware, we then see how to connect everything and begin writing the code. Each chapter will close with how to execute the project along with a sample of it running and suggestions for embellishing the project.

© Charles Bell 2022
C. Bell, *Beginning MicroPython with the Raspberry Pi Pico*, Maker Innovations Series,
https://doi.org/10.1007/978-1-4842-8135-2_6

Before we jump into our first electronics project for the Pico, let's discuss a few best practices and other practical advice for developing projects. These apply to all projects in this chapter and likely any future project you may have in mind.

Getting Started with Pico Projects

If you have never worked with microcontrollers before, you have no knowledge of building electronics projects, or you are not familiar with the hardware on the Pico, you may be wondering how to get started building such projects.

In this section, we will see some helpful tips and best practices for how to get started working with the Pico hardware. Most of this advice applies to any electronics or microcontroller project. They are included here for the beginner and those that need a refresher.

One Step at a Time!

Another very common mistake beginners make is sitting down and wiring all of their electronics together and then writing all their code in one pass without testing anything ahead of time. This creates a situation where if something doesn't work, it can be masked by a host of problems.

For example, if there is some logic error or data produced is incorrect, it may cause other parts of the project to fail or produce incorrect results. This is made worse when the project doesn't work at all – there are too many parts to try and diagnose what went wrong. This often places beginners in a desperate situation of confusion and frustrations. You students out there know exactly what I am talking about.

This can be avoided easily by building your project one step at a time. That is, build your project one aspect at a time. For example, if you're working with LEDs to signal something, get that part working first. Similarly, if you're reading data from a sensor, ensure you can do that correctly in isolation before wiring it all together and hoping it all works.

Even the very experienced can make this mistake, but they are more equipped to fix it if something goes wrong (and they know better, but it's a "do as I say not as I do" situation). We will build the examples in this book one step at a time. Some are small enough that there may be only one step, but the practice is one you should heed for any project you undertake.

Some Assembly Required

Some vendors offer Pico and breakout boards with and without headers soldered. Not soldering the headers saves on production and in some cases shipping costs and makes the boards a bit cheaper. If you know how to solder (or know someone who does), you may be able to save a little going with the boards without headers.

Another reason you may want a board without headers is if you want to install your board in a project enclosure or some other form of embedded installation. In this case, having the headers soldered may take up more space that you have or make the completed project a bit bulkier.

You may also encounter some add-on boards, breakout boards, or other discrete components that are not soldered with headers (or connectors). If you want to use these, you may have to solder the header or connector yourself. For example, most of the breakout boards from Adafruit (`adafruit.com`) and SparkFun (`sparkfun.com`) do not come with the headers soldered.

Handle with Care!

You should consider your Pico as a very sensitive device susceptible to electrostatic discharge (ESD). Unless you place your board in a case or on a nonmetal surface, you should handle your board carefully, always placing it on a nonconductive surface before powering it on. ESD can be caused by many things (think back to when you were a child with sneakers on carpet). This discharge can harm the board. Always ensure you handle your board so that ESD is controlled and minimized.

You should also never move the board when it is powered on. Why? The board has components soldered on with many pins exposed on both sides. Should any two or more of those pins touch something that conducts electricity, you can risk damaging the board.

Also, always store your board in an ESD safe container – one that is expressly made to store electronics. Your average, everyday inexpensive plastic box should be avoided (many generate static electricity when handled). However, if you do not have a container made for electronics, you can use static-free bags to place the board in while it is being stored. Many of the boards and components you buy come in such packaging. So, don't throw it away!

You should take care to make sure your body, your workspace, and your project are grounded to avoid electrostatic discharge (ESD). ESD can damage your electronics – permanently. The best way to avoid this is to use a grounding strap that loops around your wrist and attaches to an antistatic mat like these: `uline.com/BL_7403/Anti-Static-Table-Mats`.

Finally, be extra careful when connecting your USB cable to your board. The micro-USB connector is prone to breakage (more so than other connectors). In most cases, it is not the cable that breaks but the connector on the board itself. When this happens, it can be very difficult to repair (or may not be repairable). It is also possible that the cable itself will stop working or only work when you hold the cable in place. If this happens, try a new cable, and if that fixes the problem, throw the old one away. If it does not fix the problem, it may be the connector on the board. Fortunately, extra care when plugging and unplugging the cable can avoid these issues. For example, always plug the micro-USB side first and use the full-sized USB end to plug and unplug from your PC. The fewer times you use the micro-USB connector, the less chance you have of damaging it.

Now, let's get started on our very first MicroPython project!

Overview

In this chapter, we will design and build a MicroPython clock. We will use both an SPI and I2C breakout board. We will use a small organic light-emitting diode (OLED) display that uses an SPI interface and a hardware-based real-time clock (RTC) that uses the DS1307 chip and a battery for keeping time while the project is turned off. Rather than simply connecting to a network time protocol (NTP) server on the Internet, we will use the hardware-based RTC and display the current date and time on the small OLED display. This not only keeps the project a bit smaller but also demonstrates how to use an RTC for projects that may not be connected to the Internet.

While the Pico has a hardware RTC, it must be initialized each time you connect the board to your PC (via Thonny or rshell), making it less than ideal for a project that you power on periodically. To make it possible for the Pico to know what time it is even after being powered off and on again without connecting to your PC, we will use an external RTC.

As you will see, there is a fair amount of wiring needed, and an understanding of the hardware capabilities is required to write the code. Which is why we spent time in previous chapters talking about the firmware and various low-level hardware control. You will need those skills and knowledge to complete this project.

While a clock may sound rather simple, this project will walk you through all the steps needed to assemble the hardware and write the code. Further, the project is small and simplistic, so we can focus on the process, which we can then apply to more advanced projects. In fact, we will see that even a relatively simple project can have an unexpected level of difficulty. But don't worry, as this chapter documents all the things you need to do to complete the project.

The sources for this project are many. The following links include background data used for this project including documentation and links to the MicroPython library (also called a driver) we will need to download for this project:

- *OLED display information*: `https://learn.adafruit.com/monochrome-oled-breakouts/wiring-128x32-spi-oled-display`

- *OLED display library*: `https://github.com/adafruit/micropython-adafruit-ssd1306`

- *RTC breakout board documentation*: `https://learn.adafruit.com/ds1307-real-time-clock-breakout-board-kit`

- *RTC library*: `https://github.com/adafruit/Adafruit-uRTC`

Note   The Adafruit MicroPython libraries are marked as deprecated, which only means no one is actively maintaining them; however, they will work with your Pico board without modification.

Notice the sites used. A good practice is to start with the Adafruit and MicroPython learning, blobs, and forums. Then check out the libraries. That is, do the research first and find all the references you can. If you find nice tutorials like those from Adafruit or SparkFun, you may want to download them to your PC or tablet or print them out for later reading. More importantly, take the time to read the references so that you understand as much as you can before you start working with the hardware or writing your code. You can save yourself a lot of time by understanding simple things like how to wire your board to the device and how the library is expected to be used.

WHICH LIBRARY DO I USE?

You may encounter a situation where you find more than one library for the hardware you want to use. In fact, I found several libraries for the OLED display. The differences among them are subtle, and it appears at least one does not support text, another is written for a specific platform, and another is written in C++ for the Pico.

The one listed earlier is the best one to use. Even so, it needs some minor changes for use. I will show you those changes, and, as you will see, they are not too difficult to spot and fix (e.g., when MicroPython throws exceptions, it will show you the source of the issue).

If you encounter a similar situation – having more than one library to choose from – you may want to try each until you find one that works best for your hardware and project. Sometimes, and in this case it is true, one library may not be viable, or another may be lacking features you need. The trick is to find the library that works best with the least amount of modification.

Now let's see what components are needed for this project, and then we will see how to wire everything together.

Required Components

Table 6-1 lists the components you will need in addition to your Pico board. You can purchase the components separately from Adafruit (adafruit.com), SparkFun (sparkfun.com), or any electronics store that carries electronic components. Links to vendors are provided should you want to purchase the components. When listing multiple rows of the same object, you can choose one or the other – you do not need both. Also, you may find other vendors that sell the components. You should shop around to find the best deal. Costs shown are estimates and do not include any shipping costs.

Table 6-1. *Required Components*

Component	Qty	Description	Cost	Links
OLED display	1	ssd1306-based SPI display	$17.5	www.adafruit.com/ product/661
RTC breakout board	1	RTC module with battery backup	$15.95	www.sparkfun.com/ products/12708
			$7.50	www.adafruit.com/ product/3296
Breadboard	1	Prototyping board, full-sized	$5.95	www.sparkfun.com/ products/12615
			$5.95	www.adafruit.com/ product/239
Jumper wires	11	M/M jumper wires, 7" (set of 30)	$2.25	www.sparkfun.com/ products/12615
		M/M jumper wires, 6" (set of 20)	$1.95	www.adafruit.com/ product/1950
Coin cell battery	1	CR1225 (SparkFun RTC)	$1.95	www.sparkfun.com/ products/337
		CR1220 (Adafruit RTC)	$0.95	www.adafruit.com/ product/380

The OLED breakout board used in this project is a small module from Adafruit. It has a tiny but bright display that you can mount on the breadboard. The resolution is 128 pixels wide by 32 pixels high. The OLED breakout board comes without headers installed, but they are easy to add if you know how to solder (now might be a good time to practice), or you can get a friend to help you. Figure 6-1 shows the Adafruit OLED SPI breakout board.

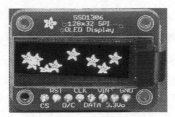

Figure 6-1. *Monochrome 128x32 SPI OLED graphic display (courtesy of adafruit.com)*

There are several OLED breakout boards available, and so long as they have the SPI interface and use the ssd1306 controller chip (the description will tell you this), you can use an alternate OLED display. The reason we need to use one with that controller chip is because the library is written for that controller. Other controller chips will require a different library.

The RTC breakout board used in this project is a DS1307 breakout board from Adafruit. The board also comes without headers installed (but includes them), nor does it come with a battery, so you must purchase a CR1220 coin cell battery. Adafruit has those as well if you want to save yourself a trip to the store. Figure 6-2 shows the RTC breakout board.

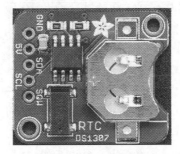

Figure 6-2. *DS1307 real-time clock assembled breakout board (courtesy of adafrui.com)*

There are several DS1307 RTC clocks available. In fact, SparkFun has one, or you can build your own! See the sidebar "Building Your Own RTC Module" for more details. Fortunately, the library we will use supports breakout boards with DS1307, DS3231, or PCF8523 RTC chips.

Tip   Small, discrete components like LEDs, resistors, etc. and even jumper wires and breadboards can be found in the kits mentioned in Chapter 2 – the Adafruit Parts Pal (`www.adafruit.com/product/2975`) or the SparkFun Beginner Parts Kit (`www.sparkfun.com/products/13973`). I recommend one of these kits.

Now, let's see how to wire the components together.

Set Up the Hardware

This project has a lot of connections. There are seven needed for the OLED and four needed for the RTC. To help keep things easier, we will plan for how things should connect. We will use a full-sized breadboard to mount the breakout boards making the connections easier. We will use male/male jumper wires to make these connections via a breadboard.

But first, we will learn what connections are needed for each component and where they need to be connected to our board, writing them down to keep things straight. Doing this small amount of homework will save you time later (and a small bit frustration).

As you will see, mapping out the connections like this makes it easy to check the connections. This table along with a wiring drawing is the tool you will see in this book and other example projects on the Internet or elsewhere. Thus, learning how to read maps and wiring drawings is a skill you should have to make your project successful.

Table 6-2 shows the connections needed for this project. Traditionally, we use black for ground (negative) and red for power (positive) at a minimum, but you can use whatever color wires you want. We will start with physical pin 40 and work our way down to the lowest number pin used. As you will see in the drawing, this is working clockwise.

Table 6-2. *Connections for the MicroPython Clock*

Physical Pin	GPIO Num/Function	Breakout Board	Pin Label
40	VBUS	RTC	VCC
37	GND	RTC	GND
37	GND	OLED	GND
26	GP20	OLED	RST
25	GP19	OLED	DATA
24	GP18	OLED	CLK
22	GP17	OLED	D/C
21	GP16	OLED	CS
10	GP9	RTC	SCL
9	GP8	RTC	SDA

Wow, that's a lot of connections! As we saw in Chapter 5, a breadboard allows us to plug our components in and use jumper wires to make the connections. This simplifies wiring the project and allows you to move things around if you need to make more room.

When plugging in components, always make sure the pins are mounted parallel to the center channel. Recall breadboards have the pins wired together in rows perpendicular to the center channel. This allows you to make more than one connection to the component (or pin on the board).

Caution   Never plug or unplug jumper wires when the project is powered on.

Finally, always make sure you wire your project, carefully double-checking all the connections – especially power, ground, and any pins used for signaling (will be set to "high" or "on") such as those pins used for SPI interfaces. Most importantly, never plug or unplug jumper wires when the project (or your board) is powered on. This will very likely damage your board or components.

For this project, I mounted the Pico on the left side of the breadboard with the OLED in the center above the center channel and the RTC module on the right below the channel. Notice the RTC board uses a different power connection. The OLED board uses 3.3V and the RTC board 5V. Always check the power requirements of your components before powering on the project. Double-check and triple-check your connections.

Figure 6-3 shows the wiring drawing for the MicroPython clock project.

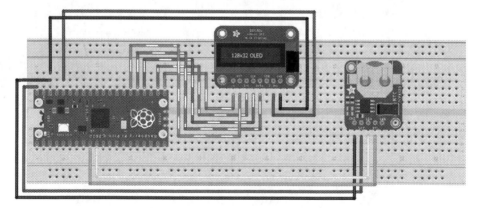

Figure 6-3. *Wiring the clock project (full-sized breadboard)*

If you do not have a full-sized breadboard, you can use two of the more popular half-sized breadboards and clip them together. If you look closely, you will see nubs on two sides and corresponding notches on the other.

Note   While you can use a half-sized breadboard for most of the projects in this book, a full-sized breadboard is a bit easier to use. The choice is mainly about being able to connect the wires without the breakout boards too closely placed.

If you'd rather use a single half-sized breadboard, you can, but the wiring will get a bit complex as shown in Figure 6-4.

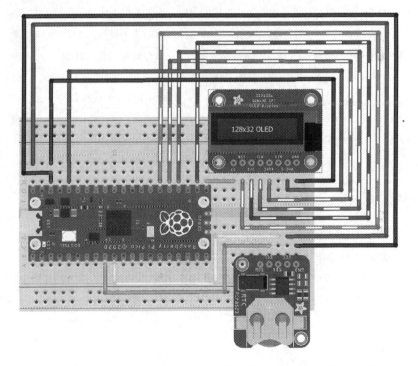

Figure 6-4. *Wiring the clock project (half-sized breadboard)*

Caution   Always double- and triple-check your connections, especially all power and ground connections. Be sure to examine the power connections to ensure the correct power (3V or 5V) is being connected to the components correctly. Connecting the wrong voltage can damage the component.

If you chose a different RTC board than the one shown in the drawing, be sure to adjust the connections as needed. For example, the SparkFun DS1307 breakout board has the pins in a different order, so don't go by this drawing alone – especially if you use alternative components!

Once again, always make sure to double-check your connections before powering the board on. Now, let's talk about the code we need to write. Don't power on your board just yet – there is a fair amount of discussion needed before we're ready to test the project.

Write the Code

Now it's time to write the code for our project. Since we are working with several new components, I will introduce the code for each in turn. The code isn't overly complicated but may not be as clear as some of the code from previous projects. Let's begin with a look at the design of the project.

Design

Once you have the hardware sorted out and how to connect the components to your board, it is time to start designing the code. Fortunately, this project is small enough to make the design simple. In short, we want to display the time on our OLED once every second. Thus, the "work" of the code is to read the date and time from the RTC and then display it on the OLED. The following lists the steps that summarize how to design and implement the code for this project or any project for that matter:

- *Libraries*: We will need to select and import libraries for the RTC and OLED.

- *Setup*: We will need to set up the interfaces for I2C and SPI.

- *Initialize*: We will need to initialize object instances for the classes in the libraries.

- *New functions*: We will write some helper functions to better organize the code.

- *Core code*: We will write the core code for the project.

- *Test the breakout boards*: We will take an extra step to test each breakout board separately before trying to execute the entire code.

- *Copy to the Pico*: Name the file main.py and copy the file to the Pico.

These elements are what we will use for most of the projects in this book, and, indeed, it is a good pattern to follow for all your MicroPython projects. The new function step allows us to wrap the operational portion of the code in a separate function to make it easy to call from the main function. We'll see more about this later when we execute and test the project.

Now that we know how the project code will be implemented, let's review the libraries needed.

Libraries Needed

Recall from earlier we need two libraries: one for the OLED display and another for the RTC. The library for the OLED display is found at `https://github.com/adafruit/micropython-adafruit-ssd1306`, and the library for the RTC can be found at `https://github.com/adafruit/Adafruit-uRTC`.

Go ahead and download both libraries now. You should be able to go to the sites and click the *Clone* or *Download* link and then the *Download Zip* button to download the files to your PC. Then, open the location of the downloaded files and unzip them. You should find the following files:

- `ssd1306.py`: The OLED display library

- `urtc.py`: The RTC library

Ordinarily, we would create a new folder for each project we want to place on our Pico, but since we will be making this project run on the Pico when it is booted (powered on), the main code file will have to be named `main.py` and placed in the root folder. The Pico will automatically execute this file on boot unless you connect it to your PC.

However, we will be creating a new folder to place the library files (drivers) for the breakout boards. Once you have your Pico connected, create a new folder named `project1` in the root folder by right-clicking the Pico in Thonny and selecting `New directory...`. Then, double-click the `project1` folder on the Pico and upload the library files to that folder. You should see a folder structure and file list similar to Figure 6-5.

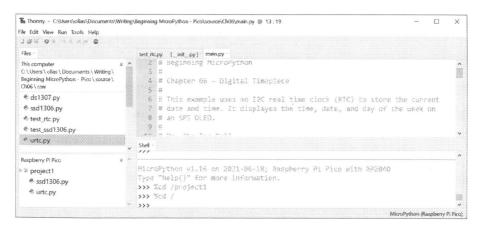

Figure 6-5. *New project folder and files (Thonny)*

Now that we have the libraries copied, let's look at the code we will need to write.

Planning the Code

Now that we have our design and have downloaded and modified the libraries, we can begin writing the code. Rather than show you a long listing and say, "comprehend or perish," let's walk through all the parts of the code first so that we understand each part. As we walk through the code, feel free to test the parts yourself, but if you prefer to wait until the end to test the code, you can. Some of this will be familiar and perhaps rudimentary to those who've worked the examples so far in this book, but a little refresher never hurts. Let's begin with a look at the import section.

Imports

The import section for the project comes before all other statements but after the comment block at the top of the file. You should also include some level of documentation at the top of the file to explain what the code does. You don't have to write a lengthy tutorial – just a short statement or so that describes the program including your name and other information. This is important if you want to share your code with others and if you ever go back to the code later to reuse it.

If you want to type in the code as we go along, you can open a new file named main.py on your PC with Thonny or your favorite code (or text) editor. We will copy the file to the Pico in a later step.

The following shows the imports for this project.

```
# Import libraries
from project1.urtc import DS1307
from project1.ssd1306 import SSD1306_SPI
from utime import sleep
from machine import SPI, Pin, SoftI2C
```

Notice we specified project1 in the first two imports because we placed these libraries (drivers) in the project1 folder. The main.py file will be copied to the root of the Pico filesystem. Also, we use the SoftI2C library instead of I2C because the RTC library doesn't work well with the I2C library. Recall, we discussed these differences in Chapter 5.

Setup

Next, we need to set up the interfaces for I2C and SPI for use in the RTC and ssd1306 libraries. That is, the classes in those libraries need object instances of the interfaces passed to the constructor. The code we will use is like the code we saw in previous examples. The following shows the interface setup code:

```
sda = Pin(8)
scl = Pin(9)
# Software I2C (bit-banging) for the RTC
i2c = SoftI2C(sda=sda, scl=scl, freq=100000)
...
# SPI for the OLED
spi = SPI(0, 100000, mosi=Pin(19), sck=Pin(18))
```

Notice we use different parameters for the SPI, and we specify pins for the I2C. You can use other pins if you'd like, but just remember to use the correct pins when you wire the components together.

Initialize

Next, we initialize object instances for the classes in the libraries. This is the point where you need to read the documentation for each library to understand what is needed to initialize the objects. For the ssd1306 library, the class constructor requires the number of pixels (the resolution is the number of pixels in rows and columns) for the display, the interface instance (SPI from the last section), and the pins we will use for the D/C, RST, and CS pins. For the RTC library, we need only pass in an interface instance (SoftI2C from the last section). The following shows how to do both steps:

```
# Initialize class instance variables for RTC, OLED
rtc = DS1307(i2c)
#start_datetime = (2021, 08, 12, 5, 14, 54, 22)
#rtc.datetime(start_datetime)
oled = SSD1306_SPI(128, 32, spi, dc=Pin(17), res=Pin(20),
cs=Pin(16))
```

Notice there are some commented out lines in there. When we first use the RTC or when we replace the battery, we must initialize the date and time. We can use the library features to do this. In this case, we simply call the datetime() function for the RTC instance passing in a tuple containing the new start date and time – the order of the tuple elements is shown in the following. Once set, we do not need to run it again. In fact, running it again will reset the RTC, and we don't need to do that. Thus, we leave this code commented out for normal operation and uncomment it when we need to reset the RTC. When you run your project for the first time, uncomment this code supplying the correct current date and time but later comment it out.

New Helper Functions

Now that all the setup and initialization code are figured out, we can create a few helper functions to allow us to organize the code.

Recall we want the project to read the date and time from the RTC and display it on the OLED once every second. Thus, we expect to see some sort of loop that performs these two steps. However, we must again refer to the library documentation where we find that the RTC returns data as a tuple (year, month, day, weekday, hour, minute, second, millisecond). This means we must format the date and time to make it easier for humans to read and to fit on the small OLED screen. This is a perfect candidate for a helper function.

Let's create a function named write_time() that takes an instance of the OLED display and the RTC and then read the date and time with the datetime() function (with no parameters) and print it to the OLED screen using the text() function, which takes a starting column (called the X position in the documentation) and row (Y position) for the location on the screen to print the message when the show() function is called. This is the essence of the project. Placing it in a separate function allows you to isolate the behavior and make it easier to maintain or modify the code – because the "core" is in one place:

```
# Display the date and time
def write_time(oled, rtc):
    # Get datetime
    dt = rtc.datetime()
    # Print the date
    oled.text("Date: {0:02}/{1:02}/{2:04}".format(dt[1], dt[2],
    dt[0]), 0, 0)
    # Print the time
    oled.text("Time: {0:02}:{1:02}:{2:02}".format(dt[4], dt[5],
    dt[6]), 0, 10)
    # Print the day of the week
    oled.text("Day:  {0}".format(get_weekday(dt[3])), 0, 20)
    # Update the OLED
    oled.show()
```

Notice we use the text() function and the format() function to take the data from the RTC and format it in an expected format that most clocks use: HH:MM::SS and MM/DD/YYYY. Notice there is an additional function here named get_weekday(). This function takes the number of the day of the week as returned from the RTC and returns a string for the name of the day. The following shows the code for this function:

```
# Return a string to print the day of the week
def get_weekday(day):
    if day == 1: return "Sunday"
    elif day == 2: return "Monday"
    elif day == 3: return "Tuesday"
    elif day == 4: return "Wednesday"
    elif day == 5: return "Thursday"
    elif day == 6: return "Friday"
    else: return "Saturday"
```

There is one more function added – a function to clear the screen. This function simply blanks the screen to allow us to overwrite the screen with new data. Normally, this is not needed, but it is a good practice to clear the screen in case the library doesn't do it for you. In this case, it does now. This function is named `clear_screen()` and is shown in the following. It simply uses the `fill()` and `show()` functions from the ssd1306 library. Passing in 0 for the `fill()` function tells the library to fill the screen with no data (blank or off):

```
# Clear the screen
def clear_screen(oled):
    oled.fill(0)
    oled.show()
```

Core Code

Now we are ready to code the new `main()` function for the project. We have our helper functions developed, so we need only call them and wait for a second on each pass. We will use a `main()` function so that when the script is executed (the name check will fail if the code is imported from another script), the `main()` function is called. We do this with the following code:

```
if __name__ == '__main__':
    try:
        main()
    except (KeyboardInterrupt, SystemExit) as err:
        print("\nbye!")
        sys.exit(0)
```

We use a try...except block so that we can capture the keyboard interrupt (*CTRL+C*) so that we can stop it. This construct is typical of how we would write scripts that are intended to be executed.

Recall, when a Python script is loaded (read), each line of code is executed. If we place all of our code in functions (or a class), we need some way to start execution in a controlled manner. The preceding code accomplishes this task, and we will use it in all of our projects. It does not matter what you call the function for the core code, but main is a common practice.

Next, we can create the main() function. The following shows the function with the setup and initialization code discussed earlier:

```
def main():
    sda = Pin(8)
    scl = Pin(9)
    # Software I2C (bit-banging) for the RTC
    i2c = SoftI2C(sda=sda,scl=scl,freq=100000)
    # SPI for the OLED
    spi = SPI(0, 100000, mosi=Pin(19), sck=Pin(18))
    # Initialize class instance variables for RTC, OLED
    rtc = DS1307(i2c)
    #start_datetime = (2021,08,12,5,14,54,22)
    #rtc.datetime(start_datetime)
    oled = SSD1306_SPI(128, 32, spi, dc=Pin(17), res=Pin(20),
      cs=Pin(16))
```

```
for i in range(10):
    clear_screen(oled)
    write_time(oled, rtc)
    sleep(1)
```

Notice how "clean" this function is – we can see only three statements: clear the screen, show the time, and wait for one second.

Let's put this code together with the import section and the helper functions. Listing 6-1 shows the complete code for the main.py file.

Listing 6-1. Completed Code for the MicroPython Clock (main.py)

```
#
# Beginning MicroPython
#
# Chapter 06 - Digital Timepiece
#
# This example uses an I2C real time clock (RTC) to store
the current
# date and time. It displays the time, date, and day of
the week on
# an SPI OLED.
#
# Dr. Charles Bell
#
# Import libraries
from project1.urtc import DS1307
from project1.ssd1306 import SSD1306_SPI
from utime import sleep
from machine import SPI, Pin, SoftI2C

# Return a string to print the day of the week
def get_weekday(day):
```

```
    if day == 1: return "Sunday"
    elif day == 2: return "Monday"
    elif day == 3: return "Tuesday"
    elif day == 4: return "Wednesday"
    elif day == 5: return "Thursday"
    elif day == 6: return "Friday"
    else: return "Saturday"

# Display the date and time
def write_time(oled, rtc):
    # Get datetime
    dt = rtc.datetime()
    # Print the date
    oled.text("Date: {0:02}/{1:02}/{2:04}".format(dt[1], dt[2],
    dt[0]), 0, 0)
    # Print the time
    oled.text("Time: {0:02}:{1:02}:{2:02}".format(dt[4], dt[5],
    dt[6]), 0, 10)
    # Print the day of the week
    oled.text("Day:  {0}".format(get_weekday(dt[3])), 0, 20)
    # Update the OLED
    oled.show()

# Clear the screen
def clear_screen(oled):
    oled.fill(0)
    oled.show()

def main():
    sda = Pin(8)
    scl = Pin(9)
    # Software I2C (bit-banging) for the RTC
    i2c = SoftI2C(sda=sda,scl=scl,freq=100000)
    # SPI for the OLED
```

```
    spi = SPI(0, 100000, mosi=Pin(19), sck=Pin(18))
    # Initialize class instance variables for RTC, OLED
    rtc = DS1307(i2c)
    #start_datetime = (2021,08,12,5,14,54,22)
    #rtc.datetime(start_datetime)
    oled = SSD1306_SPI(128, 32, spi, dc=Pin(17), res=Pin(20),
      cs=Pin(16))
    for i in range(10):
        clear_screen(oled)
        write_time(oled, rtc)
        sleep(1)

if __name__ == '__main__':
    try:
        main()
    except (KeyboardInterrupt, SystemExit) as err:
        print("\nbye!")
        sys.exit(0)
```

Take some time to read through the code so you can see how it is organized. We will use this as a template in future projects. You can save it to your PC, but don't execute it on the Pico yet because we need to test the code for the breakout boards.

Test the Breakout Boards

Now that we have planned the code and know how to code each of the parts, we have one more thing to do – test the breakout boards separately. We do this by wiring one breakout board and testing it, then powering off and unwiring that breakout board, and then wiring the other breakout board and testing it.

This is a good practice to get into the habit of doing for one primary reason. You will save yourself a lot of grief by testing the individual parts of the project – especially the hardware – one at a time. This not only makes it easier to narrow down any issues, but it also ensures you can identify the source of the problem. That is, if you plugged all the hardware in and wired everything and wrote the code, deployed it, then powered it on, and nothing works, how do you know which part is to blame? This is one of my mantras: build and test one piece at a time.

Tip   Testing code one part at a time is a familiar pattern to me, and it is highly recommended you adopt the process yourself, that is, coding a part of the project at a time and testing each individually.

For this project, there are two parts – the RTC and the OLED. Let's see how to test them individually. The code presented is intended to be run via a REPL console via Thonny.

Test the RTC Breakout Board

To test the RTC, use the following code. Listing 6-2 is a condensed form of the code we saw in Listing 6-1 with only the bare minimum code added. You can name this file test_rtc.py if you'd like to save it, but we will execute the code via the REPL console.

Listing 6-2. Test Code for the RTC Breakout Board (test_rtc.py)

```
from project1.urtc import DS1307
from utime import sleep
from machine import Pin, SoftI2C

sda = Pin(8)
scl = Pin(9)
i2c = SoftI2C(sda=sda,scl=scl,freq=100000)
rtc = DS1307(i2c)
```

```
start_datetime = (2021,08,16,8,11,0,0)
rtc.datetime(start_datetime)
for i in range(0,10):
    # Get datetime
    dt = rtc.datetime()
    print("\nTest:", i+1)
    # Print the date
    print("Date: {0:02}/{1:02}/{2:04}".format(dt[1],
    dt[2], dt[0]))
    # Print the time
    print("Time: {0:02}:{1:02}:{2:02}".format(dt[4],
    dt[5], dt[6]))
    sleep(3)
```

Notice we set the date and time in this test. When you run this for yourself, you should change the date and time tuple to include the current date and time when you run the test. What you should see in the REPL console is a tuple representing the date and time. It should be the same as what you set since the code will execute much less than a second from the time you set it to the time you query the RTC. Go ahead and reenter that last statement several times to ensure the time changes as you'd expect. That is, wait a few seconds and try it again – several seconds should have elapsed. Listing 6-3 shows what the output should look like for a successful test.

Listing 6-3. Test RTC Output

```
Test: 1
Date: 08/16/2021
Time: 11:00:00

Test: 2
Date: 08/16/2021
```

Time: 11:00:03

Test: 3
Date: 08/16/2021
Time: 11:00:06

Test: 4
Date: 08/16/2021
Time: 11:00:09

Test: 5
Date: 08/16/2021
Time: 11:00:12

Test: 6
Date: 08/16/2021
Time: 11:00:15

Test: 7
Date: 08/16/2021
Time: 11:00:18

Test: 8
Date: 08/16/2021
Time: 11:00:21

Test: 9
Date: 08/16/2021
Time: 11:00:24

Test: 10
Date: 08/16/2021
Time: 11:00:27

If any of the statements fail, be sure to check your wiring and look for any typos. Also, ensure you are using the correct, modified version of the libraries (and that you have copied them to the board).

Test the OLED Breakout Board

To test the OLED, use the following code. Listing 6-4 is a condensed form of the code we saw in Listing 6-1 with only the bare minimum code added. You can name this file test_oled.py if you'd like to save it, but we will execute the code via the REPL console.

Listing 6-4. Test Code for the OLED Breakout Board (test_oled.py)

```
from project1.ssd1306 import SSD1306_SPI
from machine import Pin, SPI
from utime import sleep_ms

spi = SPI(0, 100000, mosi=Pin(19), sck=Pin(18))
oled = SSD1306_SPI(128, 32, spi, dc=Pin(17), res=Pin(20),
cs=Pin(16))
for i in range(40):
    for j in range(32):
        oled.fill(0)
        oled.show()
        oled.text("HELLO WORLD", i, j)
        oled.show()
        sleep_ms(100)
```

When you run this code, you should see the screen blank (it should be blank from the start), then display the hello message in different places in the range of the OLED screen, and may "scroll" off the screen (can you spot why?).

If you do not see any output, power off your board, check all the connections, and verify the correct pins are used and that you have the correct modified version of the library copied to your board.

Tip   The OLED breakout boards from Adafruit (and presumably others) come with a protective cover over the lens. You can and should leave that in place to ensure the lens does not get damaged. Plus, the OLED is bright enough to see through the protective cover.

OK, now we're ready to execute and test the completed project.

Execute

We are finally at the point where we can copy all the files to our board and execute the project code. There are several recommended steps in this process as shown in the following. You should follow this process each time you want to deploy and test a project:

1. Double-check all hardware connections (wiring).

2. Connect your Pico to your PC.

3. Copy the libraries and code file to the board.

4. Test the code, fix any issues found, and recopy the file(s) if needed.

5. Disconnect and reconnect the board.

The first step cannot be overstated. Always check your wiring connections every time before you power on the board. This is in case curious hands have wandered by and "examined" your project or you've moved it, or some other event has occurred to unplug wires. It never hurts to be extra careful.

Next, we connect the Pico to our PC to power on the board and check for any issues. Yes, this is the smoke test! Simply make sure all LEDs that are supposed to illuminate do (like those on the board) and that things that should not be on are off. For example, if you see a solid bar on the OLED when you power it on, that's not a good sign. If ever in doubt, disconnect the Pico and check your connections. If things still aren't right, disconnect everything and test your board. Sometimes, a damaged component can cause strange behavior.

Next, we copy all the libraries and code we want to use to the board. Recall, we copy the libraries for the RTC and OLED to a folder on the Pico named `project1` and copy the `main.py` file to the root folder on the Pico.

Caution   Be sure to uncomment out the lines to initialize the RTC on your first execution. You can comment them out immediately after your test (be sure to do so!).

At this point, the code isn't running, but we can execute it via Thonny. Simply click the Run button and watch your code run! If everything is connected correctly, and the code is correct, you will see the date and time appear on the OLED. You should see something like Figure 6-6, which shows the project running in all its glory.

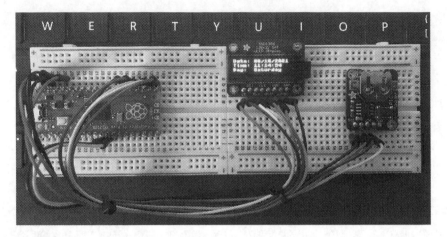

Figure 6-6. *A MicroPython clock!*

Notice in the figure I am using two half-sized breadboards connected together, which is the same size as a full-sized breadboard. Notice all of the wiring. If we used a single half-sized breadboard, the wiring would be a snaggle that could obscure the OLED. Ever the neat freak, I've zip-tied the wiring so that it is out of the way.

If something doesn't work, go back and check your code. If you left the two lines of code to initialize the RTC uncommented, you may see the same date and time appear each time you run the code. Be sure to comment those out on subsequent executions. Or, if you forgot to uncomment out those lines, you may see some strange date and time values.

It is at this point that you should be basking in the wonder of your first successful MicroPython hardware project. Take some time to bask in your delight of a job well done.

However, we're not done. There's one more step. Disconnect your Pico and exit Thonny and then reconnect it to your PC to power it on again. If the date and time show up after a few seconds, you've done it! You have successfully created a project you can package and run anywhere you want, and so long as the coin cell battery has a charge, it won't lose time.

Taking It Further

This project has a lot of potential for embellishment. If you liked the project, you should consider taking time to explore some embellishments. Here are a few you may want to consider. Some are easy and some may be a challenge:

- Use a different RTC.

- Calculate AM/PM and display it.

- Use a larger display and display the Julian date.

- Use a light sensor to dim the display in direct sunlight.

- Add a speaker and implement an alarm feature (hint: some RTCs have this feature).

- Format the date and time using different world standards such as YYYY/MM/DD.

Of course, if you want to press on to the next project, you're welcome to do so, but take some time to explore these potential embellishments – it will be a good practice.

- DS1307 chip

- Coin cell battery breakout board

- 3V coin cell battery

- 32.768kHz crystal

- (2) 1K resistor

If you're thinking this project is rudimentary now that we have solved the problems with the libraries, consider this: most sensor-based projects and indeed most projects that generate data that must be associated with a date and time when the events are sampled. Thus, using an RTC to read the date and time will be a consideration for many IoT projects.

BUILDING YOUR OWN RTC MODULE

If you're like me and like to tinker, you can build your own RTC module using an RTC DS1307 chip, two resistors, a crystal, and a coin cell battery breakout board. You can find these components at most online electronics stores such as Adafruit (www.adafruit.com), SparkFun (www.sparkfun.com), and Mouser (www.mouser.com). The component list is as follows:

That's it! The following shows how to connect the components on a breadboard.

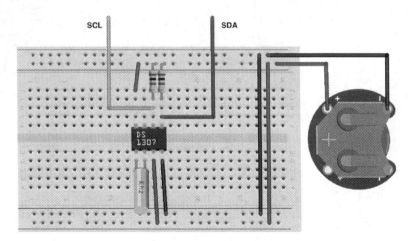

See www.learningaboutelectronics.com/Articles/DS1307-real-time-clock-RTC-circuit.php for an example walk-through for assembling this side project.

If you plan to build a lot of projects that use an RTC, buying these components in bulk and wiring up your own RTC 1307 module may be more cost-effective. Plus, it ups the cool factor of your kit.

Summary

Working with hardware such as breakout boards and the libraries we need to talk to them over specialized interfaces such as I2C and SPI can be a challenge. Sometimes, like we saw in this chapter, you need the Soft version of the SPI or I2C libraries. The reason for this is the growing array of boards that vendors are creating specialized versions of the MicroPython firmware that may not work 100% with the Pico.

The trick then is understanding why the changes are necessary and taking the time to make the changes yourself. It is so easy to just give up when something doesn't work – don't do that! Take your time and understand the problem and then solve it systematically.

In this chapter, we saw a detailed walk-through of a MicroPython clock. We used an OLED display to display time we read from an RTC. Along the way, we learned how to plan our projects, make hardware connections, and write code for use in deploying on our Pico.

In the next chapter, we will explore a project that uses more low-level hardware in the form of discrete components such as LEDs, resistors, and buttons. These are the building blocks you will need to form more complex solutions.

CHAPTER 7

Project: Pedestrian Crossing

Now that we've had a tutorial of how to design, wire, and implement a MicroPython project, let's now look at a more advanced project. In this case, we will use some very basic components to learn further how to work with hardware. The hardware of choice for this project will be LEDs, resistors, and a button. A button is the most basic of sensors. That is, when the button is pressed, we can make our MicroPython code respond to that action.

Working with LEDs is perhaps more of a "Hello, World!" style project for hardware because turning LEDs on and off is easy, and except for figuring out what size of current limiting resistor is needed, wiring LEDs is also easy.

However, to make it more interesting and a bit of a challenge, we will be implementing a simulation. More specifically, we will implement a traffic light and a pedestrian walk button. The walk button is a button pedestrians can use to trigger the traffic signal to change and stop traffic so they can cross the street.

Simulation projects can be a lot of fun because we already have an idea of how it should work. For example, unless you've lived in a very rural area, you most likely have encountered a traffic signal at an intersection that included walk/don't walk signs with a button. If you live in the city, you will have encountered these in various configurations. When a pedestrian

© Charles Bell 2022
C. Bell, *Beginning MicroPython with the Raspberry Pi Pico*, Maker Innovations Series, https://doi.org/10.1007/978-1-4842-8135-2_7

(or bicyclist) presses the walk button, the traffic lights all cycle to red and the walk sign is illuminated. After some time (30 seconds or so), the walk sign flashes, and then about 15 seconds later, the walk signal cycles to don't walk and the traffic signals resume their normal cycle.

Note   The word "cycle" refers to a set of states that are linear in action. Thus, cycle refers to the changing of one state to another.

Overview

In this chapter, we will implement a traffic signal with a pedestrian walk button. This project works with LEDs, which allows us to see the state of our code as it executes. For the traffic light (also called a stoplight), we will use a red, yellow, and green LED to match the same colored lights on the traffic light. We will also use a red and yellow LED to correspond to the don't walk (red) and walk (yellow) lights.

We will use a pushbutton (also called a momentary button) because it triggers (is on) only when pushed. When released, it is no longer triggered (is off). Trigger is the word used to describe the state of the button where triggered means the connections from one side of the button to another are connected (on). A button that remains triggered (latched) is called a latching button, which typically must be pressed again to turn off.

We will simulate the traffic light and walk signal by first turning on only the green traffic light LED and the red walk LED signal. This is the normal state we will use. When the button is pressed, the traffic light will cycle to yellow for a few seconds and then cycle to red. After a few seconds, the walk signal will cycle to yellow and after a few seconds will begin flashing. After a few more seconds, the walk signal will cycle back to red and the traffic light to green.

Now let's see what components are needed for this project, and then we will see how to wire everything together.

Required Components

Table 7-1 lists the components you will need in addition to your Pico and USB cable. Links to vendors are provided should you want to purchase the components. I include both value packages and single unit prices where available.

Table 7-1. *Required Components*

Component	Qty	Description	Cost	Links
Red LED	2	Pack of 25	$4.00	www.adafruit.com/product/299
		Single	$0.35	www.sparkfun.com/products/9590
Yellow LED	2	Pack of 25	$4.95	www.adafruit.com/product/2700
		Single	$0.35	www.sparkfun.com/products/9594
Green LED	1	Pack of 25	$4.00	www.adafruit.com/product/298
		Single	$0.35	www.sparkfun.com/products/9592
220 or 330 Ohm resistors	5	Variety Kit	$7.95	www.sparkfun.com/products/10969
		Pack of 25	$0.75	www.adafruit.com/product/2780

(continued)

Table 7-1. (*continued*)

Component	Qty	Description	Cost	Links
Button	1	Momentary button, breadboard friendly (pack)	$2.50	www.adafruit.com/ product/1119
		Single	$0.50	www.sparkfun.com/ products/9190
Breadboard	1	Prototyping board, full-sized	$5.95	www.sparkfun.com/ products/12615
			$5.95	www.adafruit.com/ product/239
Jumper wires	11	M/M jumper wires, 7" (set of 30)	$2.25	https://www.sparkfun. com/products/11026
		M/M jumper wires, 6" (set of 20)	$1.95	https://www.adafruit. com/product/11709

You can purchase the components separately from Adafruit (adafruit.com), SparkFun (sparkfun.com), or any electronics store that carries electronic components. Costs shown are estimates and do not include any shipping costs.

Some components such as the LEDs and button can be found in a beginning electronics kit like those from the Parts Pal kit from Adafruit that we saw in Chapter 5. Other vendors may have similar kits. Buying basic components like LEDs, buttons, and resistors is much cheaper when bought in a kit.

Similarly, you can pick up a set of resistors of various sizes much cheaper than if you bought a few at a time. In fact, you most likely will find buying a small set of five or ten of each size resistor you will eventually need will be far more expensive than if you purchased a set. The set from SparkFun will provide you all the resistors you need for most projects.

Recall from Chapter 5 that LEDs require a current limiting resistor that reduces the current to safe levels for the LED. To determine what size resistor we need, we need to know several things about the LED. This data is available from the manufacturer who provides the data in the form of a data sheet or, in the case of commercially packaged products, lists the data on the package. The data we need includes the maximum voltage, the supply voltage (how many volts are coming to the LED), and the current rating of the LED.

For example, if I have an LED like the ones in the Adafruit Parts Pal, in this case a 5mm red LED, we find on Adafruit's website (`www.adafruit.com/products/297`) that the LED operates at 1.8–2.2V and 20mA of current. Let's say we want to use this with a 5V supply voltage. We can then take these values and plug them into this formula:

```
R = (Vcc-Vf)/I
```

Using more descriptive names for the variable, we get the following:

```
Resistor = (Volts_supply - Volts_forward) / Desired_current
```

Plugging our data in, we get this result. Note that we have mA so we must use the correct decimal value (divide by 1000).

```
Resistor = (5 - 1.8) / 0.020
         = 3.2 / 0.020
         = 160
```

Thus, we need a resistor of 160 Ohms. However, there is no resistor with that rating. When this happens, we use the next size up. For example, if you have only 220 or even 330 Ohm resistors, you can use those. The result will be the LEDs will not be as bright, but having a higher resistor is much safer than using one that is too small. Too much current and an LED will burn out.

Now, let's see how to wire the components together.

Set Up the Hardware

Before we look at the wiring, let's review some tips for wiring components. The best way to wire components to your board is to use a breadboard. As we saw in Chapter 5, a breadboard allows us to plug our components in and use jumper wires to make the connections. In this project, we will use one jumper wire for ground from the Pico board to the breadboard power and ground rails (those that run along the top and bottom marked with a red line for power and blue or black for ground) and then jumpers on the breadboard to connect to the button. In fact, we will use the ground rail on one side of the breadboard to plug in one side of the LEDs.

The button works in either position so long as the pins are oriented with two legs on each side of the center trough. If you orient the button with the legs that can reach either side of the trough, it will be oriented correctly. If you get it off by 90 degrees, the button either will not work or will always be triggered. If you have any doubts, use a multimeter to test the continuity of the button connections. You should find the connections open when not pressed and closed when pressed.

The only component that is polarized is the LED (it has a positive and a negative leg). When you look at the LED, you will see one leg (pin) of the LED is longer than the other. This longer side is the positive side. We will plug the LEDs in so that the negative leg is plugged into the ground rail and the positive side is plugged into the main area of the breadboard. We then plug the resistor in to jump over the center trough connecting the resistor to the GPIO pin on the Pico. It doesn't matter which direction you plug the resistor in – they will work both directions.

Table 7-2 shows the connections needed for this project. Traditionally, we use black for ground (negative) and red for power (positive) at a minimum, but you can use whatever color wires you want. We will start with physical pin 40 and work our way down to the lowest number pin used. As you will see in the drawing, this is working clockwise.

Table 7-2. *Connections for the MicroPython Clock*

Physical Pin	GPIO Num/Function	Connection
40	VBUS	Breadboard power (top)
37	GND	Breadboard ground (bottom)
17	GP13	Resistor for red LED (stoplight)
16	GP12	Resistor for yellow LED (stoplight)
15	GP11	Resistor for green LED (stoplight)
12	GP9	Button side A (bottom)
11	GP8	Resistor for red LED (walk light)
10	GP7	Resistor for green LED (walk light)
N/A	Breadboard power (top)	Button side B (top)
N/A	Breadboard ground	All LED negative side
N/A	Resistor	All LED positive side

Wow, that's a lot of connections! As we saw in Chapter 5, a breadboard allows us to plug our components in and use jumper wires to make the connections. This simplifies wiring the project and allows you to move things around if you need to make more room.

Caution   Never plug or unplug jumper wires when the project is powered on. You risk damaging your board or the components.

Figure 7-1 shows the wiring drawing for the pedestrian crossing project.

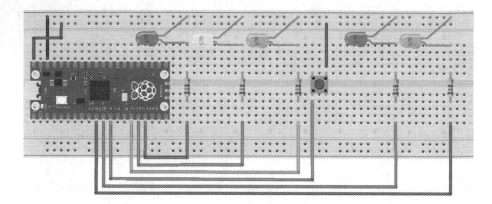

Figure 7-1. *Wiring the pedestrian crossing project (full-sized breadboard)*

Once again, always make sure to double-check your connections before powering the board on. Now, let's talk about the code we need to write. Don't power on your board just yet – there is a fair amount of discussion needed before we're ready to test the project.

Write the Code

Now it's time to write the code for our project. The code isn't overly complicated, but it is a bit longer than the examples thus far. We will see how to write code to simulate the pedestrian crosswalk button and traffic light. We will need to monitor the button and, when pressed, cycle the lights as described earlier. We also need code to initialize the LEDs, setting them to off initially. We can write functions for monitoring the button and cycling the LEDs. We will use an interrupt to tie the function for the button to the hardware so that we can avoid using a polling loop.

Imports

The imports for the project will require the Pin class from the machine library and the utime library. The following shows the imports for the project:

```
from machine import Pin
import utime
```

Setup

The setup code for this project will need to initialize the button and LED instances and then turn off all the LEDs (as a precaution) and turn on the green stoplight LED and the red walk signal LED. Listing 7-1 shows the code for setup and initialization.

Listing 7-1. Setup and Initialization of the Button and LEDs

```
# Setup the button and LEDs
stoplight_red = Pin(13, Pin.OUT)
stoplight_yellow = Pin(12, Pin.OUT)
stoplight_green = Pin(11, Pin.OUT)
button = Pin(9, Pin.IN, Pin.PULL_DOWN)
pedestrian_red = Pin(8, Pin.OUT)
pedestrian_green = Pin(7, Pin.OUT)

# Setup lists for the LEDs
stoplight = [stoplight_red, stoplight_yellow, stoplight_green]
pedestrian_signal = [pedestrian_red, pedestrian_green]

# Turn off the LEDs
for led in stoplight:
    led.off()
```

```
for led in pedestrian_signal:
    led.off()
```

```
# Start with green stoplight and red pedestrian_signal
stoplight[2].on()
pedestrian_signal[0].on()
```

One thing to notice is how the button is initialized. This is a Pin object instance that is set up as an input (read), and the pull-up resistors are turned on. This allows the board to detect when the button is pressed because the value of the pin will be a positive value when the connection is made (the button is pressed).

Notice also I create a list that contains the LEDs for the stoplight and walk signal (named pedestrian_signal in the code). This is mostly for demonstration so you can see how to manage lists of class objects. As you can see, it makes it easier to call the same function for all the objects in the list using a loop. Take note of this technique as you will need it from time to time in other projects.

Functions

There are two functions needed for this part of the project. First, we need a function to cycle through the lights. Second, we need a function to monitor the button press. Let's look at the cycle light function.

We will name the cycle light function cycle_lights(). Recall we need to control how the lights change state. We do this with a specific cycle as described earlier. To recap, we call this function when we want to simulate changing the stoplight when the walk request button is pressed. Thus, this function will be called from the code for the button. Listing 7-2 shows the code for the cycle_lights() button. As you will see, the code is rather straightforward. The only tricky part may be the loop used to flash the yellow walk LED. Be sure to read through it so that you understand how it works.

Listing 7-2. The cycle_lights() Function

```python
# We need a method to cycle the stoplight and pedestrian_signal
#
# We toggle from green to yellow for 2 seconds
# then red for 20 seconds.
def cycle_lights():
    # Go yellow.
    stoplight[2].off()
    stoplight[1].on()
    # Wait 2 seconds
    utime.sleep(2)
    # Go red and turn on walk light
    stoplight[1].off()
    stoplight[0].on()
    utime.sleep_ms(500)  # Give the pedestrian a chance
                          to see it
    pedestrian_signal[0].off()
    pedestrian_signal[1].on()
    # After 10 seconds, start blinking the walk light
    utime.sleep(1)
    for i in range(0,10):
        pedestrian_signal[1].off()
        utime.sleep_ms(500)
        pedestrian_signal[1].on()
        utime.sleep_ms(500)

    # Stop=green, walk=red
    pedestrian_signal[1].off()
    pedestrian_signal[0].on()
    utime.sleep_ms(500)  # Give the pedestrian a chance
                          to see it
```

```
stoplight[0].off()
stoplight[2].on()
```

We will name the button function button_pressed(). This function is used as a callback for the button press interrupt. Technically, we tell MicroPython to associate this method with the pin interrupt, but we will see that in a moment. However, there is another element to this function that requires explanation.

When we use a component like a button and the user (you) presses the button, the contacts in the button do not go from an off state to an on state instantaneously. There is a very small period where the value read is erratic. Thus, we cannot simply say "when the pin goes high" because the value read on the pin may "bounce" from low to high (or high to low) rapidly. This is called bouncing. We can overcome this artificially with code (as well as other techniques) – called debouncing.

In this case, we can check the value of the pin (button) over time and only "trigger" the button press if and only if the value remains stable during that time. The code for debouncing the pin is shown in Listing 7-3. Notice in the loop we wait for a value of 50. This is 50 milliseconds. If the trigger is long enough, we call the cycle_lights() function.

Listing 7-3. The button_pressed() Function

```
# Create callback for the button
def button_pressed(line):
    cur_value = button.value()
    active = 0
    while (active < 50):
        if button.value() != cur_value:
            active += 1
        else:
            active = 0
        utime.sleep_ms(1)
```

```
        print("")
    if active:
        cycle_lights()
    else:
        print("False press")
```

Tip   For more information about debouncing and the techniques available to avoid it, see www.eng.utah.edu/~cs5780/ debouncing.pdf.

Finally, we need to set up the button to call the button_pressed() function when the board detects the interrupt. The following sets the callback function using the interrupt setting for the button pin:

```
# Create an interrupt for the button
button.irq(trigger=Pin.IRQ_RISING, handler=button_pressed)
```

Now we're all set to test the code. Go ahead and open a new file named pedestrian_crossing.py and enter the preceding code. Listing 7-4 shows the complete code for the project.

Listing 7-4. Pedestrian Crossing Simulation Code

```
#
# Beginning MicroPython
#
# Chapter 07 - Pedestrian Crossing
#
# This example implements a Pedestrian Crossing Simulator
# controlling LEDs and button as input
#
# Dr. Charles Bell
#
```

```python
# Import libraries
from machine import Pin
import utime

# Setup the button and LEDs
stoplight_red = Pin(13, Pin.OUT)
stoplight_yellow = Pin(12, Pin.OUT)
stoplight_green = Pin(11, Pin.OUT)
button = Pin(9, Pin.IN, Pin.PULL_DOWN)
pedestrian_red = Pin(8, Pin.OUT)
pedestrian_green = Pin(7, Pin.OUT)

# Setup lists for the LEDs
stoplight = [stoplight_red, stoplight_yellow, stoplight_green]
pedestrian_signal = [pedestrian_red, pedestrian_green]

# Turn off the LEDs
for led in stoplight:
    led.off()
for led in pedestrian_signal:
    led.off()

# Start with green stoplight and red pedestrian_signal
stoplight[2].on()
pedestrian_signal[0].on()

# We need a method to cycle the stoplight and pedestrian_signal
#
# We toggle from green to yellow for 2 seconds
# then red for 20 seconds.
def cycle_lights():
    # Go yellow.
    stoplight[2].off()
    stoplight[1].on()
```

```python
    # Wait 2 seconds
    utime.sleep(2)
    # Go red and turn on walk light
    stoplight[1].off()
    stoplight[0].on()
    utime.sleep_ms(500)  # Give the pedestrian a chance
                          to see it
    pedestrian_signal[0].off()
    pedestrian_signal[1].on()
    # After 10 seconds, start blinking the walk light
    utime.sleep(1)
    for i in range(0,10):
        pedestrian_signal[1].off()
        utime.sleep_ms(500)
        pedestrian_signal[1].on()
        utime.sleep_ms(500)

    # Stop=green, walk=red
    pedestrian_signal[1].off()
    pedestrian_signal[0].on()
    utime.sleep_ms(500)  # Give the pedestrian a chance
                          to see it
    stoplight[0].off()
    stoplight[2].on()

# Create callback for the button
def button_pressed(line):
    cur_value = button.value()
    active = 0
    while (active < 50):
        if button.value() != cur_value:
            active += 1
```

```
        else:
            active = 0
        utime.sleep_ms(1)
        print("")
    if active:
        cycle_lights()
    else:
        print("False press")

# Create an interrupt for the button
button.irq(trigger=Pin.IRQ_RISING, handler=button_pressed)
```

OK, now we're ready to execute the project.

Execute

We are finally at the point where we can copy all the files to our board and execute the project code. Once again, be sure to check all hardware connections before connecting the Pico to your PC. Then, copy the code files to your Pico and execute the script. You can create a directory on your Pico to place the code if you'd like to keep things tidy. For example, you can create a directory named project2 and place the files there as shown in Figure 7-2.

Figure 7-2. Pedestrian crossing files on the Pico

Once you've downloaded the file (`pedestrian_crossing.py`) to your Pico, simply click the *Run* button and watch your code run! If everything is connected correctly, and the code is correct, you will see the green LED for the stoplight illuminated and the red LED for the pedestrian cross walk illuminated.

You can then press the button and watch the stoplight change from green to yellow and then red. The cross walk will then change from red to green and start flashing. When the timer expires, the cross walk will change from green to red and the stoplight from red to green. If something doesn't work, go back and check your code.

Taking It Further

This project shows excellent prospects for reusing the techniques in other projects. This is especially true since we have now learned how to use analog devices (LEDs). You should now consider taking time to explore some embellishments. Here are a few you may want to consider. Some are easy and some may be a challenge or require more research and more complex coding:

- Use NeoPixels (`www.adafruit.com/category/168`) instead of LEDs. These are RGB LEDs, so you need only two – one for the stoplight and one for the walk light. See `https://github.com/JanBednarik/micropython-ws2812` for more information and examples.

- Use OLED from the last project in place of the LEDs for the walk sign to show "WALK" or "DON'T WALK."

- Add another stoplight to complete the simulation for a pedestrian crossing.

- Add three more stoplights and extend the simulation to include controlling stoplights in two directions. By this point, you will have a lot of wires in your breadboard, so you may need to use a second breadboard to keep all of the wiring tidy.

- Once you have four stoplights working, add a second pedestrian crossing for the other intersection.

Of course, if you want to press on to the next project, you're welcome to do so, but take some time to explore these potential embellishments – it will be a good practice.

Summary

Working with discrete electronic components can be a lot of fun. Just making the circuit work is a real thrill when you're just starting out with electronics. Now that we know a lot more about controlling our Pico and hardware connected to the GPIO, we can see how powerful having an easy-to-program language like MicroPython at our disposal is to make things easy.

In this chapter, we implemented a simulation of a pedestrian crossing button and stoplight. We used a series of LEDs to represent the stoplight and walk signal. We also added a hardware button to simulate pressing the real walk. If you liked this project, you would enjoy the next two projects even more.

In the next chapter, we will explore our first sensor project[1] to read values and then archive the data and display it on an OLED.

---

[1] Actually, a button is a primitive sensor, so this chapter is our first sensor project.

CHAPTER 8

Project: Soil Moisture Monitor

One of the most common forms of electronics projects is those that monitor events using sensors providing the data either to another machine, cloud service, or local server (like a web server). One way to do that is to wire your Pico up to a set of sensors and then log the data. You can find several examples of general data loggers on the Internet, but few combine the logging of data with a visualization component. Indeed, making sense of the data is the key to making a successful project.

In this chapter, we won't jump directly into making our project run on the Internet. Rather, we will start with the basics and explore combining data logging with data visualization. We will use a different OLED made specifically for the Pico using a third-party host board. We will also see how to use an analog sensor that produces analog data that we will then have to interpret. In fact, we will rely on the analog-to-digital conversion (ADC) capabilities of our Pico to change the voltage reading to a value we can use. Finally, we will be reusing the RTC module from Chapter 6.

However, this chapter includes a few hardware challenges that are great examples of incompatibilities among components that you may encounter in your own projects. We will explore these issues in detail along with solutions and ways to mitigate the issues. With that comes added complexity that makes this project the most complex so far in the book.

© Charles Bell 2022
C. Bell, *Beginning MicroPython with the Raspberry Pi Pico*, Maker Innovations Series,
https://doi.org/10.1007/978-1-4842-8135-2_8

As you will see, the code used in this chapter is more modular and uses more functions than previous projects, but not much more than the previous examples. However, the use of a third-party host board makes the project quite different. As you will see, the code isn't difficult to learn and uses concepts we have seen in previous chapters. It is the hardware that is the most challenging.

Overview

In this chapter, we will implement a plant soil moisture monitoring solution (plant monitor for brevity). This will involve using one or more soil moisture sensors connected to our Pico. We will set up a timer alarm (an interrupt) to run periodically to read the data from the sensors and store it in a comma-separated value (CSV) file as well as display the last value read and average over time.

The project also supports a rudimentary user interface that includes four buttons whose functions include turning the display off, turning it back on, and clearing the data log (the extra button is used to confirm the delete). We will also use an LED to indicate when a sensor is being read.

We will be separating the code for reading the sensor from the display. This means we can reuse or modify either without confusing ourselves as we dig into the code. For example, so long as the visualization component reads the sensor data from the file, it doesn't matter to the sensor reading code how it is used. The only interface or connection between these two parts is the format of the file, and since we're using a CSV file, it is very easy to read and use in our code.

To make things more interesting and to make it easier to code, we will place all the sensor code in a separate code module. Recall, this is a technique used to help reduce the amount of code in any one module, thereby making it easier to write and maintain.

Now let's see what components are needed for this project, and then we will see how to wire everything together.

Note   Since we are well into our third project and have seen many of the techniques employed in this project, some topics such as wiring and setup of the hardware shall be brief in favor of discussing the hardware details.

Required Components

The components for this project include a new host board that you can plug your Pico into that supports two additions (copies) of the GPIO headers, allowing you to use up to two modules made for the Pico.

One of those modules is called the Pico Display, which has a nice RGB OLED screen that is about 75% of the size of the Pico. Onboard that module are four buttons and an RGB LED, making this module very handy in creating simple user interfaces like the one for this project.

However, as mentioned previously, we will encounter some problems using the Pico Display without our RTC and soil moisture sensors. Before we look at those details, Table 8-1 lists the components you will need in addition to your Pico and USB cable. Links to vendors are provided should you want to purchase the components.

Table 8-1. *Required Components*

Component	Qty	Description	Cost	Links
Soil moisture	1+	Sensor	$6.95	www.sparkfun.com/products/13637
RTC breakout board	1	RTC module with battery backup	$15.95	www.sparkfun.com/products/12708
			$7.50	www.adafruit.com/product/3296
Coin cell battery	1	CR1225 (SparkFun RTC)	$1.95	www.sparkfun.com/products/337
		CR1220 (Adafruit RTC)	$0.95	www.adafruit.com/product/380
Host board	1	Omnibus	$7.75	https://thepihut.com/collections/pico/products/pico-omnibus-dual-expander
OLED	1	Pico Display	$14.00	https://thepihut.com/collections/pico/products/pico-display-pack
Jumper wires	3	M/M jumper wires, 7" (set of 30)	$2.25	https://www.sparkfun.com/products/11026
		M/M jumper wires, 6" (set of 20)	$1.95	https://www.adafruit.com/product/1956
Jumper wires	4	F/F jumper wires, 6" (set of 20)	$1.95	www.sparkfun.com/products/11709
		F/F jumper wires, 6" (set of 40)	$3.95	www.adafruit.com/product/266

You can purchase the components separately from Adafruit (`adafruit.com`), SparkFun (`sparkfun.com`), or any electronics store that carries electronic components. Costs shown are estimates and do not include any shipping costs.

Notice we are using two different forms of jumper cables. The usual we've seen before with a male connector on each end as well as a female/female cable, which we will use to connect to the RTC from the host board. However, the number of M/M jumper wires needed will vary depending on how many sensors you plan to use.

Now, let's discuss the new components we will be using.

Pico Omnibus

The host board (sometimes called a host adapter) is the Pico Omnibus from Pimoroni (`https://shop.pimoroni.com/products/pico-omnibus`). The board has two sets of male headers that replicate the Pico GPIO. Together with modules that have female headers, you can place your Pico in the center and one module on either side. Or, as we will do in this project, one module and use the other headers for connecting to other hardware. Figure 8-1 shows the Pico Omnibus with a Pico in the center and two popular modules installed.

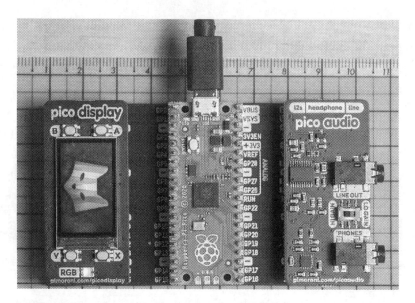

Figure 8-1. *Pico Omnibus (courtesy of thepihut.com)*

Pimoroni sells a variety of modules you can connect to the Pico Omnibus. See https://shop.pimoroni.com/collections/pico for more details and the latest offerings. You can purchase Pimoroni components at adafruit.com, sparkfun.com, and thepihut.com or directly from pimoroni.com.

Pico Display

The Pico Display shown on the left is the OLED we will use for this project. Figure 8-2 shows the Pico Display. Notice it has four buttons as well as a single red, green, and blue (RGB) LED that you can use as an indicator. Nice.

Figure 8-2. *Pico Display (courtesy of thepihut.com)*

Soil Moisture Sensor

Soil moisture sensors come in a variety of formats, but most have two
prongs that are inserted into the soil and, using a small electrical charge,
measure the resistance between the prongs. The higher the value read, the
more moisture is in the soil. However, there is a bit of configuration needed
to obtain reliable or realistic thresholds. While the manufacturer will have
threshold recommendations, some experimentation may be needed to
find the right values.

These sensors can also be affected by environmental factors including
the type of pot the plant is in, the soil composition, and other factors.
Thus, experimenting with a known overwatered soil, dry soil, and
properly tended soil will help you narrow down the thresholds for your
environment.

Figure 8-3 shows a soil moisture sensor from SparkFun that has a
terminal mount instead of pins. You can find several varieties of these
sensors. Just pick the one you want to use, keeping in mind you may need
different jumpers to connect it to your board.

Figure 8-3. *Soil moisture sensor (courtesy of sparkfun.com)*

Of special note is how these soil moisture sensors work. If you were to leave the sensors powered on, they can degrade over time. The metal on the prongs can become degraded due to electrolysis, thereby dramatically reducing its lifespan. You can use a technique of a GPIO pin to power the sensor by turning the pin on when you want to read a value. Keep in mind there will be a small delay while the sensor settles, but we can use a simple delay to wait and then read the value and turn the sensor off. In this way, we can extend the life of the sensor greatly.

The soil moisture sensors come using a variety of connectors from a terminal block to one of several connectors with pins. Be sure to check your soil moisture sensors to ensure you use the correct jumper wires. For example, you can use a male-to-female jumper wire for the terminal block version or a female-to-female connector for those using standard pins.

Potential Hardware Conflicts

Now, let's talk about a subject that occurs more often than you think – conflicts between hardware components. Most times, conflicts can be resolved by changing the software libraries we use like using SoftI2C or SoftSPI or even a different driver, but other times it's simply because of how the hardware is wired internally.

In this case, we have a potential conflict between the Pico Display and the pins needed for the soil moisture sensors as well as the RTC module. Yes, all three have a potential to make your project miserable! Since this can happen in other projects, we need to examine the issue in more detail to prepare you to diagnose and overcome the situation.

Let's begin by looking at the interface pins that the Pico Display uses. The nice folks at Pimoroni have provided us with an excellent color-coded chart that has on the left a view from the top of the module (looking at the OLED), and on the right is a view from the underside.

Looking at the left side, notice the blocks that have a text box next to them. These are the pins the Pico Display uses. To be safe, we should avoid using these pins for other hardware. That is normally an easy thing to do, but in this case, we will need three pins for each soil moisture sensor (although you can combine the ground pins) and four for the I2C interface for the RTC. Since we must avoid using the same pins as the Pico Display, we must make our choices for the power and signal pins for the soil moisture carefully.

Figure 8-4 shows the pinout chart of the Pico Display.

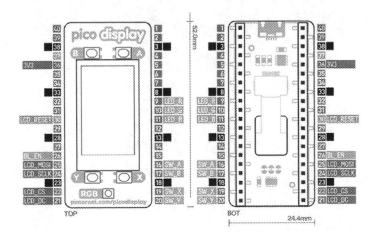

Figure 8-4. *Pico Display GPIO (courtesy of pimoroni.com)*

For example, if you were to use pins numbered 9 and 10 for the power pins on the soil moisture sensors, these are wired to the RGB LED on the Pico Display. So, each time you power the soil moisture on, you will see the RGB LED turn on. That might be fine if you want to turn the LED on when reading, but it is a good example of hardware conflicts.

Another thing to consider is the signal pins for the soil moisture sensors require analog-to-digital (ADC) pins for the soil moisture sensors. However, the Pico has only three pins that can do ADC conversions, GPIO26, GPIO27, and GPIO28, which limits us to at most three soil moisture sensors.

However, you can employ an external ADC module like those from Adafruit and SparkFun. These modules provide additional pins with ADC capabilities, allowing you to make more ADC pins available for your project. For example, the ADS1015 12-Bit ADC – 4 Channel from Adafruit (`www.adafruit.com/product/1083`) uses an I2C interface, and a driver is available for use with MicroPython. Figure 8-5 shows the ADS1015 12-Bit ADC – 4 Channel.

Figure 8-5. *ADS1015 12-Bit ADC – 4 Channel (courtesy of adafruit.com)*

Now, let's see how to wire the components together.

Set Up the Hardware

Since we are using the Pico Omnibus, we need to take a slight detour and load a custom image provided by Pimoroni. It is much easier to load the custom image than to try and install all of the libraries needed to use the Omnibus and Pico Display. We will need the same library we used in Chapter 6 for the RTC, but the custom image has all of the other libraries we will need.

Another thing that complicates our hardware setup is the layout of the Pico Omnibus. Recall, this host board has two GPIO headers for modules with male pins that you can use to mount modules with female headers soldered on the bottom of the board. However, the pinout for the GPIO headers on the Omnibus is reversed. That means you cannot start counting the physical pin number starting in the upper-left corner; rather, it is numbered from one starting in the upper-right corner. Figure 8-6 shows the correct layout of the GPIO module headers on the Omnibus enlarged for clarity.

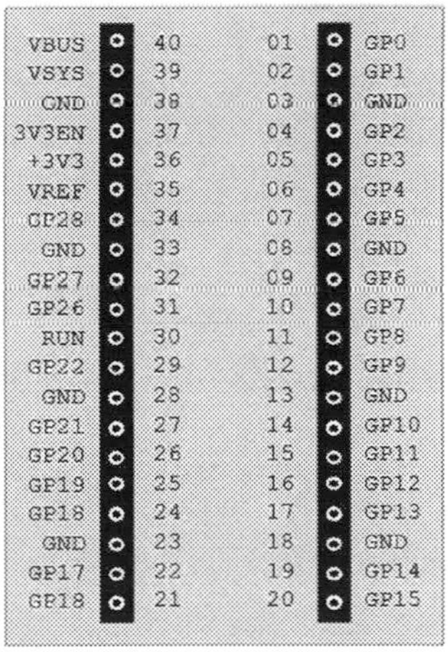

Figure 8-6. *Pico Omnibus GPIO pinout*

Fortunately, the pins are labeled on the Omnibus, so you can find them without having a map like before. Figure 8-7 shows the Omnibus GPIO. Notice I've mounted the Pico Display on the left. You can mount it on either side.

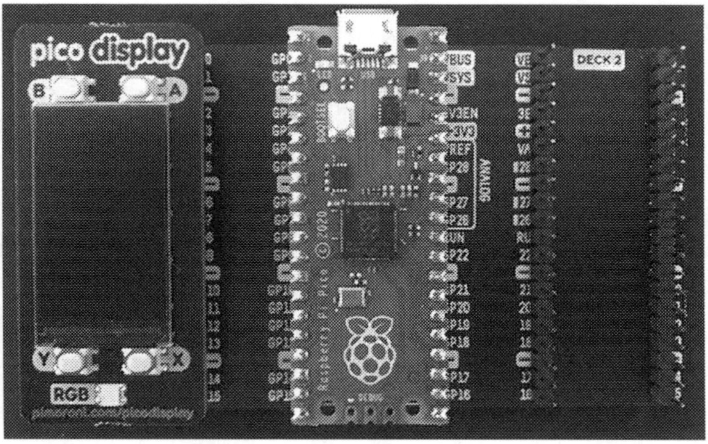

Figure 8-7. Pico Omnibus module GPIO

Now that we're aware of the limitation of the pins we need to use and the layout change for the Omnibus, let's first discuss how to install the custom image before we discuss how to connect the hardware.

Load the Pimoroni Image on the Pico

Pimoroni has prepared a special, custom image that includes all of the libraries we will need to use the host board and the display. Recall from Chapter 1, to install an image, we first download the .uf2 file and then copy the file to our Pico in boot select mode.

For the Pimoroni image, begin by visiting https://github.com/ pimoroni/pimoroni-pico/releases/ and click the link to download the MicroPython .uf2 image for the latest version. For example, the latest version at the time of this writing was version 0.2.5, and the link to the

.uf2 file is `https://github.com/pimoroni/pimoroni-pico/releases/download/v0.2.5/pimoroni-pico-v0.2.5-micropython-v1.16.uf2`.

Next, unplug your Pico from your PC and hold down the *BOOTSEL* button and reconnect to your PC. Release the *BOOTSEL* button and then drag and drop the `.uf2` file to the RPI-RP2 drive. Once the copy is finished, you can then disconnect and reconnect the Pico.

Finally, open Thonny and verify the new image has loaded. You may not see any banner that identifies the MicroPython image as the Pimoroni custom image. However, you can check that you are using the correct image by using the REPL console to import the Pimoroni library. This command will succeed if you have the Pimoroni custom image and fail for others. The following shows a successful test with the Pimoroni custom image. Notice there wasn't an error when the `import` statement was executed:

```
MicroPython v1.16 on 2021-08-19; Raspberry Pi Pico with RP2040

Type "help()" for more information.
>>> import pimoroni
>>>
```

Now that we have our custom image installed, let's see how to connect the hardware.

Connecting the Hardware

Table 8-2 shows the connections needed for this project. This shows the use of two soil moisture sensors, but you can use a single sensor or three if you'd like. However, it is recommended you start with one sensor until you get the project working and then add additional sensors.

Table 8-2. *Connections for the Plant Monitor*

Omnibus	Pin Number	Component	Pin
VBUS	40	RTC	5V
GND	38	RTC	GND
GP11	15	RTC	SCL
GP10	14	RTC	SDA
GND	8	Soil #1	GND
GP21	27	Soil #1	VCC
GP27	32	Soil #1	SIG
GND	3	Soil #2	GND
GP22	29	Soil #2	VCC
GP28	34	Soil #2	SIG

Of course, you must insert the soil moisture sensors into the soil of your plants. If your plants are located further away from your power source, you may need to use longer wires to connect the sensors. You should start with a single, small plant and one sensor (or for testing, two sensors in one plant) that you can place close to your PC (or power source).

Caution   You will need soil moisture sensors that can operate at 3.3–5V. Some MicroPython boards may limit output on the pins to 3.3V. The sensors from SparkFun are compatible.

To connect the wiring, start by installing the Pico in the center of the Omnibus with the Pico Display installed to the left (or right if you prefer). Once you've done that, lay out the RTC and soil moisture sensors as well as your kit of jumper wires. Figure 8-8 shows a pictorial representation of how the modules are wired with the correct Omnibus GPIO header enlarged for clarity.

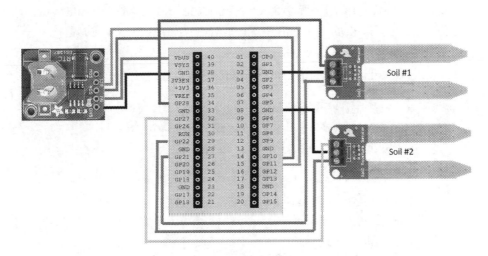

Figure 8-8. *Wiring the plant monitor*

Once again, always make sure to double-check your connections before powering the board on. Now, let's talk about the code we need to write. Don't power on your board just yet – there is a fair amount of discussion needed before we're ready to test the project.

Write the Code

Now it's time to write the code for our project. The code is longer than what we've seen thus far, and due to all the bits and bobs we're working with, it is best to divide the project into parts. So, we are going to write the code in stages. We won't have a working project until the end, so most of the discussion will be about the individual parts. We will put it all together before testing the project.

For this project, we will rely more on classes than we did in previous examples. We will create a main code file (main.py) that we can use to download to the Pico for automatic execution, which will set up the sensors for reading by a dedicated class module and display the data using a different class module. We will use a third class to control how often we read the sensor(s). Thus, we will create three class modules as follows. We will see the details of each of these in a later section:

- ReadTimer: A class to control how often the code reads the sensors. Recall, the soil moisture sensors need some time to power on, stabilize, and read.

- SoilMoisture: A class to read one or more soil moisture sensors and return the data. The class will also save the data collected to a comma-separated value file (CSV).

- PlantDisplay: A class to display the data to the Pico Display.

However, before we examine the class modules, we need to work on calibrating our sensors.

Calibrating the Sensor

Calibration of sensors is very important. This is especially true for soil moisture sensors because there are so many different versions available. These sensors are also very sensitive to the soil composition, temperature, and even the type of pot in which the plant lives. Thus, we should experiment with known soil moisture, so we know what ranges to use in our code.

More specifically, we want to classify the observation from the sensor so that we can determine if the plant needs watering. We will use the values "dry," "Ok," and "wet" to classify the value read from the sensor.

Seeing these labels is much easier for us to determine – at a glance – whether the plant needs watering. In this case, the raw data such as a value of 1756 may not mean much, but if we see "dry," we know it needs water.

Since the sensors are analog sensors, we will use the analog-to-digital conversion on the board. When we read the data from the pin, we will get a value in a range starting at zero. This value is related to the resistance the sensor reads in the soil. Low values indicate dry soil, and high values indicate wet soil.

However, the sensors from different vendors can vary widely in the values read. For example, sensors from SparkFun tend to read values in the range 0–32768, but sensors from other vendors can read as high as 65535. Fortunately, they all seem to be consistent in that the lower the value, the drier the soil.

So, we must determine thresholds for the three classifications. Again, there are several factors that can influence the values read from the sensor. Thus, you should select several pots of soil including one that you feel is dry, another that is correctly watered, and a third that is overwatered. The best thing to do is select one that is dry, take measurements, then water it until the soil moisture is correct, measure that, then water it again until there is too much water.

To determine the threshold, we must first write a short bit of code to set up our board for reading values from the sensor. This includes choosing a GPIO pin that supports ADC. We also need to choose a pin to use to power the board. This is also an analog output pin. We will use GP27 for the sensor signal pin to read data and GP21 for the power pin. The ground for the sensor can be connected to any of the ground pins on the Pico.

Finally, we will write a loop to read several values every five seconds and then average them. Five seconds is an arbitrary value, and it was derived from reading the data sheet for the sensor. Check your sensors to see how much time is needed for the read to settle (maybe under the heading of frequency of reads).

Listing 8-1 shows the code needed to set up the analog-to-digital channel, a pin to use for powering the sensor, and a loop for reading ten values and averaging them.

Listing 8-1. Calibrating the Soil Moisture Threshold

```
# Import libraries
from machine import ADC, Pin
from utime import sleep

print("Beginning MicroPython - Soil Moisture threshold test.")
# Setup the GPIO pin for powering the sensor. We use Pin 19
power = Pin(21, Pin.OUT)
# Setup the ADC for the signal pin
adc = ADC(Pin(27))
# Turn sensor off
power.low()

# Loop 10 times and average the values read
print("Reading 10 values.")
total = 0
for i in range (0,10):
    # Turn power on
    power.high()
    # Wait for sensor to power on and settle
    sleep(5)
    # Read the value
    value = adc.read_u16()
    print("Value read ({0:02}): {1}".format(i+1, value))
    total += value
    # Turn sensor off
    power.low()
```

```
# Now average the values
print("The average value read is: {0}".format(total/10))
```

If you enter this code in a file named threshold.py, you can download it to your Pico and execute it. Listing 8-2 shows the output of running this calibration code in a plant that is correctly watered.

Listing 8-2. Running the Calibration Code

```
Beginning MicroPython - Soil Moisture threshold test.
Reading 10 values.
Value read (01): 752
Value read (02): 720
Value read (02): 752
Value read (04): 784
Value read (05): 832
Value read (06): 736
Value read (07): 800
Value read (08): 784
Value read (09): 784
Value read (10): 752
The average value read is: 769.6
```

Here, we see an average value of 770 (always round the number – you need integers). Further tests running the code on dry soil resulted in a value of 425 and for a wet plant, 3100. Thus, the thresholds for this example are 500 for dry and 2500 for wet. However, your results may vary greatly, so make sure to run this code with your sensors, board, and plant of choice.

Tip   To make things easier for calibrating the thresholds, use sensors from the same vendor. Otherwise, you may have to use a different set of thresholds for each sensor supported.

Notice the values read. As you can see, the values can vary from one moment to another. This is normal for these sensors. They are known for producing some jumpy values. Thus, you should consider sampling the sensor more than once to get an average over a short period rather than a single value. Even taking an average can be skewed slightly if one or more of the samples is off by a large margin. However, sampling even ten values and averaging will help reduce the possibility of getting an anomalous reading. We will do this in our project code.

Now that we have our threshold values for our sensors, we can begin with the code modules for the classes.

Class Modules

The first part of the project will be to create the code modules to contain the new classes that contain all the functionality to read data from the sensors, save the data to a file, and display the information on a display. In this section, we will see how to write the code for the class modules starting with the timer.

ReadTimer

We will use a new class named ReadTimer to create a hardware timer that we can use to read the values from the sensor. Since we will use a loop to read the sensor waiting 5 seconds for each read, we will need a minimum of 50–55 seconds to read ten values. Thus, we cannot set the update frequency to anything less than about one minute. While you may want to set this to a low value for testing, you certainly do not want to check the soil moisture of your plants every minute. That is, how often do you check your plants normally? Once every few days or once a day? Why check it sooner than normal?

SAMPLING FREQUENCY

How often you sample data from a sensor (also called sampling rate) is often overlooked when designing sensor networks. The tendency is to store as many values as you can, thinking more data is better. But that is not applicable in the general case. Consider the plant monitoring project. If you normally check your plants once per day, how can sampling the sensors once every five minutes benefit you? It won't!

Sampling rate must be calculated carefully to deliver the data you need to draw conclusions without creating too much data. While more data is always better than too little data, saving data too often at unrealistic frequencies can generate so much data that it could exceed the storage capacity of your device.

You should carefully consider the sampling rate when designing projects that sample sensors. Choose a sampling rate that is based on realistic expectations. Generally, if you are sampling data that can change very slowly, the sampling rate should be long. Sampling data that can change more quickly should have a higher (shorter time between samples) sampling rate.

For this project, we will set the frequency at two minutes (120,000 microseconds).

The design of this class is a bit new and may seem a bit unorthodox at first. Rather than use a timer as a callback function and assign it to a hardware timer, we will use the hardware timer to set a variable named data_read_event to True when the timer fires. We can then create a function to get the value of that variable as well as reset it (set it to False). This way, we can use the hardware timer to periodically set the data_read_event to True, and once we've read the data, set it to False. This allows the code for our soil moisture class to run independently from the timer.

In all, we will need three functions aside from the constructor as follows:

- read_data_event(): The callback function as described earlier to set the read data event variable.

- time_to_read(): A function callers can use to get the read data event variable.

- reset(): A function callers can use to reset the read data event variable.

We will use this class in the soil moisture class where we only read the data when the data read event has fired (the variable is True). We will name the code module read_timer.py and place it on our Pico in the project3 folder (or similar). Listing 8-3 shows the completed code for the ReadTimer class. Take a moment to read through the code to see how it works.

Listing 8-3. The ReadTimer Class

```python
# Import libraries
from machine import Timer

# Constants
DATA_READ_INTERVAL = 120000          # Increase this interval
                                     # as needed

# Class to control reading data with a timer
class ReadEvent:
    def __init__(self):
        # Create and start the timer interrupt to read data
        self.data_read_event = True
        self.read_timer = Timer()
```

```
    self.read_timer.init(period=DATA_READ_INTERVAL,
        mode=Timer.PERIODIC, callback=self.read_data_event)

# Callback for reading the data on the interval.
def read_data_event(self, timer_obj):
    self.data_read_event = True

# Check to see if it is time to read
def time_to_read(self):
    return self.data_read_event

# Reset the read event boolean (timer doesn't reset)
def reset(self):
    self.data_read_event = False
```

SoilMoisture

This class is where we will read the soil moisture sensors and record the data in a CSV file. We will write the class so that most of the work in writing data to the CSV file will be functions used only within the class, but we will expose one function to clear the CSV file. Recall, the user interface has a button that clears the log file. The code is designed to create the file even if it doesn't exist.

Constructor

The class is designed to read any number of sensors via a list of dictionaries passed when the class is instantiated. Thus, we will write the constructor to accept the list and set up the sensors. To do so, we will use a new list of dictionaries that contain the Pin class instantiations for controlling the power (turning on or off) and the ADC class instantiations for reading data (signal pin).

347

The dictionary required for the list passed to the constructor is defined as follows. Notice we specify the pin for reading the data, the power pin, as well as a nickname (for the display) and a location or description (for the log file):

```
sensor = {
  'pin': sensor_pin,
  'power': power_pin,
  'location': location or description
  'nick': nickname for the sensor
}
```

The code we will use in the main code to pass the data to the SoilMoisture class is as follows. Here, we define two sensors:

```
sensor_list = [
    {
        'pin': 27,
        'power': 21,
        'location': 'Green ceramic pot on top shelf',
        'nick': 'Ivy',
    },
    {
        'pin': 28,
        'power': 22,
        'location': 'Fern on bottom shelf',
        'nick': 'Fern',
    }
]
```

The code for the constructor is easy to follow, but one portion that needs examination is the code for creating a new list from the dictionaries passed to the constructor. We will use one GPIO pin to turn on the power for the sensor and another pin to read it from the ADC class. Thus, we create the instances of the Pin and ADC classes as we build the new list of dictionaries as follows. This piece of code is a good example of how dictionaries can help keep multiple instantiations of classes organized:

```
self.sensors = []
for sensor in sensor_list:
    # Setup the dictionary for each soil moisture sensor
    soil_moisture = {
        'sensor': ADC(Pin(sensor['pin'])),
        'power': Pin(sensor['power'], Pin.OUT),
        'location': sensor['location'],
        'nick': sensor['nick']
    }
    self.sensors.append(soil_moisture)
```

We also need to pass in the RTC class and the file name of the log file. Thus, calling the constructor requires passing three values as follows:

```
plants = SoilMoisture(rtc, DATA_FILENAME, sensor_list)
```

Public Functions

Other than the constructor, we need the following functions that will be called from our main code. Recall, we call these functions "public" functions since they can be used outside the class (by the caller):

- clear_log(): Clears the log file (erases all data in the file)

- get_values(): Returns the values read

- read_sensors(): Reads the data from the sensor if the read timer has fired (data_read_event is True)

The code for these functions are simple enough, but some explanation is needed for the read_sensors() function. In this function, we use a private function to read the value from the sensor by passing the power and signal pin variables to the private function named _get_value() as defined in the following:

```
# Read the sensor 10 times and average the values read
def _get_value(self, adc, power):
    total = 0
    # Turn power on
    power.high()
    for i in range (0,10):
        # Wait for sensor to power on and settle
        sleep(5)
        # Read the value
        value = adc.read_u16()
        total += value
    # Turn sensor off
    power.low()
    return int(total/10)
```

Notice we use the same code from the threshold.py example to turn on the power pin, wait five seconds, then read the value using the ADC class. We do this ten times and then average the values.

Private Functions

There are a number of other functions used only within the class. Recall, we name these with an underscore as the first character in the name signifying them as private. The following lists the functions and their uses. We leave the examination of the code for these functions as an exercise:

- `_format_time()`: Format the time (epoch) for a better view

- `_get_value()`: Read the sensor ten times and average the values read

- `_convert_value()`: Convert the raw sensor value to an enumeration

If you are wondering about the data file, you need not worry. The following shows a mock-up of data you can use in your tests:

9/6/2021 6:22	Ivy	760	ok	Green ceramic pot on top shelf
9/6/2021 6:22	Fern	772	ok	Fern on bottom shelf
9/6/2021 6:23	Ivy	742	ok	Green ceramic pot on top shelf
9/6/2021 6:23	Fern	756	ok	Fern on bottom shelf
9/6/2021 6:25	Ivy	761	ok	Green ceramic pot on top shelf
9/6/2021 6:25	Fern	763	ok	Fern on bottom shelf
9/6/2021 6:26	Ivy	768	ok	Green ceramic pot on top shelf
9/6/2021 6:26	Fern	760	ok	Fern on bottom shelf
9/6/2021 6:27	Ivy	763	ok	Green ceramic pot on top shelf
9/6/2021 6:27	Fern	756	ok	Fern on bottom shelf
9/6/2021 6:28	Ivy	760	ok	Green ceramic pot on top shelf
9/6/2021 6:28	Fern	753	ok	Fern on bottom shelf
9/6/2021 6:29	Ivy	753	ok	Green ceramic pot on top shelf

If you want to start with some sample data, you can do so, but just make sure it is comma separated with no spaces and one line of data per row.

We will name the code module soil_moisture.py and place it on our Pico in the project3 folder (or similar). Listing 8-4 shows the completed code for the SoilMoisture class. Take a moment to read through the code to see how it works. Notice the constants that define the thresholds for wet and dry soil measurements. Recall, we got these through experimenting with the preceding threshold example code:

Listing 8-4. The SoilMoisture Class

```
# Import libraries
from machine import ADC, Pin
from utime import sleep
import os

# Thresholds for the sensors
LOWER_THRESHOLD = 500
UPPER_THRESHOLD = 2500
UPDATE_FREQ = 120    # seconds

class SoilMoisture:
    # Initialization for the class (the constructor)
    def __init__(self, rtc, csv_filename, sensor_list):
        self.rtc = rtc

        # Try to access the file system and make the new path
        self.sensor_file = csv_filename

        # Loop through the sensors specified and setup a new
          dictionary
        # for each sensor that includes the power and ADC pins
          defined.
```

```python
        self.sensors = []
        for sensor in sensor_list:
            # Setup the dictionary for each soil
              moisture sensor
            soil_moisture = {
                'sensor': ADC(Pin(sensor['pin'])),
                'power': Pin(sensor['power'], Pin.OUT),
                'location': sensor['location'],
                'nick': sensor['nick']
            }
            self.sensors.append(soil_moisture)

        self.values_read = None
        print("Soil moisture sensors are ready...")

    # Clear the log
    def clear_log(self):
        log_file = open(self.sensor_file, 'w')
        log_file.close()

    # Get the values read
    def get_values(self):
        return self.values_read

    # Format the time (epoch) for a better view
    def _format_time(self):
        # Get datetime
        dt = self.rtc.datetime()
        return "{0:02}/{1:02}/{2:04} " \
               "{3:02}:{4:02}:{5:02}".format(dt[1], dt[2],
               dt[0], dt[4], dt[5], dt[6])
```

```python
# Read the sensor 10 times and average the values read
def _get_value(self, adc, power):
    total = 0
    # Turn power on
    power.high()
    for i in range (0,10):
        # Wait for sensor to power on and settle
        sleep(5)
        # Read the value
        value = adc.read_u16()
        total += value
    # Turn sensor off
    power.low()
    return int(total/10)

# Monitor the sensors, read the values and save them
def read_sensors(self):
    log_file = open(self.sensor_file, 'a')
    self.values_read = []
    for sensor in self.sensors:
        # Read the data from the sensor and convert
          the value
        value = self._get_value(sensor['sensor'],
        sensor['power'])
        print("Value read: {0}".format(value))
        # datetime,num,value,enum,location
        message = ("{0},{1},{2},{3},{4}"
                    "".format(self._format_time(),
                              sensor['nick'], value,
                              self._convert_value(value),
                              sensor['location']))
```

```
        log_file.write("{0}\n".format(message))
        value_read = {
            'timestamp': self._format_time(),
            'raw_value': value,
            'value': self._convert_value(value),
            'location': sensor['location'],
            'nick': sensor['nick']
        }
        self.values_read.append(value_read)
    log_file.close()

# Convert the raw sensor value to an enumeration
def _convert_value(self, value):
    # If value is less than lower threshold, soil is dry
      else if it
    # is greater than upper threshold, it is wet, else all
      is well.
    if (value <= LOWER_THRESHOLD):
        return "dry"
    elif (value >= UPPER_THRESHOLD):
        return "wet"
    return "ok"
```

PlantDisplay

The last class we will create is a class to display data to the Pico Display. We place this code in a separate class to keep the display portion of the code separate from the data. There are no surprises in this code other than how to initialize and communicate with the Pico Display.

Recall, the user interface allows the user to turn the screen off and back on, so this class will need to take care of those operations. Also, there are cases where we want to display a message to the user, so the class will provide that feature as well.

The class has the following functions. The code for these functions is easy to understand, and the discovery of how the code works is left as an exercise:

- clear_screen(): Clear the screen

- _write_text(): Write data to the screen

- screen_on(): Turn the screen on

- screen_off(): Turn the screen off

- show_data(): Show the data on the OLED

- show_message(): Clear the screen and write a message

- is_screen_on(): Return True if the display is turned on

- button_pressed(): Return the button pressed or None if no buttons are pressed

We will name the code module plant_display.py and place it on our Pico in the project3 folder (or similar). Listing 8-5 shows the completed code for the PlantDisplay class. Take a moment to read through the code to see how it works.

Listing 8-5. The PlantDisplay Class

```
# Import libraries
from utime import sleep
import picodisplay as display

# Constants
DEFAULT_FONT_SCALE = 2
WRAP_SIZE = 240
BUTTON_A = 10
BUTTON_B = 20
BUTTON_X = 30
BUTTON_Y = 40
```

```python
class PlantDisplay:
    """

    This class displays data from one or more soil moisture
    sensors.
    """

    # Initialization for the class (the constructor)
    def __init__(self):
        # Setup the Pico Display with a bytearray
          display buffer
        buf = bytearray(display.get_width() * display.get_
        height() * 2)
        display.init(buf)
        display.set_backlight(0.5)
        self.clear_screen()
        self.display_on = True
        self.led_on = False

    # Function to clear the screen
    def clear_screen(self):
        display.set_pen(0, 0, 0)
        display.clear()
        display.update()
        display.set_pen(255, 255, 255)

    # Function to write data to the screen
    def _write_text(self, message, x, y, scale=DEFAULT_
    FONT_SCALE):
        self.clear_screen()
        display.text(message, x, y, WRAP_SIZE, scale)
        display.update()
```

```python
# Turn screen on
def screen_on(self):
    # Turns on the display and reads the data
    display.set_backlight(0.5)
    self._write_text("Display ON", 10, 10, 3)
    sleep(2)
    self.display_on = True

# Turn screen off
def screen_off(self):
    # Turns off the display
    self._write_text("Display OFF", 10, 10, 3)
    sleep(2)
    self.clear_screen()
    display.set_backlight(0)
    self.display_on = False

# Show the data on the LED
def show_data(self, soil_data):
    y = 40
    self.clear_screen()
    display.text("Plant Monitor", 10, 10, WRAP_SIZE, 3)
    for data in soil_data:
        display.text(data['nick'], 10, y, WRAP_SIZE, 3)
        display.text(str(data["value"]), 105, y, WRAP_
        SIZE, 3)
        display.text(str(data["raw_value"]), 160, y, WRAP_
        SIZE, 3)
        y = y + 20
    display.update()
```

```
# Clear the screen and write a message.
def show_message(self, message):
    self._write_text(message, 10, 10, 3)

# Return True if the display is turned on
def is_screen_on(self):
    return self.display_on

# Return the button pressed or None if no buttons
  are pressed
def button_pressed(self):
    if display.is_pressed(display.BUTTON_A):
        return BUTTON_A
    if display.is pressed(display.BUTTON_B):
        return BUTTON_B
    if display.is_pressed(display.BUTTON_X):
        return BUTTON_X
    if display.is_pressed(display.BUTTON_Y):
        return BUTTON_Y
    return None
```

Now, let's see the main code for this project.

Main Code

The main code for this project is stored in a file named main.py. It is a
continuation of the pattern we saw previously where we create a function
named main() and call it from the conditional at the bottom of the file. So,
there's nothing new there, but it is best to take a slower walk through this
code as it defines how the project works.

What is new for this project is the use of the three classes we created
along with the RTC class we saw in Chapter 6. Thus, the import section is
a bit longer. In fact, we will need to import a number of things from our

classes as well as the I2C and Pin classes from the machine library. The following shows the imports for the main code:

```
from machine import Pin, SoftI2C
from utime import sleep
from project3.plant_display import PlantDisplay, BUTTON_A,
BUTTON_B, BUTTON_X, BUTTON_Y
from project3.urtc import DS1307
from project3.soil_moisture import SoilMoisture
from project3.read_timer import ReadEvent
import sys
```

We also create a constant to store the log file name that we pass to the SoilMoisture class when we instantiate it:

```
DATA_FILENAME = 'plant_data.csv'
```

The instantiation of the class variables is a bit longer but not difficult. The following shows how we create each of the class variables:

```
# Setup the display
display = PlantDisplay()
display.clear_screen()
# Setup I2C for RTC
sda = Pin(10)
scl = Pin(11)
# Software I2C (bit-banging) for the RTC
i2c = SoftI2C(sda=sda, scl=scl, freq=100000)
# Initialize class instance variables for the RTC
rtc = DS1307(i2c)
```

Next, we create the list of dictionaries that define the sensors we want to use where we specify the pin numbers for the power and signal lines as well as a description (location) and nickname. We then pass that to the soil moisture class to complete the instantiation:

```
# Setup the sensors
sensor_list = [
    {
        'pin': 27,
        'power': 21,
        'location': 'Green ceramic pot on top shelf',
        'nick': 'Ivy',
    },
    {
        'pin': 28,
        'power': 22,
        'location': 'Fern on bottom shelf',
        'nick': 'Fern',
    }
]
# Setup the soil moisture object instance from the
SoilMoisture class
plants = SoilMoisture(rtc, DATA_FILENAME, sensor_list)
```

After that, we enter a loop that simply calls the data_read_event.time_
to_read() function, and if it returns True, we read the sensors and display
the data. We also call the display.button_pressed() function, and if it
returns a value other than null, we act for the specific button press detected.
Listing 8-6 shows the complete code for the main.py code file. Take a
moment and scan the code to see how the button features are implemented.

Listing 8-6. Plant Monitor Complete Code (main.py)

```
# Import libraries
from machine import Pin, SoftI2C
from utime import sleep
from project3.plant_display import PlantDisplay, BUTTON_A,
BUTTON_B, BUTTON_X, BUTTON_Y
```

```python
from project3.urtc import DS1307
from project3.soil_moisture import SoilMoisture
from project3.read_timer import ReadEvent
import sys

# Constants
DATA_FILENAME = 'plant_data.csv'

def main():
    # Global variables
    data_read_event = False
    print("Hello! Welcome to the plant monitor program.")
    # Setup the Pico Display
    display = PlantDisplay()
    display.clear_screen()
    # Setup I2C for RTC
    # Note: RGB LED is on 6, 7, and 8. If you use these, the
      LED will blink when you read the sensor
    sda = Pin(10)
    scl = Pin(11)
    # Software I2C (bit-banging) for the RTC
    i2c = SoftI2C(sda=sda, scl=scl, freq=100000)
    # Initialize class instance variables for the RTC
    rtc = DS1307(i2c)
    #start_datetime = (2021, 08, 12, 5, 14, 54, 22)
    #rtc.datetime(start_datetime)
    # Setup the sensors
    sensor_list = [
        {
            'pin': 27,
            'power': 21,
```

```
        'location': 'Green ceramic pot on top shelf',
        'nick': 'Ivy',
    },
    {
        'pin': 28,
        'power': 22,
        'location': 'Fern on bottom shelf',
        'nick': 'Fern',
    }
]
# Setup the soil moisture object instance from the
  SoilMoisture class
plants = SoilMoisture(rtc, DATA FILENAME, sensor_list)
display.show_message("Reading data...")
data_read_event = ReadEvent()
while True:
    # Check to see if it is time to read the data
    if data_read_event.time_to_read():
        data_read_event.reset()
        if display.is_screen_on():
            print("Reading data...")
            plants.read_sensors()
            values = plants.get_values()
            display.show_data(values)
    sleep(1)
    # Check to see if a button was pressed
    button_pressed = display.button_pressed()
    if not button_pressed:
        continue
    print("Button pressed", button_pressed)
    # Turning the log off only works when the screen is on.
```

```
    if button_pressed == BUTTON_A and display.is_
screen_on():
        # Clear the log.
        display.show_message("Press B to clear the log.")
        # wait for 5 seconds then ignore the call
        for i in range(10):
            if display.button_pressed() == BUTTON_B:
                display.show_message("Log cleared.")
                print('Requesting clear log.')
                plants.clear_log()
                sleep(2)
                display.show_message("Reading data...")
                data_read_event.reset()
                break
            else:
                sleep(0.5)
    # Allow user to turn on the screen if it is off
    elif button_pressed == BUTTON_X and not display.is_
screen_on():
            display.screen_on()
            display.show_message("Reading data...")
            data_read_event.reset()
    # Allow user to turn off the screen if it is on
    elif button_pressed == BUTTON_Y and display.is_
screen_on():
            display.screen_off()
        sleep(1)

if __name__ == '__main__':
    try:
        main()
    except (KeyboardInterrupt, SystemExit) as err:
```

```
print("\nbye!")
sys.exit(0)
```

Now, let's run this project!

Execute

Now is the fun part! We've got the code all set up to read soil moisture from our plants and display the data. But first, we have to copy all of our files to the Pico. Go ahead and create a folder named `project3` on the Pico and then copy the `soil_moisture.py`, `plant_display.py`, `read_event.py`, and `urtc.py` (from Chapter 6) to the `project3` folder on the Pico. Finally, copy the `main.py` file to the root folder of the Pico.

Next, we need to insert our soil moisture sensors into our plants. If you need to relocate the plants to your work area, go ahead and do so while you test the project. You may find you will need longer jumper wires if you plan to mount your Pico near the normal location for your plants. Both Adafruit and SparkFun sell longer jumper wires (or you can make your own).

Once those files are copied and the soil moisture sensors are inserted into your plants, you can test the main.py code by running it from Thonny. You should see data appear on the screen after about two minutes similar to Figure 8-9.

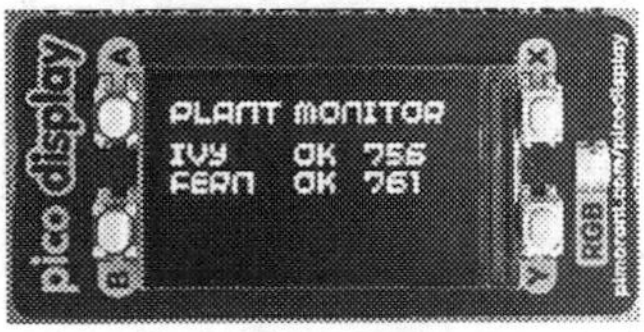

Figure 8-9. *Plant monitor project*

The code has some debug statements inserted which you can view in the REPL console if you run the `main.py` from Thonny. The following shows an example of the output you will see:

```
Hello! Welcome to the plant monitor program.
Soil moisture sensors are ready...
Reading data...
Value read: 760
Value read: 764
Reading data...
Value read: 752
Value read: 764
...
```

If you do not see the output or the Pico Display does not show any data, be sure to double-check all of your wiring and make sure you've copied all of the files to the proper locations on the Pico.

Once everything is working, you can disconnect your Pico and connect it to a 5V power supply to run the project on boot. Cool!

Taking It Further

This project, like the last one, shows excellent prospects for reusing the techniques in other projects. If you liked seeing your sensor data on the display or want to examine the soil moisture data collected, you should consider taking time to explore some embellishments. Here are a few you may want to consider. Some are easy and some may be a challenge or require more research:

- Add more sensors to expand your project to more plants.

- Add LEDs to your board to illuminate when the plants need watering.

- Change the color of the text where OK is green, dry is red, and wet is blue.

- Make RGB light each time a sensor is read. Use a different color for each sensor.

- Change the frequency of the sensor read.

- Make the *B* button force a new sensor read.

- Save the sensor configuration to a file and read it from the main application instead of hard-coding the data.

- Move the log write/read to a new class and control it from the `main.py` module.

Of course, if you want to press on to the next project, you're welcome to do so, but take some time to explore these potential embellishments – it will be a good practice.

Summary

One of the more common forms of electronics or IoT projects is those that generate data (sometimes called data collectors). The implementation of data collectors can vary greatly, but they generally store the data in some location and provide a way to view the data. The simplest forms are those that log the data locally (sometimes called data loggers), as opposed to these that transmitted to a remote server, where the data is stored in a database or a cloud service.

In this chapter, we saw a MicroPython project that logs data read from a series of soil moisture sensors. We created a plant monitoring solution that saved the data to the local SD card. The project also displayed the data on a Pico Display so that we can see the data at any time. This project can

be used as a template for a host of data collection projects. You can simply
follow the pattern established in this chapter and build your own data
logging project.

In the next chapter, we will take a look at a technology that
makes creating electronics projects easier using a component system
called Grove.

## CHAPTER 9

Introducing Grove

Thus far in the book, we have learned how to use two discrete components to build electronics projects on a breadboard without a lot of soldering. We saw several examples and three projects that demonstrated how to build electronic solutions with discrete components and modules.

While we can continue to build our electronics projects with breadboards and jumper wires, there are better alternatives available to us. There are component systems designed to unify wiring by providing a modular cabling system to connect modules. One such component system that has been around for a while and is available for use with the Pico is called Grove.

The Grove component system has a rich host of modules we can use to build our projects simply by connecting the hardware together using polarized connectors (you can't plug them in incorrectly). Grove expands your opportunities for building more complex projects, freeing you to concentrate on the code for your project.

In this chapter and the next three chapters, we will explore the third component system named Grove from Seeed Studio (`https://wiki.seeedstudio.com/Grove/`).

Overview

In this section, we will discover the Grove component system. We will learn about the capabilities and limitations of the systems as well as examples of the components available. The chapter also includes details on how to start using the components in projects.

© Charles Bell 2022

C. Bell, *Beginning MicroPython with the Raspberry Pi Pico*, Maker Innovations Series, https://doi.org/10.1007/978-1-4842-8135-2_9

Grove is designed to make building projects faster using pluggable modules containing sensors, input, output, and other functions. Unlike other component systems, the Grove component system supports a variety of protocols[1] that operate over the same set of wires!

Grove supports the analog, digital, I2C, SPI, and universal asynchronous receiver-transmitter (UART[2]) protocols. Furthermore, Grove supports all of these protocols using the same wiring and connectors, so there's no need to remember what cables go with what protocols. Cool!

Now that we know what protocols Grove supports and how the cables are wired, let's see how easy the Grove component system makes using the modules.

The Grove Component System

Grove was created and released in 2010 by Seeed Studio (`seeedstudio.com`). They wanted to create an open source, modular component system to simplify rapid prototyping. But they didn't stop there. They continued to refine and develop more modules to include an impressive array of modules that contain small circuits that include sensors, input devices, output devices, and more. They also produce host adapters for many platforms.

Note   Seeed Studio also uses the term breakout board for host adapters.

---

[1] You can call them "interfaces" or "connections" if it helps keep them sorted.
[2] A form of serial communication. `https://en.wikipedia.org/wiki/Universal_asynchronous_receiver-transmitter`

Each host adapter supports many Grove connectors that match the capabilities of the host board. If the host board supports all of the protocols that Grove supports, the host adapter will have several connectors for each of the protocols.

These host adapters simply connect to your host board enabling the use of Grove modules without the need for additional electronics such as breadboards and discrete components without soldering.

The Grove cabling system is not designed for daisy chaining. Rather, Grove modules are connected to the host adapter directly. So, connections form a "star" layout where the modules plug into one of the connectors on the host adapter. That's why most host adapters have so many Grove connectors. We will see some examples of host adapters in a later section.

Each Grove module is self-contained; all of the supporting electrical components are on the module mounted on a small PCB (most come in a pretty blue color in fact) of various sizes. All you need to do is connect the modules to your host adapter using a Grove cable, and your hardware is done.

Capabilities

The capabilities of the Grove system include the following:

- Modularized cabling supporting four protocols (I2C, digital, analog, and UART)

- Easy, polarized connectors (no incorrect or reversed connections[3])

- No soldering required!

---

[3] Perhaps the greatest bane of anyone working with I2C is inadvertently reversing the data and clock connections. Qwiic eliminates that guesswork entirely.

How Does It Work?

Grove wiring is polarized – you can only connect the cable to the device one way, so you always know the connections are correct. Grove uses a four-wire cable of various lengths with a larger keyed connector. So, you can't misconnect a Grove cable. Nice. Figure 9-1 shows a typical Grove cable and connectors.

Figure 9-1. *Grove connectors (courtesy of seeedstudio.com)*

Figure 9-2 shows a close-up of the Grove connector.

Figure 9-2. *Comparing Qwiic and Grove connectors (courtesy of sparkfun.com)*

We will discuss how the cables are used for each of the protocols; let's discuss each of these in more detail.

I2C

Recall from Chapter 4, I2C is a fast digital protocol that uses two wires (plus power and ground) to read data from circuits (or devices). I2C over the Grove cabling system uses all four wires as shown in Table 9-1.

Table 9-1. *Grove Cable (I2C)*

Pin	Color	Description
1	Yellow	SCL
2	White	SDA
3	Red	VCC (power)
4	Black	GND (ground)

Digital

The digital protocol is used for modules that produce a digital value, typically a positive integer in the range 0–1024 or larger. Digital wiring uses three wires: ground (GND), power (VCC of 3.3V or 5V), and signal. The digital protocol for Grove allows for up to two signal lines (named D0 and D1) using two of the four wires as shown in Table 9-2. Some modules may be labeled in such a way to indicate three signal lines (D0/D1 and D1/D2), but the interface supports only two signal lines. Signal lines can be used for input or output.

Table 9-2. *Grove Cable (Digital)*

Pin	Color	Description
1	Yellow	D0 – primary signal line
2	White	D1 – secondary signal line
3	Red	VCC (power)
4	Black	GND (ground)

Analog

The analog protocol supports communicating with modules using voltage. Like the digital protocol, the analog protocol supports up to two analog lines as well as the ground (GND) and power (VCC). The first analog line is named A0 and the second A1. Similar to the digital protocol, some modules may label the analog lines A0/A1 and A1/A2. Table 9-3 shows the layout of the analog protocol over the Grove cabling.

Table 9-3. *Grove Cable (Analog)*

Pin	Color	Description
1	Yellow	A0 – primary analog line
2	White	A1 – secondary analog line
3	Red	VCC (power)
4	Black	GND (ground)

UART

The UART protocol is a special serial protocol that uses two lines for transmit (TX) and receive (RX). Pins 1 and 2 are used for these lines, and the other two are the common ground and power lines as shown in Table 9-4.

Table 9-4. *Grove Cable (UART)*

Pin	Color	Description
1	Yellow	RX – serial receive
2	White	TX – serial transmit
3	Red	VCC (power)
4	Black	GND (ground)

Having all of the cables wired the same means you don't need to have any special cables for each of the four protocols, but there are some cases where we may need a slightly different cable. We will discuss the available Grove cables in a later section.

Grove modules come in a variety of sizes, and most have only a single Grove connector but may host a number of other connectors depending on the features supported. Grove modules are designed to support a single function using a dedicated circuit.

While Grove modules are not uniform in size, they do conform to one of several formats as shown in Table 9-5. Most of the formats support a Grove connector in either a vertical (cable plugs in at a right angle to the board) or horizontal orientation.

Table 9-5. *Grove Module Sizes (Courtesy of seeedstudio.com)*

Format	Size	Example
1x1	20x20mm	
1x2	20x40mm	
1x3	20x60mm	
2x2	40x40mm	
2x3	40x60mm	

The host adapter has multiple Grove connectors that you can use to connect modules (depending on the protocol as their dedicated connectors for each protocol). There are a variety of host adapters available for a growing list of host boards. This includes several for the Arduino, NodeMCU, Raspberry Pi Pico, and many more. You can discover the latest offerings by visiting `https://wiki.seeedstudio.com/ Grove_System/#how-to-connect-grove-to-your-board`.

Now that we know what the Grove system is and how it works, let's examine some of the limitations.

Limitations

Like most systems, there are some limitations. Fortunately, there are few and only the largest or most complex projects may need to heed. The limitation you may encounter for larger projects is that the maximum number of modules that can be supported is limited to the number of connections available on the host adapter, which is often limited by the host device or by the size of the host adapter.

For example, if you want to use the Grove Pico host adapter, it has only two Grove I2C connectors and thus can use only two I2C modules. Similarly, most Grove host adapters have limited numbers of digital and analog connectors. However, there are some things you can do to mitigate some of these limitations. Seeed Studio offers a number of modules that can help out (called interfaces).

Tip You can discover the latest interface boards available for a variety of uses at `https://www.seeedstudio.com/category/Grove-c-1003.html`.

For example, if you want to use more I2C connections than what are available on the host adapter, you can use the Grove 8-Channel I2C Hub (`www.seeedstudio.com/Grove-8-Channel-I2C-Hub-TCA9548A-p-4398.html`) to extend the number of I2C connections. With this module, you can use one I2C connector on your host adapter and connect up to eight I2C modules to the hub. Figure 9-3 shows the Grove 8-Channel I2C Hub.

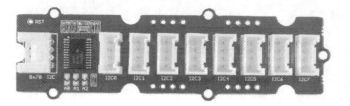

Figure 9-3. *Grove 8-Channel I2C Hub (courtesy of seeedstudio.com)*

To increase the number of connections for analog sensors, you can take a different route and use an analog-to-digital (ADC) module. The Grove ADS1115 16-bit ADC module (`www.seeedstudio.com/Grove-ADS1115-16-bit-ADC-p-4599.html`) allows you to connect up to four analog sensors connected via the onboard screw terminals. Figure 9-4 shows the Grove ADS1115 16-bit ADC module.

Figure 9-4. *Grove ADS1115 16-bit ADC module (courtesy of seeedstudio.com)*

Another limitation is the length of the Grove cables. Currently, the longest Grove cable from Seeed Studio is 50cm. If you need to use a longer cable, you can use two Grove Screw Terminal modules and a set of twisted pair wires (such as an Ethernet cable) to create your own longer cable. Figure 9-5 shows the Grove Screw Terminal module.

Figure 9-5. *Screw Terminal module (courtesy of seeedstudio.com)*

Tip   See `https://www.seeedstudio.com/category/`
`Grove-c-1003/accessories-c-945/cables-c-949.html` for
the list of Grove cables from Seeed Studio.

Now that we know more about Grove, let's see what components (host
adapters and modules) are available.

Components Available

There are a lot of components available for the Grove system. This section
highlights some of the categories of modules available. We won't see
everything that is available because the catalog is quite large. Since the
product has been around for some time, there are several versions of some
of the modules. Rather than attempt to view all of the latest modules, we
will see the more popular host adapters and modules as well as those we
will use in upcoming chapters. Figure 9-6 shows a snapshot of the top-level
index from the Seeed Studio Grove online store. As you can see, there are a
lot of categories!

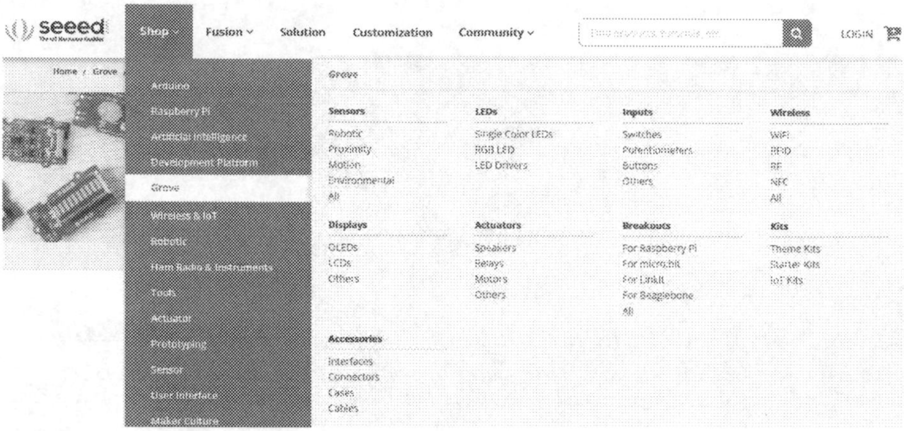

Figure 9-6. *Seeed Studio Grove online store index*

Note   While you may encounter older versions of some Grove components, the older versions are still usable and can sometimes be found used for a discount.

Host Adapters

Aside from the impressive list of modules, the list of host adapters available from Seeed Studio is very impressive. Since we are working with Arduino and Raspberry Pi in this book, let's look at versions of each for these platforms.

The host adapter most will want to use for the Raspberry Pi Pico is named Grove Shield for Pico (`www.seeedstudio.com/Grove-Shield-for-Pi-Pico-v1-0-p-4846.html`). We saw this host adapter in Chapter 1. It provides ten Grove connectors as well as GPIO headers that can be accessed with the Pico installed. Figure 9-7 shows the Grove Shield for the Raspberry Pico.

Figure 9-7. *Grove Shield for Raspberry Pi Pico (courtesy of seeedstudio.com)*

Notice the most commonly used GPIO pins are exposed on the upper-left corner. This allows you to use the header for additional connections. Another cool feature!

There are other Grove host adapters for the Pico. One of the most popular is the Maker Pi Pico Base, which we saw in Chapter 1. The Maker Pi Pico Base (without Pico) is available from Cytron (`https://thepihut.com/products/maker-pi-pico-base-without-pico`). You can get this board with the Pico already soldered in place or with a header ready for you to plug in your Pico with male headers soldered on. Figure 9-8 shows the Maker Pi Pico Base.

Figure 9-8. *Maker Pi Pico Base (without Pico) (courtesy of thepihut.com)*

Modules

Seeed Studio offers a wide variety of modules that contain sensors, input, output, and display capabilities similar to those available for Qwiic. However, the categories and number of modules available are several times that of the other systems. So many that it is not possible to list them all here. Table 9-6 lists the categories of modules available with a link to each category for further reading. You will find most have subcategories that you can explore to find more about the modules in the category. All URLs (links) begin with www.seeedstudio.com/category/.

Table 9-6. *Categories of Grove Modules*

Category	Description	Category Link
Sensors	Modules that allow you to sample the world around us	`Sensor-for-Grove-c-24.html`
LEDs	Modules that contain various forms of LEDs	`leds-c-891.html`
Input	Modules that contain devices that permit input of data or input actions like buttons	`Input-c-21.html`
Wireless	Modules that support wireless technologies	`wireless-c-899.html`
Displays	Modules with output devices	`displays-c-929.html`
Actuators	Modules with devices that produce movement, drive motors, or produce sound	`actuators-c-940.html`
Accessories	Grove accessories such as cables, headers, and more	`accessories-c-945.html`

So, what are the modules available in these categories? We will use the same list of subcategories we used for the other component systems. You will find the Seeed Studio website organized a bit different, but all of these subcategories are present:

- *Sensors*: Typically contain a single sensor that produces output (readings or values) on the I2C bus. Examples include temperature, humidity, pressure, distance, magnometer, light, and environmental (gases) sensors.

- *Displays*: Modules that contain an output device for displaying data. Examples include OLED and LED displays.

- *Relays*: Modules that contain relays that permit you to switch higher power devices on or off.

- *Motors*: Modules that permit you to control small electric motors.

- *Input*: Modules that contain one or more buttons, potentiometers, keypads, or switches.

- *ADC/DAC*: Modules that provide analog-to-digital conversion (ADC) or digital-to-analog conversion (DAC) that permit incorporation of other circuits into your project.

- *Accessory*: Various modules that provide handy operations such as data loggers, cryptographic operations, and more.

Now, let's look at a sample of the Grove modules we will be using in the upcoming chapters as we explore how to write the code for IoT projects using the Grove system beginning with an output device.

We will make use of several Grove LED modules. These modules contain one LED of a particular color. Figure 9-9 shows a Grove LED module. You can discover all of the Grove LED modules at `https://www.seeedstudio.com/category/Grove-c-1003/leds-c-891/single-color-leds-c-914.html`.

Figure 9-9. *Grove Red LED module (courtesy of seeedstudio.com)*

We will also use an LCD screen in some of the projects. The Grove – OLED Display 0.96" (`www.seeedstudio.com/Grove-OLED-Display-0-96-SSD1315-p-4294.html`) is a nifty, small OLED similar to the one we used in the Qwiic projects. Figure 9-10 shows the OLED display.

Figure 9-10. *Grove – OLED Display 0.96" (SSD1315) (courtesy of seeedstudio.com)*

The Grove Sound Sensor module (`https://www.seeedstudio.com/Grove-Sound-Sensor-Based-on-LM358-amplifier-Arduino-Compatible.html?queryID=4e7fe5323cfe7b455a38a1b11c3889c0&objectID=1820&indexName=bazaar_retailer_products`) provides the ability to detect sound or noise as an analog value similar to a microphone. Figure 9-11 shows the module with the sensor-facing side.

Figure 9-11. *Grove Sound Sensor (courtesy of seeedstudio.com)*

We will also use input devices such as the Grove Dual Button module that has two buttons mounted (`www.seeedstudio.com/Grove-Dual-Button-p-4529.html`). The module comes with a variety of colored caps permitting you to match the color of the cap to your project features. Figure 9-12 shows the module with caps on the buttons. You can also use them without the caps. Note that the Grove connector is located on the bottom of the board.

Figure 9-12. *Grove Dual Button module (courtesy of seeedstudio.com)*

The Grove – AHT20 I2C Temperature and Humidity Sensor module can measure both temperature and humidity (`www.seeedstudio.com/Grove-AHT20-I2C-Industrial-grade-temperature-and-humidity-sensor-p-4497. html`). Figure 9-13 shows the module with the sensor-facing side.

Figure 9-13. *Grove – AHT20 I2C Temperature and Humidity Sensor (courtesy of seeedstudio.com)*

Notice this module has additional pins for advanced users. In this case, we see the I2C pins broken out on the right side of the module. Modules with these features typically come without headers mounted.

Once again, there are many modules available. These are just a sampling of the modules available from Seeed Studio. A compact list of all Grove devices and modules is available at `www.seeedstudio.com/category/Grove-c-1003.html`.

Cabling and Connectors

The Grove system includes cables of various lengths including 5, 20, 30, 40, and 50cm. Most modules produced by Seeed Studio include a 20cm cable or longer. The 5cm cables are great for projects that include modules mounted in close proximity or inside an enclosure.

There are also special cables available for a variety of uses such as a branch or "Y" cable that lets you connect two modules to a single source, a Grove to servo cable for using servos connected directly to a host, and even cables for connecting directly to your host board with a Grove connector on one side and the other side broken out with individual male or female pins.

See `www.seeedstudio.com/cables-c-949.html` for a list of cables and connectors to support the Grove system.

Where to Buy Grove Components

You can purchase Qwiic components directly from Seeed Studio (seeedstudio.com), which is based in China. They often ship products quickly, but shipping may take longer than expected. Fortunately, you can often find Grove modules on popular online retail sites such as amazon.com and online auction sites. In fact, I have seen select starter kits in brick-and-mortar stores that sell electronic components. If you live in the United States, check out the online retail stores first or buy in bulk to save on shipping from Seeed Studio.

Now, let's discuss how to use these systems in your projects.

Using the Components with Your Pico

Plugging your choice of Grove host adapter onto your host board and plugging the modules together with the cables is pretty easy. Recall, the connectors only go one way, so you can't cross-connect anything.

However, Grove modules are not designed to be hot pluggable. You should not connect and disconnect modules while your board is powered on. This could lead to damaging the module(s) or your host board.

Caution   Do not plug or unplug Grove modules while your board is powered on.

Once the hardware is plugged together, the next step is to start working on the code to enable your modules and complete your project. To do so, you are likely required to load one or more software libraries.

Like the vast array of modules, the software libraries required for the Grove modules vary and depend on the module itself. Fortunately, Seeed Studio is very good about providing samples for use of each of their hundreds of modules.

The following summarizes the steps necessary for the Pico. The following does not include all of the steps needed for all of the projects in the book; rather, the section is an overview of what you can expect to configure your PC to implement the projects. Specific details for each example are included in each chapter.

Fortunately, most Grove modules have examples on how to use them that include, at a minimum, sample code for the Arduino. For example, there is a Wiki page for the OLED Display 0.96 module that shows you how to get started using it (https://wiki.seeedstudio.com/Grove-OLED_ Display_0.96inch/).

Software libraries for the Pico are available for download to your PC, but some Python libraries are designed for use with the Raspberry Pi, not the Pico. So, you may need to copy/download one or more additional code modules to the Pico to get them to work. Be aware that some libraries may require changes in order to work with the Pico.

Most often, this is changing the use of I2C to SoftI2C, but sometimes you may need to change additional things in the code modules (library) to accommodate the Pico hardware. This makes using the Grove system a bit more of a challenge, but not burdensome once you experience how to make a few work as we will see in the next three chapters. Most can be used with little or no changes.

If you encounter a Grove module where there isn't a Python library, do not despair. Again, most Grove modules have a Wiki page that will show you how to get started. But if there isn't a specific Python library, you most likely can find a similar one from the Internet that you can use. All it takes is a bit of exploring, and you can find Python libraries for what you need.

Summary

Grove provides a simple, no-error connector that you can use to connect a variety of components together using several protocols – all from the same board.

Now that the hardware challenges have been nearly eliminated, we can turn our attention back to learning how to write the code for our projects. As you saw in this chapter, this may require installing software libraries to support the modules you are using or adapting existing libraries to suit your needs.

The next chapter begins a series of projects that use Grove components to teach you how to work with the systems for the Pico. As you will see, except for the hardware itself, the pattern of building the projects is the same as the previous project chapters.

CHAPTER 10

Project: Sound Activated Lights

As we saw in Chapter 9, the Grove component system can help make your hardware connections much simpler with less risk of incorrectly wiring your components. Indeed, except for making sure you are plugging in the Grove cables to the correct ports, you can't make a wrong or reversed connection.

The Grove modules are all self-contained boards that have everything the main component needs, so there is no need to wire up additional hardware like resistors. The challenge lies in writing your code to talk to the components. Most Grove modules have examples you can use, and some have libraries you can download. However, some do not have any Python examples, or the Python examples are written for the Raspberry Pi rather than the Pico. In those cases, you may need to either write the code yourself using the examples as a guide or modify existing Python libraries for use on the Pico.

Since this is our first Grove project, in this chapter we will keep those issues to a minimum and instead spend some time looking at the Grove hardware and how to connect things to our Pico.

© Charles Bell 2022
C. Bell, *Beginning MicroPython with the Raspberry Pi Pico*, Maker Innovations Series,
https://doi.org/10.1007/978-1-4842-8135-2_10

Overview

In this chapter, we begin our tour of example Grove projects with a simple project that demonstrates how to use a sound sensor and an RGB LED to display assorted colors based on the sound detected. The idea is the LED will light up whenever sound is detected, and the color will differ based on the loudness of the sound. So, we will be creating a sound detector.

The code for this project will need to read from an analog sensor (the sound sensor) and convert that value to a range of red, green, and blue values to convert the integer that the analog-to-digital converter returns from the sensor. As you will see, there is a bit of trickery needed to ensure the higher the value of the sensor, the brighter (higher values) the RGB values. We use those values to turn on an RGB LED.

Now let's see what components are needed for this project, and then we will see how to wire everything together.

Required Components

The components for this project include a Grove host board that you can plug your Pico into that supports multiple Grove connectors. Recall, Grove connectors on the host board support one of several protocols including analog, digital, and I2C. We will need two Grove modules: a sound sensor and an RGB LED.

Table 10-1 lists the components you will need in addition to your Pico and USB cable. Links to vendors are provided should you want to purchase the components.

Table 10-1. *Required Components*

Component	Qty	Description	Cost	Links
Sound Sensor	1	Sensor	$5.40	www.seeedstudio.com/Grove-Sound-Sensor-Based-on-LM358-amplifier-Arduino-Compatible.html
Chainable RGB	1	RGB LED	$6.60	www.seeedstudio.com/Grove-Chainable-RGB-Led-V2-0.html
Grove Shield for Pi Pico V1.0	1	Host board	$4.30	www.seeedstudio.com/Grove-Shield-for-Pi-Pico-v1-0-p-4846.html
Grove Cable	2	See note	Varies	https://www.seeedstudio.com/category/Grove-c-1003/accessories-c-945/cables-c-949.html

Note   Each Grove module comes with a short cable. If you need longer cables, see the link in the table for options.

You can purchase the components directly from Seeed Studio via the links in the table, or you can often find them at online retailers such as Adafruit (adafruit.com), SparkFun (sparkfun.com), or any electronics store that carries electronic components. Costs shown are estimates and do not include any shipping costs.

Now, let's discuss the new components we will be using.

Grove Shield for Pi Pico

We saw the Grove Shield for Pico in Chapter 9, but let's explore its features in more detail. There are ten Grove connectors that include three analog ports, three digital ports, two UART ports, and two I2C ports. There is also an SPI header and a switch that allows you to choose between 5V and 3.3V to power the Grove connectors. Figure 10-1 shows the Grove Shield for Pico.

Figure 10-1. *Grove Shield for Pi Pico v1.0 (courtesy of seeedstudio.com)*

Notice the 5V/3.3V switch is located in the upper left, and the SPI breakout is located in the lower right. Notice also that the board is marked *USB* to orient the Pico with the USB connector to the left. Finally, notice the two rows of double female headers. You connect your Pico to the centermost set leaving headers open for use with jumper wires. Cool!

Like all Grove components, Seeed Studio provides a Wiki page devoted to documenting the component and providing example code. The Wiki page for this host adapter is found at https://wiki.seeedstudio.com/ Grove_Shield_for_Pi_Pico_V1.0/.

Sound Sensor

The Grove Sound Sensor is an analog module that incorporates a microphone and a small amplifier. It can be used to detect sound in the area and even the intensity of the sound. We will use both features in this project. Figure 10-2 shows the Grove Sound Sensor.

Figure 10-2. Grove Sound Sensor (courtesy of seeedstudio.com)

Grove RGB LED

The lamp used in this project is a bright red, green, and blue (RGB) LED that can be used to produce a vast array of colors by specifying a value of 0–255 for each color. The higher the value, the brighter (intensity) that color is shown. By mixing the intensity, we can see a wide range of colors.

For example, values of (255, 0, 0) for red or (127, 0, 127) for purple. To see what this might look like, an RGB chooser (www.w3schools.com/colors/colors_rgb.asp) can help you visualize the color. Navigate there now and try it out yourself.

The Grove Chainable RGB LED module allows you to produce any color you want. Figure 10-3 shows the Grove Chainable RGB LED.

Figure 10-3. *Grove Chainable RGB LED (courtesy of seeedstudio.com)*

So, what does the chainable in the name mean? It means if you want to use more than one RGB LED, you can "chain" the modules together. In fact, on the bottom of the module you will see two Grove connectors, one marked "IN" and another "OUT." Figure 10-4 shows what the connectors look like. Notice the labels for each.

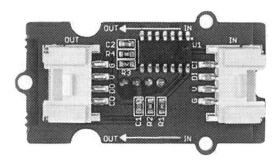

Figure 10-4. *Grove Chainable RGB LED connectors on the bottom (courtesy of seeedstudio.com)*

To chain multiple modules together, simply connect the first Grove cable from your host adapter to the "IN" connector, then another Grove cable to the "OUT," and then the "IN" to the next module, and so on. You can connect up to 1024 RGBs together.

Grove Kits

Seeed Studio also sells kits for some platforms that include a host adapter and several modules. An excellent alternative kit for this project that has many of the sensors you will need is the Grove Starter Kit for Raspberry Pi Pico (`www.seeedstudio.com/Grove-Starter-Kit-for-Raspberry-Pi-Pico-p-4851.html`). Figure 10-5 shows the kit.

Figure 10-5. *Grove Starter Kit for Raspberry Pi Pico (courtesy of seeedstudio.com)*

Notice we see the Pico host adapter and the source sensor along with an LCD, environment sensors, LEDs, and much more. If you decide to purchase the kit, you can visit the Wiki at `www.seeedstudio.com/Grove-Starter-Kit-for-Raspberry-Pi-Pico-p-4851.html` to learn more about the components and see sample projects.

Now, let's see how to connect the components together.

Set Up the Hardware

Connecting the hardware for a Grove project is really easy. Since the cables are keyed, you don't have to worry about incorrect connections. Rather, we have to consider which Grove connectors we need to use. For this project, we need only two connectors, one for the I2C interface on the Chainable RGB module and an analog connector for the sound sensor. We will use the *I2C0* connector for the RGB module and the *A0* connector for the sound sensor as shown in Figure 10-6.

Figure 10-6. *Connections for the sound detector project*

Caution   Be sure to plug the Grove cable into the RGB module on the side that is indicated as "IN." Plugging it into the "OUT" port may prevent the LED from illuminating. Recall, we use the "OUT" port to chain the RGB modules together by connecting the "OUT" of one module to the "IN" of the next in the chain.

Once again, always make sure to double-check your connections before powering the board on. Now, let's talk about the code we need to write. Don't power on your board just yet – there is a fair amount of discussion needed before we're ready to test the project.

Write the Code

Now it's time to write the code for our project. The code is a bit less complicated than the previous project but has its own interesting twists. Specifically, we will need a function to convert the value read from the sound sensor into a tuple of three values in the range 0–255 for the RGB values. Before we look at the code, let's look at the library we will need to communicate with the Chainable RGB module that uses an I2C interface.

Libraries Needed

We need only one library for the Chainable RGB module since the sound sensor is an analog device that we can read with functions from the MicroPython machine library. If you visit the Wiki for the Chainable RGB module (https://wiki.seeedstudio.com/Grove-Chainable_RGB_LED/), you will discover a section that demonstrates how to use the module with Python on the Raspberry Pi. However, this example is for Python, not MicroPython. In fact, most of the Wiki pages for the Grove modules have only Python examples. So, what do we do? We turn to Google for help!

Tip   When researching Grove modules to use with the Pico, be sure to Google for a MicroPython driver. Most Python drivers for Grove modules require additional libraries or libraries that only work in Python.

A quick Google search for "chainable rgb grove micropython" will return a number of entries. Among them are example libraries for the p9813 chip, which is the controller chip used on the Chainable RGB module. The library found to work best for the Pico is the micropython-p9813 library from Mike Causer (`https://github.com/mcauser/micropython-p9813`).

We need only download the library to our PC and then upload it to our Pico. The best way to do that is to use the command `git clone https://github.com/mcauser/micropython-p9813` to make a copy (clone) of the repository as follows. This copies all of the files including examples and documentation to your PC:

```
$ git clone https://github.com/mcauser/micropython-p9813
Cloning into 'micropython-p9813'...
remote: Enumerating objects: 36, done.
remote: Total 36 (delta 0), reused 0 (delta 0), pack-reused 36
Unpacking objects: 100% (36/36), done.
```

Once you clone the repository, you can locate the `p9813.py` file in the `<root of clone>/micropython-p9813` folder. You can then download that to your Pico.

Now, let's take a look at the code for the project.

Note   Since writing the code for a Grove project does not require any special programming, we will skip the line-by-line explanation and instead talk about the high-level parts of the code.

Code Layout

We will follow a similar code layout as we did in the previous project. We will create a `main()` function that will run when the Pico boots and helper functions for the more complicated parts. Thus, we will place all of our setup and the main execution loop in the main() function. Finally, we will add a conditional at the bottom of the script to call the main() function if the script is executed (loaded by MicroPython for execution).

Since we are familiar with how we write the code for our projects, let's look at the code in overview starting from the top of the script file. We will name the file main.py.

Imports

Recall, we place the imports at the top of the file. The imports for the project will require the ADC and Pin classes from the machine library and the sleep library. We also need to import the p9813 library from the project4 folder. The following shows the imports for the project:

```
from machine import ADC, Pin
from time import sleep
from project4.p9813 import P9813
```

Functions

There are three helper functions needed for this project. We need a function to read a value from the sensor. We also need a function to translate the value read from the sound sensor to a tuple in the range of 0–255, 0–255, and 0–255 for the RGB values. We will break this operation into two parts to help with code comprehension.[1]

---

[1] Separating complex parts of a function is a tool you can use to help isolate and solve complex problems. It also helps with code readability.

Listing 10-1 shows the code for the get_value() function. Here, we pass in an instance of the ADC class and use that to read ten values waiting for 100ms before each read. Like we have with the last analog sensor, we will read a series of values from the sensor and return an average to help reduce sporadic values from reading the sensor.

Listing 10-1. The get_value() Function

```
# Read the sensor 10 times and average the values read
def get_value(adc):
    total = 0
    for i in range (0,10):
        # Wait for sensor to settle
        sleep(0.1)
        # Read the value
        value = adc.read_u16()
        total += value
    return int(total/10)
```

Translating the value read from the sensor to a tuple is a bit more complicated than you may expect. There are two steps. First, we need to map the values to an integer. One mechanism[2] to do this is to think of the tuple as three hexadecimal values in the range 0–255, which in hexadecimal is 0x00–0xFF. Now, if you arrange them consecutively such as 0xFFFFFF, you get a value of 16,777,215 or a range of 0–16,777,215. The second step is to convert to the RGB tuple; we shift the value 8 bits at a time to get each range.

We name the first step translate() and call that from within the second function named num_to_rbg(), which will call from the main() function.

---

[2] I am certain there are others.

Listing 10-2. The translate() Function

```
# Translate from range 1-65353 to 1-16,777,215
def translate(x, in_min, in_max, out_min, out_max):
    return int((x - in_min) * (out_max - out_min) /
    (in_max - in_min) + out_min)
```

Listing 10-3 shows the num_to_rgb() function. Take a moment to read the lines of code that do the bitwise shifts to ensure you understand how it works. In short, we first shift 16 bits to capture the leftmost value for red, then 8 bits and mask the extra bits (with the logical and operation) for green, and finally mask all except the rightmost value to capture the value for blue.

Listing 10-3. The num_to_rgb() Function

```
# Map range 0-0xFFFFFF to (R,G,B) tuple
def num_to_rgb(sensor_value):
    mapped_value = translate(sensor_value, LOW_THRESHOLD, 0xFFFF,
                                    1, 0xFFFFFF)
    r = mapped_value >> 16
    g = (mapped_value >> 8) & 0x00FF
    b = (mapped_value & 0x0000FF)
    return (r,g,b)
```

Now let's look at the main function.

Main Function

Next is the main() function. Here, we will initialize the variables we will need as well as implement the loop to keep the script running until cancelled or until the Pico shut down. Let's begin with the setup code and then look at the main loop execution.

Setup

The setup code for this project will need to initialize the ADC class instance and create variables of the Pin class for use with the I2C interface for the Chainable RGB module. We also turn off the RGB LED by assigning the values of zero for each color in the tuple. There are two steps to setting the color for the RGB. First, we set the values for red, green, and blue and then call the write() function to tell the library to turn the LED on with those values. Listing 10-4 shows the code for setup and initialization.

Listing 10-4. Setup and Initialization

```
# Setup the sound sensor
sound = ADC(Pin(26))

# Setup the RGB module
scl = Pin(7, Pin.OUT)
sda = Pin(6, Pin.OUT)
rgb_chain = P9813(scl, sda, 1)
rgb_chain[0] = (0, 0, 0) # turn RGB off
rgb_chain.write()
sleep(1)
```

One thing to notice is that the P9813 class returns an array, not a single class instance. Thus, when we want to assign values to the RGB for the color, we must use the array index [0].

Execution Loop

Next, we examine the loop code. Here, we will greet the user and then get the value from the sound sensor. If the value is greater than the lowest threshold we established, we then convert the "sound" read to color and set the RGB to the new tuple (red, green, and blue). If the value from the sound sensor is lower or equal to the threshold, we turn the LED off. Listing 10-5 shows the code for the execution loop.

Listing 10-5. Execution Loop

```
print("Welcome to the sound to light detector!")
while True:
    value = get_value(sound)
    if value > LOW_THRESHOLD:
        rgb = num_to_rgb(value)
        print("Value read: {0:05} Color: {1}".
        format(value, rgb))
        rgb_chain[0] = rgb
        rgb_chain.write()
        sleep(1)
        continue
    rgb_chain[0] = (0, 0, 0)
    sleep(0.25)
    rgb_chain.write()
```

Now we're all set to evaluate the code. We will write the code to execute automatically when we power on the Pico. Recall, we do this by naming the code main.py and placing the libraries we want to use in a folder named project4. Listing 10-6 shows the complete code for the project.

Listing 10-6. Sound Detector Code

```
#
# Beginning MicroPython
#
# Chapter 10 - Sound to Light Detector
#
```

```python
# This example implements a sound detector that turns on a RGB
# LED based on the value from the sound sensor. We use a Grove
# Sound Sensor and a Grove Chainable RGB LED.
#
# Dr. Charles Bell
#
# Import libraries
from machine import ADC, Pin
from time import sleep
from project4.p9813 import P9813

# Constants
LOW_THRESHOLD = 10000    # Threshold of the smallest sound
value - tune to your environs

# Read the sensor 10 times and average the values read
def get_value(adc):
    total = 0
    for i in range (0,10):
        # Wait for sensor to settle
        sleep(0.1)
        # Read the value
        value = adc.read_u16()
        total += value
    return int(total/10)

# Translate from range 1-65353 to 1-16,777,215
def translate(x, in_min, in_max, out_min, out_max):
    return int((x - in_min) * (out_max - out_min) / (
                in_max - in_min) + out_min)
```

```python
# Map range 0-0xFFFFFF to (R,G,B) tuple
def num_to_rgb(sensor_value):
    mapped_value = translate(sensor_value,
    LOW_THRESHOLD, 0xFFFF, 1, 0xFFFFFF)
    r = mapped_value >> 16
    g = (mapped_value >> 8) & 0x00FF
    b = (mapped_value & 0x0000FF)
    return (r,g,b)

def main():
    # Setup the sound sensor
    sound = ADC(Pin(26))

    # Setup the RGB module
    scl = Pin(7, Pin.OUT)
    sda = Pin(6, Pin.OUT)
    rgb_chain = P9813(scl, sda, 1)
    rgb_chain[0] = (0, 0, 0) # turn RGB off
    rgb_chain.write()
    sleep(1)

    print("Welcome to the sound to light detector!")
    while True:
        value = get_value(sound)
        if value > LOW_THRESHOLD:
            rgb = num_to_rgb(value)
            print("Value read: {0:05} Color: {1}".format
            (value, rgb))
            rgb_chain[0] = rgb
            rgb_chain.write()
            sleep(1)
            continue
        rgb_chain[0] = (0, 0, 0)
```

```
        sleep(0.25)
        rgb_chain.write()

if __name__ == '__main__':
    try:
        main()
    except (KeyboardInterrupt, SystemExit) as err:
        print("\nbye!")
        sys.exit(0)
```

OK, now we're ready to execute the project.

Execute

Now we can copy all of our code to our Pico. If you haven't already done so, you should create a folder named project4 on your Pico and then upload the P9813.py file to the project4 folder. Next, upload the main.py file to the root folder of your Pico.

Recall, there are two ways to test or execute the code. We could use Thonny to connect to the Pico and simply run the main.py script. Or we can reboot the Pico by unplugging it and plugging it back in to the USB port on your PC.

The difference is if you run the main.py file manually, you will see the debug statements show in the output at the bottom of Thonny. Running the script automatically may not show those statements if you do not use Thonny or a similar application to connect to the Pico.

Once the program starts, you can then make some noise! Simply clap your hands or snap your fingers, or if you are careful, tap the sensor with a pen or pencil. Depending on the ambient noise in the room, you may need to adjust the minimal sound threshold so that the RGB illuminates only for louder noises. When values greater than the threshold are detected, the program writes debug statements to the REPL console. The following shows an example of the output you will see:

```
Welcome to the sound to light detector!
Value read: 15371 Color: (24, 194, 60)
Value read: 14249 Color: (19, 150, 46)
Value read: 13089 Color: (14, 61, 72)
Value read: 10904 Color: (4, 42, 204)
Value read: 13457 Color: (15, 239, 142)
Value read: 14291 Color: (19, 199, 191)
Value read: 12906 Color: (13, 101, 84)
Value read: 11816 Color: (8, 95, 9)
...
```

If you do not see the RGB illuminate and change colors when noises are varied in loudness, or the REPL console does not show any data, be sure to notice the sound values read and adjust the threshold up or down as needed.

Once everything is working, you can disconnect your Pico and connect it to a 5V power supply to run the project on boot and watch the colors change with sound. Cool!

Taking It Further

This project, like the last one, shows excellent prospects for reusing the techniques in other projects. Sound sensors can be applied to many problems, and if you want to consider taking time to explore some embellishments, here are a few you may want to consider:

- Experiment with different sounds in the room like opening and closing doors or windows and adjust the code to detect those sounds. Perhaps even assign special colors to those sound levels.

- Add more RGB LEDs to your chain and program the code to send the color codes to all of the RGBs in the chain.

- Adapt the code to use a set of colors for differing loudness (sounds). This could be helpful or interesting if you want to display color changes to sound levels such as applause from an audience.

Of course, if you want to press on to the next project, you're welcome to do so, but take some time to explore these potential embellishments – it will be a good practice.

Summary

As you can see, using Grove modules is much easier than trying to connect a set of jumper wires to breakout boards or building a circuit on a breadboard. In this regard, the Grove system is a grand success. Best of all, it allows you to quickly assemble the hardware of your project so you can concentrate on the code.

In this chapter, we took a look at a sample Grove project that uses an I2C device and an analog sensor. We saw how to connect the modules to our host board as well as how to adapt code to work with the Pico. This small project has also shown us how easy it is to use Grove modules, and now that we've had some practice with a simple example, we are ready to jump into a more complex project.

In the next chapter, we will see another project that demonstrates how to use more Grove modules to create a classic electronic game called Simon Says. It's time to have some fun!

CHAPTER 11

Project: Simon Game

If you like vintage electronic games, you have played a game named Simon.[1] It is a round tabletop game that has four large colored buttons on top. One or more players can play with the objective to repeat a sequence from memory. The game presents the player with a sequence of colored lights in a random pattern. The player's goal is to press the buttons for each color in the sequence before time runs out. If the player repeats the sequence correctly, the game continues and adds another light to the sequence. The game starts with a single light, so early levels are pretty easy, but as the sequence gets longer, it becomes harder to play. Throw in several players and you've got a cool, Internet-free game party!

In this chapter, we will see how to create a version of the Simon game using Grove modules using analog, digital, and I2C protocols. Let's get started.

Overview

The project for this chapter is designed to demonstrate how to use analog, digital, and I2C devices on the same Grove host adapter to build a Simon game. It works very much like the original game but with an LCD for displaying messages. We will use a Grove Buzzer for sound and two Grove Dual Button modules. For the lights, we will use one Grove RGB LED module.

---

[1] https://en.wikipedia.org/wiki/Simon_(game)

© Charles Bell 2022
C. Bell, *Beginning MicroPython with the Raspberry Pi Pico*, Maker Innovations Series,
https://doi.org/10.1007/978-1-4842-8135-2_11

While this seems like a simple project build, the number of modules in use and integrating all of the code for those modules makes this project the most ambitious of the book. If you haven't read and worked on the other projects, you may want to work on the earlier chapters first and save this one until you've mastered a few of the others.

For those with access to a 3D printer, we will also see a simple mounting plate you can print and install the modules onto to protect them and make it easier to use in playing the game.

Let's see what hardware we will need.

Required Components

The hardware needed for this project is listed in Table 11-1. We will use a Grove Dual Button, Grove Buzzer, Grove LCD RGB Backlight, Grove Dual Button modules, and a Grove Chainable RGB LED V2.0.

Table 11-1. *Hardware Needed for the Mood Detector Project*

Component	Qty	Description	Cost	Links
Grove Dual Button	3	Buttons	$2.20	www.seeedstudio.com/Grove-Dual-Button-p-4529.html
Grove Buzzer	1	Buzzer	$1.90	www.seeedstudio.com/Grove-Buzzer.html
Grove LCD RGB Backlight	1	LCD	$11.90	www.seeedstudio.com/Grove-LCD-RGB-Backlight.html
Grove Chainable RGB LED V2.0	1	LED	$6.60	www.seeedstudio.com/Grove-Chainable-RGB-Led-V2-0.html
Grove Cable	5	Cable	$0.95	www.sparkfun.com/products/14426
Grove Shield for Pi Pico V1.0	1	Host board	$4.30	www.seeedstudio.com/Grove-Shield-for-Pi-Pico-v1-0-p-4846.html

Let's discuss these components briefly. We will discover how to work with the hardware in more detail later in the chapter. We saw the Grove Shield for Pico, Grove Buzzer, and the Grove Chainable RGB LED in the last chapter, so let's look at the new Grove components for this chapter.

Grove Dual Button

The Grove Dual Button is a digital module that has two momentary buttons. While there are two buttons on the module, we need only a single Grove cable to connect to the host adapter. This is because digital modules use only three wires: ground, 3.3/5V, and one for signal. Since we have four cables available, we can use the extra wire for the second button.

The button comes with a set of colored button caps that you can use to help color code your button choices, which is a nice option.

You may have noticed we need three of these modules. Two modules are used for the four color buttons, and another is used for a mode and start option. We will see these functions later when we start the code for the project.

Figure 11-1 shows the Grove Dual Button.

Figure 11-1. *Grove Dual Button (courtesy of seeedstudio.com)*

Grove LCD RGB Backlight

If you've used monochrome LCD displays in the past, you may appreciate the interesting option on the Grove LCD RGB Backlight. While the text color remains dark gray, you can change the background using an RGB color similar to the Chainable RGB LED. Figure 11-2 shows the Grove LCD RGB Backlight.

Figure 11-2. *Grove LCD RGB Backlight (courtesy of seeedstudio.com)*

While this module does not offer the option, some Grove I2C modules support address changes by opening or closing jumpers on the bottom of the board. Now, let's see how to connect the components together.

Set Up the Hardware

Once again, connecting the hardware for a Grove project is really easy. Since the cables are keyed, you don't have to worry about incorrect connections. Rather, we have to consider which Grove connectors we need to use. For this project, we need six connections for the six modules we will be using. The connections and their types are shown in Table 11-2.

Table 11-2. *Simon Game Connections*

Module	Description	Pico Shield Connector
Dual Button 1	Start/mode	D16/D17
Dual Button 2	Red/green buttons	D18/D19
Dual Button 3	White/blue buttons	D20/D21
Buzzer	Sound	A0
RGB LCD	Display	I2C0
Chainable RGB LED	Color cue	I2C1

Thus, we will need six Grove cables, and each will plug into one spot on the Pico Shield. Figure 11-3 shows how the connections will look once all of the modules are connected to the Pico Shield.

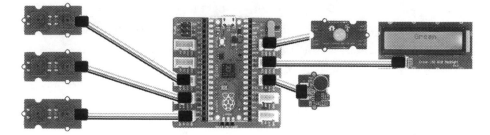

Figure 11-3. *Connections for Simon Game*

Wow! That's a lot of connections, right? Not really, though, considering we're only using six cables. If we had wired everything together using breadboards, we would have used over 30 jumper wires!

Note   Be sure to switch the Pico Shield to the 5V setting. This is because the Grove RGB LED works best with 5V power.

You can play the game with the modules connected loosely, but for best results, you may want to consider using a small board about 4" wide and 8" long to attach the modules using small wood screws. This will make gameplay much better.

Or, better, you could build yourself a mounting plate!

Using a Mounting Plate

Since we have so many components and a bunch of cables connecting them all together, using the project can take a little bit of space, and with all of those modules dangling by their cables tethered only to the Grove host adapter, you run the risk of accidentally unplugging a module, or, worse, the electronics on the module may come into contact with conductive material. Even so, using them to play a game like Simon can become a lesson in patience.

You can mitigate this by using a double-sided tape to tape them to your desk, but a better solution is to create a mounting plate. We could create a full enclosure, but as you will see, leaving the modules exposed gives the project a genuine cool factor.

If you have your own 3D printer or have access to a 3D printer, you can print a mounting plate. The source code for this chapter includes the 3D printing files you need to create a simple enclosure to mount the modules arranged in a manner that enables gameplay. Figure 11-4 shows the mounting plate.

Figure 11-4 shows an example mounting plate for the game. There are places to bolt all of the modules as well as the Pico Shield.

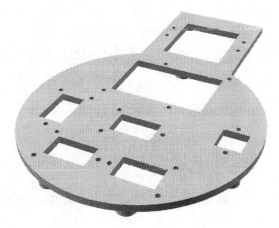

Figure 11-4. *3D mounting plate design for the Simon Says project*

While this looks like nothing more than a coaster, there are feet on the bottom of the plate and places for M2 nuts. In fact, you will need to print this plate upside down.

There is also a set of spacers you will need to print as shown in Figure 11-5.

Figure 11-5. *3D spacers design for the Simon Says project*

Notice there are (2) short M2 spacers for the buzzer module, (12) medium spacers for the Dual Button modules and the Chainable RGB LED (each take 3), and (4) long spacers for the LCD RGB Backlight.

To mount the modules, you will need the following hardware. You may use longer bolts if you cannot find the exact sizes, but be sure to adjust the constant FOOT_HEIGHT in the simon.scad file to allow for the extra length:

- (22) M2 nuts

- (6) M2x10mm bolts

- (12) M2x12mm bolts

- (4) M2x19mm bolts

To assemble the enclosure, begin by mounting the Dual Button and Chainable RGB LED modules. Arrange the mounting plate with the Pico section (the square section) facing away from you (call it the top). Find the four mounting positions that match the holes in the modules.

Mount one Dual Button module on the far left of the plate (oriented vertically) and the two along the bottom edge (oriented horizontally). The last position where the button module fits is in the center. This spot is for the Chainable RGB LED. Mount the Chainable RGB LED in the remaining spot in the center.

You will need three bolts and three medium spacers for each. Place the M2 nuts in the nut traps on the bottom of the mounting plate and tighten.[2]

Next, mount the Buzzer to the spot on the right side of the mounting plate using two small spacers and two bolts and nuts.

Next, mount the LCD using the four long spacers and long bolts. Be sure to orient the LCD so the Grove connector is on the same side as the RGB LED.

Finally, mount the Pico Shield. You will need two bolts and nuts (no spacers). You will need to mount the Pico Shield before you mount the Pico to the shield. When you have the Pico Shield mounted, insert the Pico.

Now you are ready to run the Grove cables. It is recommended you make the connections in the following order, routing the cables under the LCD to keep them away from the buttons:

1. Connect the leftmost Dual Button to D16/D17 on the Pico Shield. The topmost button will be the mode and the bottom the start button.

2. Connect the next Dual Button module to D18/D19 on the Pico Shield. This is the left module on the bottom of the plate.

3. Connect the last Dual Button module to D20/D21 on the Pico Shield.

4. Connect the Chainable RGB LED to I2C0 on the Pico Shield.

5. Connect the RGB LCD to I2C1 on the Pico Shield.

6. Connect the Buzzer to A0 on the Pico Shield.

---

[2] Do not overtighten! You only need to tighten them enough to keep the modules on the mounting plate.

Tip   If you plan to partially disassemble the game to use parts for other projects temporarily, be sure to use a small piece of painter's or masking tape to note where each cable is used. That way, you can replace the module and reconnect it without guessing the connection.

The Dual Button modules come with colored caps for the buttons. I used a white cap for the mode button and a blue cap for the start button (but any color will do for these). The game button caps should be, from left to right, red, green, white, and blue.

You should also make all of the cable connections as well since we will route all wiring under the LCD RGB Backlight. You can use a small zip tie to bundle the cables, but be sure to avoid kinking or putting strain on the Grove connectors. Figure 11-6 shows the completed Simon game.

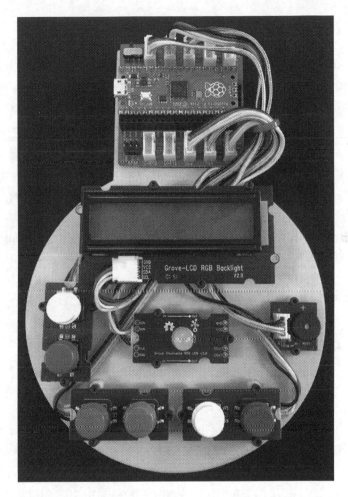

Figure 11-6. *Mounting the modules to the 3D printed plate*

If you have experience creating 3D models for printing, feel free to experiment with creating your own enclosure – one that also includes a battery so you can make the project a handheld game.

Now that we know more about the hardware for this chapter, let's write the code!

Write the Code

The code for this project uses analog and digital modules as well as two I2C devices. The Dual Buttons are digital, the Buzzer is an analog module, and the RGB LCD and Chainable RGB LED are I2C devices. As you will see, the code isn't overly complicated, but there is a lot of code to work through as well as some new modules for working with the hardware.

Like the previous projects, we will use classes to wrap our functionality. We'll focus on making the Simon game its own class and general control of the game system in the main code. We will also be making a number of class modules, which will be presented before we look at the main code. Briefly, we will need three class modules. We will write class modules for the buzzer, buttons, and the gameplay.

Let's first look at the software libraries we will need to download.

Install Software Libraries

We will need to download two libraries, one for the RGB LCD and another for the Chainable RGB LED.

The library we will need for the RGB LCD is found on a web page to a Chinese GitLab that shows the contents of the code module (http://47.106.166.129/Embeded/pico-micropython-grove/blob/master/I2C/lcd1602.py). Rather than download the file, you can open a new file in Thonny, copy the code from the web page, and paste it in the new file and save it as lcd1602.py. We will use the code library unchanged once we upload it to the Pico.

We will be using the same library for the Chainable RGB LCD that we used in Chapter 10 (https://github.com/mcauser/micropython-p9813). Recall, to download the library, we use the command git clone https://github.com/mcauser/micropython-p9813 to make a copy (clone) of the repository as follows. This copies all of the files including examples and documentation to your PC:

```
$ git clone https://github.com/mcauser/micropython-p9813
Cloning into 'micropython-p9813'...
remote: Enumerating objects: 36, done.
remote: Total 36 (delta 0), reused 0 (delta 0), pack-reused 36
Unpacking objects: 100% (36/36), done.
```

Once you clone the repository, you can locate the `p9813.py` file in the `<root of clone>/micropython-p9813` folder. You can then download that to your Pico.

Now, let's take a look at the class modules for the project.

Create the Class Modules

While we will not dive into every line of code, we will see some of the more complex code and those areas discussed that differ significantly from what you may have experienced thus far in your MicroPython journey. You can read the code and learn more about how it works at your leisure.

Since there are several code modules (files) for this project, it is recommended that you create a project folder (e.g., named `project5`) and save all of the files there. It will make copying them to your Pico easier later.

Let's start with writing the classes starting with the `Buzzer` class.

Buzzer Class

The `Buzzer` class provides a mechanism to play tones. Specifically, we will create functions for each of the sounds that the Simon game uses. In this case, we need the following tones (or tone sequences):

- *play_theme_song( )*: An introductory song played when the game starts

- *play_ready_set_go( )*: A tone to indicate the player can begin entering the sequence of buttons

- *play_success( )*: A tone to indicate the sequence entered matches the challenge sequence

- *play_ failure( )*: A set of tones to indicate the sequence is not correct and the player's turn ends

- *play_color( )*: Play a unique tone for each of the four LED buttons

Aside from those functions, we will also create a constructor so we can set up the class and additional helper functions: one for playing a set of tones (song), another to get the frequency for the tone, and another to play a single tone (note).

We will also use a scale of notes and their frequencies stored in private variables. In this way, we can record the notes in variables for each of the tones/sounds earlier and then use the frequency function to retrieve the frequency of the note. The frequency defines how long the buzzer will sound. By varying the frequency, we can get different notes.

We can also define how long to hold (play) each tone, which will help us determine a cadence or primitive rhythm. We will call these "beats" where each beat is a quarter note (so we'll be using 4/4 time). Thus, a 1 is one quarter, 2 is half, etc. We also use a tempo that we can use to determine the speed, which we will set globally, but you could easily modify the code to allow different tones played at different speeds. This way, we can make the song faster or slower depending on our aesthetic requirements.

Rather than use a tuple, we will use one of the more powerful Python data storage called a dictionary. A dictionary allows us to create a structure where we can store one or more key-value pairs where we can store all of the parts of the song, the number of notes, notes, and beats. We will also see how to store the tempo for each song.

The following shows the layout of the dictionary we will use for each song. Here, we use the keys `tempo`, `num_notes`, `notes`, and `beats` which will be used in the code to reference the value for each:

```
# Success tones dictionary
self.success = {
    'tempo': DEFAULT_TEMPO,
    'num_notes': 3,
    'notes': "CCC",
    'beats': [1, 1, 1]
}
```

Let's get started writing the code. Open the Thonny Python IDE and create a new file named `buzzer.py` in the project folder. As usual, we begin with the imports and constants followed by the class definition. For this class, we will define in the constructor the songs we will be using for the Simon game. Along with the default tempo, we also define the Pico GPIO pin in the code module. Recall, we are using the analog (A0) connector on the Pico Shield, but we will be using the pin as a digital output. This is perfectly fine since that pin can be used as either an analog or a digital pin. We refer to the pin by its pin number (26). In fact, we will be using a technique called pulse-width modulation[3] (PWM) to rapidly turn the pin on and off over a period of time to change the sound produced.

Listing 11-1 shows the first part of the code with documentation removed for brevity.

Listing 11-1. Buzzer Class (Part 1)

```
from machine import Pin
from utime import sleep

# CONSTANTS
```

---

[3] https://learn.sparkfun.com/tutorials/pulse-width-modulation/all

```python
DEFAULT_TEMPO = 0.095
BUZZER_PIN = 26
NOTES_IN_SCALE = 8
HIGH = 1
LOW = 0

def tone(buzzer_pin, frequency, duration):
    """Generate a tone on the buzzer."""
    half_wave = 1 / (frequency * 2)
    waves = int(duration * frequency)
    # pylint: disable=unused-variable
    for i in range(waves):
        buzzer_pin.on()
        sleep(half_wave)
        buzzer_pin.off()
        sleep(half_wave)

class Buzzer:
    """Buzzer Class"""
    note_names = ['c', 'd', 'e', 'f', 'g', 'a', 'b', 'C']
    frequencies = [131, 147, 165, 175, 196, 220, 247, 262]
    failure = {}
    success = {}
    theme_song = {}
    ready_set_go = {}
    colors = [{}, {}, {}, {}]

    def __init__(self):
        """Constructor"""
        # Failure tones dictionary
        self.failure = {
            'tempo': DEFAULT_TEMPO,
            'num_notes': 5,
```

```
        'notes': "g c",
        'beats': [4, 1, 4, 1, 10]
}
# Success tones dictionary
self.success = {
        'tempo': DEFAULT_TEMPO,
        'num_notes': 3,
        'notes': "CCC",
        'beats': [1, 1, 1]
}
# Theme song dictionary
self.theme_song = {
        'tempo': DEFAULT_TEMPO,
        'num_notes': 18,
        'notes': "cdfda ag cdfdg gf ",
        'beats': [1, 1, 1, 1, 1, 1, 4, 4, 2,
                  1, 1, 1, 1, 1, 1, 4, 4, 2]
}
# Start signal dictionary
self.ready_set_go = {
        'tempo': DEFAULT_TEMPO,
        'num_notes': 1,
        'notes': "e",
        'beats': [2]
}
# Tones for the colors
for i in range(0, 4):
        self.colors[i]['tempo'] = DEFAULT_TEMPO
        self.colors[i]['num_notes'] = 1
        self.colors[i]['beats'] = [1]
```

```
    self.colors[0]['notes'] = "a"
    self.colors[1]['notes'] = "g"
    self.colors[2]['notes'] = "C"
    self.colors[3]['notes'] = "f"

    # Setup the buzzer
    self.buzzer_pin = Pin(BUZZER_PIN, Pin.OUT)
```
. . .

Notice the tone() function. This function is used by the play_song() function to play the note on the buzzer. Notice here we do some math first where we get the half wave of the frequency. We are getting one half of the sine wave so that we can turn the buzzer for half the wave and off for half the wave, which is the frequency times the duration and, hence, a pulse. Again, there are other ways to generate a PWM, but this works well for the buzzer.

Next are the various functions defined to play the specific songs. We won't go into too much detail as the code is not complicated.

Listing 11-2 shows the rest of the code for the class with documentation removed for brevity.

Listing 11-2. Buzzer Class (Part 2)

. . .

```
    def play_theme_song(self):
        """Play theme_song tones."""
        self.play_song(self.theme_song)

    def play_success(self):
        """Play success tones."""
        self.play_song(self.success)

    def play_failure(self):
        """Play failure tones."""
        self.play_song(self.failure)
```

```python
def play_color(self, color):
    """Play button_color tones."""
    self.play_song(self.colors[color])

def play_ready_set_go(self):
    """Play ready_set_go tones."""
    self.play_song(self.ready_set_go)

def frequency(self, note):
    """Get frequency for a note."""
    # Search through the letters in the array, and
    # return the frequency for that note.
    for i in range(0, NOTES_IN_SCALE):
        if self.note_names[i] == note:
            return self.frequencies[i]
    return 0

def play_song(self, song):
    """Play a song."""
    for i in range(0, song['num_notes']):
        duration = song['beats'][i] * song['tempo']
        if song['notes'][i] == ' ':
            sleep(duration)
        else:
            freq = self.frequency(song['notes'][i])
            tone(self.buzzer_pin, freq, duration)
        sleep(duration)
        sleep(song['tempo']/10)
```

Now, let's look at the Buttons class file.

Buttons Class

The Buttons class is designed to manage the six buttons in the game. Since the code for reading each button is the same, we can combine the code to make it easier to use. We also use a digital pin on the GPIO for each button. We use an array to define the buttons and the index of the button in the array to refer to a specific button.

There are two functions for the class. We will use the get_button_pressed() function to return the number of the button that is being pressed (or –1 if no button is pressed) and the get_button_value() function to return the current state for a specific button.

We will also need two helper functions to make using the buttons easier. First, we will create a function named button_name(), which simply returns a string to match the button number. This is for diagnostic purposes since the game doesn't need it for gameplay. But it does make it easier to debug!

Second, we create a function named debounce(), which has a very unique and key role. When mechanical switches (buttons) are pressed, the mechanics can produce a lot of noise initially and thus can vary in value rapidly. We call this "bouncing," which can make reading buttons problematic.[4] One way to reduce the noise is to use a loop to sample the value of the button over a brief period of time to stabilize the fluctuations. This function is one way we can achieve that goal.

Let's look at the completed code for this class. It is not complicated and does not need a lot of explanation. However, you should examine the debounce() code to see how it works so that you can use it in other projects where buttons are employed. Listing 11-3 shows the code for the class with documentation removed for brevity.

---

[4]https://docs.micropython.org/en/v1.8.4/pyboard/pyboard/tutorial/debounce.html

Listing 11-3. Buttons Class

```
from machine import Pin
from utime import sleep

def button_name(button_num):
    """Return the name of the button for diagnostics."""
    name = ""
    if button_num == 0:
        name = "START_BUTTON"
    elif button_num == 1:
        name = "MODE_BUTTON"
    elif button_num == 2:
        name = "RED_BUTTON"
    elif button_num == 3:
        name = "GREEN_BUTTON"
    elif button_num == 4:
        name = "WHITE_BUTTON"
    else:
        name = "BLUE_BUTTON"
    return name

def debounce(pin):
    """Debounce button presses."""
    # wait for pin to change value
    # it needs to be stable for a continuous 20ms
    cur_value = pin.value()
    active = 0
    while active < 20:
        if pin.value() != cur_value:
            active += 1
        else:
            active = 0
```

```
        sleep(0.01)

class Buttons:
    """Class to manage buttons for Simon game."""

    START_BUTTON = 0
    MODE_BUTTON = 1
    RED_BUTTON = 2
    GREEN_BUTTON = 3
    WHITE_BUTTON = 4
    BLUE_BUTTON = 5

    def __init__(self):
        self.button_list = []
        self.button_list.append(Pin(17, Pin.IN, Pin.PULL_
        UP))  # START
        self.button_list.append(Pin(16, Pin.IN, Pin.PULL_UP))
        # MODE
        self.button_list.append(Pin(19, Pin.IN, Pin.PULL_UP))
        # RED
        self.button_list.append(Pin(18, Pin.IN, Pin.PULL_UP))
        # GREEN
        self.button_list.append(Pin(20, Pin.IN, Pin.PULL_UP))
        # WHITE
        self.button_list.append(Pin(21, Pin.IN, Pin.PULL_UP))
        # BLUE

    def get_button_pressed(self):
        """Return the button (index) pressed."""
        for button_num in range(0,6):
            if self.button_list[button_num].value() == 0:
                debounce(self.button_list[button_num])
                return button_num
```

```
        return -1

    def get_button_value(self, button_num):
        """Check a button for status."""
        return self.button_list[button_num].value()
```

At this point, you might be wondering how one could write classes like this and expect them to work when put with the main code. Indeed, it is often unlikely this will happen smoothly unless you do some testing and debugging.

If you recall from earlier projects, we used a main() function and a condition at the end of the module to call it if the module were executed. Well, we can do that with class modules! The following shows how to write a short test for this class module. Simply place it at the end of the file and then execute the code. This code simply runs a loop that reports the button pressed. You can simply wire up the three Dual Button modules and test them. It is also a terrific way to figure out which buttons correspond to the button functions.

```
...
if __name__ == '__main__':
    try:
        buttons = Buttons()
        while True:
            index = buttons.get_button_pressed()
            if index >= 0:
                print("{} = {} pressed".format(index, button_
                name(index)))

    except (KeyboardInterrupt, SystemExit) as err:
        print("\nbye!\n")
```

To create the class file, open a new file in Thonny and save it as buttons.py in the project folder.

When you execute this code in Thonny, you will see something similar to the following (buttons were pressed randomly for this example). Now we see where that button_name() function comes in handy!

```
>>> 0 = START_BUTTON pressed
>>> 4 = WHITE_BUTTON pressed
>>> 2 = RED_BUTTON pressed
>>> 1 = MODE_BUTTON pressed
>>> 3 = GREEN_BUTTON pressed
>>> 5 = BLUE_BUTTON pressed
...
```

Now, let's look at the Simon class file.

Simon Class

This class is responsible for running the Simon gameplay. That is, it generates the random sequences for the player to press and then checks the results to see if there is a match. If the sequence matches, gameplay continues.

The mode and start buttons discussed previously are not part of this class. Rather, this class only contains code to detect the four color buttons, the Chainable RGB LED, and the RGB LCD. The main code will manage the mode and start buttons.

We will use functions for the setup routine where we can change the number of players (setup_mode()), start the game (start_game()), show the number of players (show_players()), and play the game (play()).

Aside from that, we will also need a number of helper functions that are a bit more complicated. We need functions to control the LCD, play a challenge sequence, read a sequence of buttons from the player, generate the challenge sequence using the randint() function to generate a random integer from zero to three to correspond to the button array index, and even determine a winner for the multiplayer mode. The following lists the private functions and their uses:

- num_alive(): Determine the number of players still active (alive)

- reset_screen(): Reset the LCD and display a new message

- show_winner(): Show the winner on the LCD

- generate_sequence(): Generate a challenge sequence

- play_sequence(): Play a challenge sequence by turning on the corresponding LED and playing the tone for the button

- read_sequence(): Read a sequence from the player

Finally, we will need a number of variables to store information including an instance of the LCD class and the buttons (stored as an array). The constructor will also need to be added to set up the hardware.

Since there are a lot of functions in the class, we will first discuss each function in overview and then highlight some of the more complex ones in more detail, but none are overly difficult. You can discover how the other functions work as an exercise. We will begin with the public functions.

The constructor is where we set up the hardware for the class, which includes the new Buttons class, Buzzer class, RGB LCD, and the Chainable RGB LED.

We also initialize the random number generator using a read from an analog pin as the seed. This will simulate using a different seed each time because reading an uninitialized pin will generate an unpredictable value. We then place the game in setup mode with the setup_mode() function, which simply resets the RGB LCD to indicate we are in the setup mode.

The start_game() function takes an integer for the number of players and simply zeros out the player scores, plays the theme song, and sets the RGB LCD for the start of gameplay.

The play() function is a bit more complicated. Here is where the gameplay is coded. At the highest level, the function loops generating a challenge sequence, playing it to the user, then reading the player's response. If the challenge is met, the loop continues with an extra button added and a new random sequence generated.[5]

When there are more than one player, the loop cycles through each player in turn. If a player misses the sequence, that player is removed from the cycle (considered no longer playing or "alive"). Play continues until there are no more players alive and a winner is determined and the game ends. When the game ends, the code pauses and then resets the game class for the next game.

Next, let's look at the private functions. Recall, private functions are used internally to the class and not visible to the caller.

The num_alive() function loops through the player scores to determine how many players are still playing. It is used in the play() function to determine when the game ends.

The reset_screen() takes as a parameter a message to be displayed on the LCD. The function clears the display and then adds the message. It is used to control the LCD during gameplay.

The show_winner() function loops through the player scores to determine which player has the highest score. Since the play() function is designed to keep going until all players have failed to complete a sequence, it is possible for two or more players to have the same score. This is an intentional omission that you are encouraged to solve as an exercise. Hint: You can simply declare a tie.

---

[5] I've seen many examples of the Simon game for Arduino and other platforms that use the same sequence adding a new button each time. To me, that's nowhere near as challenging as having a new sequence each turn.

The generate_sequence() function takes as a parameter the number of buttons and returns an integer array allocated from memory that includes a set of random integers in the range 0–3 to represent the buttons in the sequence. To create a random integer in that range, we call randint(0, 3), which returns the correct range.

The play_sequence() function uses two parameters, one for the button (challenge) sequence and another for the number of notes. It simply loops through the array turning on the Chainable RGB LED with the appropriate color and playing the tone for each button using a delay between each. This is used by the play() function to present the challenge sequence to the player.

The read_sequence() function also uses two parameters, one for the button (challenge) sequence and another for the number of notes. It simply loops through the array reading the button presses from the player. If the correct button is pressed, the next button is read and so forth. If all buttons were pressed in the correct order (the sequence pressed equals the challenge sequence), the function returns true, or false is returned on the first incorrect button press in the sequence. This is used by the play() function to read the player's response.

OK, that's a lot of functions! Let's now look at the complete code for the class. Take a few moments to read it (there's a lot of code) to ensure you understand how it all works.

Listing 11-4 shows the complete code for the class with documentation removed for brevity. Take a few moments to read the code so that you understand all of the parts of the code. As you will see, it is not complicated, but there is a lot of code to sift through.

Listing 11-4. Simon Class

```
import time
import urandom
from machine import ADC, I2C, Pin
```

```python
from project5.buttons import Buttons
from project5.buzzer import Buzzer
from project5.lcd1602 import LCD1602_RGB, LCD1602
from project5.p9813 import P9813

# Constants
MIN_BEATS = 2          # Starting number of beats
MAX_PLAYERS = 4        # Max number of players
MAX_TIMEOUT = 5.0      # Seconds to wait to abort read
KEY_INTERVAL = 0.500 # Interval between button playback
# RGB Values
RED_LED = (255, 0, 0)
GREEN_LED = (0, 255, 0)
WHITE_LED = (200, 200, 200)
BLUE_LED = (0, 0, 255)
RGB_COLORS = (RED_LED, GREEN_LED, WHITE_LED, BLUE_LED)

def generate_sequence(num_notes):
    """Generate a new button sequence."""
    if num_notes == 0:
        return []
    # Create a new sequence adding a new beat
    challenge_sequence = []
    i = 0
    while i < num_notes:
        challenge_sequence.append(urandom.randint(0, 3))
        i = i + 1
    return challenge_sequence

class Simon:
    """Simon Class"""

    i2c = I2C(0,scl=Pin(9), sda=Pin(8), freq=400000)
```

```python
lcd = LCD1602(i2c, 2, 16)              # LCD
lcd_rgb = LCD1602_RGB(i2c, 2, 16)      # LCD RGB control
buzzer = Buzzer()                      # Buzzer
buttons = Buttons()                    # Buttons
num_players = 1
player_scores = []
# Setup the RGB module
scl = Pin(7, Pin.OUT)
sda = Pin(6, Pin.OUT)
rgb_chain = P9813(scl, sda, 1)
rgb_chain[0] = (0, 0, 0) # turn RGB off
rgb_chain.write()

def __init__(self):
    """Constructor"""
    # Setup the LCD
    self.lcd.clear()
    # Set background color?
    self.lcd_rgb.set_rgb(127, 127, 127)

    # if analog input pin 0 is unconnected, random analog
    # noise will cause the call to randomSeed() to generate
    # different seed numbers each time the sketch runs.
    # random.seed() will then shuffle the random function.
    urandom.seed(ADC(0).read_u16())

    print("Playing theme...")
    self.buzzer.play_theme_song()
    print("done.")

    # Put game in setup mode
    self.setup_mode()

def start_game(self, players):
```

```python
    """Start a new game."""
    self.num_players = players
    for player in range(0, players):
        player_score = {
            'number': player,
            'is_alive': True,
            'high_score': 0
        }
        self.player_scores.append(player_score)
    self.reset_screen("Get ready!")

def play(self):
    """Play game."""
    game_over = False
    num_notes = 1

    # Main game loop
    while not game_over:
        # For each player, generate a new sequence and
        test skills
        for player in range(0, self.num_players):
            if self.player_scores[player]['is_alive']:
                num_notes = self.player_scores[player]
                ['high_score'] + 1
                self.reset_screen("Player {0}".
                format(player + 1))
                challenge_sequence = generate_
                sequence(num_notes)
                self.play_sequence(challenge_sequence,
                num_notes)
                self.buzzer.play_ready_set_go()
                self.reset_screen("Go!")
                print("Go!")
```

```python
            if self.read_sequence(challenge_sequence,
            num_notes):
                self.buzzer.play_success()
                self.reset_screen("Success!")
                print("Success!")
                time.sleep(0.500)
                self.player_scores[player]['high_
                score'] = num_notes
            else:
                self.reset_screen("FAILED")
                print("Fail")
                self.player_scores[player]['is_
                alive'] = False
        # Check to see if any players remain alive
        # and show winner if multiple players
        players_remaining = self.num_alive()
        if players_remaining == 0:
            self.reset_screen("GAME OVER")
            if self.num_players > 1:
                self.show_winner()
            game_over = True
            print("Game over...")
            time.sleep(2)
    self.player_scores = []

def setup_mode(self):
    """Enter setup mode."""
    self.lcd.clear()
    self.lcd.setCursor(0, 0)
    self.lcd.print("Simon Says!")
    self.lcd.setCursor(0, 1) # column 1, row 2
    self.lcd.print("Setup Mode")
```

```python
    def show_players(self, num_players):
        """Show players."""
        self.lcd.clear()
        self.lcd.setCursor(0, 0)
        self.lcd.print("Simon Says!")
        self.lcd.setCursor(0, 1) # column 1, row 2
        if num_players == 1:
            self.lcd.print("single player")
        else:
            self.lcd.print(chr(num_players + 0x30))
            self.lcd.print(" players")

    def show_winner(self):
        """Show the winner."""
        winner = -1
        score = 0
        for player in range(0, self.num_players):
            if self.player_scores[player]['high_score']
              > score:
                winner = player
                score = self.player_scores[player]
                          ['high_score']
        self.lcd.setCursor(0, 0)
        self.lcd.print("Player ")
        self.lcd.print(winner + 1)
        self.lcd.print("WON!")
        self.lcd.setCursor(0, 1) # column 1, row 2
        self.lcd.print("Score = ")
        self.lcd.print(score)

    def num_alive(self):
        """Number of players still playing."""
        count = 0
```

```python
        for player in range(0, self.num_players):
            if self.player_scores[player]['is_alive']:
                count = count + 1
        return count

    def reset_screen(self, message):
        """Reset the LCD."""
        self.lcd.clear()
        self.lcd.setCursor(0, 0)
        self.lcd.print("Simon Says! (")
        self.lcd.print("{0}".format(self.num_players))
        self.lcd.print(")")
        self.lcd.setCursor(0, 1) # column 1, row 2
        self.lcd.print(message)

    def read_sequence(self, challenge_sequence, num_notes):
        """Read button sequence from the player."""

        def show_challenge_sequence():
            colors = ""
            for color in challenge_sequence:
                if color == 0:
                    colors += "R "
                elif color == 1:
                    colors += "G "
                elif color == 2:
                    colors += "W "
                elif color == 3:
                    colors += "B "
            return colors

        button_read = -1
        index = 0
        start_time = time.time()
```

```python
        # Loop reading buttons and compare to stored sequence
        while index < num_notes:
            button_read = self.buttons.get_button_pressed() - 2
            # if a color button is pressed, check the sequence
            if button_read >= 0:
                # print(">", button_read, show_challenge_
                sequence())
                if challenge_sequence[index] != button_read:
                    self.buzzer.play_failure()
                    self.reset_screen("FAIL SEQUENCE")
                    time.sleep(5)
                    return False
                print("MATCH!")
                start_time = time.time()
                index = index + 1
                button_read = -1
            if (time.time() - start_time) > MAX_TIMEOUT:
                print("ERROR: Timeout!")
                self.buzzer.play_failure()
                self.reset_screen("FAIL TIMEOUT")
                time.sleep(5)
                return False
            time.sleep(0.050)
        return True

    def play_sequence(self, challenge_sequence, num_notes):
        """Play the tones and illuminate the buttons in the
        sequence."""
        for beat in range(0, num_notes):
            button_index = challenge_sequence[beat]
            self.rgb_chain[0] = RGB_COLORS[button_index]
            self.rgb_chain.write()
```

```
self.buzzer.play_color(button_index)
time.sleep(KEY_INTERVAL)
self.rgb_chain[0] = (0, 0, 0) # turn RGB off
self.rgb_chain.write()
time.sleep(KEY_INTERVAL)
```

To create the class file, open a new file in Thonny and save it as `simon_says.py` in the project folder.

Notice one interesting feature of this code. Look at the `read_sequence()` function. Notice there is another function declared inside that one named `show_challenge_sequence()`. This is a common technique for removing duplicate code. The inner function simply encapsulates a few lines of code that are called repeatedly from the outer function. What is this function used for, you may wonder? It is placed there so you can cheat while debugging your code. It simply prints to the console the sequence of buttons, making it easy for you to evaluate the game. I'll leave it up to you as to where you can place a call to this function. Hint: Look for a line of code commented out. Cool, eh?

Now we can write our main code.

Main Code Module

Now we can write the main code. Open a new file and name it `main.py`. Since we are placing most of the hardware work in the Simon game class, all we need to do here is write code to interact with the Simon game class.

We use a simple loop for controlling the *mode* button to set the number of players and the *start* button to start the game. We will make the code allow the use of the mode button so long as a game is not in process.

Note   The *mode* button is closest to the Grove connector. If you orient the module with the Grove connector on top, the *mode* button is the top button and *start* is the bottom button.

Recording the number of players is done using a variable that we allow up to four players. So, pressing the *mode* button continually will cycle through the options (e.g., 1, 2, 3, 4, 1, 2, 3, 4…). We will use this value when the player presses the *start* button.

When the *start* button is pressed, we use the Simon class to start a new game with the start_game() method passing in the number of players selected. Then we call the play() function turning control over to the Simon class. Once the game ends, we place the Simon instance back to the setup mode with the setup_mode() function. A few short delays are added to make the game flow better.[6]

By placing all of the game control in its own class, we've simplified the main code. Listing 11-5 shows the complete code for the main script for this project. You can read it to see how all of the code works.

Listing 11-5. Main Code Module

```
from time import sleep
from project5.simon_says import Simon, MAX_PLAYERS
from project5.buttons import Buttons

def main():
    """"Main"""
    print("Welcome to the Simon Says game!")
    simon = Simon()
```

---

[6] Purists may say the use of delays or sleep is a poor replacement for excellent code, but they are handy for controlling flow and execution speed. Plus, there are (good) side effect benefits in some languages such as Python related to threading.

```python
game_started = False
start_button = False
mode_button = False
num_players = 1
buttons = Buttons()
while True:
    if not game_started:
        # Show number of players
        start_button = buttons.get_button_value(Buttons.
        START_BUTTON) == 0
        mode_button = buttons.get_button_value(Buttons.
        MODE_BUTTON) == 0
        if start_button:
            print("Start button pressed.")
            simon.start_game(num_players)
            sleep(1)
            simon.play()
            sleep(1)
            simon.setup_mode()
        elif mode_button:
            num_players = num_players + 1
            if num_players > MAX_PLAYERS:
                num_players = 1
            print("Mode button pressed - {0} players."
                "".format(num_players))
            sleep(0.050)
            simon.show_players(num_players)
            sleep(2)
            simon.setup_mode()
```

```
if __name__ == '__main__':
    try:
        main()
    except (KeyboardInterrupt, SystemExit) as err:
        print("\nbye!\n")
```

OK, that's it! We've written the code. We're now ready to execute the project!

Execute

Now that we've spent many pages exploring the Grove modules and writing the code to interact with them, it is time to test the project by executing (running) it. Recall, we can copy all of our code to our Pico. If you haven't already done so, you should create a folder named project5 on your Pico and then upload the buttons.py, buzzer.py, lcd1602.py, p9813.py, and simon_sys.py files to the project5 folder. Next, upload the main.py file to the root folder of your Pico.

Recall, there are two ways to test or execute the code. We could use Thonny to connect to the Pico and simply run the main.py script. Or we can reboot the Pico by unplugging it and plugging it back in to the USB port on your PC.

The difference is if you run the main.py file manually, you will see the debug statements show in the output at the bottom of Thonny. Running the script automatically may not show those statements if you do not use Thonny or a similar application to connect to the Pico.

Once the program starts, you will see some diagnostic messages written to the terminal. You will also see a welcome message appear on the LCD. You can then press the *mode* button to set the number of players, and when you're ready, press the start button to *start* the game. Figure 11-7 shows examples of the LCD when in setup mode.

Figure 11-7. *Executing the Simon Says project*

When you run the code from Thonny, you will see output similar to the following:

```
Welcome to the Simon Says game!
Mode button pressed - 2 players.
Mode button pressed - 3 players.
Mode button pressed - 4 players.
Mode button pressed - 1 players.
Start button pressed.
Playing theme...
...
```

If everything worked as executed, congratulations! You've just built your second Grove project. If something isn't working, check your connections to ensure you've connected everything correctly.

Since we named the main code file main.py, you can restart the Pico and run the game on boot. If you connect a power supply to the Pico, or a 5V battery pack, you can play the game as a handheld game. Cool!

Taking It Further

While we didn't discuss them in this chapter, there are some ideas where you could make this project into an IoT project. Here are just a few suggestions you can try once we have learned how to take our projects to the cloud. Put your skills to work!

- *Complete the enclosure*: Use the sample base plate and create a cover for the game.

- *Handheld version*: Find someone with a 3D printer and print out the mounting plate. Once assembled, purchase a portable 5V battery and attach it to the bottom of the mounting plate. This will allow you to run the game without the need of a PC or USB power from a wall wart.

- *Increase the difficulty*: One of the ways you can enhance gameplay is to make the timeout time for a player to enter a sequence shorter as gameplay continues. For example, for the first n sequences, use the default timeout; for the next n sequences, reduce the timeout by a portion; and so on until the timeout gets to a minimum timeout. If you do the same thing for the delay used in playing the challenge sequence, it will ensure the game will become much more difficult and more fun to play.

Summary

In this chapter, we completed a more complex project to explore Grove modules. Along the way, we learned more about how to work with Grove modules including how to write our own classes for managing multiple modules and sensors (buttons are sensors after all).

Rather than build something that has an "OK, that's cool" factor, we built a working Simon game that we can play with our friends. Since we wrote all of the code for the game, we can also expand it however we want, including making it more difficult to play as the game progresses.

Using the examples in this chapter, you will discover other uses for the code to build other games and replicate another vintage handheld electronic game.

In the next chapter, we will look at one more project using Grove modules, returning to building projects that use sensors. We will build an environmental project that allows you to monitor your environment.

CHAPTER 12

Project: Monitoring your Environment

One of the most common examples of electronics projects is a project to monitor the environment. Given the current ongoing health crisis, this project may be something useful to help us understand the conditions of our indoor environment. There are several products you can buy to monitor indoor air quality, and for those with severe allergies and similar health conditions (some can be life-threatening), an indoor air monitor may be a requirement to treat their condition.

In this chapter, we will see how to create a simple indoor environment monitor that detects air quality (the presence of harmful gases), dust concentration, barometric pressure, and temperature, displaying the data on a small OLED. We'll see more analog and digital modules as well as the use of multiple I2C Grove modules.

Let's get started.

Project Overview

The project for this chapter is designed to demonstrate how to use analog, digital, and multiple I2C devices on the same Grove host adapter to build an indoor environment monitor. It uses several sensors to sample the air for gases and dust as well as sampling the temperature and barometric

© Charles Bell 2022
C. Bell, *Beginning MicroPython with the Raspberry Pi Pico*, Maker Innovations Series,
https://doi.org/10.1007/978-1-4842-8135-2_12

pressure. As you will see, this is the most challenging of the projects in this book not only for the number of modules used but also for the complexity of the code.

Caution   The project for this chapter should not be used for treating life-threatening health disorders. It is meant to be a demonstration of what is possible and should not be relied upon for critical health choices.

We will use a simple loop to sample the sensors every minute. For most uses, that is actually too frequent as indoor air quality may not change quickly. If you choose to install this project for long-term use, you may want to experiment with longer sampling times especially if you plan to log the data.

If you haven't read and worked on the other projects, you may want to work on the earlier chapters first and save this one until you've mastered a few of the others.

For those with access to a 3D printer, we will also see a simple mounting plate you can print and install the modules onto to protect them and make it easier to use in running the project.

Let's see what hardware we will need.

Required Components

The hardware needed for this project is listed in Table 12-1. URLs for each component are included for ease of ordering including duplicate entries for alternative vendors. We will use a Grove OLED 0.96 and Buzzer along with Grove High Accuracy Temperature, Barometer, Air Quality, and Dust sensors. While this project doesn't include any Qwiic components, three of these sensors use I2C.

Table 12-1. *Hardware Needed for the Environment Monitor Project*

Component	Qty	Description	Cost	Links
Grove OLED 0.96 v1.3	1	Display	$16.40	www.seeedstudio.com/Grove-OLED-Display-0-96.html
Grove Buzzer	1	Buzzer	$2.10	www.seeedstudio.com/Grove-Buzzer.html
Grove I2C High Accuracy Temperature Sensor	1	MCP9808	$5.20	www.seeedstudio.com/Grove-I2C-High-Accuracy-Temperature-Sensor-MCP9808.html
Grove Temperature and Barometer Sensor	1	BMP280	$9.80	www.seeedstudio.com/Grove-Barometer-Sensor-BMP280.html
Grove Air Quality Sensor	1	Air quality	$10.90	www.seeedstudio.com/Grove-Air-Quality-Sensor-v1-3-Arduino-Compatible.html
Grove Dust Sensor	1	Dust	$12.70	www.seeedstudio.com/Grove-Dust-Sensor-PPD42NS.html

(continued)

455

Table 12-1. (*continued*)

Component	Qty	Description	Cost	Links
Grove — I2C Hub (6 Port)	1*	I2C Hub	$1.70	www.seeedstudio.com/Grove-I2C-Hub-6-Port-p-4349.html
			$6.95	shop.switchdoc.com/collections/grove/products/grove-6-port-12c-hub
Grove Cable	7	Cables		www.sparkfun.com/products/14426
Grove Shield for Pi Pico V1.0	1	Host board	$4.30	www.seeedstudio.com/Grove-Shield-for-Pi-Pico-v1-0-p-4846.html

* You need only one of these.

About the Hardware

Let's discuss these components briefly. We will discover how to work with the hardware in more detail later in the chapter. We saw the buzzer in Chapter 11, but the remaining five modules are new.

Grove OLED 0.96

Since we have more data than can fit on two short lines, we must change our display of choice to use a small OLED module. The Grove OLED 0.96 is a monochrome 128×64 dot matrix display with high brightness and contrast ratio and low power consumption. You can address all of the pixels (dots) on the screen too. Note that there are several versions of this module. We will be using the version that uses the SSD1308 chip. If you use a different version, you may need to use a different software library. Figure 12-1 shows the Grove OLED Display.

Figure 12-1. *Grove OLED Display (courtesy of seeedstudio.com)*

Grove I2C High Accuracy Temperature Sensor (MCP9808)

The Grove – I2C High Accuracy Temperature Sensor (or simply MCP9808) is a high accuracy digital module based on the MCP9808 microchip. It features high accuracy measuring temperatures ranging from –40 to 125 degrees Celsius. While there are other temperature sensors available for use, this module is not only reliable and accurate, but it also uses I2C for easy integration into our environment monitor. Figure 12-2 shows the Grove I2C High Accuracy Temperature Sensor (MCP9808).

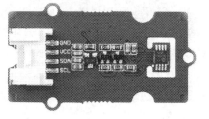

Figure 12-2. *Grove I2C High Accuracy Temperature Sensor (courtesy of seeedstudio.com)*

If you recall from our Qwiic modules, most permit you to alter the I2C address and other features using jumpers. This module is similar, and you can change the I2C address by soldering the jumpers on the back of the module. Figure 12-3 shows what the jumpers look like. Notice the labels for each.

Figure 12-3. *Grove I2C Jumpers – Temperature Sensor (courtesy of seeedstudio.com)*

You can change the I2C address by soldering across the jumpers as shown in Table 12-2.

Table 12-2. *I2C Address Map for the Grove High Accuracy Temperature Sensor*

A0	A1	A2	Address
0	0	0	0x18
0	0	1	0x19
0	1	0	0x1A
0	1	1	0x1B
1	0	0	0x1C
1	0	1	0x1D
1	1	0	0x1E
1	1	1	0x1F

You may need to change the address if you add another I2C module with the same address or if you want to use multiple Grove I2C High Accuracy Temperature Sensors.

Grove Temperature and Barometer Sensor (BMP280)

Since we are capturing temperature, we may also want to measure the barometric pressure. The Grove Temperature and Barometer Sensor (or simply BMP280) is an excellent choice for that data. While it can also measure temperature and can be used to determine altitude, we will use it solely for the barometric pressure. If you'd like to see how to do that, visit `www.seeedstudio.com/Grove-Barometer-Sensor-BMP280.html` for more information. Figure 12-4 shows the Grove Temperature and Barometer Sensor.

Figure 12-4. *Grove Temperature and Barometer Sensor (courtesy of seeedstudio.com)*

Like the High Accuracy Temperature Sensor, you can also change the I2C address for this module using the jumpers on the back as shown in Figure 12-5.

Figure 12-5. *Grove I2C Jumpers – Barometric Pressure Sensor (courtesy of seeedstudio.com)*

Here, our choices are a bit narrower. We can use the jumpers to change the address from 0x76 (default) to 0x77.

Grove Air Quality Sensor

The Grove Air Quality Sensor is an analog sensor designed for indoor air quality testing and measures certain gases including carbon monoxide, alcohol, acetone, thinner, formaldehyde, and similar slightly toxic gases. While it does not differentiate among the gases, it provides a general value that you can use to determine thresholds for "safe" air quality. In fact, we will write the code to determine ranges for good, fair, and poor air quality. Figure 12-6 shows the Grove Air Quality Sensor.

Figure 12-6.   *Grove Air Quality Sensor (courtesy of seeedstudio.com)*

Grove Dust Sensor

We will also be measuring the dust or particles in the air. The Grove Dust Sensor is a digital module and an excellent choice because it provides a percentage of particles found in the air. We can therefore write our code to test for a threshold of particulates in the air to determine dusty or even smoky conditions. Figure 12-7 shows the Grove Dust Sensor.

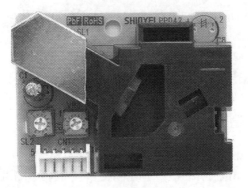

Figure 12-7. *Grove Dust Sensor (courtesy of seeedstudio.com)*

There is one more unexpected component that we will need. We have three modules that use I2C connections. Most Pico adapter boards (shields) offer only two I2C connections: I2C0 and I2C1. However, recall that I2C connections are not limited to only one per bus. Rather, we can connect multiple modules to the same I2C bus where each module is referenced by its address.

To achieve this, we will need a little help from another component. We need a Grove I2C Hub. Seeed Studio sells one that is the same 40mm format as the sensors we will be using (`www.seeedstudio.com/Grove-I2C-Hub-6-Port-p-4349.html`). SwitchDoc Labs also offers a Grove I2C Hub (`https://shop.switchdoc.com/collections/grove/products/grove-6-port-12c-hub`) which is a bit larger but has the same number of connectors for Grove I2C modules. Figure 12-8 shows the Grove I2C Hub.

Figure 12-8. *Grove I2C Hub (courtesy of seeedstudio.com)*

Figure 12-9 shows the SwitchDoc Labs I2C Hub.

Figure 12-9. *SwitchDoc Labs I2C Hub (courtesy of switchdoc.com)*

As you may surmise, we will be connecting all of our I2C modules to the hub and then the hub to I2C0 on the Pico Grove Shield.

Set Up the Hardware

For this project, we need six connections for the six modules we will using. The connections and their types are shown in Table 12-3.

Table 12-3. *Environment Monitor Connections*

Module	Description	Pico Shield Connector
I2C Hub	Hub	I2C0
OLED	Display	I2C Hub
MCP9808	Temperature	I2C Hub
BMP280	Barometer	I2C Hub
Buzzer	Sound	A0
Dust Sensor	Dust	D20/21
Air Quality	Air quality	A1

Thus, we will need seven Grove cables. Figure 12-10 shows how the connections will look once all of the modules are connected to the Pico Shield and I2C Hub.

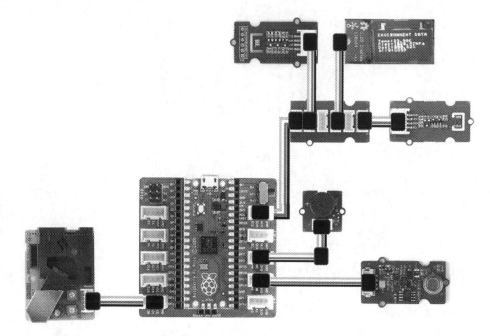

Figure 12-10. *Environment monitor project Grove connections*

Using a Mounting Plate

Since we have so many components and a bunch of cables connecting them all together, using the project can take a little bit of space, and with all of those modules dangling by their cables tethered only to the Grove Pico Shield, you run the risk of accidentally unplugging a module, or, worse, the electronics on the module may come into contact with conductive material. You can mitigate this somewhat by using a double-sided tape to tape them to your desk, but a better solution is to create a mounting plate. We could create a full enclosure, but as you will see, leaving the modules exposed gives the project a genuine cool factor.

If you have your own 3D printer or have access to a 3D printer, you can print a mounting plate. The source code for this chapter includes the

3D printing files you need to create a simple mounting plate to mount the modules arranged in a space-efficient manner. Figure 12-11 shows the mounting plate.

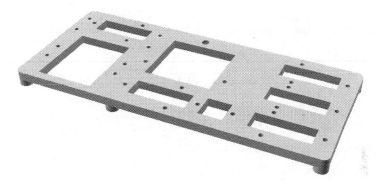

Figure 12-11. *3D mounting plate design for the environment monitor project*

Notice there are mounting points for all of the sensor modules along with the OLED, Pico Shield (on the left side), and an I2C Hub for both the Seeed Studio and SwitchDoc Labs versions (above the Pico Shield on the left).

If you're thinking this resembles a simple plank of wood (which would work equally as well), there are feet on the bottom of the plate and places for the nuts on the bottom as well. In fact, you will need to print this plate upside down.

There is also a set of spacers you will need to print as shown in Figure 12-12.

Figure 12-12. *3D spacers design for the Simon Says project*

Notice from left to right, there are (11) short M2 spacers for the MCP9808, BMP280, air quality, and buzzer modules. There are (3) long M2 spacers for the OLED module. Finally, there is (1) M4 spacer for the dust sensor.

To mount the modules, you will need the following hardware:

- (19) M2 nuts

- (1) M4 nut

- (16) M2x8mm bolts

- (3) M2x19mm bolts

- (1) M4x5mm bolt

To assemble the mounting plate, begin by mounting the dust sensor in the center, the buzzer below it, the OLED in the upper left, and the air quality, BMP280, and MCP9808 on the bottom and right (any order is fine). Finally, mount the I2C Hub in the upper left and the Pico Shield on the left. Figure 12-13 shows the completed project with the cables routed to the top.

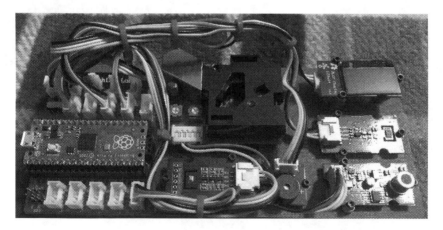

Figure 12-13. *Mounting the modules to the 3D printed plate*

Before you celebrate by plugging all of your modules into your host adapter, take a few moments to carefully label each of the cables using a piece of masking or painter's tape. Write the connector label on the tape so you don't have to worry about connecting them to the wrong connectors. The I2C cables can be plugged into any of the I2C connectors. Figure 12-14 shows a close-up of how the I2C Hub is mounted.

Figure 12-14. *I2C Hub mounting on the 3D printed plate*

If you have experience creating 3D models for printing, feel free to experiment with creating your own enclosure – perhaps one that also includes a battery and a small form factor host board. If you decide to build a complete enclosure, make sure to place holes or a grid opening over the sensors for airflow. The dust and air quality sensors are the modules that need openings most.

Now that we know more about the hardware for this chapter, let's write the code!

Write the Code

The code for this project involves following the usual pattern. For this project, that means using analog and digital modules as well as multiple I2C devices. The air quality sensor is an analog sensor, the buzzer and dust sensors are digital modules, and the MCP9808, BMP280, and OLED are I2C devices.

Like the previous projects, we will use a class to wrap our functionality. Let's first look at the software libraries we will need to download.

Install Software Libraries

We will need to download three libraries. Specifically, we need a library for the BMP280, OLED, and MCP9808. However, there is no MicroPython library for the Dust Sensor, so we will be writing our own library for that sensor.

We can get the BMP280 library from `https://github.com/dafvid/micropython-bmp280`, the OLED library from `https://github.com/micropython/micropython/tree/master/drivers/display`, and the MCP9808 library from `https://github.com/adafruit/Adafruit_CircuitPython_MCP9808`. You can install them with the following commands:

```
$ pip3 install bmp280
$ pip3 install adafruit-circuitpython-mcp9808
```

Once you have those libraries installed, we're ready to write the code.

Create the Class Modules

While we will not dive into every line of code, we will see some of the more complex code and those areas discussed that differ significantly from what you may have experienced thus far in your MicroPython journey. You can read the code and learn more about how it works at your leisure.

Since there are several code modules (files) for this project, it is recommended that you create a project folder (e.g., named `project6`) and save all of the files there. It will make copying them to your Pico easier later.

Let's start with the most difficult: a solution to read the dust sensor. As mentioned, there is no library currently available to read this sensor on the Pico (but there are some available for other platforms), so we must write the code ourselves. As you will see, it is a bit tricky.

DustSensor Class

While this module is a class, it contains a single function. This may seem strange, and you may tend to implement the single function in either the main code file or as a separate code module. That will work just fine, but it is not the recommended mechanism.

A class module is a very useful tool for developers because it allows us to place code in a single container that works on a common set of data. Thus, it models an object or concept in our projects. It also allows us to keep state (a set of assignments or initializations) for the object during its lifetime.

For example, if you have a single function that initializes some data variables based on data passed as parameters and then initializes another class instance variable (or several), each time the function is called, it repeats all of the setup, which is wasteful. Using a class allows us to do that setup code once.

Thus, the code for the dust sensor is placed in a class module named `dust_sensor.py`, and the class is named `DustSensor`. You can create the file now in Thonny.

As mentioned, there is a single function named `read()` that reads the data from the dust sensor. Unlike other read functions you may be accustomed to, this function cannot simply query another class or abstract function to get the data. In this case, we are reading directly from the hardware via a digital pin on the Pico. We will allow the caller to specify the pin to use in the constructor, but we also have a default value of the pin number (`DUST_SENSOR_PIN = 20`) for the dust sensor data.

But there is a catch. We cannot simply read the value once. It doesn't work like that. The sensor is designed to emit a pulse over a period of time during which it will turn "on" and "off" in a variable frequency. Note this is essentially the pulse-width modulation (PWM) that we've seen in controlling LEDs and other devices to limit power to the device.

To determine what this "pulse" means for this sensor, we learn from the data sheet that we can determine the amount of dust read by counting the number of times the value is set to "on" (high) over a period of 30 seconds. Figure 12-15 shows an excerpt of the data sheet that documents this process.

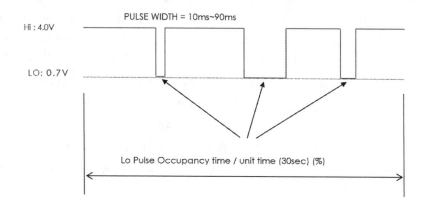

Figure 12-15. *Excerpt of the Grove Dust Sensor data sheet (LPO)*

The data sheet for the dust sensor can be found at
https://raw.githubusercontent.com/SeeedDocument/Grove_Dust_
Sensor/master/resource/Grove_-_Dust_sensor.pdf

What we are seeing there is the dust sensor sends a pulse of low (off) over a period of 30 seconds. These pulses can occur at various times and can last for a short period of time. The total of the time spent in the "off" state over the interval (30 seconds) is called the low pulse occupancy time (LPO) and is represented as a percentage. Easy, right? Well, sort of.

There are two implications for our code we must adhere. First, we must read the sensor over a 30-second period. Thus, there will not be anything else going on during that time (unless you want to do some form of threading or interrupts). This means, at a minimum, our read function will run for 30 seconds. Second, we must write our code to quickly capture when the pin goes to 0 (off), and total the time spent in that state. This is the most difficult aspect of the code.

Fortunately, we can view the other libraries for the dust sensor to learn how it was done for other platforms. In fact, the code from a similar Python implementation will work just fine. Cool. The following is an excerpt for the code to capture the time spent in the off state:

```
while time.time() - starttime <= SAMPLETIME_S:  # in
sampling window
    if self.dust_sensor_pin.value() == 0:
        start = time.ticks_us()
    elif start > 0:
        value = time.ticks_diff(time.ticks_us(), start)
        # Low Pulse Occupancy Time (LPO Time) in microseconds
        low_pulse_occupancy += value
        start = 0
```

As you can see, we simply sum the time for a variable named low_ pulse_occupancy. Now, we need to convert that value into a percentage concentration, and that is where it gets tricky.

We have to take the LPO calculated and form a ratio and then take the ratio and use a formula to convert it. We find this formula on the data sheet in the form of a graph that describes the performance of the dust sensor under controlled conditions. Figure 12-16 shows an excerpt from the data sheet with this data.

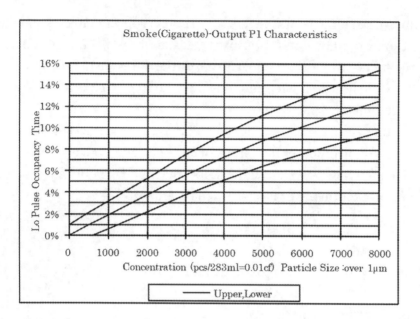

Figure 12-16. *Excerpt of the Grove Dust Sensor data sheet (graph)*

Formulating a formula to model this graph is a bit complex, but once again we can copy what others have done and implement the same in our code. The following shows the formula used in a Python library for the Raspberry Pi. It is not necessary to understand every nuance of the formula; rather, for our uses, it is sufficient to understand the source of the information – the graph on the data sheet.

```
# ratio: percentage of low pulses over the sampling window
ratio = low_pulse_occupancy / (SAMPLETIME_S * 1e+6)
concentration = 1.1 * (ratio ** 3) - 3.8 * (ratio ** 2) + 520 *
ratio + 0.62
```

OK, that's the hard part of this code. The rest are techniques you've seen before, so we won't go through every line. However, you should examine the class member variables to see the use of the self.last_data variable. We use this to store the last known reading. When we calculate the concentration, we either return the concentration calculated or return the last known reading in case the dust sensor doesn't produce enough samples (pulses) to calculate the reading.

Listing 12-1 shows the complete code for the DustSensor class with comments removed for brevity.

Listing 12-1. DustSensor Class Module

```
import machine
import time

SAMPLETIME_S = 30
DUST_SENSOR_PIN = 20

class DustSensor:
    """DustSensor Class"""

    def __init__(self, sensor_pin=DUST_SENSOR_PIN):
        """Constructor"""
        # Setup dust sensor
        self.dust_sensor_pin = machine.Pin(sensor_pin,
        machine.Pin.IN)
        self.last_reading = 0.62 # Minimal value possible from
        data sheet

    def read(self):
        """Read dust sensor"""
        # start time of sampling window in seconds
        starttime = time.time()
        # ratio of LPO time over the entire sampling window
        ratio = 0
        #  Low Pulse Occupancy Time (LPO Time) in microseconds
        low_pulse_occupancy = 0
```

```
        # concentration based on LPO time and characteristics
        graph (datasheet)
        concentration = 0
        start = 0
        while time.time() - starttime <= SAMPLETIME_S:  # in
        sampling window
            if self.dust_sensor_pin.value() == 0:
                start = time.ticks_us()
            elif start > 0:
                value = time.ticks_diff(time.ticks_us(), start)
                # Low Pulse Occupancy Time (LPO Time) in
                microseconds
                low_pulse_occupancy += value
                start = 0

        # ratio: percentage of low pulses over the
        sampling window
        ratio = low_pulse_occupancy / (SAMPLETIME_S * 1e+6)
        concentration = 1.1 * (ratio ** 3) - 3.8 * (ratio ** 2)
        + 520 * ratio + 0.62
        if concentration != 0.62:
            print("PM concentration: {} pcs/0.01cf".
            format(concentration))
            self.last_reading = concentration
        else:
            concentration = self.last_reading
            print("PM last reading: {} pcs/0.01cf".
            format(concentration))
        return concentration

if __name__ == '__main__':
    try:
```

```
# Setup dust sensor
dust_sensor = DustSensor()
while True:
    print("Reading dust sensor...")
    print("Dust = {}".format(dust_sensor.read()))
    time.sleep(5)

except (KeyboardInterrupt, SystemExit) as err:
    print("\nbye!\n")
```

Notice what we have at the bottom of the class. This is another example of how to write some rudimentary testing code. With this, we can execute the code module by itself and test our read function. It is recommended you do that once you have your hardware wired and before you attempt to run the entire project. You should see output similar to the following:

```
Reading dust sensor...
PM concentration: 0.634378 pcs/0.01cf
Dust = 0.634378
Reading dust sensor...
Reading dust sensor...
PM concentration: 0.621001 pcs/0.01cf
Dust = 0.621001
Reading dust sensor...
PM last reading: 0.621001 pcs/0.01cf
Dust = 0.621001
Reading dust sensor...
PM concentration: 0.649432 pcs/0.01cf
Dust = 0.649432
Reading dust sensor...
PM concentration: 0.7309418 pcs/0.01cf
Dust = 0.7309418
...
```

Notice we see one case where the sensor did not generate enough samples to compute the dust concentration. This illustrates the technique of saving the last reading in case the next reading is out of bounds or there is an error.

Now, let's look at the next class module, a class to manage reading from all of the sensors.

AirMonitor Class

One of the things you may encounter in building projects with many sensors is that it can sometimes be a challenge to ensure all of the sensors are read in a timely manner, especially if the sampling rate of the sensors varies. More specifically, some sensors may need time to "warm up" or simply need time to reset before reading the next value. Making your main code accommodate all of these nuances may be a challenge.

CHOOSING A SAMPLE RATE

One of the things that you must consider when writing IoT solutions is how often you need to read data called the sample rate (or sampling rate). There are several factors you must consider, all of which should help you determine how often you should read data.

First, you must consider how often you can get data from the sensors. Some sensors may require as much as several minutes to refresh values. Most of those either let you read stale data (the last value read) or emit an error if you read the data too frequently.

Aside from the sensors, you also need to consider how often the data changes or how often you need to check/retrieve the data. The application will play a big factor in determining an optimum rate. For example, if you are sampling a sensor for data that doesn't change often, there is no point in reading it more frequently.

Another factor to consider concerns storing the data. If you are planning to store the data, reading the data every second could generate more data than your storage mechanism can handle.

Finally, the criticality of the data may also be a factor. More specifically, if the data is used to make critical decisions for industrial, mechanical, or health decisions, the sample rate may need to be high (fast). For example, it would be far too late to detect oncoming vehicles every 30 seconds.

When choosing a sample rate, you must consider all of these elements: refresh rates of your sensors, how often the data will change, how much data you want to store, and the criticality of the data.

Fortunately, we can move coordination like this to a helper class. That is, we can create a class to read all of the sensors and provide data to the main code for display. For this project, we will create a class module named `air_monitor.py` that contains a class named `AirMonitor`. You can create the file now in Thonny.

In this class, we will set up all of the sensors initializing any libraries needed and create two functions for use by our main module, a function to read the data named `read_data()` and a function to retrieve the data named `get_data()`. All of the work to read the sensors appears in the `read_data()` function. The data returned by the `get_data()` function is a dictionary that contains the four sensor values, making it easy to display the data.

We will also need a number of helper functions to read from the sensors as described in the following:

- `read_pressure()`: Read the pressure from the BMP280

- `read_temperature()`: Read the temperature from the BMP280

- `translate()`: Translate a range of values from one range to another. Used to transform the values from the air quality sensor from 1–65535 to 1–1024 to classify the air quality.

Let's return to the sample time for the class. Recall, our dust sensor needs 30 seconds to read, but other sensors need additional time. Specifically, the air quality sensor requires a 20-second startup and 2+ seconds of read time. Thus, the minimal sample rate we can accommodate is 52–60 seconds. Now you can see why it is important to group all of your sensor read mechanisms into a single class/function.

Now, let's go through some of the details of the class implementation. Once again, we won't see every detail, so you should read through the code on your own to discover how it works.

We use a dictionary in the class to store the sensor data and return it with the `get_data()` function. The following shows the new dictionary. Once returned to the main sketch, we simply use the key to retrieve the sensor data. For example, `data["temperature"]` fetches the temperature value:

```
data = {
    "temperature": 0.0,
    "pressure": 0.0,
    "dust_concentration": 0.0,
    "air_quality": AIR_GOOD,
}
```

Notice we will use a series of constants for the air quality. The following shows the constants used that map to relative quality values. We can use these values in the main code to print text to match the constant value:

```
AIR_POOR = 0
AIR_FAIR = 1
AIR_GOOD = 2
AIR_ERR = 3
```

Listing 12-2 shows the complete code for the class with documentation removed for brevity. Take a few moments to read through the code so that you understand all of the parts of the code. As you will see, it is not overly complicated; rather, just a lot of code due to the number of sensors we are reading.

Listing 12-2. AirMonitor Class Module

```
from machine import ADC, I2C, Pin
import time
from project6.bmx280x import BMX280
from project6.mcp9808 import MCP9808
from project6.dust_sensor import DustSensor

# Constants
DUST_SAMPLE_RATE = 60 # 60 seconds
AIR_SENSOR_PIN = 1
AIR_POOR = 0
AIR_FAIR = 1
AIR_GOOD = 2
AIR_ERR = 3

class AirMonitor:
    """AirMonitor Class"""

    data = {
        "temperature": 0.0,
        "pressure": 0.0,
        "dust_concentration": 0.0,
        "air_quality": AIR_GOOD,
    }

    def __init__(self, i2c):
        """Constructor"""
```

```python
        # Initialize the BMP280
        self.i2c = i2c
        # Setup BMP280
        self.bmp280 = BMX280(i2c, 0x77)
        # Setup MCP9808
        self.mcp9808 = MCP9808(i2c)
        # Setup dust sensor
        self.dust_sensor = DustSensor()
        # Setup air quality sensor
        self.air_quality = ADC(28)
        self.to_volts = 5.0 / 1024

    def read_pressure(self):
        """Read the pressure from the BMP280."""
        return self.bmp280.pressure/100

    def read_temperature(self):
        """Read the temperature from the BMP280."""
        return self.bmp280.temperature

    def translate(self, x, in_min=1, in_max=65535, out_min=1,
    out_max=1024):
        """Translate from range 1-65353 to 1-1024."""
        return int((x - in_min) * (out_max - out_min) /
                    (in_max - in_min) + out_min)

    def read_data(self):
        """read_data"""
        print("\n>> Reading Data <<")
        # Read temperature
        try:
            print("> Reading temperature = ", end="")
            self.data["temperature"] = self.mcp9808.read_temp()
```

```python
            print(self.data["temperature"])
        except Exception as err:
            print("ERROR: Cannot read temperature: {}".
            format(err))
            return False

        # Read pressure
        try:
            print("> Reading pressure = ", end="")
            self.data["pressure"] = self.read_pressure()
            print(self.data["pressure"])
        except Exception as err:
            print("ERROR: Cannot read pressure: {}".
            format(err))
            return False

        # Read dust
        self.data["dust_concentration"] = 0.10
        try:
            print("> Reading dust concentration")
            self.data["dust_concentration"] = self.dust_
            sensor.read()
            print("> Dust concentration = {}".format(self.
            data["dust_concentration"]))
        except Exception as err:
            print("ERROR: Cannot read dust concentration: {}".
            format(err))
            return False

        # Read air quality
        try:
            print("> Reading air quality = ", end="")
            raw_value = self.air_quality.read_u16()
```

```
        sensor_value = self.translate(raw_value)
        if sensor_value > 700:
            self.data["air_quality"] = AIR_POOR
        elif sensor_value > 300:
            self.data["air_quality"] = AIR_FAIR
        else:
            self.data["air_quality"] = AIR_GOOD
        print(self.data["air_quality"])
    except Exception as err:
        print("ERROR: cannot read air quality: {0}".
        format(err))
        self.data["air_quality"] = AIR_ERR
        return False

    return True

def get_data(self):
    """get_data"""
    return self.data
```

Notice there are a number of debugging print statements in the code. You may want to take those out once you get everything working.

Tip   If you have any trouble getting the code to work, you may want to comment out the lines of code for reading the dust sensor so that you do not have to wait 30 seconds for each read. Similarly, you can comment out the read to other sensors to give you a chance to solve any problems using the class in your project.

Now we can write our main code.

Main Code Module

Now we can write the main code. Open a new file and name it `main.py`. Since we are placing all of the sensor work in the `AirMonitor` class, all we need to do here is set up the I2C bus, instantiate the new class instance (stored in a variable named `air_quality`), initialize the OLED and buzzer, and then print the greeting.

The `main()` function simply calls the `read_data()` method, and if it returns true, we get the data and display it on the OLED. The only extra work we need to do is determine what the air monitor sensor is returning and print the correct value and examine the data to ensure it is below established levels (to determine air quality). If the air quality is low, we display a message and play an alarm sequence on the buzzer.

We will also use a helper function to sound a tone on the buzzer. This isn't absolutely necessary, but it does help reduce the amount of code, and this concept will help you understand the way we use the buzzer in the next chapter.

However, the software library we will be using for the OLED doesn't contain methods that allow macro functions like writing a string to the display or setting up (initializing) the display. We will create those helper functions named `oled_write()` and `setup_oled()`.

The following shows the code for the oled_write() function:

```
def oled_write(oled, column, row, message):
    """oled_write"""
    oled.text(message, column*8, row*8, 255)
    oled.show()
```

The following shows the code for the setup_oled() function:

```
def setup_oled(i2c):
    """setup_oled"""
    # Setup OLED
```

```
display = SSD1306_I2C(128, 64, i2c)  # Grove OLED Display
display.text('Hello World', 0, 0, 255)
display.show()
oled_write(display, 0, 1, "Environment")
oled_write(display, 0, 2, "Monitor")
oled_write(display, 0, 4, "Starting...")
return display
```

Since we will only use the buzzer to sound if there is a poor air quality condition, rather than use the Buzzer class we created in Chapter 11, we will create a more simplistic beep() helper function that simply plays a tone using the same PWM we created in the Buzzer class. The following shows the simplified beep() function. We will use pin 26 (an analog pin) for the buzzer.

```
def beep(buzzer_pin, duration=0.150):
    """beep"""
    buzzer_pin.on()
    time.sleep(duration)
    buzzer_pin.off()
```

Finally, let's discuss the sampling rate again. Recall from the AirMonitor class, we have a minimal sampling rate of 60 seconds hard-coded. In the main() function, we also have a sampling rate constant. This should be used to control how often we call the read_data() function rather than how long it takes to read the data. A minor distinction, but the result is we must consider both how long it takes to read the data and how often we want to start the read.

Listing 12-3 shows the complete code for the main script for this project. You can read through it to see how all of the code works.

Listing 12-3. Main Code Module

```
# Import libraries
from machine import Pin, I2C
import time
from project6.air_monitor import AirMonitor, AIR_POOR, \
AIR_FAIR, AIR_GOOD, AIR_ERR
from project6.ssd1306 import SSD1306_I2C

# Constants
SAMPLING_RATE = 5 # 5 second wait to start next read
BUZZER_PIN = 26
WARNING_BEEPS = 5
HIGH = 1
LOW = 0

# Constants for environmental quality
MAX_TEMP = 30.0
MAX_DUST = 40.0

def beep(buzzer_pin, duration=0.150):
    """beep"""
    buzzer_pin.on()
    time.sleep(duration)
    buzzer_pin.off()

def oled_write(oled, column, row, message):
    """oled_write"""
    oled.text(message, column*8, row*8, 255)
    oled.show()

def setup_oled(i2c):
    """setup_oled"""
    # Setup OLED
```

```python
    display = SSD1306_I2C(128, 64, i2c)  # Grove OLED Display
    display.text('Hello World', 0, 0, 255)
    display.show()
    oled_write(display, 0, 1, "Environment")
    oled_write(display, 0, 2, "Monitor")
    oled_write(display, 0, 4, "Starting...")
    return display

def main():
    """Main"""
    print("Welcome to the Environment Monitor!")
    # Setup buzzer
    buzzer = Pin(BUZZER_PIN, Pin.OUT)
    i2c = I2C(0,scl=Pin(9), sda=Pin(8), freq=100000)
    print("Hello. I2C devices found: {}".format(i2c.scan()))
    oled = setup_oled(i2c)
    # Start the AirMonitor
    air_quality = AirMonitor(i2c)
    time.sleep(3)
    oled_write(oled, 11, 4, "done")
    beep(buzzer)
    oled.fill(0)
    oled.show()

    while True:
        if air_quality.read_data():
            # Retrieve the data
            env_data = air_quality.get_data()

            oled_write(oled, 0, 0, "ENVIRONMENT DATA")
            oled_write(oled, 0, 2, "Temp: ")
            oled_write(oled, 6, 2, "{:3.2f}C".format(env_
            data["temperature"]))
```

```
oled_write(oled, 0, 3, "Pres: ")
oled_write(oled, 6, 3, "{:05.2f}hPa".format(env_
data["pressure"]))
oled_write(oled, 0, 4, "Dust: ")
if env_data["dust_concentration"] == 0.0:
    oled_write(oled, 6, 4, "--           ")
else:
    oled_write(oled, 6, 4, "{:06.2f}%".format(env_
    data["dust_concentration"]))
oled_write(oled, 0, 5, "airQ: ")
if env_data["air_quality"] in {AIR_ERR, AIR_POOR}:
    oled_write(oled, 6, 5, "POOR")
elif env_data["air_quality"] == AIR_FAIR:
    oled_write(oled, 6, 5, "FAIR")
elif env_data["air_quality"] == AIR_GOOD:
    oled_write(oled, 6, 5, "GOOD")
else:
    oled_write(oled, 6, 5, "--       ")

# Check for environmental quality
if ((env_data["dust_concentration"] > MAX_DUST) or
        (env_data["temperature"] > MAX_TEMP) or
        (env_data["air_quality"] == AIR_POOR) or
        (env_data["air_quality"] == AIR_ERR)):
    #pylint: disable=unused-variable
    for i in range(0, WARNING_BEEPS):
        oled_write(oled, 3, 7, "ENV NOT OK")
        beep(0.250)
        time.sleep(0.250)
        oled_write(oled, 3, 7, "          ")
        time.sleep(0.250)
```

```
        else:
            oled.fill(0)
            oled.show()
            oled_write(oled, 0, 2, "ERROR! CANNOT")
            oled_write(oled, 0, 3, "READ DATA")

        time.sleep(SAMPLING_RATE)

if __name__ == '__main__':
    try:
        main()
    except (KeyboardInterrupt, SystemExit) as err:
        print("\nbye!\n")
sys.exit(0)
```

OK, that's it! We've written the code and we're now ready to execute the project!

Execute

Now it is time to test the project by executing (running) it. Recall, we can copy all of our code to our Pico. If you haven't already done so, you should create a folder named project6 on your Pico and then upload the air_ monitor.py, dust_sensor.py, bmx280x.py, mcp98008.py, and ssd1306.py files to the project6 folder. Next, upload the main.py file to the root folder of your Pico.

Recall, there are two ways to test or execute the code. We could use Thonny to connect to the Pico and simply run the main.py script. Or we can reboot the Pico by unplugging it and plugging it back in to the USB port on your PC.

The difference is if you run the main.py file manually, you will see the debug statements show in the output at the bottom of Thonny. Running the script automatically may not show those statements if you do not use Thonny or a similar application to connect to the Pico.

Once the program starts, you will see some diagnostic messages written to the terminal. You will also see a welcome message appear on the LCD. When you run the code from Thonny, you will see output similar to the following:

```
Welcome to the Environment Monitor!
Hello. I2C devices found: [24, 60, 119]

>> Reading Data <<
> Reading temperature = 20.8125
> Reading pressure = 1022.359
> Reading dust concentration
> Dust concentration = 0.649432
> Reading air quality = 2

>> Reading Data <<
> Reading temperature = 20.8125
> Reading pressure = 1022.394
> Reading dust concentration
> Dust concentration = 0.649432
> Reading air quality = 2
...
```

Figure 12-17 shows examples of the OLED output.

Figure 12-17. Executing the environment monitor project

If everything worked as executed, congratulations! If something isn't working, check your connections to ensure you've connected everything correctly.

Since we named the main code file main.py, you can restart the Pico and run the project on boot. If you connect a power supply to the Pico, or a 5V battery pack, you can run it continuously without your PC.

Going Further

While we didn't discuss them in this chapter, there are some ideas where you could make this project into an IoT project. Here are just a few suggestions you can try once we have learned how to take our projects to the cloud. Put your skills to work!

- *Environment portal*: You can display the values of the last sensor(s) read in a web page to allow you to see the condition of your environment from anywhere in the world. If you also add the date and time, you can see how your environment changes over time. See Chapter 13 for ideas on how to implement this suggestion.

- *Additional sensors*: Implement additional sensors to read more data such as specific gases such as CO_2, O_2, and a light sensor to detect day and night cycles. You could also include a vibration sensor if you live in areas prone to seismic tremors. Interestingly, you can use vibration sensors to detect when someone walks into the room.

- *Sampling rate*: Adjust the sampling rate to match your environmental needs. For example, if you live in a very clean apartment or house with good climate control, your sampling rate may be lower than if you live in a dusty area prone to temperature changes such as an RV or typical rustic cabin.

Summary

In this chapter, we got more hands-on experience making projects with Grove analog and digital modules as well as multiple I2C devices. We used these modules to create an environment monitor that displays the temperature, barometric pressure, air quality, and dust (particle) concentration in the air – in other words, an indoor air monitoring solution.

Along the way, we learned more about how to work with Grove modules including how to write our own classes for managing multiple sensors. We also saw how to use alternative software libraries in both the Arduino and Python versions of our project. Finally, we saw some potential to make this project better as well as some ideas for how to adapt the project for practical uses.

In the next chapter, we will see how to extend our projects into an exciting new realm – the Internet. We will see how to connect our Pico to the Internet and learn how to make our projects into an Internet of Things (IoT) project.

CHAPTER 13

Introducing IoT for the Cloud

Thus far in the book, we have learned that the Raspberry Pi Pico is a great small microcontroller that has a lot of power in such a small package. It's inexpensive and easy to program. However, there is one thing missing – there is no way to connect it to the Internet. At least, not directly because it doesn't have WiFi support. We will see how to add WiFi support in this chapter.

In previous chapters, you've seen a number of projects, ranging from very basic to advanced in difficulty; it is time to discuss how to make your IoT data viewable by others via the cloud. More specifically, you will get a small glimpse at what is possible with the more popular cloud computing services and solutions.

I say a glimpse because it is not possible to cover all viable solutions available in cloud services solutions for IoT in a single chapter. Once again, this is a case where learning a little bit about something and seeing it in practice will help you get started.

In this chapter, we will get an overview of what the cloud is and how it is used for IoT solutions. The chapter also presents a concise overview of the popular cloud systems for IoT as well as a short example using two of our earlier projects to give you a sense of what is possible and how projects can be modified to use the Internet.

© Charles Bell 2022
C. Bell, *Beginning MicroPython with the Raspberry Pi Pico*, Maker Innovations Series,
https://doi.org/10.1007/978-1-4842-8135-2_13

THE CLOUD: ISN'T THAT JUST MARKETING HYPE?

Don't believe all the hype or sales talk about any product that includes "cloud" in its name. Cloud computing services and resources should be accessible via the Internet from anywhere, available to you via subscription (fee or for free), and permit you to consume or produce and share the data involved. Also, consider the fact that you must have access to the cloud to get to your data. Thus, you have no alternative if the service is unreachable (or down).

Since the technologies presented are quite unique in implementation (but straightforward in concept), I keep the project hardware and programming to a minimal effort.

Overview

Unless you live in a very isolated location, you have been bombarded with talk about the cloud and IoT. You've seen advertisements in magazines and on television, or read about it in other books, or attended a seminar or conference. Unless you've spent time learning what cloud means, you are wondering what all the fuss is about.

What Is the Cloud?

Simply stated,[1] the cloud is a name tagged to services available via the Internet. These can be servers you can access (running as a virtual machine on a larger server), systems that provide access to a specific software or environment, or resources such as disks or IP addresses that

---

[1] Experienced cloud researchers will tell you there is a lot more to learn about the cloud.

you can attach to other resources. The technologies behind the cloud include grid computing (distributed processing), virtualization, and networking. The correct scientific term is cloud computing. Although a deep dive into cloud computing is beyond the scope of this book, it is enough to understand that you can use cloud computing services to store your sensor data.

What Is Cloud Computing Then?

The term *cloud computing* is sadly overused and has become a marketing term for some. True cloud computing solutions are services that are provided to subscribers (customers) via a combination of virtualization, grid computing (distributed processing and storage), and facilities to support virtualized hardware and software, such as IP addresses that are tied to the subscription rather than a physical device. Thus, you can use and discard resources on the fly to meet your needs.

These resources, services, and features are priced by usage patterns (called *subscription plans* or *tiers*), in which you can pay for as little or as much as you need. For example, if you need more processing power, you can move up to a subscription level that offers more CPU cores, more memory, and so forth. Thus, you only pay for what you need, which means that organizations can potentially save a great deal on infrastructure.

A classic example of this benefit is a case where an organization experiences a brief and intense level of work that requires additional resources to keep their products and services viable. Using the cloud, organizations can temporarily increase their infrastructure capability and, once the peak has passed, scale things back to normal. This is a lot better than having to rent or purchase a ton of hardware for that one event.

Sadly, there are some vendors that offer cloud solutions (typically worded as *cloud enabled* or simply *cloud*) that fall far short of being a complete solution. In most cases, they are nothing more than yesterday's

Internet-based storage and visualization. Fortunately, Microsoft Azure is authentic: a full cloud computing solution with an impressive array of features to support almost any cloud solution you can dream up.

Tip   If you would like to know more about cloud computing and its many facets, see `https://en.wikipedia.org/wiki/Cloud_computing`.

How Does the Cloud Help IoT?

OK, so now that we know what cloud systems are, how do they help me with my IoT projects? There are a variety of ways, but most common are mechanisms for storing and presenting your data rather than storing it locally or even remotely on another system such as a dedicated database server. That is, you can send the data you collect from your sensors to the cloud for storage and even use additional cloud services to view the data using charts, graphs, or just plain text. The sky is the limit with respect to how you can present your data.

But storing data isn't the only feature you can leverage in the cloud. There are other services that you can use to link to yet other services to form a solution. For example, most paid IoT cloud systems provide features that can "talk" to each other allowing you to link them together to quickly build a solution. The features are often called components rather than services, but both terms apply.

For example, in Microsoft Azure, you can store your data with one of several components and then link it to others that allow you to modify the data via queries, others to route the data to other places (even to another cloud service vendor), and to one of several components for displaying the data. Yes, it really is a set of building blocks like that.

Now that we've had a general overview of cloud systems, let's look at those that support IoT projects directly.

IoT Cloud Systems

There are a number of IoT cloud vendors that offer all manner of products, capacities, and features to match about anything you can conjure for an IoT project. With so many vendors offering IoT solutions, it can be difficult to choose one. The following is a concise list of the more popular IoT offerings from the top vendors in the cloud industry:

- *Oracle IoT*: www.oracle.com/internet-of-things/

- *Microsoft Azure IoT Hub*: https://azure.microsoft.com/en-us/product-categories/iot/

- *Google IoT Core*: https://cloud.google.com/iot-core

- *IBM IoT*: www.ibm.com/internet-of-things

- *Arduino IoT Cloud*: www.arduino.cc/en/IoT/HomePage

- *Adafruit IO*: https://io.adafruit.com/

- *If This Then That (IFTTT)*: https://ifttt.com/

- *MathWorks ThingSpeak*: https://thingspeak.com/

Most of the vendors offer commercial products, but a few like Google, Azure, Arduino, IFTTT, and ThingSpeak offer limited free accounts. A few are free like Adafruit IO and Arduino IoT Cloud but may limit you to a particular platform or a smaller set of features. As you may surmise, some of the offerings are complex solutions with steep learning curve, but the IFTTT and ThingSpeak offerings are simple and easy to use. Since we want a solution that is easy to use (and free!), we will then use ThingSpeak in the next chapter to round out our introduction to IoT cloud systems.

Tip   If you want or need to use one of the other vendors, be sure to read all of the tutorials thoroughly before jumping into your code.

Let's look at some of the types of services available in cloud systems that support IoT projects.

IoT Cloud Services Available

IoT projects offer an amazing opportunity to expand our knowledge of the world around us and to observe events from all over the world no matter where we are located. To address these capabilities, IoT cloud services provide an array of services that you can leverage in your applications.

There are services for collecting data, managing your devices, performing analytics, and even application and processing extensions for you to exploit. For example, some vendors include complete user management where you can provide user accounts for people to log in and use your cloud solution and see your data.

The following lists a number of the types of services available. Some vendors may not offer all of the services, and a service common among the vendors may work very differently from one vendor to another. However, this should give you an idea of what services are available and a general idea of the feature set:

- *Device management*: Allows you to set up, manage, and track what devices are in your IoT network.

- *Data storage*: Permits storage of your IoT data either on a temporary (typically free for a number of days) or permanent (paid) storage.

- *Data analytics*: Allows you to perform analysis on your data to find trends, outliers, or any form of analytical query.

- *Data query and filters*: You can perform queries or filter your IoT data after it has been sent to the cloud service for detailed presentations or transformations.

- *Big data*: Permits you to store vast amounts of data and perform operations on the data (think data warehousing).

- *Visualization tools*: Various dashboards and graphics you can use to help present your data in meaningful ways (spreadsheet, pie charts, etc.).

- *High availability*: Provides features that allow you to operate even if portions of your cloud servers (or the vendor's) fail or go offline due to network issues.

- *Third-party integration*: Allows you to connect your IoT services to other IoT servers from other vendors. For example, connecting your Adafruit IO data to IFTTT for triggering an SMS message.

- *Security (data, user)*: Provides support for managing user accounts, security access, and more for your applications.

- *Encryption*: Allows you to encrypt your data either in the cloud or when transmitting the data from one service to another.

- *Deployment*: Similar to device management, but on a grander scale where you build IoT devices using common profiles, operating systems, configurations, etc.

- *Scalability*: The ability to scale from a small number of devices and services to many devices. This is often only available in the larger, paid vendor services.

- *APIs (Rest, programming)*: Allow you to write code to communicate directly with the services instead of issuing web requests. Often part of the larger, paid vendor services.

For our beginning IoT projects, we will be focusing on a subset of these services, which can be grouped into several categories. Let's look at a few of the most common services you may want to start using right away.

Data Storage

These services allow you to store your data in the cloud rather than on your local device. Some data such as alerts or notices do not need to be stored, and you should think about if you would need the data in the future and will be project dependent. For example, if you wanted to create a weather alert project, you may not care what the temperature was a week or even a month ago. However, if you want to do some amateur weather forecasting, you will want to store data for some time (perhaps years). You may consider storing the data locally, which may be possible for some platforms such as the Raspberry Pi, but the Arduino and similar boards have very limited storage capabilities.

Thus, if you need to store your data for some period and storing it locally is not an option, you should consider this when selecting a cloud vendor. Look for how data will be stored, the mechanisms needed to send the data to the service, and how to get the data out of the service.

Data Transformation (Queries)

These services allow you to perform queries on the data as it flows to or through the cloud services. You may want to show only a subset of the data to your users, or you may want to filter the data so that data from certain devices, dates, etc. are shown for one of several views.

The case where you'd want to consider these are for IoT projects that collect data from multiple sensors and multiple devices, and the data is stored for a period of time. For example, if you have devices geographically distributed over a wide area, you may only want to see data from a subset of those devices. Similarly, if you have data from several time periods, hours, days, and weeks, you may only want to see data from a specific time.

Visualization Tools

These services along with routing and messaging are the most commonly used for beginning IoT projects. These are simply services that allow you to see your data on the Internet. It may be nothing more than a simple list of the data, or it may be an elaborate data dashboard complete with controls that users can use to manipulate the display. Fortunately, most cloud vendors provide a robust set of tools (some more than one) that you can use to present your data to yourself or your users.

Routing and Messaging

These services are the heart or the bones of the IoT cloud. They encompass the glue to bind different services together. More specifically, they provide mechanisms for you to connect your devices to services and those services to other services such as queries, filters, and visualization tools, permitting you to build an IoT solution using several cloud services. We'll see an example of such a service in the next section.

Now that we've had an overview of the IoT cloud services and the most common services we will encounter, let's jump into a simple example using a web page to control hardware.

But first, let's talk about basic networking capabilities for the Pico.

Connecting Your Pico to the Internet

At the time when the Pico was launched, there were no options available for you to connect your Pico to the Internet except through connecting your Pico to another microcontroller (or Raspberry Pi) to provide the connectivity. Those options are still available (and valid), but they are not simple to set up and program. What we want is a module that we can connect to our Raspberry Pi to connect it to the Internet and provide basic TCP/IP operability. Fortunately, such a module exists! Before we look at that module, let's review what modules are available for us today.

Pico WiFi Modules

There are currently few modules available for connecting our Pico to the Internet. These include the following. While this is a concise list, there are sure to be more options available in the future:

- *ESP8266 WiFi Module for Raspberry Pi Pico*: `https://thepihut.com/collections/pico/products/esp8266-wifi-module-for-raspberry-pi-pico` ($9.94)

- *DiP-Pi WiFi Master for Raspberry Pi Pico*: `https://thepihut.com/collections/pico/products/dip-pi-wifi-master-for-raspberry-pi-pico` ($16.89)

- *Maker Pi Pico Base*: `https://thepihut.com/collections/pico/products/maker-pi-pico-base-without-pico` ($8.81)

- *Pico Wireless Pack*: `https://shop.pimoroni.com/products/pico-wireless-pack` ($13.20)

Most are made to work as an external module that you have to program separately and then use either a serial or similar code library to transfer data back and forth. This is the same concept as connecting your Pico to another microcontroller, which isn't sufficient for getting started quickly or making it easy.

Let's discover a bit more about each of these options.

ESP8266 WiFi Module for Raspberry Pi Pico

This module is a WiFi add-on that allows you to connect your Pico to the Internet via an intermediate module. Specifically, the ESP8266 WiFi Module has an ESP-12 chip onboard that is designed to process commands via a serial connection. Figure 13-1 shows the module. Notice the ESP-12 module on the right. There are also two buttons used for programming the ESP-12 module (reset and boot). On the bottom of the board is a set of female headers that permit you to attach the module directly to your Pico or use it with the Pico Omnibus host board that we've seen in previous chapters (https://shop.pimoroni.com/products/pico-omnibus).

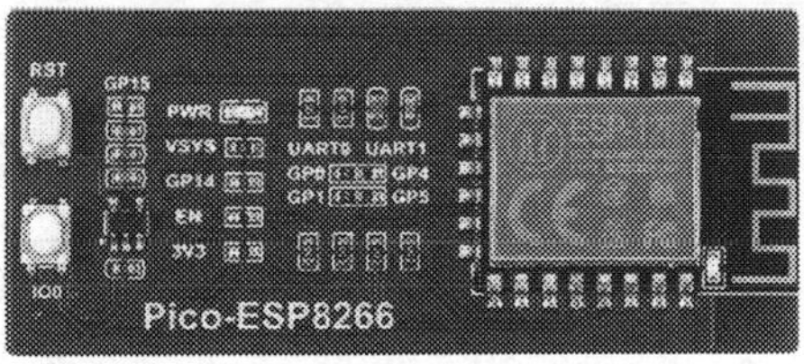

Figure 13-1. *ESP8266 WiFi Module (courtesy of thepihut.com)*

The module is controlled via UART AT commands supporting the TCP/UDP communication protocol. The following shows an excerpt from one of the sample code files found on the product website:

```
sendCMD("AT","OK")
sendCMD("AT+CWMODE=3","OK")
```

```
sendCMD("AT+CWJAP=\""+SSID+"\",\""+password+"\"","OK",20000)
sendCMD("AT+CIFSR","OK")
sendCMD("AT+CIPSTART=\"TCP\",\""+ServerIP+"\","+Port,"OK",10000)
sendCMD("AT+CIPMODE=1","OK")
sendCMD("AT+CIPSEND",">")
```

As you can see, we are not using any special libraries; rather, we're sending AT commands over a UART (think serial) connection to the module. While this helps eliminate GPIO issues (pins used by modules that you need for other modules), it is a bit tedious to program TCP/IP connections this way. Fortunately, there are several working examples on the product website.[2]

See www.waveshare.com/wiki/Pico-ESP8266 for documentation and more information about using this module.

DiP-Pi WiFi Master for Raspberry Pi Pico

This module is similar to the last module in that it also has a female header on the bottom to allow you to connect it to your Pico, and it supports a similar WT8266 WiFi chip that you access via AT commands. Figure 13-2 shows the DiP-Pi WiFi Master.

---

[2] Portions of the site are shown with Chinese text and may be difficult to read for some.

Figure 13-2. *DiP-Pi WiFi Master for Raspberry Pi Pico (courtesy of thepihut.com)*

Sadly, while there are WiFi code examples listed on their list of examples (`https://dip-pi.com/ready-to-use-examples`), the WiFi links are not active, suggesting there may be examples in the future. However, the operating manual for the product has details on the features of the WiFi module as well as links to the AT commands supported.

See `https://dip-pi.com/installation-and-operating-manuals` to download the documentation for this module.

Maker Pi Pico Base

We first saw the Maker Pi Pico Base in Chapter 1. Recall, it supports Grove modules as well as a host of other nice features. While it does not have a WiFi module, the Pico Base has a special connector on the right side that allows you to connect an ESP-01 module to the board to provide Internet capabilities. Figure 13-3 shows the base with the ESP-01 connector highlighted.

Figure 13-3. *Maker Pi Pico Base (courtesy of thepihut.com)*

Like the other modules, this requires programming the ESP-01 via AT commands similar to the ESP8266 WiFi Module. Fortunately, you can load MicroPython on the ESP-01 and write your Python code to connect to the Internet. Sadly, there are no examples on the product website at this time to show you how to do that, but you could follow similar examples from the other modules as a guide.

If you already own a Maker Pi Pico Base and an ESP-01 (or similar module), this may be the least expensive option. So long as you can sort the AT commands, you can make this option work for you.

See `https://github.com/CytronTechnologies/MAKER-PI-PICO` for documentation and more information about using this module.

Pico Wireless Pack

The Pico Wireless Pack is another excellent product of `pimoroni.com`. The module has the familiar female header on the bottom so that you can use it to connect directly to your Pico. It also has an SD card! Wow.

While it too is based on an ESP32 chip, you do not have to use AT commands to access it. In fact, Pimoroni provides a custom MicroPython uf2 image that contains all of the Pimoroni Pico–specific libraries including the network library. Figure 13-4 shows the Pico Wireless Pack.

Figure 13-4. *Pico Wireless Pack (courtesy of thepithut.com)*

The Pico Wireless Pack is a departure from the last modules that require you to use AT codes to control the onboard ESP processor. Instead, we can use a library designed to simplify the use of the WiFi module. To illustrate the difference in how it is programmed, the following shows the same code as the preceding AT command example. Which one do you think is more intuitive?

```
import project8.ppwhttp as ppwhttp
WIFI_SSID = "your SSID here!"
WIFI_PASS = "Your PSK here!"
ppwhttp.start_wifi(WIFI_SSID, WIFI_PASS)
```

This is much easier to understand than using the AT commands, unless, of course, you are proficient in their use.

There is also a user-configurable button, an RGB LED, and an SD card reader on the module, which is a nice touch. See https://shop.pimoroni. com/products/pico-wireless-pack for documentation and more information about using this module.

Caution   The documentation for the Pico Wireless Pack states that the library for the SD card is experimental, but so long as you use it for base file reading and writing, you should not have a problem.

So, Which One Do You Choose?

Only one of these modules supports a programming interface other than the UART-based AT commands. That means there is only one choice for those of us who want to connect our Pico to the Internet and use code that resembles how other platforms use networking code. Thus, we will use the one module that allows us to use our Pico to work with TCP/IP connections – the Pico Wireless Pack from `pimoroni.com`.

Using the Pico Wireless Pack

To use the Pico Wireless Pack, you must download all of the Pimoroni-specific libraries and set up your Pico to use them, which is a potentially time-consuming process. Fortunately, you can avoid all that and simply download their custom Pico boot image and copy it to your Pico.

Start by visiting `https://github.com/pimoroni/pimoroni-pico/releases/` and download the file located in the `v0.3.2` folder named similar to the following (the version number of the folder and file may differ):

```
v0.3.2/pimoroni-pico-v0.3.2-micropython-v1.17.uf2
```

You can refer to Chapter 1 for how to set up your Pico to use the new boot image, but, briefly, you simply remove the Pico from your PC, press and hold the *BOOTSEL* button, then connect the Pico to your PC. Once the Pico opens as a drive, you can copy the `.uf2` file to the drive and then remove the Pico and reconnect it.

Note   You must use the custom `.uf2` from Pimoroni to use the Pico Wireless Pack examples and the projects in this chapter and the next.

Unlike some of the other WiFi offerings for the Pico, the Pico Wireless Pack has several simple examples available on the Pimoroni GitHub site. You can find example WiFi code for the Wireless Pack at `https://github.com/pimoroni/pimoroni-pico/tree/main/micropython/examples/pico_wireless`.

Let's look at a couple of simple examples so we can ensure the module is working on our WiFi. One is a simple utility, but the other is a nifty example of how you can build a simple web server and run it on your Pico. Specifically, it is a simple HTTP (hypertext transfer protocol[3]) listener that accepts commands on a specific port and responds by sending preformatted HTML back to the client.

We won't go through the code at this time; rather, we will concentrate on the mechanics of getting the examples to work. We will see more about the details of how the HTTP server works in a later section.

Download the entire repo by visiting `https://github.com/pimoroni/pimoroni-pico` and clicking the *Code* button and choosing *Download Zip*. Once downloaded, you can unzip the file and navigate to the folder to see the code for the examples.

We will look at two examples. The first is a simple WiFi scanner that finds the WiFi access points within the area. To use this example, open Thonny and navigate to the `<download dir> pimoroni-pico/tree/main/micropython/examples/pico_wireless` where `<download dir>` refers to the location on your PC where you downloaded and unzipped the GitHub code.

Next, connect your Pico and copy the `pphttp.py` and `scan_networks.py` files to your Pico. You can then open and run the `scan_networks.py` file. You should see output that lists the WiFi access points in your area like the following. You should see your own WiFi on this list. If you do not, try moving your Pico closer to the router. Once you find your WiFi, you are ready to try to connect to it.

---

[3] `https://developer.mozilla.org/en-US/docs/Web/HTTP`

```
Found 5 network(s)...
0: FrogPond
1: DIRECT-FB-HP OfficeJet Pro 8730
2: Snapping1
3: Snapping2
4: ATT-WIFI-0123
```

Once you determine your Pico can find your wireless network, you can then test it further by running the rgb_http.py example. This example lets you control the RGB LED on the Pico Wireless Pack using your browser. It demonstrates how you can control hardware over the Internet, which is a large part of what the IoT is all about!

To run this example, you will need to copy the pphttp.py, rgb_http.py, and secrets.py files to your Pico. Then, you will need to open the secrets.py file and enter the SSID and password for your WiFi. For example, if your SSID is named Snapper1 and password is secret_code, open the secrets.py file and edit it as shown. Be sure to save the file on your Pico.

```
WIFI_SSID = "Snapper1"
WIFI_PASS = "secret_code"
```

Once you've saved the file, you can open the rgb_http.py file and run it. When the code starts, you will see the Pico will connect to your WiFi and then print out several messages. The one we must find is the one that shows the IP address that the Pico is using to host the HTTP server. This is known as "listening" since the code is waiting for a connection on that IP and port. The following shows an example of the messages you should see with the IP and port for the listening message shown in bold:

```
Connecting to Snapper1...
Connected!
Starting server...
Server listening on 192.168.1.20:80
```

510

Once you run the server, connect to it with the IP address and port shown in the output using your web browser on your PC. Using the information in the preceding example, you would use http://192.168.1.20:80 in the URL box. Your browser would then connect to the HTTP server on the Pico and display the web page.

Go ahead and try it out. Open your browser and specify the IP address shown in the console output. Figure 13-5 shows what you should see in your browser window.

Figure 13-5. *RGB HTTP example website*

If you do not see the web page, be sure to double-check that your PC is connected to the same network as your Pico. This can happen if you have multiple WiFi networks, or your PC is hardwired to a networking device on another network.

You can now use the drop-down boxes to change the value for each of the red, green, and blue variables. You can use the drop-down or type in a specific value for each. Let's try several examples. Just type in the value for each of the boxes and then click *Set LED*. For example, you could try the base colors such as red (255,0,0), green (0,255,0), and blue (0,0,255). You should see the RGB LED on the Pico Wireless Pack change to match the values you entered.

Back in the Thonny console, you can see the diagnostic messages printed each time you connect to the Pico and change the values for the RGB LED. Notice we see there are two commands being processed: *GET* for retrieving data from the server and *PUT* for sending data to the server. The *GET* returns the result of changing the web page data, and the *PUT* is where the RGB values are sent to the server:

```
Client connected!
Serving GET on /...
Success! Sending 200 OK
Client connected!
Serving POST on /...
Set LED to 255 0 0
Success! Sending 200 OK
Client connected!
Serving POST on /...
Set LED to 255 255 0
Success! Sending 200 OK
Client connected!
Serving POST on /...
Set LED to 255 255 255
Success! Sending 200 OK
Client connected!
Serving POST on /...
Set LED to 0 0 0
Success! Sending 200 OK
```

Once that works, you are ready to start adding networking to your projects. Let's look at some of the projects in this book and see how we can turn them into simple IoT projects.

IoT Project Examples

Let's see how to apply what we learned to two of our example projects to complete the IoT portion for each. We are going to use the pedestrian crossing example from Chapter 7 and the soil moisture monitor project from Chapter 8. We will be creating a rudimentary web server for each project running on the Pico. This will allow you to access the project from anywhere on your network (or beyond).

Rather than develop the web server code from scratch, we will be mimicking the code from the Pimoroni example code for the Pico Wireless Pack. If you have not yet downloaded the code, please visit `https://github.com/pimoroni/pimoroni-pico` and download the code. Once downloaded, we will want to copy the example code files from `<download dir> pimoroni-pico/tree/main/micropython/examples/pico_wireless` and into your own project folder.

For example, you can create `project7` and `project8` folders for the next two projects. Then, copy the `secrets.py` files in the example source code to each of the project folders and modify it for your WiFi. Now you are ready to start working on the following examples.

Example 1: Pedestrian Crossing

In this example, we will use the pedestrian crossing example from Chapter 7. Recall, this project simulates a pedestrian crossing signal where the pedestrian presses a button to request the traffic lights cycle to allow them to cross the street. Instead of a button, we will use a web page to trigger the walk request. Yes, we will see how to remotely control the hardware and our code over the network. Let's get started!

Set Up the Hardware

For this project, you will need to refer to Chapter 7 and set up the hardware using a breadboard and the LEDs and resistors just like you did before. However, this time we will be using the Pico Omnibus host board from Pimoroni. Table 13-1 shows an updated hardware list for the project.

Table 13-1. Required Components for the Pedestrian Crossing Web Example

Component	Qty	Description	Cost	Links
Red LED	2	Pack of 25	$4.00	www.adafruit.com/product/299
		Single	$0.35	www.sparkfun.com/products/9590
Yellow LED	1	Pack of 25	$4.95	www.adafruit.com/product/2700
		Single	$0.35	www.sparkfun.com/products/9594
Green LED	2	Pack of 25	$4.00	www.adafruit.com/product/298
		Single	$0.35	www.sparkfun.com/products/9592
220 or 330 Ohm resistors	5	Variety Kit	$7.95	www.sparkfun.com/products/10969
		Pack of 25	$0.75	www.adafruit.com/product/2780
Pico Omnibus	1	Pico host board	$8.25	https://shop.pimoroni.com/products/pico-omnibus
Pico Wireless Pack	1	WiFi	$13.20	https://shop.pimoroni.com/products/pico-wireless-pack
Breadboard	1	Prototyping board, full-sized	$5.95	www.sparkfun.com/products/12615
			$5.95	www.adafruit.com/product/239
Jumper wires	6	M/F jumper wires, 7" (set of 30)	$2.25	https://www.sparkfun.com/products/11026

Notice the jumper wires need to be the M/F type since the GPIO on the Pico Omnibus has male pins. Go ahead and plug your Pico into the Pico Omnibus and the Pico Wireless Pack onto the right side of the board. We will use the left-side GPIO headers for the LEDs. But use care, because the GPIO header rows are reversed to make it easy to add modules designed to mount to the bottom of the Pico. Thus, you must read the label on the Pico Omnibus carefully to ensure you use the correct pins.

Figure 13-6 shows the Pico Omnibus with the Pico Wireless Pack installed. Notice the left side (Deck 1) is where you will connect the jumper wires for the LEDs.

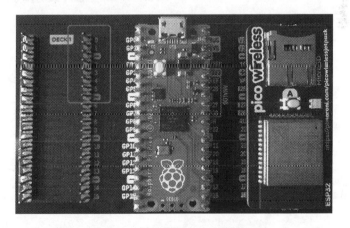

Figure 13-6. *Pico Omnibus with the Pico Wireless Pack*

There is one other change. The Pico Wireless Pack uses some of the GPIO pins that we had in the Chapter 7 implementation. Thus, we must use different pins. Table 13-2 shows the pins we will use for the LEDs. The changes are shown in bold.

Table 13-2. *Connections for the Pedestrian Crossing Web Example*

Physical Pin	GPIO Num/Function	Connection
3	GND	Breadboard ground (bottom)
6	**GP5**	**Resistor for red LED (stoplight)**
5	**GP4**	**Resistor for yellow LED (stoplight)**
4	**GP3**	**Resistor for green LED (stoplight)**
1	**GP1**	**Resistor for red LED (walk light)**
0	**GP0**	**Resistor for green LED (walk light)**
N/A	Breadboard ground	All LED negative side
N/A	Resistor	All LED positive side

Figure 13-7 shows a schematic of how the wiring should be oriented for the Pico Omnibus to the breadboard hosting the LEDs.

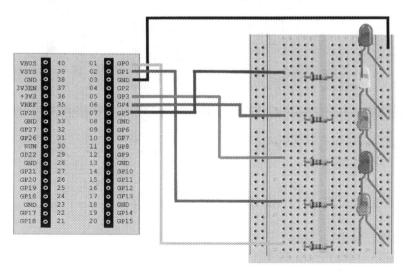

Figure 13-7. *Stoplight simulation wiring (web version)*

Once you have the code wired, you are ready to start writing the code.

Write the Code

The code for this example will use the core code from the project in Chapter 7, but we will not be using the `main()` function. Rather, we will see how to use the Pimoroni library to create a simple HTTP server (also called a listener). The code will send a short HTML-based response (a simple web page) to the client that includes a form containing a single button for the walk request. The listener will listen on port 80.

We will also see an advanced technique using the threading library available on the Pico. As you will see, this library permits us to execute a function in a second core processor on the Pico. It is an excellent way to keep two things going at the same time and get a bit more processing at the same time.

The concept of the HTML server is quite simple. The code listens for a connection on the socket port and then receives the request (in this case, in the form of an HTML `GET` method) and sends an HTML response (the web page). If the button is pressed, the walk cycle will commence by calling the `cycle_lights()` function from the Chapter 7 project.

If you've never used HTML code before, don't worry as the example code will provide everything you need. You don't have to learn HTML for this chapter, but a basic knowledge would be helpful if you want to elaborate on the project or use the HTML server concept for your own projects. A reliable source of information about HTML can be found at `www.w3schools.com/html/`.

Since this is all new code, we will step through all of the parts so you can see how it works, but we will skip the code for controlling the LEDs. Please refer to Chapter 7 if you have not completed that project.

We will create a new file named `pedestrian_crossing_web.py`. Go ahead and open a new file in Thonny if you want to follow along.

Let's begin with the code needed for the import section.

Imports

We need a few libraries in the import section. We need the Pin, _thread, utime, and sys libraries, which are standard libraries for the Pico. The Pimoroni-specific library is named ppwhttp. Notice we place the import statement in a try...else block and print a message if the library cannot be found (the ImportError is raised). This is a common way to test to see if a library is present on the Pico:

```
# Import libraries
from machine import Pin
import _thread
import utime
import sys

# Check for the Pimoroni http class library.
try:
    import ppwhttp
except ImportError:
    raise RuntimeError("Cannot find ppwhttp. Have you copied
    ppwhttp.py to your Pico?")
```

Let's look at the global variables we need.

Global Variables

We will need to define the web page we will send to the client and variables for the LEDs. The HTML for the page is represented as a string. If the HTML code were complex or longer, it is best to store the code in a separate file, but since the code is short, we will leave it in the code. Again, don't worry about learning all the details for the HTML code. As you can see, it is simple to understand, but the tags (those in the square brackets) may not be familiar:

```
# HTML web page for the project
MAIN_PAGE = """<!DOCTYPE html>
<html>
  <head>
    <title>Beginning MicroPython</title>
  </head>
  <center><h2>Pedestrian Crosswalk Simulation</h2></center><br>
  <center>A simple project to demonstrate how to control
  hardware over the Internet.</center><br><br>
  <form>
    <center>
      <button name="WALK" value = "PLEASE" type="submit"
      style="height: 50px; width: 100px">REQUEST WALK</button>
    </center>
  </form>
</html>
"""

# Setup the button and LEDs
stoplight_red = Pin(5, Pin.OUT)
stoplight_yellow = Pin(4, Pin.OUT)
stoplight_green = Pin(3, Pin.OUT)
pedestrian_red = Pin(1, Pin.OUT)
pedestrian_green = Pin(0, Pin.OUT)

# Setup lists for the LEDs
stoplight = [stoplight_red, stoplight_yellow, stoplight_green]
pedestrian_signal = [pedestrian_red, pedestrian_green]
```

We will also need to create a number of functions to manage the HTML server and control the LEDs.

Functions Needed

We will create five functions as follows:

- `cycle_lights()`: The same function from Chapter 7. You can copy it from the Chapter 7 project unchanged.

- `get_home()`: A callback function for the HTML server. This function is called when a client connects to the server. It simply returns the web page.

- `get_walk()`: A callback function for the HTML server. This function is called when the client clicks the button on the web page.

- `server_loop_forever()`: A special function that contains the main loop for the HTML server. It is used as a parameter for the threading module enabling the HTML server to run on the other microcontroller core on the Pico.

- `main()`: The main function we will call when the script is loaded and executed.

Let's look at the code for these functions.

As mentioned, the `cycle_lights()` function is unchanged from the Chapter 7 project, so we will skip the details.

The two functions for the HTML server are very simple. The following shows the code for both functions:

```
@ppwhttp.route("/", methods=["GET", "POST"])
def get_home(method, url, data=None):
    return MAIN_PAGE
```

```
@ppwhttp.route("/?WALK=PLEASE", methods=["GET"])
def get_walk(method, url, data=None):
    if method == "GET":
        cycle_lights()
    return MAIN_PAGE
```

The key to how these functions work is the decorator before each function. Notice the @ppwhttp.route() decorator. This is used by the pwhttp library to identify functions used to "route" control when a client connects and sends a GET or POST method. The first parameter to the decorator defines the path portion of the URL sent. This is how the route is determined. For example, if the client enters http://192.168.1.20:80, the get_home() function is called. Similarly, if the client enters http://192.168.1.20:80/?WALK=PLEASE, the get_walk() function is called. Finally, notice inside the get_walk() function, we test the method, and if it is a GET operation, we call cycle_lights(). This completes the simple HTML web server!

Note   The port (:80) of the URL is optional since port 80 is the default for HTML.

Next is the function we use for the threading library, server_loop_forever(), as shown in the following. When this function is called from the threading library (it is only called once), it starts the HTML server and then drops into a loop calling the handle_http_request() function of the pwhttp library:

```
def server_loop_forever():
    server_sock = ppwhttp.start_server()
    while True:
        ppwhttp.handle_http_request(server_sock)
        utime.sleep(0.01)
```

Finally, we have the main() function, which is where everything comes together. We place the LED setup code, call the start_wifi() function of the pwhttp library to connect to our WiFi, then call the start_new_ thread() function of the threading library to launch a new thread. The following shows the main() function:

```
def main():
    # Turn off the LEDs
    for led in stoplight:
        led.off()
    for led in pedestrian_signal:
        led.off()

    # Start with green stoplight and red pedestrian_signal
    stoplight[2].on()
    pedestrian_signal[0].on()

    ppwhttp.start_wifi()

    # Handle the server polling loop on the other core!
    _thread.start_new_thread(server_loop_forever, ())
```

Recall, we place the SSID and password of our WiFi router in the secrets.py file, which must be uploaded to the Pico. The pwhttp library will open the file and read the values when the start_wifi() function is called.

The main() function is called using the normal mechanism we've used in previous projects located at the bottom of the file.

That's all there is to it. Listing 13-1 shows the completed code for this project with comments and code for the LEDs removed for brevity.

Listing 13-1. Completed Code for the Pedestrian Crossing
Web Example

```
# Import libraries
from machine import Pin
import _thread
import utime
import sys

# Check for the Pimoroni http class library.
try:
    import project7.ppwhttp
except ImportError:
    raise RuntimeError("Cannot find ppwhttp. "
                       "Have you copied ppwhttp.py to
                       your Pico?")

# HTML web page for the project
MAIN_PAGE = """<!DOCTYPE html>
<html>
  <head>
    <title>Beginning MicroPython</title>
  </head>
  <center><h2>Pedestrian Crosswalk Simulation</h2></center><br>
  <center>A simple project to demonstrate how to control
  hardware over the Internet.</center><br><br>
  <form>
    <center>
      <button name="WALK" value = "PLEASE" type="submit"
      style="height: 50px; width: 100px">REQUEST WALK</button>
    </center>
  </form>
</html>
"""
```

523

```python
# Setup the button and LEDs
stoplight_red = Pin(5, Pin.OUT)
stoplight_yellow = Pin(4, Pin.OUT)
stoplight_green = Pin(3, Pin.OUT)
pedestrian_red = Pin(1, Pin.OUT)
pedestrian_green = Pin(0, Pin.OUT)

# Setup lists for the LEDs
stoplight = [stoplight_red, stoplight_yellow, stoplight_green]
pedestrian_signal = [pedestrian_red, pedestrian_green]

def cycle_lights():
    print("START WALK")
...
    print("END WALK")

@ppwhttp.route("/", methods=["GET", "POST"])
def get_home(method, url, data=None):
    return MAIN_PAGE

@ppwhttp.route("/?WALK=PLEASE", methods=["GET"])
def get_walk(method, url, data=None):
    if method == "GET":
        cycle_lights()
    return MAIN_PAGE

def server_loop_forever():
    server_sock = ppwhttp.start_server()
    while True:
        ppwhttp.handle_http_request(server_sock)
        utime.sleep(0.01)
```

```
def main():
    # Turn off the LEDs
    for led in stoplight:
        led.off()
    for led in pedestrian_signal:
        led.off()

    # Start with green stoplight and red pedestrian_signal
    stoplight[2].on()
    pedestrian_signal[0].on()

    ppwhttp.start_wifi()

    # Handle the server polling loop on the other core!
    _thread.start_new_thread(server_loop_forever, ())

if __name__ == '__main__':
    try:
        main()
    except (KeyboardInterrupt, SystemExit) as err:
        print("\nbye!\n")
sys.exit(0)
```

OK, now we're ready to execute the project.

Execute

Before executing the project, be sure to upload the pedestrian_crossing_ web.py to the root of the Pico onboard drive. You also need to create a project7 folder on the Pico and upload the Pico Wireless Pack library (ppwhttp.py) file into that folder. Finally, you also need to upload the secrets.py file from the Pico Wireless Pack library and modify it to include your WiFi SSID and password. Upload this file to the root of the Pico onboard drive.

OK, now we've got the code setup to control our LEDs, and we have the code for a simple HTML server setup to listen on 80. All we need now is the IP address of that board to point our web browser. We can get that from our debug statements by running the code. Listing 13-2 shows the initial run for the project.

Listing 13-2. Running the Pedestrian Crossing Web Project

```
Connecting to Snapper1...
Connected!
>Starting server...
Server listening on 192.168.1.20:80
Client connected!
Serving GET on /...
Success! Sending 200 OK
Client connected!
Serving GET on /?WALK=PLEASE...
START WALK
END WALK
Success! Sending 200 OK
```

Notice in this case the IP address is 192.168.1.20. All we need to do is put that in our browser as shown in Figure 13-8.

Pedestrian Crosswalk Simulation

A simple project to demonstrate how to control hardware over the Internet.

REQUEST
WALK

Figure 13-8. Executing the pedestrian crossing web project

Once you enter the URL, you should see a web page like the image shown. If you don't, be sure to check the HTML in your code to ensure it is exactly like what is shown; otherwise, the page may not display properly. You should also ensure the network your PC is connected to can reach the network to which your board is connected. If your home office is set up like mine, there may be several WiFi networks you can use. It is best if your board and your PC are on the same network (and same subnet).

Tip   If your Pico doesn't connect to your WiFi within a reasonable time, you may need to click *Stop* in Thonny and rerun the project to reset the Wireless Pack.

Once you get that sorted out, verify the green LED for the stoplight is on and the red LED for the pedestrian crossing is on. All other LEDs are off. If you do not see something similar, go back and check your connections again.

Now go ahead and click the button. Remember, the walk button will engage, and you will see the lights cycle, but you won't be able to do anything until the walk cycle is complete. This is because we don't return the response HTML until after the cycle is complete (see the code to convince yourself).

Notice in the output window in Thonny there are debug messages printed for each time the client connects (the code accepts the connection and GET request) as well as a statement about what it is doing. You should see something similar.

Now, let's look at a second example.

Example 2: Soil Moisture Monitor

In this example, we will use the plant monitoring project from Chapter 8. This project used one or more soil moisture sensors to read the relative moisture in the soil for one or more plants. While the features of the project are the same as we saw in Chapter 8, the code for this example is more complex.

Note   The example is meant to show what is possible rather than a complete project. Suggestions on how to improve the code are presented in a later section.

We will be using more advanced HTML code, but once again will not explain all of the details. If you'd like to know how each of the tags is used, you may want to consult a WWW resource or simply Google "HTML tags."

Also, while this project is based on the project in Chapter 8, we will not be using an OLED screen because we will be writing code to a file and reading it when a client connects to the web server returning as a table. As you will see, writing data to a file is much easier and uses less complex code.

We will also be using a different real-time clock (RTC) module. We will use the Pico RTC from waveshare.com because it has a set of pass-through (also called stacking) headers so you can mount the Pico on top and the RTC module to the Pico Omnibus saving us from wiring it to the GPIO headers. Figure 13-9 shows the Pico RTC DS3231 module. See `www.waveshare.com/wiki/Pico-RTC-DS3231` for more details about this module.

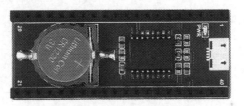

Figure 13-9. Pico RTC DS3231 (courtesy of thepihut.com)

Let's look at the hardware for this example.

Set Up the Hardware

For this project, you will need to refer to Chapter 8 and set up the hardware using a breadboard and the soil moisture modules just like you did before. However, this time we will be using the Pico Omnibus host board from Pimoroni and a micro-SD card to store the data. Table 13-3 shows an updated hardware list for the project.

Table 13-3. *Required Components for the Plant Monitoring Example*

Component	Qty	Description	Cost	Links
Soil moisture	1+	Sensor	$6.95	www.sparkfun.com/products/13637
RTC module	1	Pico RTC DS3231	$14.88	https://thepihut.com/products/precision-rtc-module-for-raspberry-pi-pico-ds3231
CR1220 coin cell	1	Battery	$0.88	https://thepihut.com/products/cr1220-12mm-diameter-3v-lithium-coin-cell-battery
Pico Omnibus	1	Pico host board	$8.25	https://shop.pimoroni.com/products/pico-omnibus
Pico Wireless Pack	1	WiFi	$13.20	https://shop.pimoroni.com/products/pico-wireless-pack
Breadboard	1	Prototyping board, full-sized	$5.95	www.sparkfun.com/products/12615
			$5.95	www.adafruit.com/product/239
Jumper wires	6	F/F jumper wires, 6" (set of 10)	$5.95	www.sparkfun.com/products/11710
Micro-SD card	1	Micro-SD card (any size)	Varies	Commonly sourced

Notice the jumper wires need to be the F/F type since the GPIO on the Pico Omnibus has male pins and the soil moisture sensors also have male pins. Go ahead and plug your Pico into the Pico Omnibus and the Pico Wireless Pack onto the right side of the board like we did in the last example.

Note   Remember, the GPIO header is reversed on the Pico Omnibus. Be sure to read the label on the host board to ensure you have the right pin selected.

There is one other change. The RTC module uses some of the GPIO pins that we had in the Chapter 8 implementation. Thus, we must use different pins. Table 13-4 shows the pins we will use for the LEDs. The changes are shown in bold.

Table 13-4. *Connections for the Plant Monitoring Web Example*

Physical Pin	GPIO Num/Function	Connection
3	GND	Ground for Sensor 1
8	GND	Ground for Sensor 2
21	**GP18**	**Power for Sensor 2**
22	**GP17**	**Power for Sensor 1**
33	GP27	Signal for Sensor 1
34	GP28	Signal for Sensor 2

Figure 13-10 shows a schematic of how the wiring should be oriented for the Pico Omnibus to the breadboard hosting the soil moisture sensors.

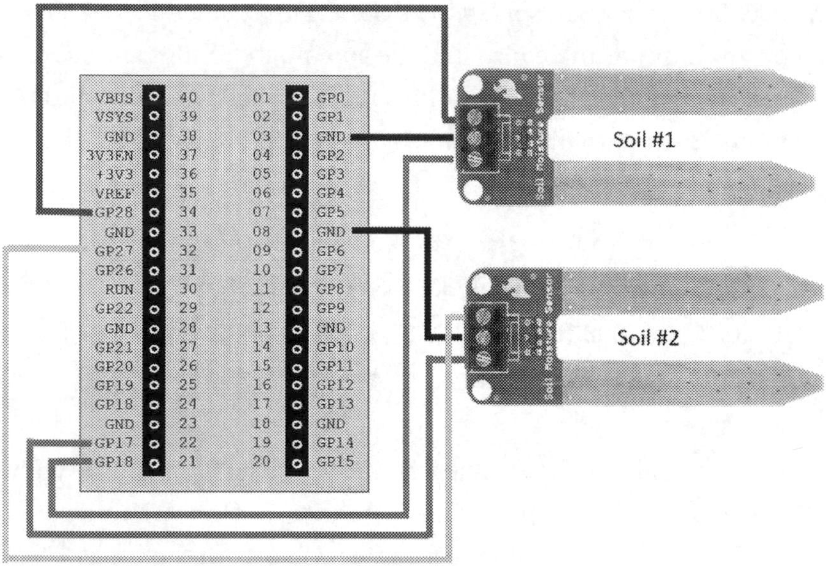

Figure 13-10. *Plant monitoring wiring (web version)*

Once you have the code wired, you are ready to start writing the code.

Write the Code

The code for this example will use some of the code from the project in Chapter 8. We will use the read_timer.py file without changes. We must modify the SoilMoisture class (soil_moisture.py) to work with a file instead of storing the values read in memory. Finally, we will not need the display library.

Note   We will examine the new and changed code in this section. Other code modules used are unchanged from Chapter 8. Refer to Chapter 8 for details on those modules.

However, there are two additional libraries we will need for this project. We will need a library for the SD card and another for the RTC module.

Once again, the SD card support on the Pico Wireless Pack is considered experimental, but the basic operations for file reading and writing work just fine. While Pimoroni does not currently supply a MicroPython library, we can find one elsewhere. The library that works best is found at `https://forums.pimoroni.com/t/pico-wireless-how-to-access-sd-card/17751/3`. Simply open Thonny and create a new file, then copy the code from the website into the file and name it `sdcard.py`. You will upload this file to the `project8` folder on the Pico later.

The library for the RTC module can be found on the vendor's website in the form of a zip file (`www.waveshare.com/w/upload/2/26/Pico-rtc-ds3231_code.zip`). Download the file and unzip it and then locate the file named `ds3231.py` in the `python` folder. You will upload this file to the `project8` folder on the Pico later.

However, the library function named `read_time()` prints a string for the time. That won't work for us since we need to get the time either as a tuple like we did in Chapter 8 or, since the `read_time()` function already formats the datetime for printing, return the string instead. Thus, you will need to modify this class slightly for use with this project.

To do so, first copy the file named `ds3231.py` to your project folder and then open it and apply the following changes shows a unified difference file where the lines marked with a – are removed and those with a + are added.[4] You will copy this file to the `project8` folder on your Pico later:

```
diff.exe" -u  ..\..\raw\Pico-rtc-ds3231_code\Pico-rtc-ds3231_
code\python\ds3231.py ds3231.py
--- ..\..\raw\Pico-rtc-ds3231_code\Pico-rtc-ds3231_code\python\
ds3231.py       2021-12-18 17:51:19.863781600 -0500
```

---

[4] `www.gnu.org/software/diffutils/manual/html_node/Detailed-Unified.html`

```
+++ ds3231.py    2021-12-21 15:31:55.456127500 -0500
@@ -55,7 +55,7 @@
        d = t[3]&0x07   #week
        e = t[4]&0x3F   #day
        f = t[5]&0x1F   #month
-       print("20%x/%02x/%02x %02x:%02x:%02x %s" %(t[6],t[5],
        t[4],t[2],t[1],t[0],self.w[t[3]-1]))
+       return "20%x/%02x/%02x %02x:%02x:%02x" %(t[6],t[5],
        t[4],t[2],t[1],t[0])

    def set_alarm_time(self,alarm_time):
        #    init the alarm pin
```

Notice we are only changing the print() statement to return the string without the day of the week.

Now that we have the libraries we need and the RTC library modified, let's start by looking at the main code.

Main Code

The main code is like the code for the last project. However, this time we will use a file to store the HTML code (since it doesn't change) and a list of HTML-formatted strings for populating an HTML table with the data from the file.

Unlike the last project, the HTML code does not include a button, but we can format a command manually on the URL. We can use this technique to allow access to commands without using buttons or other user interface features. It also helps to make these commands harder to use to prevent overuse. For example, we can provide a clear log command. We would use a URL like http://192.168.42.140/CLEAR, which submits a GET request to the HTML server. We can capture that command and clear the log when it is issued.

The following sections explain the initialization code and the functions needed. We will see the complete code in a later section. Let's start with the HTML code.

HTML Code (Files)

We will store the HTML code needed in files to save memory. Recall by reading a row at a time, we do not have to take up space with the strings in our code. As your projects grow in complexity, this could become an issue. Thus, this project demonstrates a way to save some memory.

The HTML for this project creates a web page with a simple table that includes all the data in the file at the time of the request. To make things easier, we will use three files. The first file (named part1.html) will contain the HTML code up to the table rows, and the second file (named plant_data.csv), which is populated by the SoilMoisture class, and the third (named part2.html) will contain the remaining HTML code.

The first file, part1.html, is shown in Listing 13-3. This file establishes the table HTML code. It also establishes characteristics for the table including text alignment, border size, and padding – all through cascading style (<style> tag). Don't worry if this looks strange or alien. You can google for W3C standards to see how we use the tag to control the style of the web page.

Listing 13-3. HTML Code (part1.html)

```
<!DOCTYPE html>
<html>
  <head>
    <title>Beginning MicroPython - Project 8</title>
    <meta http-equiv="refresh" content="30">
```

```
    <style>
      table, th, td {
          border: 1px solid black;
          border-collapse: collapse;
      }
      th, td {
          padding: 5px;
      }
      th {
          text-align: left;
      }
    </style>
  </head>
  <center><h2>Beginning MicroPython - Project 8</h2>
  </center><br>
  <center>A simple project to demonstrate how to retrieve
  sensor data over the Internet.</center>
  <center><br><b>Plant Monitoring Data</b><br><br>
    <table style="width:75%">
      <col width="180">
      <col width="120">
      <col width="125">
      <col width="125">
      <tr><th>Datetime</th><th>Sensor Number</th><th>Raw
      Value</th><th>Moisture</th><th>Location</th></tr>
```

Notice the meta tag. Here is an example of how we can add HTML code to automatically refresh the page periodically. In this case, it will refresh every 30 seconds.

Notice the table code. Again, don't worry if this seems strange. It works and it is very basic. Those familiar with HTML may want to embellish and improve the code. The last line establishes the header for the table.

The second file, `plant_data.csv`, contains the data. We will use a constant to populate a properly formatted HTML table row. The following shows an example of what a row of data would look like in the file and how that data is transformed to HTML. We will see the HTML for the table row in the next section.

```
# Raw data
2021-08-08 17:26:17,1,78,dry,Small fern on bottom shelf
# HTML table row
<tr><td>2021-08-08 17:26:17</td><td>1</td><td>78</td><td>dry
</td><td>Small fern on bottom shelf </td></tr>
```

The last file, `part2.html`, contains the closing tags so it isn't very large. But since we're reading from files, we include this file. The following shows the code in the second file:

```
    </table>
  </center>
</html>
```

So, how do we use these files? When we send a response back to the client (the web page), we read the first file sending one row at a time, then read the data file sending one row at a time, then read the last file sending one row at a time. We will use a helper function to read the data file in the `SoilMoisture` class.

Imports

The imports we need for the main code include those for the threading (`_thread`), operating system (`uos`), time (`utime`), system (`sys`), RTC (`ds3231`), the read timer (`read_timer`), the soil moisture sensors (`soil_moisture`), and finally the Pimoroni Wireless Pack library (`pwhttp`). The complete list of imports is shown in Listing 13-4. If you want to follow along, open a new file and name it `main.py` in Thonny.

Listing 13-4. Imports for main.py

```
# Import libraries
import _thread
import uos
import utime
import sys
from project8.ds3231 import ds3231              # RTC library
from project8.read_timer import ReadEvent        # Read event
                                                 timer class
from project8.soil_moisture import SoilMoisture  # SoilMoisture
                                                 class

# Check for the Pimoroni http class library.
try:
    import project8.ppwhttp as ppwhttp
except ImportError:
    raise RuntimeError("Cannot find ppwhttp. Have you copied
    ppwhttp.py to your Pico?")
```

Now let's look at the constants.

Constants

We need a string we can use to create the rows for the table as it is read from the file. The following shows the string used. Notice we use replacement syntax so that we can use the format() function to fill in the details:

```
# HTML web page for the project
HTML_TABLE_ROW = "<tr><td>{0}</td><td>{1}</td><td>{2}</td>
<td>{3}</td><td>{4}</td></tr>"
```

Recall we will be using a special command in the form of /CLEAR to clear the log, for example, `http://192.168.1.20/CLEAR`. Once you enter that URL, unless redirected, the web browser will remain at that locator. To force the browser to return to the home page, we use a meta tag that we will populate with the IP address for our web server later. The following shows the format string we will use:

```
HTML_REDIRECT = '<meta http-equiv="Refresh" content="0;
url=''{0}''" />'
```

Now let's look at the setup code.

Setup Code

Unlike other forms of the `main.py` code we've seen in other examples, we will keep this one simple and place the setup code at the global level. We will need to open the HTML files and read them into memory, set up the RTC module, and set up the `SoilMoisture` class. Listing 13-5 shows the setup code. Since the latter is similar to the project from Chapter 8, we will skip the details. Refer to Chapter 8 for how to format the dictionary data for specifying the soil moisture sensors.

Listing 13-5. Setup Code

```
# Setup code
print("Welcome to the Plant Monitor Web Version!\n")

# Read base HTML pages
with open("/part1.html") as html_file:
    WEB_PART1 = "".join(html_file.readlines())
with open("/part2.html") as html_file:
    WEB_PART2 = "".join(html_file.readlines())
```

```
# RTC Setup
I2C_SDA = 20
I2C_SCL = 21
rtc = ds3231(0, I2C_SCL, I2C_SDA)

# Setup Sensors class
sensor_list = [
    {
        'pin': 27,
        'power': 17,
        'location': 'Green ceramic pot on top shelf',
        'nick': 'Ivy',
    },
    {
        'pin': 28,
        'power': 18,
        'location': 'Fern on bottom shelf',
        'nick': 'Fern',
    }
]
# Setup the soil moisture object instance from the
SoilMoisture class
plants = SoilMoisture(rtc, sensor_list)
```

Next, we will need three helper functions for the web server operations.

Helper Functions

For the routing operations, we will create a function named get_home()
to route the home GET request that calls the get_html_sensor_data()
function from the SoilMoisture class (explained in a later section) and
another function named clear_log() to route the /CLEAR to route the GET
request that calls the clear_log() function of the SoilMoisture class.
Listing 13-6 shows the code for these functions.

Listing 13-6. Web Server Functions

```
@ppwhttp.route("/", methods=["GET", "POST"])
def get_home(method, url, data=None):
    # Read data and return web page.
    DATA_PART = ""
    try:
        DATA_PART = plants.get_html_sensor_data(HTML_TABLE_ROW)
        except Exception as err:
        print("Error reading data.", err)
    return "".join([WEB_PART1, DATA_PART, WEB_PART2])

@ppwhttp.route("/CLEAR", methods=["GET"])
def clear_log(method, url, data=None):
    if method == "GET":
        plants.clear_log()
    addr = ".".join(map(str, ppwhttp.get_ip_address()))
    redirect = HTML_REDIRECT.format("http://{0}:80".
    format(addr))
    return "".join([WEB_PART1, redirect, WEB_PART2])
```

We will also need a function to read the values from the sensor. To make the web server responsive to client requests, we will use a thread to run the soil moisture sensor reads. Recall, the soil moisture sensors need a length startup time to read data. The following shows the helper function we will use:

```
def read_sensors(plants):
    print("Reading sensors...")
    plants.read_sensors()
    print("Sensor read complete. Sleeping.")
```

Finally, we will use a function for the main portion of the code.

Main Function

The main() function will be called when the code module is loaded on startup. It is responsible for starting the WiFi, web server, and a loop to read the sensor data when the read event fires. Listing 13-7 shows the main() function. Since most of the code is familiar, we will leave the details as an exercise.

Listing 13-7. Main Function

```python
def main():
    ppwhttp.start_wifi()
    server_sock = ppwhttp.start_server()
    utime.sleep(2)

    # Main loop for reading client requests
    data_read_event = ReadEvent()
    while True:
        ppwhttp.handle_http_request(server_sock)
        utime.sleep(0.01)
        # Check to see if it is time to read the data
        if data_read_event.time_to_read():
            data_read_event.reset()
            # Handle the sensor reading loop on the other core!
            try:
                _thread.start_new_thread(read_sensors,
                [plants])
            except Exception as ex:
                print("ERROR: Cannot read sensors:", ex)
                sys.exit(1)
```

Let's look at the completed code.

Complete Code

Now that we have seen all the parts of the code module, let's look at the completed code. Listing 13-8 shows the complete code for the main code module with comments removed for brevity. Once again, we can save this file as main.py.

Listing 13-8. Main Code Module

```
# Import libraries
import _thread
import uos
import utime
import sys
from project8.ds3231 import ds3231           # RTC library
from project8.read_timer import ReadEvent    # Read event
                                             #  timer class
from project8.soil_moisture import SoilMoisture  # SoilMoisture
                                                 #  class

# Check for the Pimoroni http class library.
try:
    import project8.ppwhttp as ppwhttp
except ImportError:
    raise RuntimeError("Cannot find ppwhttp. Have you copied
    ppwhttp.py to your Pico?")

# Constants
# HTML web page for the project
HTML_TABLE_ROW = "<tr><td>{0}</td><td>{1}</td><td>{2}</
td><td>{3}</td><td>{4}</td></tr>"
HTML_REDIRECT = '<meta http-equiv="Refresh" content="0;
url=''{0}''" />'
```

```python
# Global Variables
WEB_PART1 = ""
WEB_PART2 = ""

# Setup code
print("Welcome to the Plant Monitor Web Version!\n")

# Read base HTML pages
with open("/part1.html") as html_file:
    WEB_PART1 = "".join(html_file.readlines())
with open("/part2.html") as html_file:
    WEB_PART2 = "".join(html_file.readlines())

# RTC Setup
I2C_SDA = 20
I2C_SCL = 21
rtc = ds3231(0, I2C_SCL, I2C_SDA)

# Setup Sensors class
sensor_list = [
    {
        'pin': 27,
        'power': 17,
        'location': 'Green ceramic pot on top shelf',
        'nick': 'Ivy',
    },
    {
        'pin': 28,
        'power': 18,
        'location': 'Fern on bottom shelf',
        'nick': 'Fern',
    }
]
```

```python
# Setup the soil moisture object instance from the
SoilMoisture class
plants = SoilMoisture(rtc, sensor_list)

@ppwhttp.route("/", methods=["GET", "POST"])
def get_home(method, url, data=None):
    # Read data and return web page.
    DATA_PART = ""
    try:
        DATA_PART = plants.get_html_sensor_data(HTML_TABLE_ROW)
    except Exception as err:
        print("Error reading data.", err)
    return "".join([WEB_PART1, DATA_PART, WEB_PART2])

@ppwhttp.route("/CLEAR", methods=["GET"])
def clear_log(method, url, data=None):
    if method == "GET":
        plants.clear_log()
    addr = ".".join(map(str, ppwhttp.get_ip_address()))
    redirect = HTML_REDIRECT.format("http://{0}:80".
    format(addr))
    return "".join([WEB_PART1, redirect, WEB_PART2])

def read_sensors(plants):
    print("Reading sensors...")
    plants.read_sensors()
    print("Sensor read complete. Sleeping.")

def main():
    ppwhttp.start_wifi()
    server_sock = ppwhttp.start_server()
    utime.sleep(2)
```

```
    # Main loop for reading client requests
    data_read_event = ReadEvent()
    while True:
        ppwhttp.handle_http_request(server_sock)
        utime.sleep(0.01)
        # Check to see if it is time to read the data
        if data_read_event.time_to_read():
            data_read_event.reset()
            # Handle the sensor reading loop on the other core!
            try:
                _thread.start_new_thread(read_sensors,
                [plants])
            except Exception as ex:
                print("ERROR: Cannot read sensors:", ex)
                sys.exit(1)
if __name__ == '__main__':
    try:
        main()
    except (KeyboardInterrupt, SystemExit) as err:
        print("\nbye!\n")
sys.exit(0)
```

Now that we have the main code module, let's look at the soil
moisture class.

Soil Moisture Class

The SoilMoisture class is based on the class with the same name from
Chapter 8, but with some significant changes. Most significantly, the
comma-separated file on the SD card to store the data (plant_data.csv)
is saved on the SD card on the Wireless Pack, which permits easy removal
of the data to transfer it to your PC (you don't need the Pico powered on

and connected to your PC). And, instead of returning only the last value read for each sensor, it returns all rows from the file as well as any recently read values. This way, we can populate a list (table) to show the user all values read.

However, to do so reliably when run with multiple threads, we will need to use a special threading concept called a lock to protect critical portions of the code that change class variables to ensure only one thread can change the value(s) at a time. We will see how this works as we work through the code.

Note   Be sure to refer to Chapter 8 for tips on calibrating the sensors. The code to calibrate the sensors is in Chapter 8.

Other than those changes, the features of the class remain the same, so we will only look at those functions that are removed or changed.

Briefly, this class will read the soil moisture sensors and record the data in a CSV file. The class is designed to read any number of sensors via a list of dictionaries passed when the class is instantiated. Recall from Chapter 8, we will use a new list of dictionaries that contain the Pin class instantiations for controlling the power (turning on or off) and the ADC class instantiations for reading data (signal pin). The following is an example of how to define two sensors in the dictionary. Please refer to Chapter 8 for more details.

```
sensor_list = [
    {
        'pin': 27,
        'power': 17,
        'location': 'Green ceramic pot on top shelf',
        'nick': 'Ivy',
    },
```

```
    {
        'pin': 28,
        'power': 18,
        'location': 'Fern on bottom shelf',
        'nick': 'Fern',
    }
]
```

Public Functions

The Chapter 8 implementation used three public methods to clear the log (clear_log()), get the last values read (get_values()), and a long-running function to read the sensors (read_sensors()). The read_sensors( ) function has been simplified, and the changes are easy to see.

We will also use the same private functions except for _format_time( ), which is no longer needed because we modified the read_time() function from the RTC class to return a formatted time string.

The version of the class for this project uses all of these functions and the existing private functions as mentioned but renames the get_values() function to get_html_sensor_data() to describe the new behavior more accurately. The get_html_sensor_data() accepts as a parameter a format string and returns all rows in memory formatted with the format string. This function therefore is used when the user visits the home (or root) of the web service and the get_home() function is called in main.py.

The code for these functions are simple enough, and most of it is unchanged from Chapter 8, but some explanation is needed for the get_html_sensor_data() function. In this function, we loop over the rows from the file and most recently read values and use the format string to format the rows and return them. We also see how we resolve the cache of values read since the code was launched. Notice we keep track of how many values (rows) were added, and when we reach the limit for the constant

CACHE_LIMIT, we write the new rows to the end of the file. This way, if the server is stopped, we reduce the risk of losing all data stored in memory; rather, we may lose up to CACHE_LIMIT values if the code is stopped or crashes. Listing 13-9 shows the code for the function. Take some time to read through it to ensure you understand how it works. We will discuss the lock in the next section.

Listing 13-9. get_html_sensor_data() Function

```
def get_html_sensor_data(self, HTML_FORMAT_STR):
    html_sensor_data = ""
    self.rw_lock.acquire()
    print("Read lock acquired.")
    for row in self.cached_values:
        cols = row.strip("\n").split(",") # split row by commas
        html = HTML_FORMAT_STR.format(cols[0], cols[1],
        cols[2], cols[3], cols[4])
        html_sensor_data += html

    # If there is too much data in the cache, write it to disk.
    if self.values_read >= CACHE_LIMIT:
        start_index = len(self.cached_values) - self.
        values_read
        self.values_read = 0
        print("Writing cache to disk...", end="")
        try:
            log_file = open(LOG_FILE, 'a')
            for index in range(start_index, len(self.cached_
            values)):
                row = self.cached_values[index]
                log_file.write("{0}\n".format(row))
            log_file.close()
```

```
        except Exception as ex:
            print("ERROR: Cannot write cache to disk.", ex)
        print("done.")
    try:
        self.rw_lock.release()
        print("Read lock released.")
    except Exception as ex:
        print("ERROR: Cannot release read lock.", ex)
    return html_sensor_data
```

Notice the use of the lock. Let's talk about that for a moment before we see the completed code for the class.

Using Locks

Since we are working with two threads, the main execution and a thread we launch periodically to read data from the sensors when the read timer fires, we have the potential for two threads to access the same variables at the same time. More specifically, the self.cached_values variable is read by the get_html_sensor_data() function and written to in the read_sensors() function. If they are accessed at the same time, we could have one of several potentially critical errors or the code may fail, or not. It is completely unpredictable. Fortunately, there is a mechanism we can use to "lock" parts of the code so only one thread can access the critical section (the protected memory or variables) at a time.

The threading class provides a lock we can use to manage the read and write operations. To create the lock, we place the following in the constructor:

```
# Lock for read/write
self.rw_lock = _thread.allocate_lock()
```

For each section of code that accesses the critical areas, we first attempt to acquire the lock with self.rw_lock.acquire(), which by default waits until the lock is available. If it is not, it will wait indefinitely

until it is. A lock is made available (or unlocked) with the `self.rw_lock.`
`release()` function. The following illustrates how the lock is used to ensure
only one thread is reading or writing the `self.cached_values` and `self.`
`values_read` variables at one time:

```
self.rw_lock.acquire()
print("Write lock acquired.")
self.cached_values.append(value_read)
self.values_read += 1
self.rw_lock.release()
```

We also add the lock to the `clear_log()` function to ensure data isn't
being read or written when the log is cleared. See the completed code for
more details.

Caution   The threading library for MicroPython is a much simplified
version from the Python base. As such, it may not be as robust and
could fail under certain conditions such as high contention. Take care
when intentionally designing reentrant code in MicroPython.

Using the SD Card

There is one more change that is important to discuss. Recall, we are using
the SD card reader on the Wireless Pack. Recall, we will use the sdcard.py
library we downloaded earlier. This requires an SPI instance to work. The
following illustrates how we set up the SPI interface and mount the drive.
We will place this code in the constructor:

```
# Setup SD card via SPI
sck_pin = Pin(18, Pin.OUT)
mosi_pin = Pin(19, Pin.OUT)
miso_pin = Pin(16, Pin.OUT)
```

```
sd_pin = Pin(22)
sd_spi = SPI(0, sck=sck_pin, mosi=mosi_pin, miso=miso_pin)
sd = SDCard(sd_spi, sd_pin)

# Mount SD card
uos.mount(sd, "/sd")
```

Now, let's look at the completed code for the class.

Completed Code

We will name the code module soil_moisture.py and place it on our Pico in the project8 folder (or similar). Listing 13-10 shows the completed code for the SoilMoisture class. Take a moment to read through the code to see how it works. Notice the constants that define the thresholds for wet and dry soil measurements. Recall, we got these through experimenting with the threshold example code in Chapter 8.

Listing 13-10. SoilMoisture Class

```
# Import libraries
from machine import ADC, Pin, SPI
import _thread
import uos
from utime import sleep
from project8.sdcard import SDCard

# Constants
LOG_FILE = "/sd/plant_data.csv"
# Thresholds for the sensors
LOWER_THRESHOLD = 500
UPPER_THRESHOLD = 2500
UPDATE_FREQ = 120    # seconds
# Max number of rows to store in memory before writing to disk
CACHE_LIMIT = 2
```

```python
class SoilMoisture:
    def __init__(self, rtc, sensor_list):
        # Lock for read/write
        self.rw_lock = _thread.allocate_lock()

        # Setup SD card via SPI
        sck_pin = Pin(18, Pin.OUT)
        mosi_pin = Pin(19, Pin.OUT)
        miso_pin = Pin(16, Pin.OUT)
        sd_pin = Pin(22)
        sd_spi = SPI(0, sck=sck_pin, mosi=mosi_pin,
        miso=miso_pin)
        sd = SDCard(sd_spi, sd_pin)

        # Mount SD card
        uos.mount(sd, "/sd")
        # If LOG_FILE is not present, create it
        try:
            uos.stat(LOG_FILE)
        except OSError:
            print("Creating log file.\n")
            log_file = open(LOG_FILE, "w")
            log_file.close()

        # Load data into memory
        self.cached_values = []
        log_file = open(LOG_FILE, "r")
        print("Reading data from disk...", end="")
        for row in log_file:
            self.cached_values.append(row)
        log_file.close()
        self.values_read = 0
        print("done.")

        self.rtc = rtc
```

```python
        # Loop through the sensors specified and setup a new
        dictionary
        # for each sensor that includes the power and ADC pins
        defined.
        self.sensors = []
        sensor_num = 1
        for sensor in sensor_list:
            # Setup the dictionary for each soil
            moisture sensor
            soil_moisture = {
                'sensor': ADC(Pin(sensor['pin'])),
                'power': Pin(sensor['power'], Pin.OUT),
                'location': sensor['location'],
                'sensor_num': sensor_num
            }
            sensor_num += 1
            self.sensors.append(soil_moisture)

    def clear_log(self):
        print("Clearing log file")
        log_file = open(LOG_FILE, 'w')
        log_file.close()
        # Lock is on the self.cached_values variable
        self.rw_lock.acquire()
        print("Write (clear) lock acquired.")
        self.cached_values = []
        self.values_read = 0
        try:
            self.rw_lock.release()
            print("Write (clear) lock released.")
```

```
    except Exception as ex:
        print("ERROR: Cannot release write (clear)
        lock.", ex)

def get_html_sensor_data(self, HTML_FORMAT_STR):
    html_sensor_data = ""
    self.rw_lock.acquire()
    print("Read lock acquired.")
    for row in self.cached_values:
        cols = row.strip("\n").split(",") # split row
        by commas
        html = HTML_FORMAT_STR.format(cols[0], cols[1],
        cols[2], cols[3], cols[4])
        html_sensor_data i= html

    # If there is too much data in the cache, write it
    to disk.
    if self.values_read >= CACHE_LIMIT:
        start_index = len(self.cached_values) - self.
        values_read
        self.values_read = 0
        print("Writing cache to disk...", end="")
        try:
            log_file = open(LOG_FILE, 'a')
            for index in range(start_index, len(self.
            cached_values)):
                row = self.cached_values[index]
                log_file.write("{0}\n".format(row))
            log_file.close()
        except Exception as ex:
            print("ERROR: Cannot write cache to disk.", ex)
        print("done.")
```

```python
        try:
            self.rw_lock.release()
            print("Read lock released.")
        except Exception as ex:
            print("ERROR: Cannot release read lock.", ex)
        return html_sensor_data
    def _get_value(self, adc, power):
        total = 0
        # Turn power on
        power.high()
        for i in range (0,10):
            # Wait for sensor to power on and settle
            sleep(1)
            # Read the value
            value = adc.read_u16()
            total += value
        # Turn sensor off
        power.low()
        return int(total/10)

    def read_sensors(self):
        for sensor in self.sensors:
            # Read the data from the sensor and convert
            the value
            value = self._get_value(sensor['sensor'],
            sensor['power'])
            print("Reading sensor {0} - value: {1}"
                  "".format(sensor['sensor_num'], value))
            value_read = ("{0},{1},{2},{3},{4}"
                          "".format(self.rtc.read_time(),
                                    sensor['sensor_num'],
```

```
                              value, self._convert_
                              value(value),
                              sensor['location']))
        self.rw_lock.acquire()
        print("Write lock acquired.")
        self.cached_values.append(value_read)
        self.values_read += 1
        try:
            self.rw_lock.release()
            print("Write lock released.")
        except Exception as ex:
            print("ERROR: Cannot release read lock.", ex)

def _convert_value(self, value):
    # If value is less than lower threshold, soil is dry
    else if it
    # is greater than upper threshold, it is wet, else all
    is well.
    if (value <= LOWER_THRESHOLD):
        return "dry"
    elif (value >= UPPER_THRESHOLD):
        return "wet"
    return "ok"
```

OK, now it is time to give the code a go and run it.

Execute

Before executing the project, be sure to upload the main.py and secrets.
py files to the root of the Pico onboard drive. Remember to modify the
secrets.py file to include your WiFi SSID and password. You also need
to create a project8 folder on the Pico and upload the Pico Wireless Pack

library (`ppwhttp.py`), the modified library for the RTC (`ds3231.py`), the soil moisture class (`soil_moisture.py`), the SD card library (`sdcard.py`), and the read timer class (`read_timer.py`) files into that folder. Finally, you also need to upload the `secrets.py` file from the Pico Wireless Pack library. Upload this file to the root of the Pico onboard drive.

Note   You should insert the soil moisture sensors in the plant soil before powering on your Pico.

OK, now we've got the code setup to read the soil moisture in one or more plants, and we have the code for a simple HTML server setup to listen on port 80. All we need now is the IP address of that board to point our web browser. We can get that from our debug statements by running the code. Listing 13-11 shows a sample run for the project.

Listing 13-11. Running the Plant Monitor Web Project

```
Welcome to the Plant Monitor Web Version!

Reading data from disk...done.
Connecting to Snapper2...
Starting server...
Server listening on 192.168.1.20:80
Reading sensors...
Reading sensor 1 - value: 606
Write lock acquired.
Write lock released.
Client connected!
Serving GET on /...
Read lock acquired.
Read lock released.
Success! Sending 200 OK
```

```
Reading sensor 2 - value: 499
Write lock acquired.
Write lock released.
Sensor read complete. Sleeping.
Client connected!
Serving GET on /...
Read lock acquired.
Writing cache to disk...done.
Read lock released.
Success! Sending 200 OK
Client connected!
Serving GET on /...
Read lock acquired.
Read lock released.
Success! Sending 200 OK
Client connected!
Serving GET on /...
Read lock acquired.
Read lock released.
Success! Sending 200 OK
Client connected!
Serving GET on /...
Read lock acquired.
Read lock released.
Success! Sending 200 OK
```

Notice in this case the IP address is 192.168.1.20. All we need to do is put that in our browser as shown in Figure 13-11.

Beginning MicroPython – Project 8

A simple project to demonstrate how to retrieve sensor data over the Internet.

Plant Monitoring Data

Datetime	Sensor Number	Raw Value	Moisture	Location
2021/12/22 15:03:26	1	17230	wet	Green ceramic pot on top shelf
2021/12/22 15:03:36	2	13061	wet	Fern on bottom shelf
2021/12/22 15:52:35	1	628	ok	Green ceramic pot on top shelf
2021/12/22 15:52:45	2	497	dry	Fern on bottom shelf
2021/12/23 14:18:39	1	614	ok	Green ceramic pot on top shelf
2021/12/23 14:18:49	2	492	dry	Fern on bottom shelf
2021/12/23 14:28:43	1	606	ok	Green ceramic pot on top shelf
2021/12/23 14:28:53	2	499	dry	Fern on bottom shelf

Figure 13-11. *Executing the plant monitor web project*

Once you enter the URL, you should see a web page like the image shown. If you don't, be sure to check the HTML in your code to ensure it is exactly like what is shown; otherwise, the page may not display properly.

Tip   If your Pico doesn't connect to your WiFi within a reasonable time, you may need to click *Stop* in Thonny and rerun the project to reset the Wireless Pack.

If everything is working, you can click *refresh* in your browser to read all of the values read from the file including those in the cache. Or you can wait until the meta tag refresh fires, which will automatically refresh the page. Neat!

Improving the Code

This example will suffice to show you what is possible for creating a small web server to present your data collected from sensors. As such, it is not intended to be run for extended periods because of how the data is stored in memory to make retrieval fasters. Additional work is needed to make it a longer-running project. The following are suggestions on how to improve the code for a more robust, longer-running project. The first two are ways to improve the current design where the historical data is presented in the web page, and the last is an alternative to show only the last values read for each sensor:

- Change the code to always read data from the SD card (the plant_data.csv file) rather than memory. Hint: You will need to use the read/write lock to protect writing to the file when new values are read from the sensors.

- Make the code read all of the rows from the SD card on start, but store all new values read into memory writing them to the file on the SD card only after 20 or more values are read.

- Change the code to only display the latest values for the sensors writing all old values to the file on the SD card. This is the easiest and most robust option to consider making the code a long-running project.

Once you have both examples working, congratulations. You have just created your first complete IoT projects. How cool is that?

Summary

When you take a typical electronics project such as a weather station, electronic game, home automation, etc. and connect it to the Internet, you've just upped the capabilities of that small project.

We saw two simple examples of this by connecting two of our example projects to the Internet. Each used a simple web server to allow us to control hardware and get information from sensors. The technique demonstrated can help you add Internet capabilities to more of the projects in this book. You are only limited by your imagination!

In this chapter, we learned more about cloud systems and how they can be used in IoT projects. Now that you've seen how easy it is to get started and how little code is needed in your projects, you can begin to modify your own projects. But we've just scratched the surface here. There is so much more that can be done with another simple, free cloud solution.

In the next chapter, we will expand our tour of cloud systems for IoT by looking at one of the most popular free options: ThingSpeak – a popular, easy-to-use, cloud-based IoT data hosting service from MathWorks. You will learn how to send your data to the cloud and display it using nice, easy-to-use graphics using the previous example projects.

CHAPTER 14

Using ThingSpeak

Now that we've built a good foundation of experience working with basic electronics and Grove modules including how to write code to use the sensors, respond to inputs (e.g., buttons), and display data as well as how to create a simple web server solution, it's time to take our IoT skills to a new level.

Thus far, we haven't discussed how to use the data generated from our projects other than saving the data in a file on the Pico or an SD card on the Pimoroni Wireless Pack. Due to the limited size of these options, you will encounter issues you need to resolve such as how much data you want to store and for how long.

While those are things that can be solved, the bigger question is what are you going to do with the data? Would you want to see how the data changes over time, how one sensor data compares to another, how often a value changes, or more basic statistics like min, max, and average values? All of these things require processing power that the Pico doesn't have to spare.

Furthermore, you may want to see the data presented in one or more graphs that you can use for a pictorial representation. The best way to do this is to take advantage of IoT cloud services. Not only can you store the data easily, but you can also perform analysis on the data and present it in one of several graphics.

© Charles Bell 2022
C. Bell, *Beginning MicroPython with the Raspberry Pi Pico*, Maker Innovations Series,
https://doi.org/10.1007/978-1-4842-8135-2_14

In fact, you can store your data in the cloud using a popular, easy-to-use, cloud-based IoT data hosting service from MathWorks called ThingSpeak (`www.thingspeak.com`). We will see how to take several of the example projects from this book and connect them to ThingSpeak to see how we can gain more insights about the data.

But first, let's take a brief tour of ThingSpeak and how to get started using it in our projects.

Getting Started

ThingSpeak offers a free account for noncommercial projects that generate fewer than 3 million messages (or data elements) per year or around 8200 messages per day. Free accounts are also limited to four channels (a channel is equivalent to a project and can save up to eight data items). If you need to store or process more data than that, you can purchase a commercial license in one of four categories, each with specific products, features, and limitations: Standard, Academic, Student, and Home. See `https://thingspeak.com/prices` and click each of the license options to learn more about the features and pricing.

ThingSpeak works by receiving messages from devices that contain the data you want to save or plot. There are libraries available that you can use for certain platforms or programming languages such as Python or the Arduino platform.

However, you can also use a machine-to-machine (M2M) connectivity protocol (called MQTT[1]) or representational state transfer (REST[2]) API designed as a request-response model that communicates over HTTP to send data to or read data from ThingSpeak. Yes, you can even read your data from other devices.

---

[1] `http://mqtt.org/`

[2] `https://en.wikipedia.org/wiki/Representational_state_transfer`

Tip   See www.mathworks.com/help/thingspeak/channels-and-charts-api.html for more details about the ThingSpeak MQTT and REST API.

When you want to read or write from/to a ThingSpeak channel, you can either publish MQTT messages, send requests via HTTP to the REST API, or use one of the platform-specific libraries that encapsulate these mechanisms for you. A channel can have up to eight data fields represented as a string or numeric data. You can also process the numeric data using several sophisticated procedures such as summing, average, rounding, and more.

We won't get too far into the details of these protocols; rather, we will see how to use ThingSpeak as a quick start guide. MathWorks provides a complete set of tutorials, documentation, and examples. So, if you need more information about how ThingSpeak works, check out the documentation at www.mathworks.com/help/thingspeak/.

The first thing we need to do is create an account.

Create an Account in ThingSpeak

To use ThingSpeak, you must first sign up for an account. Fortunately, they provide the option for a free account. In fact, you get a free account to start with and add (purchase) a license later. To create a free account, visit https://thingspeak.com/, click *Get Started For Free*, then click Create one! as shown in Figure 14-1.

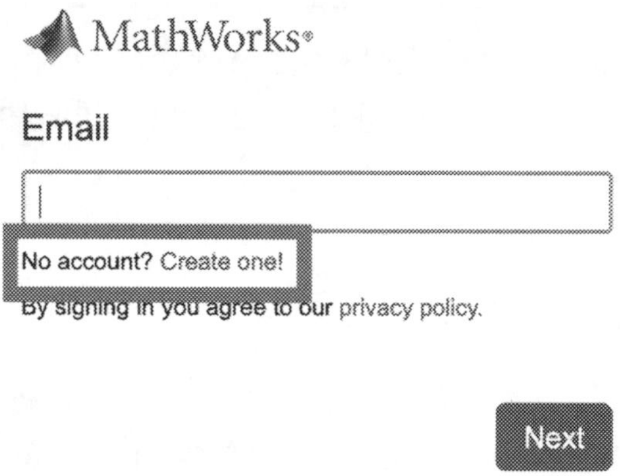

Figure 14-1. *Create a new ThingSpeak/MathLabs account*

On the next page, enter your email address, location (general geographic), and first and last names, then click *Continue*. You may be asked to set the email address as your MatLab account. To do so, tick the *Use this email for my MathWorks Account* checkbox and click *Continue*. You will then be sent a validation email. Open that and follow the instructions to verify your email and complete your free account by choosing a password and ticking the accept the *Online Services Agreement Online Services Agreement* checkbox. You may be asked to complete a short questionnaire. Be sure to log in before continuing.

Next, let's create our first channel.

Create a Channel

Once you log in to ThingSpeak, you can create a channel to hold your data. Recall, each channel can have up to eight data items (fields). From your login home page, click *New Channel* as shown in Figure 14-2.

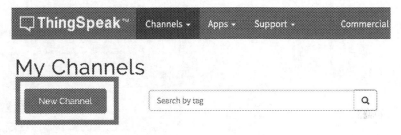

Figure 14-2. *Creating a channel in ThingSpeak*

You will be presented with a really long form that has a lot of fields that you can fill out. Figure 14-3 shows an example of the form.

New Channel

Name	
Description	
Field 1	Field Label 1 ☑
Field 2	☐
Field 3	☐
Field 4	☐
Field 5	☐
Field 6	☐
Field 7	☐
Field 8	☐
Metadata	
Tags	(Tags are comma separated)
Link to External Site	http://
Link to GitHub	https://github.com/
Elevation	
Show Channel Location	☐
Latitude	0.0
Longitude	0.0
Show Video	☐ ⦿ YouTube ○ Vimeo
Video URL	http://
Show Status	☐

Save Channel

Help

Channels store all the data that a ThingSpeak application collects. Each channel includes eight fields that can hold any type of data, plus three fields for location data and one for status data. Once you collect data in a channel, you can use ThingSpeak apps to analyze and visualize it.

Channel Settings

- **Percentage complete:** Calculated based on data entered into the various fields of a channel. Enter the name, description, location, URL, video, and tags to complete your channel.
- **Channel Name:** Enter a unique name for the ThingSpeak channel.
- **Description:** Enter a description of the ThingSpeak channel.
- **Field#:** Check the box to enable the field, and enter a field name. Each ThingSpeak channel can have up to 8 fields.
- **Metadata:** Enter information about channel data, including JSON, XML, or CSV data.
- **Tags:** Enter keywords that identify the channel. Separate tags with commas.
- **Link to External Site:** If you have a website that contains information about your ThingSpeak channel, specify the URL.
- **Show Channel Location:**
  - **Latitude:** Specify the latitude position in decimal degrees. For example, the latitude of the city of London is 51.5072.
  - **Longitude:** Specify the longitude position in decimal degrees. For example, the longitude of the city of London is -0.1275.
  - **Elevation:** Specify the elevation position meters. For example, the elevation of the city of London is 35.052.
- **Video URL:** If you have a YouTube™ or Vimeo® video that displays your channel information, specify the full path of the video URL.
- **Link to GitHub:** If you store your ThingSpeak code on GitHub®, specify the GitHub repository URL.

Using the Channel

You can get data into a channel from a device, website, or another ThingSpeak channel. You can then visualize data and transform it using ThingSpeak Apps.

See Get Started with ThingSpeak™ for an example of measuring dew point from a weather station that acquires data from an Arduino® device.

Learn More

***Figure 14-3.** New Channel form*

At a minimum, you need only name the channel, enter a description (not strictly required but recommended), and then select (tick) one or more fields naming each.

So, what are all those channel settings? The following gives a brief overview of each. As you work with ThingSpeak, you may want to start using some of these fields:

- *Percentage complete*: A calculated field based on the completion of the name, description, location, URL, video, and tags in your channel.

- *Channel name*: Unique name for the channel.

- *Description*: Description of the channel.

- *Field#*: Tick each box to enable the field.

- *Metadata*: Additional data for the channel in JSON, XML, or CSV format.

- *Tags*: A comma-separated list of keywords for searching.

- *Link to external site*: If you have a website about your project, you can provide the URL here to publish on the channel.

- *Show channel location*: Tick this box to include the following fields:

  - *Latitude*: Latitude of the sensor(s) for the project or source of the data

  - *Longitude*: Longitude of the sensor(s) for the project or source of the data

  - *Elevation*: Elevation in meters for use with projects affected by elevation

- *Video URL*: If you have a video associated with your project, you can provide the URL here to be published on the channel.

- *Link to GitHub*: If your project is hosted in GitHub, you can provide the URL to be published on the channel.

Wow, that's a lot of stuff for free! As you will see, this isn't a simple toy or severely limited product. You can accomplish quite a lot with these settings. Notice there are places to put links to video, website, and GitHub. This is because channels can be either private (only your login or API key as we will see can access) or public. Making a channel public allows you to share the data with anyone, and thus those URL fields may be handy to document your project. Cool.

Now, let's create a practice channel that we will use in the next section to see how to write data (sometimes called upload) to ThingSpeak. Use the following parameters for the fields on the New Channel form:

- *Name*: practice_channel

- *Description*: Testing ThingSpeak connection from Pico

- *Field 1*: RandInt

Enter the values as shown and then click *Save Channel* to complete the process. Now we are ready to test writing some data.

How to Add ThingSpeak to Your Projects

Once you create your channel, it is time to write some data. There are two pieces of information you will need for most projects, the API key for the channel and for some libraries the channel number (the integer value shown on the channel page). There are libraries available for many platforms, and on some platforms there may be several ways (libraries or techniques) to write data to a ThingSpeak channel.

You can find the API key on the channel page by clicking the *API Keys* tab. When you create a new channel, you will have one write and one read API key. You can add more keys if you need them so that you can use one key per device, location, customer, etc. Figure 14-4 shows the API Keys tab for the channel created previously.

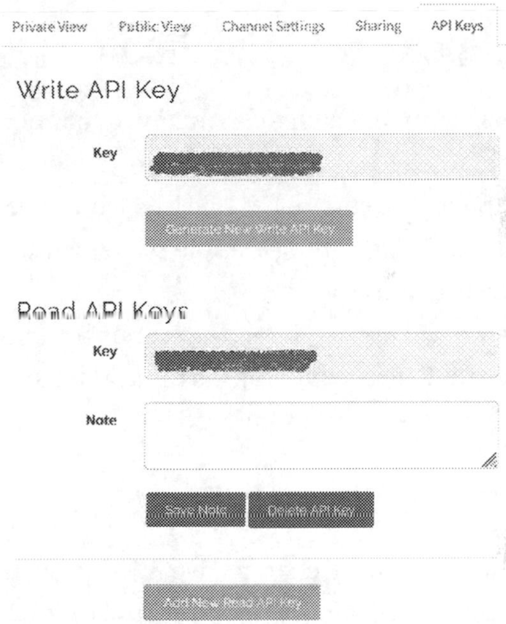

Figure 14-4. *API keys for a practice channel*

Notice I masked out the keys. If you make your channel public, do not share the write key with anyone you don't want to allow to write to your channel. You can create new keys by clicking the *Generate New Write API Key* or *Add New Read API Key* buttons. You can delete read keys by clicking the *Delete API Key* button.

We use the key in our code to allow the device to connect to and write data to the channel. So, we typically copy this string from the channel page and paste it into our code as a string. Recall, we may use a library that encapsulates the HTTP or MQTT mechanism, or, in the case of the Raspberry Pi Pico, we will use the library for the Pimoroni Pico Wireless Pack and the HTTP protocol.

Now that you understand the basics of creating a channel in ThingSpeak, let's take a look at how to do it in more detail for the Pico.

Using ThingSpeak with the Pico

This project is a very simple sketch to learn how to connect and write data to a ThingSpeak channel. For the data, we will be generating a random integer and send that to the channel. While this won't necessarily give you anything meaningful, we keep things simple so we can see the mechanics of how to interact with ThingSpeak.

The hardware we will use is our Pico Omnibus host board and Wireless Pack from Chapter 13. Refer to the projects in Chapter 13 on how to set up these components for use in this example.

Configuring the Raspberry Pi Pico

To write data to the ThingSpeak channel, we need to ensure we have the Pimoroni Pico Wireless Pack library (`ppwhttp.py`) uploaded. That's it! Now, let's write the code. As you will see, it uses a function in the `ppwhttp.py` module for uploading data to ThingSpeak.

Write the Code

While there is no library for the Raspberry Pi Pico, we can write one and use it in later examples. The class module we will create is named `thingspeak.py` and will contain a class named `ThingSpeak`. For the public methods, we need only a constructor and a function to write (upload) data to ThingSpeak. We will use three private methods for connect, disconnect, and parsing the response operations. To make it a bit more tolerant of networking issues, we will also build a retry loop into the upload procedure. While we will see the complete code for these functions, we will only discuss the highlights of each, leaving explanation of the code details as an exercise.

Note   If you want to read data from ThingSpeak, you can add that function to this class extending its use to other projects.

Let's begin with the imports and constants. In order to send data to a server, we must work with some lower-level methods defined in a class named picowireless (used by ppwhttp). We will also need the JSON and time libraries. We use the JSON library to convert a Python dictionary into a JSON string. It is very easy to use, and it is just one line of code. The following shows an example of how to convert a Python dictionary into a JSON string for use in uploading data:

```
param_str = json.dumps(param_dict)
```

We will use several constants, most of which are for communicating over HTTP with ThingSpeak including the hostname, port, mode, and delay values. We will also form a header packet as a constant that we will complete with values at runtime (so, it is a format string). Finally, we will also set a constant for the number of retries to attempt to connect and send data. This is necessary since communicating over HTTP can fail due to a number of reasons (primarily because packets are not guaranteed to be delivered).

Listing 14-1 shows the import and constant sections for the ThingSpeak class.

Listing 14-1. ThingSpeak Class Import and Constant Sections

```
# Import libraries
import json
import sys
import time
import picowireless
import ppwhttp

# Constants
MAX_RETRIES = 10
TCP_MODE = const(0)
REQUEST_DELAY = const(30)
THINGSPEAK_PORT = 80
THINGSPEAK_HOST = "api.ThingSpeak.com"
HTTP_HEADERS = """POST /update HTTP/1.1
Host: api.ThingSpeak.com
Accept: */*
Content-Length: {0}
Content-Type: application/json

{1}
"""
```

•••

Notice the HTTP_HEADERS constant. This is defined using a document string (a string with three "'s on either side), which is used as shown complete with newlines. This is important because this forms an HTTP packet which we will send to the server. If you notice the placeholders, you will find we have two: one for the length of the data and another for the data. Since we set the header variable Content-Type to application/json, we will need to format the data as a JSON string.

For the constructor, we will accept the API key and user-customized maximum retries with a default of MAX_RETRIES. Since this code is run once, we will create a socket connection to the server as well. Listing 14-2 shows the constructor.

Listing 14-2. Constructor for the ThingSpeak Class

```
def __init__(self, key, num_retries=MAX_RETRIES, with_
debug=False):
    self.api_key = key
    self.max_retries = num_retries
    self.with_debug = with_debug
    self.port = THINGSPEAK_PORT
    # Connect to WiFi
    ppwhttp.start_wifi()
    # Resolve the IP address for ThingSpeak
    self.host_address = picowireless.get_host_by_name
    (THINGSPEAK_HOST)
    if self.with_debug:
        print("DNS resolved '{}' to {}.{}.{}.{}"
            "".format(THINGSPEAK_HOST, *self.host_address))
    # Get a client socket
    self.client_sock = picowireless.get_socket()
```

For the upload_data() function, we will require a Python dictionary that includes each of the keys and their values. We have to add the API key, but we can do that easily. In the function, we will create a loop that contains a try...except block for calling the network functions we will use. Specifically, we open a connection to the ThingSpeak server, issue the POST request, then wait for a status code. We then test the code to ensure the upload worked.

If we encounter a problem with any of the network functions, we sleep for five seconds and then try the commands again. We will do this up to MAX_RETRIES or until the operation succeeds.

Listing 14-3 shows the code for the upload_data() function.

Listing 14-3. The upload_data() Function

```
def upload_data(self, param_dict, timeout=5000):
    if self.with_debug:
        print("parameters: {0}".format(param_dict))
    # Add API key to the dictionary
    param_dict.update({'api_key': self.api_key})
    param_str = json.dumps(param_dict)
    # Attempt to connect to ThingSpeak
    retry = 0
    while retry <= self.max_retries:
        try:
            print("Connecting to ThingSpeak...", end="")
            if not self._connect():
                print("Connection failed!")
                return False
            print("connected.")
            break
        except Exception as err:
            print("\nWARNING: ThingSpeak connection
            failed: {0}"
                "".format(err))
            if retry <= self.max_retries:
                print("Retrying in 5 seconds. [{}]".
                format(retry+1))
                time.sleep(5)
                retry = retry + 1
```

```
        else:
            retry = self.max_retries + 1
            print("WARNING: Cannot connect to
            ThingSpeak. "
                    "Exceeded retries. Abort.")
            self._disconnect()
            return False
# Format the POST to send data to ThingSpeak
post_header = HTTP_HEADERS.format(len(param_str),
                param_str).replace("\n", "\r\n")
if self.with_debug:
    print("POST HEADER:\n", post_header)

# Attempt to retry if the timeout fails
retry = 0
while retry <= self.max_retries:
    try:
        print("Sending data...", end="")
        picowireless.send_data(self.client_sock,
        post_header)
        print("done.")
        break
    except Exception as err:
        print("\nWARNING: ThingSpeak update failed:
        {0}".format(err))
        if retry <= self.max_retries:
            print("Retrying in 5 seconds. [{}]".
            format(retry+1))
            time.sleep(5)
            retry = retry + 1
```

```
        else:
            retry = self.max_retries + 1
            print("WARNING: Cannot upload to
            ThingSpeak. "
                    "Exceeded retries. Abort.")
            self._disconnect()
            return False

response = self._get_response(timeout)
# Check header for correct status.
if response["status"] == "200 OK":
    print("Data upload complete.")
elif response['status'] == "ERROR":
    print("ERROR: {0}".format(response['body']))
else:
    print("WARNING: data not acknowledged.")
    if self.with_debug:
        print("Header, body: {0}\n{1}"
                "".format(response['header'], response
                ['body']))
self._disconnect()
return True
```

Notice we retry both the connect and send data operations. Here is where we are using the lower-level functions from the picowireless module. Specifically, once the connect is made with the server, we call the picowireless.send_data() function to send the HTTP POST packet we created to the server. We then wait for a response from the server and parse it. This is where the three helper (private) functions come into play.

There are also three private functions: _connect(), _disconnect(), and _get_response(). We use the _connect() function to connect to the server using the client_start() function from the picowireless library and wait for a response. If we don't get a response before the timeout, we fail. In the _disconnect() function, we stop the client connection. And in the _get_response() function, we retrieve the data from the server using the avail_data() function from the picowireless library, then parse the response packet looking for a status code of 200, which indicates a successful operation. If we see any other code, we flag it as a warning and print the header. How this all works will become clear once you read the code.

Listing 14-4 shows the complete code for this class with comments removed for brevity. Take some time to read it so that you familiarize yourself with how it works.

Listing 14-4. The ThingSpeak Class (Python)

```python
# Import libraries
import json
import sys
import time
import picowireless
import ppwhttp

# Constants
MAX_RETRIES = 10
TCP_MODE = const(0)
REQUEST_DELAY = const(30)
THINGSPEAK_PORT = 80
THINGSPEAK_HOST = "api.ThingSpeak.com"
HTTP_HEADERS = """POST /update HTTP/1.1
Host: api.ThingSpeak.com
Accept: */*
Content-Length: {0}
Content-Type: application/json

{1}
"""
```

```
class ThingSpeak:
    def __init__(self, key, num_retries=MAX_RETRIES, with_
    debug=False):
        self.api_key = key
        self.max_retries = num_retries
        self.with_debug = with_debug
        self.port = THINGSPEAK_PORT
        # Connect to WiFi
        ppwhttp.start_wifi()
        # Resolve the IP address for ThingSpeak
        self.host_address = picowireless.get_host_by_
        name(THINGSPEAK_HOST)
        if self.with_debug:
            print("DNS resolved '{}' to {}.{}.{}.{}"
                "".format(THINGSPEAK_HOST, *self.host_address))
        # Get a client socket
        self.client_sock = picowireless.get_socket()
    # Attempt to connect to ThingSpeak to create a client
      connection.
    def _connect(self, timeout=1000):
        picowireless.client_start(self.host_address, self.port,
                                  self.client_sock, TCP_MODE)
        t_start = time.time()
        timeout /= 1000.0
        while time.time() - t_start < timeout:
            state = picowireless.get_client_state(self.
            client_sock)
            if state == 4:
                return True
            time.sleep(1.0)
        return False
```

```python
# Stop the client connection.
def _disconnect(self):
    # Stop the client
    picowireless.client_stop(self.client_sock)

# Upload the data in the form of a dictionary to
ThingSpeak.
def upload_data(self, param_dict, timeout=5000):
    if self.with_debug:
        print("parameters: {0}".format(param_dict))
    # Add API key to the dictionary
    param_dict.update({'api_key': self.api_key})
    param_str = json.dumps(param_dict)
    # Attempt to connect to ThingSpeak
    retry = 0
    while retry <= self.max_retries:
        try:
            print("Connecting to ThingSpeak...", end="")
            if not self._connect():
                print("Connection failed!")
                return False
            print("connected.")
            break
        except Exception as err:
            print("\nWARNING: ThingSpeak connection
            failed:"
                    " {0}".format(err))
            if retry <= self.max_retries:
                print("Retrying in 5 seconds. [{}]".
                format(retry+1))
                time.sleep(5)
                retry = retry + 1
```

```
        else:
            retry = self.max_retries + 1
            print("WARNING: Cannot connect to
            ThingSpeak. "
                    "Exceeded retries. Abort.")
            self._disconnect()
            return False

# Format the POST to send data to ThingSpeak
post_header = HTTP_HEADERS.format(len(param_str),
            param_str).replace("\n", "\r\n")
if self.with_debug:
    print("POST HEADER:\n", post_header)

# Attempt to retry if the timeout fails
retry = 0
while retry <= self.max_retries:
    try:
        print("Sending data...", end="")
        picowireless.send_data(self.client_sock,
        post_header)
        print("done.")
        break
    except Exception as err:
        print("\nWARNING: ThingSpeak update failed:
        {0}".format(err))
        if retry <= self.max_retries:
            print("Retrying in 5 seconds. [{}]".
            format(retry+1))
            time.sleep(5)
            retry = retry + 1
```

```
        else:
            retry = self.max_retries + 1
            print("WARNING: Cannot upload to
            ThingSpeak. "
                    "Exceeded retries. Abort.")
            self._disconnect()
            return False
    response = self._get_response(timeout)
    # Check header for correct status.
    if response["status"] == "200 OK":
        print("Data upload complete.")
    elif response['status'] == "ERROR":
        print("ERROR: {0}".format(response['body']))
    else:
        print("WARNING: data not acknowledged.")
        if self.with_debug:
            print("Header, body: {0}\n{1}"
                    "".format(response['header'],
                    response['body']))
    self._disconnect()
    return True

# Get the response from the server.
def _get_response(self, timeout):
    # Wait for a response
    t_start = time.time()
    while True:
        if time.time() - t_start > timeout:
            picowireless.client_stop(self.client_sock)
            err_msg = ("Timeout waiting for response
            {0}:{1}"
```

```
                        "".format(self.host_address,
                        self.port))
            return {'status':'ERROR', 'header': {}, 'body':
            err_msg}
        avail_length = picowireless.avail_data(self.
        client_sock)
        if avail_length > 0:
            break
    if self.with_debug:
        print("Got {} bytes in response.".format
        (avail_length))

    # Read the response from the server (in bytes)
    response = b""
    while len(response) < avail_length:
        data = picowireless.get_data_buf(self.client_sock)
        response += data
    response = response.decode("utf-8")
    # Break into the header and body
    head, body = response.split("\r\n\r\n", 1)
    if self.with_debug:
        print("Header:\n", head)
    status = "UNKNOWN"
    # Find the status
    for line in head.split("\r\n")[1:]:
        key, value = line.split(": ", 1)
        if key == 'Status':
            status = value
            break
    return {'status': status, 'header': head, 'body': body}
```

```
if __name__ == '__main__':
    try:
        sample_params = {'field1': 42}
        api_key = "YOUR_API_KEY_GOES_HERE"
        ThingSpeak = ThingSpeak(api_key, with_debug=True)
        ThingSpeak.upload_data(sample_params)
    except (KeyboardInterrupt, SystemExit) as ex:
        print("\nbye!\n")
    sys.exit(0)
```

Notice once again we've employed a simple mechanism to allow us to test the class. You can simply provide a value for your API write key (not the read key) and run the class module to send a single value to your channel. If you're eager to get started, try it out now.

Next is the code for the main script. We will use the new class to upload the random number we generate. We will name the main script test_thingspeak.py. If you are following along, open a new file now with that name. Be sure to place it in the same folder as the thingspeak.py module.

Listing 14-5 shows the complete code for the script for this project. It follows a now familiar pattern where we create a main() function and call it from a try...except block to catch a *CTRL+C* key sequence. The code is very simple. All you need to do is put your API key in the constant and run it.

Listing 14-5. Complete Code for the test_thingspeak.py Script

```
# Import libraries
import random
import sys
import time
from thingspeak import ThingSpeak

# API KEY
THINGSPEAK_APIKEY = 'YOUR_WRITE_API_KEY_HERE'
```

```
def main():
    """main"""
    print("Welcome to the ThingSpeak Raspberry Pi Pico
    demonstration!")
    print("Press CTRL+C to stop.")
    thingspeak = ThingSpeak(THINGSPEAK_APIKEY)
    while True:
        # Generate a random integer
        rand_int = random.randint(1, 20)
        print("Random number generated: {}".format(rand_int))
        thingspeak.upload_data({'field1': rand_int})
        # Sleep for 30 seconds
        time.sleep(30)

if __name__ == '__main__':
    try:
        main()
    except (KeyboardInterrupt, SystemExit) as err:
        print("\nbye!\n")
sys.exit(0)
```

Notice the dictionary we used to pass the data to the upload_data()
function. Here, we used field1 as the key for the channel field. As it turns
out, we must use field1, field2, etc. for the field key names regardless of
how we may name them in the channel. While this may be a little strange,
you should get in the habit of listing the fields in the dictionary in the order
they appear in the channel setup.

Note   Be sure to substitute your API key in the location marked.
Failure to do so will result in runtime errors.

Now that you have all the code entered, let's test the script and see if
it works.

Testing the Script

To run the script, enter the following command. Let the script run for several iterations before using *Ctrl+C* to break the main loop. Listing 14-6 shows an example of the output you should see without debug enabled in the ThingSpeak class.

Note   You may see retry attempts if your network drops or you lose connectivity.

Listing 14-6. Example Console Output (No Debug)

```
Welcome to the ThingSpeak Raspberry Pi Pico demonstration!
Press CTRL+C to stop.
Connecting to Snapper1...
Connected!
Random number generated: 3
Connecting to ThingSpeak...connected.
Sending data...done.
Data upload complete.
Random number generated: 7
Connecting to ThingSpeak...connected.
Sending data...done.
Data upload complete.
Random number generated: 14
Connecting to ThingSpeak...connected.
Sending data...done.
Data upload complete.
Random number generated: 9
Connecting to ThingSpeak...connected.
Sending data...done.
```

...
```
Random number generated: 13
Connecting to ThingSpeak...connected.
Sending data...done.
```

bye!

If the connection is very slow, you could encounter a situation in which you get an error code other than 200 every other or every N attempts. If this is the case, you can increase the timeout in the loop() function to delay processing further. This may help for some very slow connections, but it is not a cure for a bad or intermittent connection.

Let the sketch run for about three minutes before you visit ThingSpeak. Once the sketch has run for some time, navigate to ThingSpeak, log in, and click your channel page and then click the *Private View* tab. We use the private view because channels are private by default. You should see results similar to those shown in Figure 14-5.

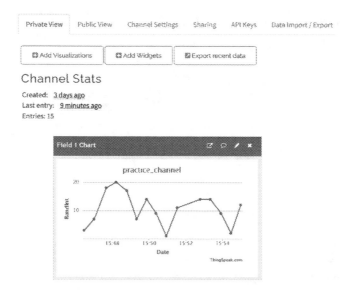

Figure 14-5. *Example channel data (Python)*

If you do not see similar data, go back and check the return codes as discussed in the last project. You should see return codes of 200 (success). Check and correct any errors in network connectivity or syntax or logic errors in your script until it runs successfully for several iterations (all samples stored return code 200).

If you see similar data, congratulations! You now know how to generate data and save it to the cloud using two different platforms.

If you run with the debug turned on, you will see a lot more data similar to what is shown in Listing 14-7. You may want to turn on debug if you encounter problems uploading your data. Notice it prints out your API key, so use this with caution in public areas.

Listing 14-7. Example Console Output (with Debug)

```
Welcome to the ThingSpeak Raspberry Pi Pico demonstration!
Press CTRL+C to stop.
Connecting to Snapper1...
Connected!
DNS resolved 'api.ThingSpeak.com' to 3.224.210.136
Random number generated: 4
parameters: {'field1': 4}
Connecting to ThingSpeak...connected.
POST HEADER:
 POST /update HTTP/1.1
Host: api.ThingSpeak.com
Accept: */*
Content-Length: 44
Content-Type: application/json

{"field1": 4, "api_key": "XXXXXXXXXXXXXXXXXXXXX"}

Sending data...done.
Got 646 bytes in response.
```

```
Header:
 HTTP/1.1 200 OK
Date: Mon, 27 Dec 2021 21:24:17 GMT
Content-Type: text/plain; charset=utf-8
Content-Length: 2
Connection: keep-alive
Status: 200 OK
X-Frame-Options: SAMEORIGIN
Access-Control-Allow-Origin: *
Access-Control-Allow-Methods: GET, POST, PUT, OPTIONS,
DELETE, PATCH
Access-Control-Allow-Headers: origin, content-type,
X-Requested-With
Access-Control-Max-Age: 1800
ETag: W/"b17ef6d19c7a5b1ee83b907c595526dc"
Cache-Control: max-age=0, private, must-revalidate
X-Request-Id: 3a8821ed-352e-450c-a541-be36d57d25a6
X-Runtime: 0.033155
X-Powered-By: Phusion Passenger 4.0.57
Server: nginx/1.9.3 + Phusion Passenger 4.0.57
Data upload complete.

bye!
```

Tip   Most issues you will encounter uploading data to your channels can be solved by ensuring you have the correct write key for the channel you want to update. Be sure to double-check the key first if you have problems.

If you encounter problems or want to run the `test_thingspeak.py` script again, you can remove all data in your channel by clicking the *Channel Settings* tab and then scrolling to the bottom and clicking the *Clear Channel* button as shown in Figure 14-6. Once you acknowledge the clear, all data from your channel will be deleted.

Want to clear all feed data from this Channel?

Clear Channel

Figure 14-6. *Delete all data in the channel*

Now, let's turn our attention to how we can modify our example projects retooling them to upload their data to ThingSpeak.

Note   ThingSpeak free accounts are limited to four channels. If you plan to implement many projects, you may need to delete one or more channels or upgrade your account to a paid subscription.

Example Project: IoT Environment Monitor

This section includes one of the projects from previous chapters that we will update to send data to ThingSpeak for visualization. We will use the environment monitor project from Chapter 12. If you have not implemented this project, you may want to do so before attempting the following examples.

The following sections present the details at a high level, and much of the detail for the original project is omitted for brevity. Rather, we will see details on the channel to create, how to prepare and modify the source files, and then a demonstration of executing the project. Let's begin with the hardware.

Required Components

The hardware for this project is the same as Chapter 12 with the exception we won't be using the Grove Shield for the Pi Pico. Rather, we will be using the Pico Omnibus so that we can add the RTC and Pico Wireless Pack.

Unfortunately, this means we will not have any Grove connectors to connect our array of Grove modules. However, there are two ways we can overcome this limitation, using Grove cables and connecting the Pico Omnibus to the Pico Grove Shield using jumper wires.

For the Grove cable option, we will use two different sets of Grove cables and a breadboard. To connect Grove modules directly to the Pico, we use the Grove – 4 pin Female Jumper to Grove 4 pin Conversion Cable (`www.seeedstudio.com/Grove-4-pin-Female-Jumper-to-Grove-4-pin-Conversion-Cable-5-PCs-per-PAck.html`) as shown in Figure 14-7.

Figure 14-7. *Grove breakout cable with female header (courtesy of seeedstudio.com)*

We may also need to use the male version named Grove – 4 pin Male Jumper to Grove 4 pin Conversion Cable (`www.seeedstudio.com/Grove-4-pin-Male-Jumper-to-Grove-4-pin-Conversion-Cable-5-PCs-per-Pack.html`) to use a breadboard to gang the ground and power cables together since there are so few of those pins on the Pico GPIO header. Figure 14-8 shows the male version of the breakout cable.

Figure 14-8. *Grove breakout cable with male header (courtesy of seeedstudio.com)*

For the jumper wire option, we will use M/F jumper wires to connect the GPIO header on the Pico Omnibus to the Grove Shield. The concept is we will "jump" all pins used by the Grove Shield from the Omnibus to the Grove Shield. This will mimic using a Pico connected to the Grove Shield (we will keep the Pico installed on the Pico Omnibus).

Since using the Grove breakout cables can be cumbersome and require the use of a breadboard to connect the ground and power cables together, we will instead jumper the GPIO header of the Pico Omnibus to the Grove Shield. While this will require a number of jumper wires, it is the easiest option to implement. However, you are welcome to use the Grove breakout cable option if that works best for you.

Set Up the Hardware

You should acquire and set up all of the modules as listed in Chapter 12. If you decide to use the 3D printed mounting plate or if you already have that done, you can leave all of the modules mounted and connected to the mounting plate and plugged into the Grove Shield. You simply remove the Pico from the Grove Shield before you start connecting it to the Pico Omnibus. Figure 14-9 shows the starting point for the hardware assuming you implemented the project in Chapter 12.

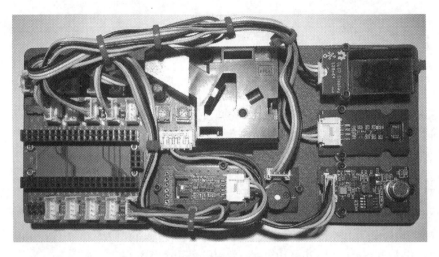

Figure 14-9. *Hardware from Chapter 12 with Pico removed*

The easiest way to connect the Grove Shield to the Pico Omnibus is to use 40 M/F jumper wires. Connecting them is very easy. Just connect the male pin of each jumper to the Pico Omnibus noting the pin number and plug it into the corresponding pin on the Grove Shield using the female pin. If you want to avoid the inevitable "bird's nest" of wires once you're done, you can purchase M/F jumper wires that are connected together. Several vendors such as SparkFun and Adafruit carry these, and if you get a set that has 20 connected together, it makes connecting the Pico Omnibus and Grove Shield easier and less messy.

For example, SparkFun has the Jumper Wires – Connected 6" (M/F, 20 pack). Since there are 20 connected together, we will need 2 of these to complete the project. Each set costs $1.95. Figure 14-10 shows the connected jumper wires from SparkFun.

Figure 14-10. *M/F Jumper Wires Connected (courtesy of sparkfun.com)*

The best way to use these jumpers is to break them into sets of ten. Connect each set of ten first to the Pico Omnibus and then the Grove Shield. When you connect across the GPIO header side, interleave the sets so that you remove most of the strain. Be sure to push the pins all the way in as it is easy to have one or more pins partially inserted.

Using a set of ten has another benefit. There are ten colors in each set, so you can visually inspect the colors to ensure you have the pins connected in order. This helps remove the need to check each pin on each GPIO header – a time-consuming and challenging task! Using groups of ten connected together will make the connections easier.

Caution   Be sure to double- and triple-check all of your connections to ensure you have all of the wires connected to the correct pins. Do not power on your Pico until you have verified all of your connections.

When you are done, you should see an arrangement similar to Figure 14-11.

Figure 14-11. *Grove Shield for Pico connected to the Pico Omnibus*

The best way to make sure you have all cables connected is to return to Chapter 12 and upload the project files to your Pico and run the `main.py` script for Chapter 12. Figure 14-12 shows the files you should have at a minimum in the `project6` folder indicated thus far in the chapter. We will create a `project9` folder in a later step. You can run main.py from Thonny on your PC.

Figure 14-12. *Environment monitor files on the Pico*

Now that we have our hardware setup, let's create the ThingSpeak channel.

Create the ThingSpeak Channel

The data for this project contains numerical data as well as categorized data (in the form of a string). We will capture the raw data rather than the label (category). The data generated includes the temperature, barometric pressure, dust concentration, and air quality. So, we will need one channel with one field for each sensor or four fields in all.

Log in to your ThingSpeak account and click *New Channel*. We will name the channel *IoT Environment Monitor*. Use the information shown in Figure 14-13 to complete the form and then click *Save Channel* at the bottom of the form. Or, you can press *Enter*, which will save the channel for you. Note that you will need to tick the checkbox for Fields 2 and 3 to get them to accept input.

Figure 14-13. *IoT Environment Monitor channel settings*

Recall, we need to remember the order of the fields. Here, we have defined *Temperature*, *Pressure*, *Dust Concentration*, and *Air Quality* where they will be referenced as field 1, field 2, field 3, and field 4 in our code.

Now that we have the channel created, go to the *API Keys* tab, and record the API key. You will need this information in the next step. Figure 14-14 shows which key you will need.

Figure 14-14. *Weather IoT channel API keys*

Prepare the Project Files

For this project, create a new folder named project9 on your Pico and upload the project files from Chapter 12 (`air_monitor.py`, `bmx280x.py`, `dust_sensor.py`, `mcp9808.py`, and `ssd1306.py`). See Chapter 12 for the details on the source for some of the files.

Most of these files do not need to be modified. However, we will need to change all occurrences of `project6` to `project9` in the `air_monitor.py` file as shown in the following:

```
# Imports
from machine import ADC, I2C, Pin
import time
from project9.bmx280x import BMX280
from project9.mcp9808 import MCP9808
from project9.dust_sensor import DustSensor
```

We also need to copy our new class module, `thingspeak.py`, to the project9 folder as well as the `ppwhttp.py` file from Chapter 13. However, we need to make one slight change to the `thingspeak.py` module. We need to change the import for the `ppwhttp` library as follows:

```
from project9 import ppwhttp
```

Finally, copy the modified `secrets.py` file to the root of the Pico filesystem.

Figure 14-15 shows the complete list of files needed on the Pico. Note that we will modify the `main.py` in the next section.

Figure 14-15. *Files needed on the Pico for the IoT Environment Monitor*

With that administrative work done, we can add the preliminary code.

Update the Main Code

In this section, we will modify the `main.py` to add the ThingSpeak code. Recall, we need only add the import statement and API key. Listing 14-8 shows an excerpt of the code with the new lines added. The rest of the code from Chapter 12 remains the same. We will update the `main()` function to add the ThingSpeak code in the next section. Notice we also need to change project6 to project9 in the imports for the air_monitor and ssd1306 libraries.

Listing 14-8. Updates to the IoT Environment Monitor Main Script (Python)

```python
from machine import Pin, I2C
import time
from project9.air_monitor import (AirMonitor,
    AIR_POOR, AIR_FAIR, AIR_GOOD, AIR_ERR)
from project9.ssd1306 import SSD1306_I2C
from project9.thingspeak import ThingSpeak

# API KEY
THINGSPEAK_APIKEY = 'YOUR_WRITE_API_KEY_HERE'

# Constants
SAMPLING_RATE = 5 # 5 second wait to start next read
BUZZER_PIN = 26
WARNING_BEEPS = 5
HIGH = 1
LOW = 0
...
```

Next, we need to declare an instance of our ThingSpeak class from the thingspeak.py library module and then, after reading the data, use the existing Python dictionary we created in the class (env_data) and pass that to our thingspeak.upload_data() function call. Listing 14-9 shows the function with changes in bold. The rest of the code for this version remains the same as we had in Chapter 12.

Listing 14-9. Updates to the IoT Environment Monitor Main Function (Python)

```
...
def main():
    """Main"""
    print("Welcome to the Environment Monitor!")
    # Setup buzzer
    buzzer = Pin(BUZZER_PIN, Pin.OUT)
    i2c = I2C(0,scl=Pin(9), sda=Pin(8), freq=100000)
    print("Hello. I2C devices found: {}".format(i2c.scan()))
    oled = setup_oled(i2c)
    # Start the AirMonitor
    air_quality = AirMonitor(i2c)
    time.sleep(3)
    oled_write(oled, 11, 4, "done")
    beep(buzzer)
    oled.fill(0)
    oled.show()

    thingspeak = ThingSpeak(THINGSPEAK_APIKEY)
    while True:
        if air_quality.read_data():
            # Retrieve the data
            env_data = air_quality.get_data()

            oled_write(oled, 0, 0, "ENVIRONMENT DATA")
            oled_write(oled, 0, 2, "Temp: ")
            oled_write(oled, 5, 2,
                       "{:3.2f}C".format(env_data
                       ["temperature"]))
            oled_write(oled, 0, 3, "Pres: ")
            oled_write(oled, 5, 3,
```

```
                     "{:05.2f}hPa".format(env_data
                     ["pressure"]))
        oled_write(oled, 0, 4, "Dust: ")
        if env_data["dust_concentration"] == 0.0:
            oled_write(oled, 5, 4, "--          ")
        else:
            oled_write(oled, 5, 4,
                     "{:06.2f}%".format(env_data
                     ["dust_concentration"]))
        oled_write(oled, 0, 5, "airQ: ")
        if env_data["air_quality"] in {AIR_ERR, AIR_POOR}:
            oled_write(oled, 5, 5, "POOR")
        elif env_data["air_quality"] == AIR_FAIR:
            oled_write(oled, 5, 5, "FAIR")
        elif env_data["air_quality"] == AIR_GOOD:
            oled_write(oled, 5, 5, "GOOD")
        else:
            oled_write(oled, 5, 5, "--       ")

        # Check for environmental quality
        if ((env_data["dust_concentration"] > MAX_DUST) or
                (env_data["temperature"] > MAX_TEMP) or
                (env_data["air_quality"] == AIR_POOR) or
                (env_data["air_quality"] == AIR_ERR)):
            #pylint: disable=unused-variable
            for i in range(0, WARNING_BEEPS):
                oled_write(oled, 3, 7, "ENV NOT OK")
                beep(0.250)
                time.sleep(0.250)
                oled_write(oled, 3, 7, "          ")
                time.sleep(0.250)
```

```
        # Send data to ThingSpeak channel
        data = {
            'field1': env_data['temperature'],
            'field2': env_data['pressure'],
            'field3': env_data['dust_concentration'],
            'field4': env_data['air_quality']
        }
        thingspeak.upload_data(data)
    else:
        oled.fill(0)
        oled.show()
        oled_write(oled, 0, 2, "ERROR! CANNOT")
        oled_write(oled, 0, 3, "READ DATA")

    time.sleep(SAMPLING_RATE)
...
```

That's it, we're ready to execute the project. We will need to let it run for a few minutes so we can get some data. If you're running the project in a controlled environment where the values do not change, you may not notice much variation. As an exercise, consider altering the environment to stimulate changes in the data. Don't use flame or touch the electronics in any way while they are running.

Execute and Visualize the Data

At this point, you can set up the hardware and run the project. Let it run for about 20 minutes and then visit your ThingSpeak channel page. You should see your data in the channel private view similar to Figure 14-16.

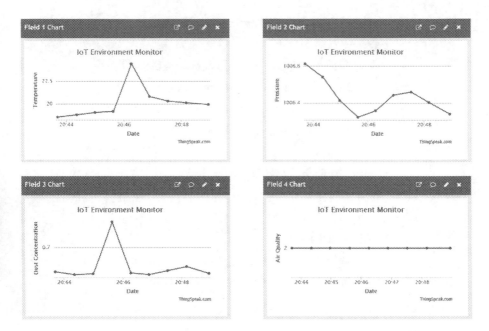

Figure 14-16. *Example results (IoT Environment Monitor example)*

Once again, you may not see a lot of variances in the data if you run it in a controlled environment. For better results in a controlled environment, you should consider changing the sample rate from 30 seconds to every 4–6 hours. This should help show how the data changes over the course of a day. Listing 14-10 shows an example execution. You should see something similar.

Listing 14-10. IoT Environment Monitor Execution

```
Welcome to the Environment Monitor!
Hello. I2C devices found: [24, 60, 119]
Connecting to Snapper1...
Connected!
```

```
>> Reading Data <<
> Reading temperature = 18.5625
> Reading pressure = 1006.613
> Reading dust concentration
> PM concentration: 0.6303307 pcs/0.01cf
> Dust concentration = 0.6303307
> Reading air quality = 2
Connecting to ThingSpeak...connected.
Sending data...done.
Data upload complete.
...
>> Reading Data <<
> Reading temperature = 20.125
> Reading pressure = 1006.402
> Reading dust concentration
> PM concentration: 0.6453933 pcs/0.01cf
> Dust concentration = 0.6453933
> Reading air quality = 2
Connecting to ThingSpeak...connected.
Sending data...done.
Data upload complete.

>> Reading Data <<
> Reading temperature = 19.9375
> Reading pressure = 1006.338
> Reading dust concentration
> PM concentration: 0.62572 pcs/0.01cf
> Dust concentration = 0.62572
> Reading air quality = 2
Connecting to ThingSpeak...connected.
Sending data...done.
...
```

However, notice the air quality line graph. That's not telling us anything, is it? What if we created an indicator widget for that data that changes color when the air quality gets poor?

In fact, you can create a gauge, numeric display, or an indicator (like an LED or light) for your data that triggers on some value or threshold. See the ThingSpeak documentation for more details about these options. For this project, an indicator is an excellent choice for the air quality to provide an at-a-glance readout.

Let's do that. Go ahead and click *Add Widgets*, then select the indicator and fill in the settings as shown in Figure 14-17, and then click *Create*. Notice I set the indicator to turn on only if the air quality (field 4) reaches three or more.

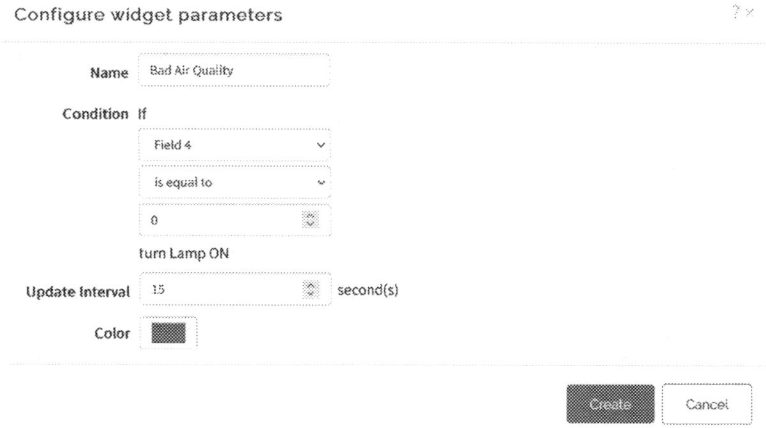

Figure 14-17. *Creating an indicator (IoT Environment Monitor example)*

When air quality (field 4) is less than or equal to three, the indicator is dim as shown in Figure 14-18.

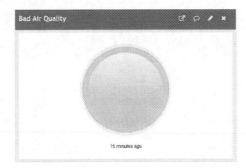

Figure 14-18. *Indicator off (IoT Environment Monitor example)*

Should the data reach a value of three to indicate poor air quality, the indicator will turn on as shown in Figure 14-19. This shows us how we can use the data to show thresholds reached. It can be used for high thresholds or low thresholds in which case you may want to choose a less alarming color such as green and so on.

Figure 14-19. *Indicator on (IoT Environment Monitor example)*

Now, we can take this a step further and create an array of indicators for the air quality. For example, we can create one for good air quality (green indicator, field 4 = 2), another for fair (yellow indicator, field 4 = 1), and another for bad (red indicator, field 4 = 0). Figure 14-20 shows an example of the indicators. Note that you can drag and drop the widgets on the view to rearrange them. Nice! Note: The indicator colors are green for good, yellow for poor, and red for bad quality.

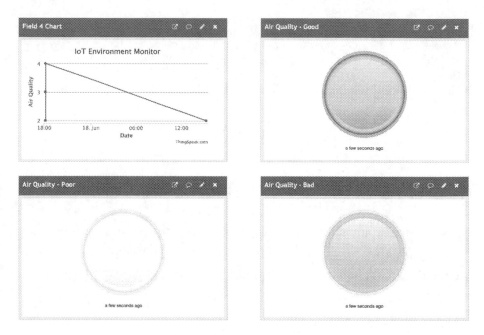

Figure 14-20. *Air quality indicators (IoT Environment Monitor example)*

Now I can see at a glance what the air quality is at the moment of last data read. Very nice!

There is just one more step you may want to consider – making the data public.

Public View

By default, your data in your channel is private. Only you can see it when you log in. However, you can share the data views to more people. You can choose one of the following options:

- *Keep channel view private*: Only you can see the data.

- *Share channel view with everyone*: Anyone can view the data via its URL on the *Public View* tab. Thus, it only shows the public widgets and such that you create.

- *Share channel view only with the following users*: Only those users that you specify can see the data on your *Private View* tab. To add a new user, enter their email address and click the *Add User* button. Each user is then emailed an invitation with the URL for the private data view. If they do not have a ThingSpeak account, they must create one to access the data. Once logged in, users can click the *Channels* ➤ *Channels Shared with Me* menu to see the shared channels.

To choose one of the public options, click the *Sharing* tab of your channel and make your selection. If you choose to share the data, you won't be given a specific URL to use. However, you can click the Public View tab and then copy the URL in your browser and share that. For example, it will resemble the following:[3]

```
https://thingspeak.com/channels/16A94A7
```

Similarly, you can do the same for those users you identified in the last option.

---

[3] This is a mock-up and not a valid URL for an existing channel. If you find a channel at this address, it is completely accidental and not associated with this work in any way.

Summary

If you have implemented all of the projects in this book, congratulations! You are now ready to tackle your own IoT projects. If you're still working on the examples, keep at it until you've learned everything you need to know to build your own IoT projects.

Our journey in learning how to build projects for the Raspberry Pi Pico using MicroPython has concluded with a dive into how to use ThingSpeak to satisfy the needs of your IoT project for storing and displaying your data. In this chapter, we learned how to get started with ThingSpeak from creating our account to creating channels to storing our data and even some insights into how to modify the visualizations. Together with the knowledge you gained in this chapter and the previous chapters, you now have the skills to complete your own IoT projects.

In fact, you can now put down this book in triumph and start thinking of some really cool ways you can implement what you have learned. You want to monitor events and data in your house, workshop, or garage. Or you want to design a more complex project that monitors sound, movement, and ambient temperature changes (like a home security system). Or you want to revisit the example project chapters and implement the suggestions at the end of each chapter. All that and more is possible with what you have learned in this book. Good luck, and happy MicroPython programming!

Correction to: Beginning MicroPython with the Raspberry Pi Pico

Correction to:

Charles Bell, *Beginning MicroPython with the Raspberry Pi Pico*
https://doi.org/10.1007/978-1-4842-8135-2

This book was published without Series ID, Print ISSN number & Electronic ISSN Number. This has now been updated in the book with the Series ID - 17311, Print ISSN: 2948-2542 & Electronic ISSN: 2948-2550.

The updated version of this book can be found at
https://doi.org/10.1007/978-1-4842-8135-2

© Charles Bell 2023
C. Bell, *Beginning MicroPython with the Raspberry Pi Pico*, Maker Innovations Series,
https://doi.org/10.1007/978-1-4842-8135-2_15

Appendix

This appendix presents a list of the hardware required to complete the projects presented in the book. While component lists are included in each chapter and discussed in greater detail, listing the components here helps when planning to purchase the components you do not already own.

Table A-1 lists the hardware common for most of the projects in this book.

© Charles Bell 2022
C. Bell, *Beginning MicroPython with the Raspberry Pi Pico*, Maker Innovations Series,
https://doi.org/10.1007/978-1-4842-8135-2

Table A-1. General Hardware Needed

Component	Qty	Chapter	Cost	Links
Raspberry Pico	1+	All	$3.77	thepihut.com/collections/pico/products/raspberry-pi-pico
Breadboard	1	04-08	$5.95	www.sparkfun.com/products/12615
			$5.95	www.adafruit.com/product/239
Jumper wires M/M	1	04-08	$2.25	www.sparkfun.com/products/11026
			$1.95	www.adafruit.com/product/1956
Jumper wires F/F	4	08	$1.95	www.sparkfun.com/products/12796
			$3.95	www.adafruit.com/product/266
OLED display	1	06	$17.50	www.adafruit.com/product/661
RTC breakout board	1	06, 08	$15.95	www.sparkfun.com/products/12708
			$7.50	www.adafruit.com/product/3296
Coin cell battery	1	06, 08	$1.95	www.sparkfun.com/products/337
CR1225 (Sparkfun RTC) CR1220 (Adafruit RTC)			$0.95	www.adafruit.com/product/380
Red LED	2	07, 13	$4.00	www.adafruit.com/product/299
			$0.35	www.sparkfun.com/products/9590

Item	Qty	Chapter	Price	Source
Yellow LED	2	07, 13	$4.95	www.adafruit.com/product/2700
			$0.35	www.sparkfun.com/products/9594
Green LED	1	07, 13	$4.00	www.adafruit.com/product/298
			$0.35	www.sparkfun.com/products/9592
220 or 330 Ohm resistors	5	07, 13	$7.95	www.sparkfun.com/products/10969
			$0.75	www.adafruit.com/product/2780
Button	1	07, 13	$2.50	www.adafruit.com/product/1119
			$0.50	www.sparkfun.com/products/9190
Soil Moisture	1+	08	$6.95	www.sparkfun.com/products/13637
RTC breakout board	1	08	$15.95	www.sparkfun.com/products/12708
			$7.50	www.adafruit.com/product/3296
Host Board - Omnibus	1	08	$7.75	thepihut.com/collections/pico/products/pico-omnibus-dual-expander
OLED - Pico Display	1	08	$14.00	thepihut.com/collections/pico/products/pico-display-pack

(continued)

Table A-1. (*continued*)

Component	Qty	Chapter	Cost	Links
Sound Sensor	1	10	$5.40	www.seeedstudio.com/Grove-Sound-Sensor-Based-on-LM358-amplifier-Arduino-Compatible.html
Chainable RGB	1	10	$6.60	www.seeedstudio.com/Grove-Chainable-RGB-Led-V2-0.html
Grove Shield for Pi Pico V1.0	1	10	$4.30	www.seeedstudio.com/Grove-Shield-for-Pi-Pico-v1-0-p-4846.html
Grove Cable	8	10	Varies	www.seeedstudio.com/cables-c-949.html?cat=949
Grove Dual Button	3	11	$2.20	www.seeedstudio.com/Grove-Dual-Button-p-4529.html
Grove Buzzer	1	11, 12	$1.90	www.seeedstudio.com/Grove-Buzzer.html
Grove LCD RGB Backlight	1	11	$11.90	www.seeedstudio.com/Grove-LCD-RGB-Backlight.html
Grove Chainable RGB Led V2.0	1	11	$6.60	www.seeedstudio.com/Grove-Chainable-RGB-Led-V2-0.html
Grove OLED 0.96 v1.3	1	12	$16.40	www.seeedstudio.com/Grove-OLED-Display-0-96.html
Grove Buzzer	1	12	$2.10	www.seeedstudio.com/Grove-Buzzer.html

Item	Quantity	Chapter	Price	Source
Grove I2C High Accuracy Temperature Sensor	1	12	$5.20	www.seeedstudio.com/Grove-I2C-High-Accuracy-Temperature-Sensor-MCP9808.html
Grove Temperature and Barometer Sensor	1	12	$9.80	www.seeedstudio.com/Grove-Barometer-Sensor-BMP280.html
Grove Air Quality Sensor	1	12	$10.90	www.seeedstudio.com/Grove-Air-Quality-Sensor-v1-3-Arduino-Compatible.html
Grove Dust Sensor	1	12	$12.70	www.seeedstudio.com/Grove-Dust-Sensor-PPD42NS.html
Grove - I2C Hub (6 Port)	1*	12	$1.70	www.seeedstudio.com/Grove-I2C-Hub-6-Port-p-4349.html
			$6.95	shop.switchdoc.com/collections/grove/products/grove-6-port-12c-hub
Pico Wireless Pack	1	13, 14	$13.20	shop.pimoroni.com/products/pico-wireless-pack
Pico Omnibus	1	13, 14	$8.25	shop.pimoroni.com/products/pico-omnibus
Micro SD Card (any size)	1	14	Varies	Commonly sourced

Table A-2 lists the optional hardware needed to complete the optional projects such as those in Chapter 4 and the suggestions in the project chapters.

Table A-2. *Optional Components*

Component	Qty	Chapter	Cost	Links
Adafruit RGB Sensor	1	04	$7.95	www.adafruit.com/ product/1334
Adafruit Thermocouple Amplifier MAX31855 breakout board	1	04	$14.95	www.adafruit.com/ product/269
Adafruit Thermocouple Type-K Glass Braid Insulated Stainless Steel Tip	1	04	$9.95	www.adafruit.com/ product/3245
Jumper Wires - Connected 6" (M/F, 20 pack)	2	14	$2.10	www.sparkfun.com/ products/12796

Index

© Charles Bell 2022
C. Bell, *Beginning MicroPython with the Raspberry Pi Pico*, Maker Innovations Series,
https://doi.org/10.1007/978-1-4842-8135-2

G

J, K

Printed in the United States
by Baker & Taylor Publisher Services